DATE DUE

JY 18 '96		
MY 27 '98		
OC 13 '98		
AP 26 '00		
DE 12 05		
OC 2 0 06		
NY 30 '06		
NO 27 '06		
FE 1 07		
AP 9 '09		
DE 22 '10		

WILLIAM R. CLINE

The Economics
of Global Warming

INSTITUTE FOR INTERNATIONAL ECONOMICS
WASHINGTON, DC

June 1992

William R. Cline, Senior Fellow at the Institute, was formerly a Senior Fellow at the Brookings Institution (1973–81); Deputy Director for Development and Trade Research at the US Treasury (1971–73); Ford Foundation Visiting Professor in Brazil (1970–71); and Assistant Professor at Princeton University (1967–70). He is the author of 19 books including *The Future of World Trade in Textiles and Apparel* (revised edition 1990), *United States External Adjustment and the World Economy* (1989), *International Debt: Systemic Risk and Policy Response* (1984), *Trade Policy in the 1980s* (1983), *World Inflation and the Developing Countries* (1981), and *Trade Negotiations in the Tokyo Round* (1978).

INSTITUTE FOR INTERNATIONAL ECONOMICS
11 Dupont Circle, NW
Washington, DC 20036-1207
(202) 328-9000 FAX: (202) 328-5432

C. Fred Bergsten, *Director*
Linda Griffin Kean, *Director of Publications*

Printed in the United States of America
94 93 92 91   3 2

Library of Congress Cataloging-in-Publication Data

Cline, William R.
    The economics of global warming /
    William R. Cline.
    p.   cm.
    Includes bibliographical references
    (p.) and index.

    1. Air—Pollution—Economic
    aspects.
    2. Global warming.
    3. Greenhouse effect, Atmospheric.
    I. Title.
    HC79.A4C55   1992
    363.73'87—dc20   92-16111
                                          CIP

ISBN 0-88132-150-8 (cloth)
ISBN 0-88132-132-X (paper)

Contents

Tables

vi

Figures

Preface

This book derives from the first research project conducted by the Institute for International Economics on an environmental issue. We decided to address global warming both because of its potentially enormous impact on the world economy and because it is the quintessential international economic problem: it transcends national borders, involves irreversible change and the risk of major adverse surprise, confronts policymakers with the need to make decisions in the face of considerable uncertainty, and calls for a coordinated and multifaceted response by a large number of countries. Global warming could prove to be one of the most difficult tests to date of international policy cooperation, and it could have major implications for current international rules and institutional arrangements.

William Cline's analysis begins with a careful evaluation of the science of global warming. He argues that valid policy decisions cannot be made without taking into account the very-long-term implications of the phenomenon over a horizon of three centuries. Because the greenhouse effect is cumulative and irreversible, the logic of the scientific analysis to date points to far greater warming than is generally associated with the problem. The standard benchmark— a doubling of atmospheric carbon dioxide—is expected to occur by the first half of the next century, and there is no reason for global warming to stop at that point. Cline argues that the ultimate damages from warming, and thus the economic stakes, are therefore far larger than currently recognized in the policy debate.

Cline's central finding is that these damages are likely to warrant major efforts to limit warming by drastically curtailing emissions of carbon dioxide and other greenhouse gases. However, he recognizes the sizable costs involved in such efforts. He therefore proposes a two-stage, contingent policy strategy. First, countries would make their best efforts (but without legally binding obligation) to limit further expansion of greenhouse gas emissions including through the adoption of such measures as modest carbon taxes, reduced deforestation and increased afforestation, and systematic pursuit of a whole range of "free" energy-efficiency gains. This initial stage would coincide with intense efforts toward further confirmation of greenhouse science. By 2000, the international community would review the scientific analysis; if the current diagnosis is confirmed, it would then be appropriate to adopt an intensified policy regime.

This study, like a number of earlier Institute studies, is being presented in two different forms to meet the needs of different audiences. In early May 1992, we released a relatively short summary of Cline's major findings and recommendations under the title *Global Warming: The Economic Stakes* as part of our POLICY ANALYSES IN INTERNATIONAL ECONOMICS series. The present volume presents Cline's full analysis including his estimates of warming in the very-long term, the logic and method for discounting distant future effects, and other detailed components of the analysis.

The Institute for International Economics is a private nonprofit institution for the study and discussion of international economic policy. Its purpose is to analyze important issues in that area, and to develop and communicate practical new approaches for dealing with them. The Institute is completely nonpartisan.

The Institute is funded largely by philanthropic foundations. Major institutional grants are now being received from the German Marshall Fund of the United States, which created the Institute with a generous commitment of funds in 1981, and from the Ford Foundation, the William and Flora Hewlett Foundation, the William M. Keck, Jr. Foundation, the Alfred P. Sloan Foundation, the C. V. Starr Foundation, and the United States–Japan Foundation. A number of other foundations and private corporations also contribute to the highly diversified financial resources of the Institute. About 14 percent of those resources in our latest fiscal year were provided by contributors outside the United States, including about 6 percent from Japan.

The Board of Directors bears overall responsibility for the Institute and gives general guidance and approval to its research program—including identification of topics that are likely to become important to international economic policymakers over the medium run (generally, one to three years), and which thus should be addressed by the Institute. The Director, working closely with the staff and outside Advisory Committee, is responsible for the development of particular projects and, after consulting with outside readers of each manuscript, makes the final decision to publish an individual study.

The Institute hopes that its studies and other activities will contribute to building a stronger foundation for international economic policy around the world. We invite readers of these publications to let us know how they think we can best accomplish this objective.

C. FRED BERGSTEN
Director
June 1992

Acknowledgments

My thanks go to Joel Darmstadter, William D. Nordhaus, Stephen H. Schneider, and Edith Brown Weiss for comments on the final manuscript. For comments on draft sections or interviews, in addition to ongoing encouragement, I thank Wilfred Beckerman, Charles R. Blitzer, Bruce A. Callander, Richard N. Cooper, Rob Coppock, Andrew Dean, Roger C. Dower, George C. Eads, Richard S. Eckaus, Jae A. Edmonds, Jessica Einhorn, Samuel Fankhauser, Christopher Flavin, Jeffrey A. Frankel, Michael Grubb, Howard K. Gruenspecht, Dale W. Jorgenson, Gordon J. MacDonald, Alan S. Manne, John P. Martin, Ruben F. Mettler, Irving Mintzer, William A. Niskanen, Joseph S. Nye, Jr., David Pearce, Rafe Pomerance, James M. Poterba, Gerald L. Potter, V. Ramanathan, John M. Reilly, Robert Repetto, Roger R. Revelle, Richard G. Richels, Norman J. Rosenberg, Cynthia Rosenzweig, Thomas C. Schelling, Richard L. Schmalensee, Katuo Seiki, Robert Shackleton, Eugene Skolnikoff, Joel B. Smith, Andrew Solow, Andrew Steer, Maurice F. Strong, Lawrence H. Summers, Eric T. Sundquist, James G. Titus, Mark Trexler, Philip K. Verleger, Jr., John Whalley, Gary W. Yohe, and H. Jay Zwally. In part because some differ from at least portions of the analysis here, none of these experts and colleagues should be held responsible for its results. Dorsati Madani and Waseem Noor provided tireless and deft research assistance. Esther Riley and Michael Treadway edited the manuscript. I dedicate this book to my daughters, Alison and Marian.

William R. Cline

Summary

Summary

Economic progress has long been recognized to involve potential adverse environmental side effects at the local or the regional level, as illustrated by air pollution from factories and automobiles. Correspondingly, it has generally been recognized that there may be a role for public policy intervention to correct such "external diseconomies," which arise because the associated damages are not included in the cost calculations of private firms and households.

In recent years it has become increasingly clear that expanding economic activity can also impose environmental damage that is global in dimension and irreversible over long time horizons. Stratospheric ozone depletion by chlorofluorocarbons (CFCs) is a major example. This study examines public policy toward the other principal area of global pollution: the "greenhouse effect." This term refers to the heat-trapping effect of rising atmospheric concentrations of carbon dioxide and certain other gases emitted from deforestation, the burning of fossil fuels, and other human activity. The eventual consequence of this effect is believed to be a warmer world, with major implications for world ecology as well as a wide range of economic effects.

As represented by the Intergovernmental Panel on Climate Change (IPCC), the majority scientific view is that the greenhouse effect will cause significant global warming by the middle of the next century in the absence of policy intervention (chapter 1). Most European countries, Japan, Canada, Australia, and New Zealand have set targets for reducing emissions of carbon dioxide, the principal greenhouse gas. US policymakers have refused to do so, on the grounds of scientific uncertainty (chapter 8).

Most economic analyses of the problem have focused on estimating the cost of abatement with the use of energy-economic models (see, e.g., Manne and Richels 1990a, 1990c; Jorgenson and Wilcoxen 1990b). Nordhaus (1991a) has gone further and examined the optimal degree of abatement by considering the benefits of damage avoidance as well. He finds that only modest action is war-

3

ranted. The present study suggests instead that social benefit-cost ratios are favorable for an aggressive program of international abatement. The difference stems in part from a longer-term perspective that takes account of much greater warming and damage (see chapter 7, annex 7A).

The Scientific Framework and Very-Long-Term Warming

Carbon dioxide and other trace gases (methane, CFCS, nitrous oxide, ozone) are transparent to incoming shortwave solar radiation but opaque to outgoing long-wave (infrared) radiation from the earth. Their natural levels raise the earth's average temperature by some 33°C (from -18°C to $+15$°C). Climatologists have applied large general circulation models (GCMS) to estimate that a doubling of carbon-dioxide-equivalent above preindustrial concentrations would increase global mean temperatures by a best-guess estimate of 2.5°C (Λ, the climate sensitivity parameter), with typical bounds of 1.5°C and 4.5°C (chapter 1).

Most analyses have focused on this rather arbitrary benchmark. Yet the doubling of carbon-dioxide-equivalent is expected to arrive as soon as the year 2025 under "business as usual," with corresponding warming already "committed" by that date actually arriving by perhaps 2050 after allowance is made for ocean thermal lag. Because global warming is cumulative and irreversible on a time scale of centuries, a much longer horizon should be considered. The IPCC itself calculates that, under business as usual, the commitment to warming would reach 5.7°C by the year 2100 (for $\Lambda = 2.5$; IPCC 1990b, figure 6.11). However, further warming would be likely to continue through at least the year 2300, when deep-ocean mixing could begin to partially reverse the increase in atmospheric concentrations (Sundquist 1990).

In view of economic growth and fossil fuel reserves, global emissions could increase from 6 billion tons of carbon (gigatons of carbon, or GtC) today to 20 GtC by the year 2100 and over 50 GtC by late in the 23rd century (chapter 2). By then, atmospheric concentrations of carbon could multiply eightfold. Global temperatures would ultimately rise by a central estimate of 10°C for $\Lambda = 2.5$ and by 18°C for the upper-bound $\Lambda = 4.5$ (based on the standard logarithmic formula for radiative forcing of carbon dioxide and incorporating the influence of other trace gases; chapter 2). Thus, *global warming potential in the very long term is far higher than the 2°C to 3°C range usually considered*—simply because the process does not stop at the conventional benchmark of a doubling of carbon dioxide.

Economic Damage

Chapter 3 attempts to estimate the size of economic damage from global warming at both the conventional benchmark (carbon dioxide doubling) and very-long-term warming levels. The analysis typically generates estimates that should be viewed as broad ranges rather than precise values, even for a specified amount of warming. They are calibrated in absolute dollar terms for the present-day US economy. The estimates are then summed and stated as a percentage of US GDP (today about $6 trillion) for application to much larger future levels of GDP in the benefit-cost analysis.

Thus, scaled to the actual size of the US economy in 1990, agricultural losses from heat stress and drought associated with benchmark (2.5°C) warming would amount to a central value of some $18 billion annually. "Carbon fertilization" effects, whereby higher carbon dioxide levels stimulate plant growth, are sometimes believed to neutralize or even overcome damages, but such calculations tend to forget that increases in other trace gases mean atmospheric carbon dioxide is considerably less than double when carbon-equivalent doubles. Similarly, farm adaptation is often cited as an offset, but at least one careful study suggests that the bulk of these losses would occur even with favorable adaptation assumptions.

Warming of the earth's surface is expected to cause a rise in mean sea levels due to thermal expansion of sea water and melting of glacial ice. Annual losses from sea-level rise would amount to an estimated $7 billion (central value, again scaled to 1990). Increased electricity requirements for air conditioning would amount to some $11 billion annually, with an offset of only about one-tenth for reduced heating costs (largely because of the much greater inefficiency of electric power in view of transmission losses). Lesser runoff in water basins would cause costs of some $7 billion annually from curtailed water supply. Increased urban pollution (tropospheric ozone) associated with warmer weather would impose an annual cost on the order of $4 billion. An increased incidence of mortality with heat stress would amount to some $6 billion in annual losses with life conservatively valued at lifetime earnings (risk pooling would suggest a higher valuation). The lumber value of forest loss would be over $3 billion annually. Ski industry losses would be some $1½ billion annually. Other tangible costs would arise from increased hurricane and forest fire damage, and there would be additional net infrastructure costs from increased immigration.

As this enumeration indicates, it is misleading to argue that damages would necessarily be small in economies in which the share of agriculture and other "outdoor" sectors is small. Several major effects are not limited to such sectors. Even agricultural effects must take account of loss of "consumer surplus" from higher prices[1] and so can be understated by consideration of agriculture's share in the economy at prewarming prices.

Overall, damages suffered in the United States for 2.5°C warming (defined as a percentage of GDP as d_0) at the present US economic scale would be close to $60 billion annually, or 1 percent of GDP. Intangible losses, particularly species loss but also human disamenity, could raise the total considerably, and total damages could reach as high as 2 percent of GDP. With upper-bound warming of 4.5°C from doubling of carbon-dioxide-equivalent, the corresponding range of damages would be 2 percent to 4 percent of GDP. For other countries, especially low-lying island nations, losses could be greater.[2]

The global damages would be much higher with very-long-term warming. Even a linear damage function would mean losses four times as high (for 10°C warming instead of 2.5°C). However, damage is likely to be nonlinear. Consider sea-level rise. In the initial range, the Antarctic does not contribute to sea-level rise, because temperature is in a low range where increased melting is more than offset by increased snow carried by air with more moisture. On the scale of 10°C warming, however, the Antarctic would likely become a major source of sea-level rise, especially if the West Antarctic ice shelf should disintegrate. Similarly, for agriculture, heat stress could be expected to impose nonlinear damage. The central estimate in chapter 3 is that the damage function is geometric with an exponent (γ) of 1.3, so that overall damages reach 6 percent of GDP with 10°C warming ($d_1 = 1$ percent $\times [10/2.5]^{1.3}$). The sensitivity analysis of chapter 7 places the prospective long-term damages under the more pessimistic assumptions at approximately 20 percent of world GDP.

Abatement Costs

Much more work has been done on the side of carbon abatement costs than on damages from global warming. As reviewed in chapter 4, several carbon-energy-economic models provide simulations of the economic cost of constraining carbon emissions. Some have more detail on alternative energy technologies (Manne and Richels 1990a, 1990c; Edmonds and Barns 1990); others emphasize economic sectoral detail (Jorgenson and Wilcoxen 1990b); still others stress international trading (Burniaux et al. 1991a). Most of the models indicate that a loss of about 2 percent of GDP would result from a reduction of carbon emissions

---

1. "Consumer surplus" refers to the benefit consumers enjoy by being able to purchase, at a lower price, food (or other goods and services) that they would be willing to buy at higher prices (albeit at smaller volumes) if necessary.

2. Developing countries tend to be located closer to the equator, where warming would be lesser. However, their economies tend to be more rigid and more exposed to hurricanes and agricultural damage.

by 50 percent from baseline levels by about the middle of the next century. The cost of the cutback rises with the percentage cut from baseline, but falls over time because of the widening range of technological alternatives from technical change.

There is another body of literature that suggests that some initial (z_0 percent) cutback can be obtained for free. The engineering tradition cites several avenues (such as compact fluorescent lights) by which energy needs may be reduced at zero or even negative cost. Market imperfections such as utility pricing rules that do not reward energy saved may contribute to this situation. As surveyed in chapter 5, studies by the US National Academy of Sciences (1991a) and others suggest that this initial tranche of zero-cost energy reduction may be on the order of 20 percent.

Abatement costs can be further cut through forestry measures. Whereas the simulation models described above indicate that the marginal cost (and tax) required to cut one ton of carbon emissions is on the order of $100 to $250 per ton (30 cents to 75 cents per gallon of gasoline), afforestation or reduced deforestation can provide the same cutback at a marginal cost of only about $10 per ton of carbon (chapter 5). But there are limits to the amount of land for which afforestation is feasible. Moreover, afforestation absorbs carbon only during the growing period of some 30 years; a steady-state forest provides no further contribution, because the carbon sequestered in new trees is offset by that released by trees that die.

Finally, carbon permit trading across nations can reduce global abatement costs by as much as one-half by shifting the cutbacks to the areas where they have the smallest impact on output (see the discussion of Burniaux et al. 1991a in chapter 5). A classic example is that carbon reductions for, say, the Netherlands can be most economically accomplished indirectly through assisting, say, Poland to reduce its high emissions levels.

Time Discounting

Policy analysis over a 300-year horizon depends crucially on the time discount rate (i.e., the real interest rate used to convert future values to comparability with today's values), especially when there is a significant lag between abatement costs and the later benefits of avoided global warming. Present practice varies widely: the US Office of Management and Budget discounts at 10 percent real; the Congressional Budget Office at the real long-term government bond rate, or 2 percent. For intergenerational issues there is a case for applying a zero discount rate (Mishan 1975, 209); and environmental degradation may "oppress" the future generation even if it is richer (Sen 1982, 347–49).

The analysis in chapters 6 and 7 conservatively remains with recent mainstream methodology, which converts all effects to consumption equivalents (using a shadow price of capital) and then discounts at the social rate of time preference (SRTP). As developed in chapter 6, the appropriate value for the SRTP is based on the rate of growth of per capita income, because it is the rising level of consumption that makes the "marginal utility" of future income worth less than that of income received today and therefore provides the underlying rationale for discounting future consumption.[3] The resulting SRTP is 1½ percent. When shadow pricing of capital is taken into account, the effective discount rate is on the order of 2 percent.

Benefit-Cost Synthesis

Chapter 7 examines a global policy of cutting carbon emissions back to 4 GtC annually and holding them at that level over three centuries. All costs are scaled up by 20 percent to cover parallel action on other greenhouse gases. Benefits are set at 80 percent of greenhouse damages, under the assumption that 20 percent cannot be avoided. Benefits are expanded to include 30 percent of carbon tax revenue, on the grounds that this revenue would reduce the economic losses imposed by the disincentive effects of the existing tax structure. For the first 30 years, much of the emissions cutback is accomplished by forestry measures at low cost. However, by the year 2100 carbon cutbacks in the rest of the economy are on the order of 80 percent from the baseline scenario of no change in policy. On the basis of the principal model estimates, carbon taxes of some $100 up to $250 per ton could eventually be required to achieve this outcome. Total abatement costs peak at about 3½ percent of GDP by about 2040 and plateau thereafter at 2½ percent (a floor is imposed; otherwise the time variable in the cost function would push costs even lower).

Using the central values of key parameters, the benefits of damage avoidance do not quite cover the costs: the ratio of the present discounted value of benefits to that of costs is approximately 3:4. However, if policymakers are risk averse and apply a weight of one-half to the central outcome and a weight three times as high to the high-damage outcome as to the low-damage case, the weighted present value of benefits exceeds that of abatement costs, with a benefit-cost ratio of approximately 1.3:1. Even if a higher discount rate of 5 percent is applied,

---

3. More specifically, the SRTP is the rate of growth of per capita income multiplied by the elasticity of marginal utility with respect to income. There is no allowance for pure myopia (as, e.g., in the biblical account of Esau's exchange of his inheritance for an immediate bowl of hot stew), an effect that is particularly inappropriate over an intergenerational horizon.

it requires only the incorporation of a small probability of a "catastrophe" to boost the benefit-cost ratio into the range favorable for aggressive action.

Policy Implications

In sum, under risk aversion it appears sensible on economic grounds to undertake aggressive abatement to sharply curtail the greenhouse effect. Chapter 8 proposes a program to do so. However, because the costs are potentially large and further scientific confirmation is desirable (especially for estimates of very-long-term warming), a two-stage approach is advisable for this purpose. In the first stage, milder measures would be implemented and machinery set in place; sharply intensified action would follow in a second phase after a decade of additional scientific confirmation.

The first stage could usefully include a "best-efforts" (but not legally binding) international commitment to limit carbon emissions by the year 2000 to their 1990 levels. "Emulatory initiative" would be encouraged so that countries prepared to take tougher measures would be encouraged to do so as an example to others. As a compensatory benefit, such leading nations could well enjoy dynamic competitive advantages as the consequence of being the first to develop the carbon-spare technologies of the 21st century. In other countries, at least moderate carbon taxes would seem appropriate, rising by perhaps $5 per year to a total of $40 per ton (12 cents per gallon of gasoline) by the year 2000. Such taxes would send a strong signal to the private sector to move away from carbon-based energy but should not cause a wrenching immediate adjustment at high cost.

An obvious measure for the initial phase is to remove existing subsidies to carbon emissions (e.g., coal subsidies in Germany, subsidized electricity in China and other developing countries). Initial action should also include an emphasis on low-cost forestry measures.

It will be important for developing countries to participate in the global abatement effort eventually, because they will provide the lion's share of future increases in global emissions. For this purpose, a moderate portion of carbon tax revenues would appropriately be channeled to developing countries to support their technological shift toward a carbon-lean economy and reduced deforestation.

In the second policy phase, after an explicit review of scientific confirmation by the year 2000, the international community would move to a stronger regime of reductions in emissions. In this phase, higher and more uniform carbon taxes across countries would be appropriate. Alternatively, the regime could involve international carbon emissions quotas, along with tradeable permits. Allocation of any such quotas would presumably have to incorporate elements of realism (e.g., by including weights for existing GDP and carbon emissions shares) and equity (e.g., by giving some weight to base-period population). By early in the 21st century, it could also prove necessary to supplement positive incentives with negative reinforcement in the form of trade penalties, as provided for in the case of CFCS under the Montreal Protocol.

1

The Scientific Basis for the Greenhouse Effect

1

The Scientific Basis for the Greenhouse Effect

"Fools rush in where angels fear to tread." —Alexander Pope

The international community may reach agreement to limit carbon emissions as early as June 1992, when Brazil will host the "Earth Summit" (chapter 8). Because the cost of switching to alternative fuels could be high, with profound implications for long-term economic growth, especially in developing countries, policy action must be based on the view that the science of the greenhouse effect is compelling. This chapter considers the scientific logic and evidence for the effect, from the viewpoint of an economist.[1] It draws heavily on the findings of the Intergovernmental Panel on Climate Change (IPCC). I will stress that both the science and the policy discussion so far (including that by the IPCC) have focused insufficiently on effects in the very long term, that is, on the order of 250 to 300 years. Chapter 2 examines global warming over this three-century period, and the benefit-cost analysis of this study (chapter 7) is based on economic effects over this very-long-term horizon.

Science and the Emergence of the Policy Issue

The theory of greenhouse warming caused by man-made emissions of carbon dioxide (CO_2) has been known for more than a century (Ausubel 1983). Tyndall (1863) had suggested that small changes in atmospheric composition could alter the climate. The Swedish scientist Svante Arrhenius (1896) made the first calculation of the effect, estimating that a doubling of carbon dioxide would raise global mean temperature by 4°C to 6°C—about the upper end of the range currently thought valid.

For most of the 20th century, however, the greenhouse effect was not considered a priority problem. Although temperatures in the Northern Hemisphere

---

1. An earlier version of this chapter appears in Cline (1991e).

had increased through the 1930s, they began a temporary cooling trend in the 1940s. Scientists then familiar with the issue tended to assume that the oceans would absorb man-made carbon dioxide emissions. Then Revelle and Suess (1957) demonstrated that the upper layer of the oceans would not rapidly absorb these emissions. They warned that "human beings are now carrying out a large-scale geophysical experiment." Their findings prompted new scientific measurements (especially at Mauna Loa, Hawaii) that subsequently documented a steady buildup in atmospheric carbon dioxide (Ausubel 1983; McKibben 1989, 10).

By the mid-1960s the greenhouse issue was well established on the agenda of environmental experts. However, it did not emerge into prominence among the broader public until the late 1980s. Indeed, in the 1970s there was concern that the earth could face cooling as a consequence of pollution from jet aircraft.[2]

Public concern about the greenhouse effect exploded in the late 1980s, primarily for three reasons. First, it was becoming evident that the decade was the warmest on record. Although not necessarily attributable to the greenhouse effect, the historically high temperatures and severe drought in the United States in 1988 in particular escalated awareness of the issue. Second, by the late 1980s numerous calculations by climatologists using general circulation models had become available. These massive computer models of the climate provided new detail on and support for the concept of global warming. Third, there was increasing awareness among scientists that other greenhouse gases (especially chlorofluorocarbons and methane) were adding substantially to the impact of carbon dioxide.

Within this policy environment, in late 1988 the United States and other nations agreed within the United Nations Environment Programme (UNEP) and the World Meteorological Organization (WMO) to establish an Intergovernmental Panel on Climate Change (IPCC). In May 1989, the Bush administration decided to propose an international conference on global warming and related environmental issues (*Financial Times*, 11 May 1989), and in April 1990 the administration hosted the White House Conference on Science and Economic Research Related to Global Change. On 22 December 1989, the United Nations General Assembly approved Resolution 44–228, which called for a global sum-

---

2. In the early 1970s the US Department of Transportation had advocated the development of a fleet of 1,000 supersonic transport airplanes. There was concern that sulfur dioxide emissions from their flights would generate stratospheric cloud formations that would reflect sunlight and potentially change the earth's temperature by a range of $-2°C$ to $+0.5°C$ (d'Arge 1975). Unlike in the lower stratum of the atmosphere—the troposphere, where turbulence, storms, and rainfall perform a cleansing function—in the stratosphere impurities persist for as long as three years (Grobecker et al. 1974). However, the issue became moot as a fleet of supersonic aircraft proved impractical and as emissions from jet engines were subsequently curtailed.

mit on environment and development issues—which became the "Earth Summit" scheduled to take place in Rio de Janeiro in June 1992 (United Nations Conference on Environment and Economic Development 1992). Although the resolution owed much to the 1987 "Brundtland Report" of the World Commission on Environment and Development (Brundtland et al. 1987), it was also stimulated by the increasing concern over the greenhouse effect. Clearly the science of global warming was being taken seriously by policymakers.

Although rarely formulated explicitly, it would seem that an important reason for the salience of the greenhouse effect has been its qualitatively different nature from that of most issues of environmental pollution. In the past, environmental issues have tended to concern local and reversible pollution (e.g., of rivers by urban waste). In contrast, greenhouse warming poses the threat of pollution that is global and, at least on a time scale of centuries, irreversible.

The Greenhouse Effect

Any body in space emits radiation. The wavelength of this radiation is inversely related to the temperature of the body. The sun's radiation reaching the earth is in the shorter wavelengths (0.2 to 4.0 micrometers [μm], with the peak at about 0.5 μm), whereas outbound radiation from the earth is in the infrared longwave bands (4 to 100 μm, with the peak near 10 μm; IPCC 1990b, 51; Rosenberg 1988, 6–10). Clouds, water vapor, and the greenhouse gases carbon dioxide, chlorofluorocarbons (CFCs), methane, nitrous oxide, and ozone are relatively transparent to shortwave radiation but much more opaque to longwave. They thus permit about half of the sun's radiation to reach the earth's surface but trap 80 percent to 90 percent of the outbound radiation from the earth's surface.

This trapping influence is called the "greenhouse effect." Without it, the earth's average surface temperature would be $-18°C$ rather than $+15°C$. The great bulk of the effect is natural, primarily from water vapor (2 percent of atmospheric volume) and nonanthropogenic carbon dioxide (which was 0.28 percent, or 280 parts per million [ppm] by volume before the Industrial Revolution). However, man-made emissions have already contributed significantly to the effect, as carbon dioxide concentrations have risen by about 25 percent from preindustrial times (to 353 ppm in 1989; IPCC 1990b, 9), largely as the consequence of the burning of fossil fuels.

The earth's radiative budget, measured in watts per square meter (wm^{-2}), is approximately as follows. Incoming ("incident") solar radiation is 340 wm^{-2}. The reflective parts of the earth's surface (snow, ice) and atmosphere (clouds, aerosols) reflect 100 wm^{-2} back to space. The remaining 240 wm^{-2} warms the earth's atmosphere and surface from absolute zero (0 degrees Kelvin, or $-273°C$)

to the equivalent of $-18°C$ (255K). The earth's surface in turn emits infrared radiation equal to 420 wm^{-2} upward into the atmosphere. The greenhouse effect sends (via reradiation) 180 wm^{-2} back to the earth, warming it by another 33°C (33K). The remainder of the outbound infrared radiation exactly balances the net incoming solar radiation ($420 - 180 = 240 = 340 - 100$ wm^{-2}; IPCC 1990b, 51, 83; Raval and Ramanathan 1989, 759).

The sensitivity of this system to anthropogenic greenhouse warming may be perceived by considering the impact of a doubling of carbon-dioxide-equivalent trace gases, the typical benchmark for analysis. As discussed below, this doubling would raise "radiative forcing" of the earth-atmosphere system by about 4 wm^{-2} and increase global mean temperatures by a central estimate of 2.5°C.[3] Higher temperatures mean more infrared emissions, and temperature rises just enough so that net outgoing radiation would once again be in balance with incoming. A substantial warming would thus result from a radiative forcing that is small relative to the total flux (4 wm^{-2} compared with 240 wm^{-2} flux in both directions at the top of the atmosphere).

The Carbon Cycle

Carbon dioxide accumulation, the primary source of warming, involves major impacts from small changes in flows relative to stocks. Fossil fuel burning contributes 5.4 ± 0.5 billion tons of carbon (gigatons of carbon, or GtC) to the atmosphere each year, and deforestation an estimated 1.6 ± 1 GtC. Annual accumulation in the atmosphere amounts to 3.4 ± 0.2 GtC. The difference is partly explained by the reabsorption of 2 ± 0.8 GtC into the ocean, but approximately 1.6 ± 1.4 GtC is missing in the annual balance (IPCC 1990b, 14). The implication is that emissions from deforestation are toward the low end of the estimated range or that there are important unknown sinks for carbon dioxide withdrawn from the atmosphere.

The annual emissions of 6 to 7 GtC are less than 1 percent of the stock of carbon contained in the atmosphere: 750 GtC. Only about half of the emissions remain in the atmosphere beyond a decade or so; thus the atmospheric concentration and stock are rising at 0.5 percent annually. Other stocks of carbon are even larger. The surface ocean holds 1,000 GtC and annually emits some 90 GtC to the atmosphere and extracts perhaps 92 GtC from it. The deep ocean holds 38,000 GtC. Land biota (forests) hold about 550 GtC, and the soil roughly 1,500 GtC. Deforestation, soil, and plant respiration and decay together emit

---

3. The IPCC (1990b, 50) defines radiative forcing as follows: "If the climate system is in equilibrium, then the absorbed solar energy is exactly balanced by radiation emitted to space by the Earth and atmosphere. Any factor that is able to perturb this balance, and thus potentially alter the climate, is called a radiative forcing agent."

about 102 GtC to the atmosphere, while photosynthesis extracts some 100 GtC from it (IPCC 1990b, 8). It is evident that small variations in these total natural flows and stocks (which have been stable over centuries) could overwhelm the net contribution of anthropogenic emissions. Hence the appeal of altering these flows by "geoengineering," for example by increasing the rate of ocean uptake (as discussed below).

A crucial aspect of carbon dioxide accumulation is that it is essentially irreversible over periods of hundreds of years. Moreover, the IPCC estimates that it would require an immediate reduction of 60 percent to 80 percent in carbon emissions just to keep atmospheric concentration from rising further (IPCC 1990b, 5).[4]

Other Trace Gases

Carbon dioxide has contributed about two-thirds of the radiative forcing from the increase in the greenhouse effect over the past 200 years, and it is expected to continue to provide approximately this share in the future. In its 1990 assessment, the IPCC reported that in the most recent decade methane had contributed, directly and indirectly, about 15 percent of total radiative forcing, CFCS 24 percent, and nitrous oxide 6 percent (IPCC 1990b, ix, 59–64). As discussed below, subsequent findings suggest that CFCS have had much less net impact.

Methane concentration has already risen to more than double preindustrial levels (in contrast to the 25 percent increase of CO_2), and its atmospheric stock is rising at 0.9 percent annually. Rice cultivation, the rearing of cattle and other domestic ruminants, biomass burning, coal mining, and natural gas leakage add to natural methane sources. However, methane is short-lived, and after 10 to 12 years in the atmosphere it reacts with hydroxyl radicals in the troposphere to end up as stratospheric water vapor, which on average accounts for one-fourth of the direct and indirect radiative forcing of methane. It might require a decrease of only 10 percent to 20 percent in anthropogenic emissions of methane to stabilize its atmospheric content (IPCC 1990b, 5).[5] For its part, nitrous oxide has recently contributed about one-tenth as much as carbon dioxide to

---

4. This estimate is consistent with a comparison of emissions (some 6 to 7 GtC) and ocean uptake (2 ± 0.8 GtC). Note, however, that ocean uptake could decline with lesser emissions because of lesser gas pressure differential between the atmosphere and the ocean surface.

5. Note, however, that in 1991 a scientific panel concluded that "the *indirect* GWP [global warming potential] of methane has not been quantified reliably" (UNEP 1991, 6). The new report noted further that for short-lived, inhomogeneously mixed gases such as the nitrogen oxides and nonmethane hydrocarbons, the GWPs identified by the IPCC (1990b) were uncertain and may have been incorrect.

greenhouse warming. Its emissions could be reduced through improved formulation of fertilizers and through reduced burning of fossil fuels and deforestation.

Atmospheric concentrations of CFCs have been rising at 4 percent annually over recent decades. CFCs are far more powerful greenhouse gases than carbon dioxide, providing about 4,000 times as much radiative forcing per unit of mass change (IPCC 1990b, 57). Governments agreed in the June 1990 London Adjustments and Amendments to the Montreal Protocol of 1987 to phase out CFC production by 1999–2000 because of damage to the ozone layer. Although the prospective replacements of CFCs, the hydrochlorofluorocarbons (HCFCS), have radiative forcing potential per unit mass comparable to the CFCs, their atmospheric residence tends to be shorter (e.g., 15 years for HCFC-22 versus 60 to 130 years for CFC-11 and -12; IPCC 1990b, 64). As a result, a favorable side effect of CFC replacement should be moderation of this source of global warming. However, this effect is modest: by the year 2100, total radiative forcing of the CFC-HCFC complex declines from a business-as-usual baseline of 1.1 wm^{-2} to 0.68 wm^{-2} under near-complete elimination of CFCs (under the "accelerated policies" scenario; IPCC 1990b, table 2.7), compared against total radiative forcing from all greenhouse gases of 9.9 wm^{-2} in the baseline.

In late 1991 an international panel of scientists released a study for UNEP (1991) that provided disturbing new evidence on the effect of CFCs. The group found that stratospheric ozone depletion had been considerably greater than expected. For the first time, decreases were shown for the spring and summer in middle and high latitudes. In the period 1979–91, stratospheric ozone declined at a rate of about 3 percent per decade for summertime and almost 5 percent for winter in the northern midlatitudes; the reductions were even faster in the Southern Hemisphere.

With respect to global warming, the panel found:

> [T]he observed ozone depletions would have tended to cool the lower stratosphere at middle and high latitudes. . . . The ozone losses . . . have increased the visible and ultraviolet incoming radiation reaching the surface/troposphere system and decreased the downward infrared radiation reaching the surface/troposphere system. . . . [T]he net effect is a decrease in radiative forcing. For middle and high latitudes . . . the magnitude of this decrease may be larger than the predicted increases in the radiative forcing due to the increased abundances of CFCs over the last decade. . . . [Globally, these radiative effects are] comparable in magnitude, but opposite in sign, to those attributed to the CFCs over the last decade. (UNEP 1991, 1, 5)

This finding meant essentially that, because ozone is a greenhouse gas, its removal by CFCs (and methyl bromides and halons) provided an offset to the greenhouse effect of increased CFC concentrations.[6] This offset effect was stronger than previously predicted and meant that the buildup of CFCs was neutral in total radiative effect because of the consequences of ozone stripping.

The new results for CFCs had important policy implications. First, they suggested that observed warming may have been closer to a *correctly* predicted rate (i.e., with proper adjustment for ozone removal) than previously thought. The past empirical data on warming may thus more fully correspond to predictions for non-CFC greenhouse gases than indicated in the IPCC report. Considering that projections of future greenhouse warming had assumed relatively little further contribution from CFCs (as just discussed), the implication is that in the future there could be less of a shortfall of actual warming from that predicted by the models, in comparison with the size of this shortfall to date (see discussion below). A further implication is the even greater primacy of carbon dioxide as the greenhouse gas to combat, as the Director General of UNEP emphasized (1991).

In sum, a broad interpretation of the new data on ozone was that the CFCs may have been "masking" warming by reducing, as a side effect, the greenhouse impact of ozone. For US policy, the results had troublesome implications. As set forth in chapter 8, the US position had been that its contribution to reducing global warming would come primarily from the reduction of CFCs. The new evidence meant that, desirable as this action would be from the standpoint of saving the ozone layer, it would do little to forestall global warming, because the effect would be essentially neutral. However, US officials depicted the unexpected findings as further evidence of scientific uncertainty and thus as confirmation of the wisdom of a "wait and see" approach.

General Circulation Models

The scientific majority view on prospective global warming is based primarily on simulations by general circulation models (GCMS). The GCMS are large mathematical models of the atmosphere that require great amounts of time to run

---

6. Note, however, that whereas most greenhouse gases trap outbound infrared radiation, the role of stratospheric ozone is more complicated. Stratospheric ozone absorbs incoming solar shortwave (ultraviolet) radiation as well as outgoing terrestrial (longwave) radiation. Reductions in stratospheric ozone thus permit more solar radiation to reach and warm the earth's surface. However, these reductions also mean that the stratosphere cools, because there is less absorption of both inbound solar and outbound longwave radiation. The cooler stratosphere emits less longwave radiation to the troposphere and thence to the earth's surface. The extent of solar shortwave warming of the earth's surface from ozone depletion depends on the total column amount of ozone, wheres the extent of the stratospheric cooling influence depends on the vertical distribution of ozone (IPCC 1990b, 29). The 1991 findings indicate that the net effect of stratospheric ozone depletion has been one of cooling, thereby offsetting the radiative forcing of CFCs.

on high-speed computers. Approximately ten research centers worldwide have provided the leading models, in some cases originally for the purpose of current weather forecasting.

The models are based on Newton's laws of mechanics and on the laws of thermodynamics (e.g., conservation of energy, flow of heat from a warmer to a cooler body). On the basis of nonlinear partial differential equations integrated forward over time, the models calculate the behavior of air or water under the influences of the earth's rotation (the Coriolis force) and differential heating (arising from the equator-pole temperature difference) in response to the sun's radiation, as augmented by the greenhouse effect. In the models the atmosphere is divided into as many as 19 vertical layers, and the earth's surface into as many as 6,912 grids. For each cell in this three-dimensional space, shaped like a coconut shell or melon rind, the models calculate climate variables including wind, temperature, humidity, surface pressure, and rainfall. Because of computational limits, the models typically must sacrifice in one area, such as grid resolution, to obtain improvement in another, such as coupling to an ocean model (Washington and Parkinson 1986; IPCC 1990b, 87–91).

Radiative Forcing and Global Warming

Global warming is calculated in terms of "commitment" to an equilibrium rise in mean global temperature. There is a lag of some two to three decades or perhaps much more between commitment and actual temperature increase, because before fully warming the earth's surface the greenhouse effect must first heat up the oceans (this is known as "ocean thermal lag").[7] In terms of commitment, warming may be estimated as follows:

$$(1.1) \quad \Delta T = R \lambda \beta$$

where ΔT is the equilibrium change in global mean surface temperature (in °C), R is radiative forcing above preindustrial levels (in wm^{-2}), λ is the warming per unit of radiative forcing to be expected as the direct impact before taking account of feedback (in °C per wm^{-2}), and β is the feedback multiplier (a pure number).

A century ago the Swedish scientist Arrhenius (1896) specified a logarithmic relationship between radiative forcing (R) and the atmospheric concentration

---

7. The lag of some two to three decades or more is, however, a phenomenon that also reflects ongoing increases in radiative forcing from persistent greenhouse gas buildup. For a discrete, once-for-all increment in greenhouse gas concentration, the time profile of warming impact would be as follows: some warming at once, about half of the equilibrium effect after some decades, and full equilibrium warming only after some three to five centuries (Stephen H. Schneider, National Center for Atmospheric Research, personal communication, 13 April 1992).

of carbon dioxide.[8] Essentially, some bands of the spectrum become saturated with respect to the blockage of infrared radiation, so that as additional carbon dioxide is added, the blocking effect rises less than linearly. The working value adopted by the IPCC for this relationship is:

$$(1.2) \quad R_c = 6.3 \ln (C/C_0)$$

where C is the atmospheric concentration of carbon dioxide and subscript 0 refers to preindustrial times (Wigley 1987; IPCC 1990b, 56). Although the IPCC notes that the relationship holds through 1,000 ppm (about $3\frac{1}{2}$ times the preindustrial concentration), it is likely to hold up to far higher multiples, because saturation of the major spectrum bands (12 to 18 μm) is offset by the increasing relative importance of the minor bands (e.g., $7\frac{1}{2}$ μm and 9 to 10 μm; V. Ramanathan, University of California, San Diego, personal communication, 21 November 1990).

Climatologists have centered much of their analysis on a key benchmark: the doubling of carbon-dioxide-*equivalent* of all trace gases (in total radiative impact) over preindustrial levels (or, considering that in preindustrial times the contribution of other trace gases was minimal, a doubling of carbon dioxide alone). From equation 1.2, this important benchmark involves radiative forcing of $R = 6.3 \ln (2) = 4.4$ wm^{-2}. Analysts of global warming have defined the *climate sensitivity parameter*, Λ, as the expected equilibrium mean global warming from a doubling of carbon-dioxide-equivalent. On the basis of GCMs, the IPCC places Λ at a lower bound of 1.5°C, a best-guess central value of 2.5°C, and an upper bound of 4.5°C. Equilibrium warming would be less than the global mean near the equator and greater than the mean at high latitudes (especially the poles). In the high latitudes, warming would be greater than the global average in the winter but less than the global average in the summer (IPCC 1990b, 142).[9]

In addition to equilibrium temperature change, the GCMs provide estimates of the impact of global warming on precipitation. A warmer atmosphere is more moist.[10] In the areas of frontal convergence, where moist air is forced to ascend, cool, and remove the resulting excess concentration of water vapor above the

---

8. "Thus if the quantity of carbonic acid increases in geometric progression, the augmentation of the temperature will increase nearly in arithmetic progression" (Arrhenius 1896, 267).

9. Warming causes sea ice to form later in the autumn. Sea ice provides great reflectivity (albedo), and its reduction permits greater solar heating of the surface. Reduced spring snow cover in northern continents above the tropics also reduces albedo. Moreover, warming is largely confined near the surface in high latitudes but mixed more thoroughly through the troposphere in the tropics, so that there is greater escape of longwave radiation at the top of the atmosphere the tropics (IPCC 1990b, chapter 5).

10. That is, there is higher specific, though not relative, humidity in the troposphere. See the discussion of cloud feedback below.

saturation point (which is reduced by this cooling), precipitation would increase. The GCMs show increased precipitation in high latitudes and the tropics through-out the year and in the middle latitudes in winter. Global mean precipitation typically rises on the order of 8 percent in the GCM simulations for a doubling of carbon-dioxide-equivalent and by about 15 percent in the high-resolution models (IPCC 1990b, 150, table 3.2).

Feedback Estimates

Of the components in equation 1.1, we have the first right-hand term from equation 1.2, a widely agreed value. The second right-hand term is also widely agreed upon: the *direct* warming effect of radiative forcing. This parameter is $0.3°C$ per wm^{-2} (Schlesinger and Mitchell 1987, 760; Cess et al. 1989, 245; IPCC 1990b, 84). It is the final term in equation 1.1, the feedback multiplier, that has caused considerable controversy and accounts for the sizable range of Λ. Applying the "best guess" of $2.5°C$ for Λ and the values just discussed for $R_{2 \times CO2}$ (4.4 wm^{-2}) and λ ($0.3°C$ per wm^{-2}), we may infer that the IPCC assigns a central value of 1.9 to the feedback multiplier β.[11] Similarly, applying the lower and upper bounds of the climate sensitivity parameter, the IPCC implicitly judges that the feedback multiplier has a minimum value of 1.1 and a maximum of 3.4. Thus, induced climate effects provide strictly positive (i.e., enhancing) rather than negative (ameliorating) feedback.

The feedback parameter β may be thought of as the product of three sub-components: β_w for water vapor, β_a for snow and ice albedo (reflectiveness of the earth's surface), and β_c for clouds:[12]

$$(1.3) \quad \beta = \beta_w \beta_a \beta_c$$

Water Vapor

The greatest agreement is on water vapor feedback.[13] Because the saturation vapor pressure rises with temperature, a warmer atmosphere holds more water vapor. As water vapor is itself a greenhouse gas, global warming produces a

---

11. That is, from equation 1.1, $2.5 = 4.4 \times 0.3 \times 1.9$.

12. This formulation takes some license by ignoring interaction among the three terms.

13. An exception is Richard Lindzen (1990). He argues that drying of the upper tropo-sphere should offset increased water vapor in the lower troposphere. Most climatologists disagree, in part because a given percentage change in water vapor has more impact in the lower troposphere than in the upper (as reviewed in Rosenberg 1992, Kerr 1990).

positive feedback from this source. Raval and Ramanathan (1989) have used satellite observations to measure the difference between longwave radiation escaping to space and that originating at the sea's surface. As expected, they find that this difference is related to sea surface temperature. Based on their results, it may be estimated that water vapor feedback reduces the amount of direct radiative forcing required for each degree Celsius of global warming from 3.3 to 2.3 wm^{-2}, and correspondingly augments the impact of parameter λ from 0.3 to an effective 0.43°C per wm^{-2} (IPCC 1990b, 84). The feedback multiplier from water vapor alone is thus approximately $\beta_w = 1.43$ (i.e., 0.43/0.3).

Snow and Ice Albedo

Feedback from reduced albedo associated with decreased snow and ice cover is more ambiguous. Typically the GCMs find positive feedback from albedo. However, the IPCC report has contradictory implications for the size (but not the direction) of this influence in different chapters with different lead authors.[14]

Clouds

There is considerable dispute on cloud feedback. Clouds perform both countergreenhouse and progreenhouse functions. They reflect back the sun's radiation (providing albedo, a countergreenhouse effect), but they also contribute to infrared trapping (a progreenhouse effect). The dominant view among GCM modelers is that global warming should change the composition and amount of clouds in a way that reduces albedo and increases infrared trapping, thereby making the cloud system a source of positive feedback. At the outset it is perhaps useful to warn against a seemingly common misconception. Because global warming should increase humidity and precipitation, it is easy to draw the wrong conclusion from this effect that there will be more clouds (see, e.g., Abelson 1990) and that because clouds today on balance are countergreenhouse, cloud feedback will be negative. Essentially the opposite is expected to occur in the GCMs (thus, Cess et al. 1989, 245, cite "diminished cloud amount").

Clouds are formed by the rise of air containing water vapor. As this air reaches higher altitudes and lower barometric pressure, it expands and thus cools adiabatically (i.e., without exchange of heat with surrounding air). The relative

---

14. Thus, chapter 3 of the report cites albedo feedback that magnifies warming from 2°C to 4°C in one GCM (the Goddard Institute's GISS model) and from 3.2°C to 4.2°C in another (the National Oceanic and Atmospheric Administration's GFDL model at Princeton), suggesting a β_w of 1.3 to 2; but chapter 5 implies that albedo feedback is only one-eighth as large as the feedback from water vapor (IPCC 1990b, 96, 145).

humidity (the mixing ratio of water vapor mass to dry air mass, r, divided by the corresponding mixing ratio at saturation, r_w, where water vapor mass is at the maximum that air of that temperature can contain) rises toward unity and water begins to condense on airborne particles.

An increase in the greenhouse effect will warm the troposphere and cool the stratosphere, where less outbound infrared radiation will reach after more atmospheric trapping. The saturation-point mixing ratio (r_w) varies positively with temperature and negatively with pressure. As a result, a warmer troposphere will mean a higher r_w and thus a lower relative humidity for a given water vapor content. With lower relative humidity, there will be less cloud formation in the troposphere. By the same reasoning, with a cooler upper atmosphere there will be greater cloud formation at higher altitudes.[15]

The GCMs tend to show that warming associated with a doubling of carbon dioxide would reduce cloud cover by 1 percent to 5 percent below an altitude of 10 km and increase cloud cover by about 1 percent above this height (Schlesinger and Mitchell 1987, 790), thereby reducing total cloud cover and redistributing it upward. Under today's conditions, lower (stratus and cumulus) clouds tend to have a negative radiative forcing effect (as much as -100 wm^{-2} for low stratus clouds), whereas high (cirrus) clouds tend to be neutral in radiative balance. Globally today, clouds on average reduce solar radiative forcing by more than they increase infrared radiative forcing (-44.5 wm^{-2} versus $+31.3$ wm^{-2}, respectively; Ramanathan et al. 1989; Cess et al. 1989, 57–61; IPCC 1990b, 84). The GCMs correspondingly tend to show that cloud change under global warming causes positive feedback, as the low clouds decrease and the high clouds increase. However, the models show a relatively wide range of variation. Cess et al. (1989) have shown that *the principal source of divergence among global warming estimates in GCMs is their differing treatment of cloud feedback.* Thus, 14 GCMs showed an average total warming coefficient for a given radiative forcing (i.e., corresponding to the product $\lambda\beta$ in equation 1.1) of 0.68°C per wm^{-2}, with a standard deviation of 0.24. In contrast, for model runs omitting clouds, this coefficient (essentially corresponding to $\lambda\beta_w\beta_a$ in the discussion here) amounts to 0.47°C per wm^{-2}, with a standard deviation of only 0.04 (Cess et al. 1989, 515).

The principal argument against positive cloud feedback is that of S. Twomey, implemented in calculations by John F. B. Mitchell of the UK Meteorological Office. The argument is that, because of the increase of the share of high-atmosphere clouds with global warming, there would be a tendency for cloud composition to shift from water droplets to ice crystals, with increased albedo as a result. In this view, higher unit cloud albedo would more than offset lower

---

15. G. L. Potter, Lawrence Livermore National Laboratory, Livermore, CA, personal communication, 5 February 1990.

total cloud cover and a greater share of infrared-trapping clouds, making β_c less than unity rather than greater, as in most GCMs. A highly publicized reduction in the UK Meteorological Office GCM calculation of global warming based on the ice crystal theory contributed to a round of skepticism in the public discussion of the greenhouse effect in 1989 (Cookson 1989). Moreover, perhaps because Mitchell was the lead author in the IPCC chapter on equilibrium climate change, that chapter adopted negative cloud feedback as a prime reason for setting the best estimate of the climate sensitivity parameter at 2.5°C rather than the mid-point of the 1.5°C-to-4.5°C range (or even higher if the most recent GCM runs are considered; IPCC 1990b, 144–45). As a consequence, the IPCC "best guess" makes relatively little allowance for the combined influences of albedo and cloud feedback.[16]

Aerosols and Masking by Urban Pollution

There is increasing evidence that aerosols (suspended microscopic particles) caused by urban pollution have masked global warming by producing an off-setting cooling effect. Sulfate aerosols, derived from industrial emissions of sulfur dioxide, are the most important. Charlson et al. (1992, 423) have concluded:

> Both the direct scattering of short-wavelength solar radiation and the modification of the shortwave reflective properties of clouds by sulfate aerosol particles increase planetary albedo, thereby exerting a cooling influence on the planet. Current climate forcing due to anthropogenic sulfate is estimated to be -1 to -2 watts per square meter, globally averaged. This perturbation is comparable in magnitude to current anthropogenic greenhouse gas forcing but opposite in sign.

Moreover, Wigley (1989) has suggested that sulfate aerosols serve as nuclei for increased formation of low (albedo-dominant) clouds.

These influences mean that urban pollution may be masking global warming. If so, this effect could help explain the shortfall of observed from predicted warming (discussed below). One implication is that there is a backlog of hidden warming potential being built up that may be expected to be revealed as industrial nations make progress in reducing urban pollution (especially acid rain). Another implication is that the IPCC's conscious downgrading of the best-guess value for the climate sensitivity parameter Λ (discussed below) may be unwarranted.

---

16. That is, with $\beta_w = 1.43$, and even suppressing β_a and β_c to 1.0 each, we have, for benchmark doubling, $\Delta T \equiv \Lambda = R_c \lambda \beta_w = 4.4 \times 0.3 \times 1.43 = 1.9°C$. Further amplification by albedo and cloud effects is thus limited, in the "best guess," to $\beta_a \beta_c = \Lambda/1.9 = 2.5/1.9 = 1.3$.

Pollution masking of the greenhouse effect raises another issue as well: should pollution simply be allowed to increase as a conscious strategy for limiting warming?[17] The answer is almost certainly in the negative. There are direct health costs of pollution. Moreover, one may expect any cooling effect from urban pollution to have diminishing returns. Even massive buildup of pollution and sulfate aerosols would thus be unlikely to be able to offset the eventual warming effects of the large future accumulation of greenhouse gases in the atmosphere that may be anticipated under business-as-usual policies.

The Empirical Evidence

One hundred years of theory and the simulations of modern computer models are the primary grounds for greenhouse science. Empirical support to date is weaker, to some extent inevitably so for reasons of long lags and natural variability.

There is unambiguous evidence on the buildup of carbon dioxide in the atmosphere. Ice core samples of trapped air provide data on preindustrial levels, and direct measurements from observations at Mauna Loa, Hawaii, since 1958 show a steady increase (from 315 to 353 ppm; IPCC 1990b, 7–9). There is no dispute that the present atmospheric concentration of carbon dioxide is about 25 percent above the preindustrial level (which was approximately 280 ppm). The more elusive evidence is on the impact of carbon dioxide and other trace gases on global warming.

Scientists support the underlying greenhouse concept with the observation that the extremely dense carbon dioxide concentration in the atmosphere of Venus and its sparse presence in that of Mars play a major role in the very hot surface temperature of the former (477°C) versus that of the latter (−47°C). However, the IPCC report fails to provide a clear accounting of what the other influences are and on what grounds the estimates are made for the net greenhouse effect (523°C for Venus, 10°C for Mars; IPCC 1990b, 3).

Further evidence for the greenhouse effect has been derived from air trapped in ice core samples dating back over 160,000 years. Isotope (deuterium) ratios provide a measure of the temperature of the atmosphere at the times of the deposits, which also contain concentrations of greenhouse gases (carbon dioxide, methane, nitrous oxide) representative of these paleological dates. These records show a relatively close correlation between the atmospheric concentration of greenhouse gases and temperature.

---

17. Such a strategy would fit into the family of geoengineering approaches discussed below and is closest to the notion of placing debris into the atmosphere to increase planetary albedo.

Interpretation is tricky, because the direction of causation is ambiguous. The most likely sequence runs as follows. Very long (Milankovitch) cycles in the earth's position (orbital eccentricity varies on a 100,000-year cycle, the obliquity of axis tilt over 41,000 years, and precession of the equinoxes over 23,000 and 19,000 years) are the most likely initial cause of temperature change (see, e.g., Berger et al. 1984, x). Poorly understood mechanisms such as changes in "ocean circulation and marine production for CO_2 . . . and fluxes of emission from natural wetlands for CH_4" then cause a rise (fall) in greenhouse gases in response to the initial rise (fall) in temperature (Lorius et al. 1990).[18] The resulting greenhouse forcing then substantially reinforces the initial temperature disturbance.

Lorius et al. have estimated that the additional influence of greenhouse forcing is necessary to explain the observed paleological temperature record. They calculate that fully one-half of observed warming between the glacial and interglacial periods in the ice core samples (i.e., 3°C of 6°C warming in the Antarctic samples from the Vostok area, corresponding to about 2°C of 4°C to 5°C globally) was contributed by greenhouse gases. Moreover, they note that this amount is consistent with a climate sensitivity parameter Λ of 3°C to 4°C, and thus with the estimates of recent GCMS.[19]

With respect to the greenhouse effect from human activity, the IPCC concluded that "there has been a real, but irregular, increase of global surface temperature since the late nineteenth century" amounting to 0.45°C ± 0.15°C (IPCC 1990b, 198). The data are from three independent sets of temperatures: air over land, air over oceans, and the sea surface. Confirming evidence is that over the same period there has been "a marked, but irregular, recession of the majority of mountain glaciers" (IPCC 1990b, 198).

The observed warming has come in two installments. There was a persistent trend toward global warming from 1910 to 1940. Then temperatures were on a modest downward trend through 1975. The second period of warming was from 1975 through 1990 (IPCC 1990b, 248, figure 8.1). The 1980s were the warmest decade on record. Indeed, as noted above, in the United States an unusually hot summer in 1988 contributed to public interest in the greenhouse effect, and one prominent scientist cited high temperatures in the 1980s as "99 percent certain" evidence of global warming. Although the global warmth in

---

18. Alternative mechanisms might include the following. Photosynthesis by the earth's biota rises with temperature but by less than the corresponding rise in carbon dioxide discharge from plant decay and respiration (Houghton and Woodwell 1989, 41). This differential should cause a net increase in biotic emissions of carbon dioxide in response to warming. Another influence is the release of enormous quantities of carbon-equivalent stored in frozen methane clathrates (MacDonald 1990a), as discussed below.

19. The combination of the ice core experiments with the information on urban pollution masking provides a further hint that the IPCC may have underestimated the "best guess" for Λ.

the 1980s probably was related to the greenhouse effect, 1988 regional climate anomalies were later attributed to the tropical Pacific cycle of the "El Niño–Southern Oscillation."

The IPCC report found that temperatures declined in the Northern Hemisphere from the 1940s to the early 1970s, but that they began to rise again thereafter; temperatures in the Southern Hemisphere were constant from the 1940s to the mid–1970s. Natural variation in temperature, and even prolonged periods of seeming trends that turn out to be random (MacDonald 1990b), mean that the nonmonotonic path of warming over the past century should be no surprise.

Despite the evidence of rising temperatures over the past century, support for the greenhouse theory has been somewhat weakened by the fact that the observed temperature increase is less than the GCM simulations show should have occurred in the absence of other influences. With an unadjusted midpoint of 3°C for the GCMs' climate sensitivity parameter (Λ), and taking an average of parameters for the relationship of observed transient warming to warming commitment (driven by the ocean lag as affected by the diffusion rate and the ratio of temperature change in regions of sinking water to global mean change), expected global mean warming from 1885 to 1990 should have amounted to 0.8°C rather than 0.45°C (calculated from IPCC 1990b, 248). One explanation of the divergence might be that ocean thermal lag is longer than the principal models suggest. Another and increasingly likely explanation is that potential warming has been masked by the effect of sulfate aerosols and cloud stimulation from urban pollution and by the ozone stripping of CFCs, as discussed above.[20] The shortfall was one reason the IPCC downgraded from 3.0°C to 2.5°C, but these offsetting influences suggest that this reduction may have been unwarranted. That is, under conditions of constant or declining (rather than rising) urban pollution, the observed warming would likely have been closer to and perhaps well in excess of the amount predicted with $\Lambda = 3$°C or higher.

Figure 1.1 shows annual temperature averages in the Northern Hemisphere over the past century. The data, displayed as deviations from the 1951–80 means, are from the Goddard Space Flight Center of the US National Aeronautics and Space Administration (NASA). Reported in Carbon Dioxide Information Analysis Center (1992), the data were derived using methodology earlier described in Hansen and Lebedeff (1987). The rising trend through the 1930s, partial decline to the 1970s, and renewed rise in the 1980s is evident in the diagram. The observations for 1881 through 1990 show statistically significant time trends at a global level, with a rate of temperature increase of 0.55°C over

---

20. Although the neutral rather than forcing effect of CFCs suggested in recent findings would work in the correct direction to explain the shortfall of observed warming, the bulk of CFC emissions may have been too recent to have contributed much to "transient" or realized, as opposed to equilibrium, expected warming, however.

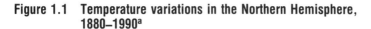

Figure 1.1 Temperature variations in the Northern Hemisphere, 1880–1990[a]

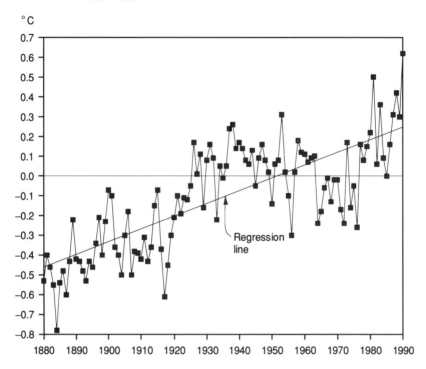

a. Data represent deviations from the mean temperature for 1951–80.

Source: Carbon Dioxide Information Analysis Center. 1992. *Trends '91.* Oak Ridge, TN: Carbon Dioxide Information Analysis Center (Hansen and Lebedeff data series).

a 100-year period.[21] The gradient is higher than the 0.45°C identified by the IPCC (although still lower than the GCM predicted 0.8°C) in part because of the inclusion of the observation for 1990, the hottest year on record.

The addition of data for 1991 would likely have further strengthened the slope of the temperature curve, because 1991 was the second-hottest year on record. Climatologists observed that the 1991 temperatures might have been

---

21. Statistical regression applying Cochrane-Orcutt correction for autocorrelation yields the following results for the coefficient on time (*t* statistics in parentheses) and adjusted R^2: global, 0.0055 (8.6), $R^2 = 0.69$; Northern Hemisphere, 0.0066 (6.8), $R^2 = 0.68$; Southern Hemisphere, 0.0043 (8.7), $R^2 = 0.60$. The finding of a higher warming trend for the Northern Hemisphere than for the Southern is contrary to the IPCC (1990b) findings reported above and reflects the specific features of the Hansen-Lebedeff data set (IPCC 1990b, figure 7.6) and, perhaps, the inclusion of 1990 data in the estimate here.

even higher in the absence of the eruption of the Philippine volcano Pinatubo.[22] The resulting sulfur dioxide is expected to increase aerosol reflection of solar radiation and mask greenhouse warming for perhaps two years (Kerr 1992).

The IPCC report found "a steady increase of cloudinesss of a few percent . . . since 1950 over the USA" (IPCC 1990b, 198). Considering that urban pollution provides an immense increase in airborne particles, which facilitate condensation and cloud formation, this phenomenon may reflect pollution trends. The lesser total warming in the Northern Hemisphere is also consistent with the influences of sulfate aerosols on direct and cloud albedo, discussed above.

As noted above, the new findings for the neutralization of CFC radiative forcing because of ozone stripping meant an additional reason to interpret the actual temperature record as adhering to a properly projected greenhouse path rather than falling short of predicted warming. When the influences of sulfate aerosols (urban pollution) and CFC neutralization are taken into account, along with the steepening of the curve by the hot years 1990–91, there could well be grounds for the return of the "best guess" for the climate sensitivity parameter Λ to 3°C or even higher, thereby reversing the modest downgrading of the IPCC report.

As for further evidence on warming and its effects, an important source is the relatively firm data from numerous studies indicating that sea level has been rising at a rate of 1 to 2 mm per year for the last 100 years. The IPCC's central estimate is that, over the past century, ocean thermal expansion from warming contributed 4 cm to sea level, melting of glaciers and small ice caps 4 cm, melting of the Greenland ice sheet 2.5 cm, and (as discussed below) the Antarctic zero, for a total rise of 10.5 cm (IPCC 1990b, 266–77).[23]

The Ecological and Economic Impact

Chapter 3 sets forth a detailed examination of the prospective impact of global warming. For the natural ecology, warming could impose loss of species and forest area. For the economy, global warming could cause agricultural losses in

---

22. Global temperatures were an average of 0.846°F above normal in 1990 and 0.702°F above normal in 1991 (*New York Times,* 9 January 1992, A11).

23. Note that Zwally (1989) has used satellite observations to conclude that the Greenland ice sheet has been growing, not declining. The IPCC reached the opposite conclusion for the past century. Schneider (1992) points out that North Atlantic temperatures actually declined in the 1977–86 observation period of Zwally's data, so that Zwally's interpretation of likely net negative contribution of the Greenland ice sheet to sea-level *rise* with global warming should be reversed (to the more usual, opposite prognosis). Schneider also notes that the recent suggestion of Miller and de Vernal that sea level could *decrease* because of Arctic ice buildup with global warming is off by a few thousand years. The Miller-de Vernal argument hinges on reduced summer solar radiation, an effect that occurs only over millennia (the Milankovitch cycle discussed above).

many regions. The level of the seas would rise, imposing costs of barrier protection of coastal cities and the loss of land area (including valuable wetlands). There would be increased electricity needs for air conditioning, potentially serious declines in the availability of water to agriculture and cities, increased urban pollution, increased intensity and frequency of hurricanes, increased mortality from heat waves, and losses in leisure activities associated with winter sports. Although effects on human amenity could be at first mixed (and favorable for cold climates), eventually with high very-long-term warming human amenity effects would tend to turn negative.

The ipcc summary of the impact of global warming included the following observations (ipcc 1990a, 5–9).

[In agriculture,] there may be severe effects in some regions, particularly . . . regions of high present-day vulnerability that are least able to adjust. . . . [F]ood production at the global level can be maintained at essentially the same level as would have occurred without climate change; however, the cost of achieving this is unclear. Nonetheless, climate change may intensify the difficulties in coping with rapid population growth.

Large losses . . . in the form of forest declines can occur. Losses from wildfire will be increasingly extensive. . . . The most sensitive areas will be where species are close to their biological limits in terms of temperature and moisture. This is likely to be, for example, in semi-arid areas. . . . Some species could be lost owing to increased stress. . . .

Relatively small climate changes can cause large water resource problems in many areas. . . . Change in drought risk represents potentially the most serious impact of climate change on agriculture at both regional and global levels.

A 1 m rise [in sea level] by 2100 would render some island countries uninhabitable, displace tens of millions of people, seriously threaten low-lying urban areas, flood productive land, contaminate fresh water supplies and change coastlines. All of these impacts would be exacerbated if droughts and storms become more severe.

Permafrost, which currently underlies 20–25% of the land mass of the Northern Hemisphere, could experience significant degradation within the next 40–50 years. . . . As a result, overlying ecosystems could be significantly altered and the integrity of man-made structures and facilities reduced. . . .

In view of these and other risks, another international body of scientists, the independent scientific Advisory Group on Greenhouse Gases, has recommended urgent international action to set an absolute upper limit of 3.5°C warming above preindustrial levels, "beyond which the risks of grave damage to ecosystems, and of non-linear responses, are expected to increase rapidly" ("Earlier Harm Seen in Global Warming," *New York Times*, 17 October 1990). Yet this ceiling would be well within the range predicted for a doubling of carbon-dioxide-equivalent.

Critiques and Response

The public policy debate on the greenhouse problem has often given the impression that scientists are hopelessly divided. Instead, the IPCC scientific report provided an important occasion to reveal a wide consensus among a substantial majority of scientists, especially those directly trained in climate sciences. The report, called for by the United Nations, assembled an international group of 170 scientists, as well as another 200 reviewers. It would be fair to say that the scientific majority accepting the report's findings is at least as large as the two-thirds threshold required for proposing constitutional amendments in the United States.

Nonetheless, some scientists have been highly vocal in their criticism of the greenhouse theory, or at least of the warming magnitudes in the mainstream projections. The IPCC report specifically rejected one influential critique. Scientists at the Marshall Institute have invoked statistical curve-fitting work by Reid to argue that variations in global temperature are largely explained by sunspot activity, not trace gas concentration (Seitz et al. 1989). The Marshall Institute concluded that the greenhouse effect would be small and might be a welcome counter to an otherwise cooling phase in the 21st century. The IPCC authors reexamined the data incorporating greenhouse radiative forcing and found that the statistical fit for the remaining influence of sunspots was consistent only with a much lower impact than suggested by Reid. They did note that an 80-year cycle of a modest 0.2°C amplitude might be caused by solar activity. More generally, however, they concluded that, because the time scale of the sunspot cycle is far shorter than that of thermal inertia of the oceans, solar radiative forcing cannot create the same sustained warming as the greenhouse effect (as trace gas concentration is strictly rising, whereas solar activity is cyclical).[24]

---

24. In late 1991, a new study reported a striking correlation between global temperature anomaly (deviation from average) and the sunspot cycle over the past century (Kerr 1991b). Danish researchers Friss-Christensen and Lassen used data on land temperatures for the Northern Hemisphere since 1870, and for the sun's energy output they used the proxy of sunspot cycle length. The interval between peaks of sunspot activity shortened from about 12 years in 1890 to about 10 years by 1940, lengthened again to nearly 11 years by 1960, and shortened again to less than 10 years by the early 1980s. The study found a remarkable 95 percent correlation between the temperature anomaly and the (negative of) sunspot cycle length. However, there is no theory that can explain how the known extent of solar variability can produce temperature changes as large as those observed over the past century. Such a theory would require some mechanism whereby the upper atmosphere magnifies the effects of known changes in irradiance. In the absence of a theoretical basis, many scientists interpreted the results as a "roll of the statistical dice"—like several sunspot relationships discerned and later discarded in the past. Moreover, the new findings gave no support whatsoever to the Marshall Institute thesis that solar activity would decline in the 21st century.

Similarly, the report did not accept the critique of greenhouse theory that data for the United States show no warming over the last 100 years. The scientists dismissed the notion that any single country could be considered globally representative. They also found that satellite data that had shown no warming in the lower atmosphere (midtroposphere) between 1979 and 1988 confirmed, rather than contradicted, the surface temperature record, and therefore increased confidence in the longer data series for surface temperatures (Kerr 1990, 481–82).

The IPCC report omitted mention of the argument by Richard Lindzen, of the Massachusetts Institute of Technology, that drying of the upper atmosphere would counteract warming of the troposphere and surface, as the IPCC scientists assessed this effect as small and greatly outweighed by other effects of greenhouse warming (Kerr 1990). As reviewed by Rosenberg (1992), most climatologists have tended to reject the Lindzen argument on water vapor.

Very-Long-Term Warming

Overall, greenhouse science holds up well to scrutiny. Its logic and physics are compelling. Although warming to date is less than predicted, the shortfall is within the range of natural variability. Alternatively, longer-than-expected ocean thermal lag and/or influences such as the hypothesized enhancement of cloud and direct aerosol albedo by sulfur dioxide pollution and the greater-than-expected stripping of ozone by CFCs may be simply masking potential warming. In any event, the scientific (IPCC) adoption of a relatively low value for the climate sensitivity parameter, with $\Lambda = 2.5°C$ for carbon-dioxide-equivalent doubling as opposed to the recent GCM averages of 3.5°C to 4°C (Rosenberg 1988, 18; IPCC 1990b, 87), is a significant bow in the direction of downgrading the estimates because of the observed temperature record to date.

My own view is that the principal shortcoming in the scientific and policy discussion to date has been the failure to extend the time horizon of analysis to the very long term, on the order of 250 to 300 years. Instead, the great bulk of the scientific work (GCM simulations in particular) has been fixated on the arbitrary benchmark of a doubling of carbon-dioxide-equivalent trace gases. However, the IPCC concluded that, under business as usual, this level of warming commitment would be achieved already by the year 2025. For purposes of planetary management, a horizon of 35 years is woefully inadequate.

Chapter 2 of this study examines the IPCC findings for warming commitment through the year 2100 and uses the report's underlying parameters to develop projections of global warming through the year 2275. As discussed in that analysis, the prospect of increased deep-ocean mixing toward the end of this horizon of 250 to 300 years holds the possibility of a partial reversal of the buildup of carbon dioxide in the atmosphere, thereby providing a natural terminal date for the planning period. The central point is that, with much greater warming over this very long horizon, economic damages could be far higher, and thus the case for preventive action is stronger than might be suggested by focusing on the usual benchmark of a doubling of carbon dioxide.

Catastrophe Scenarios

There are several possible ways in which global warming might bring catastrophic damage rather than moderate progressive decay. One possibility is that the release of carbon dioxide stored in methane clathrates submerged along continental shelves and in permafrost could cause massive positive feedback not incorporated in the GCMs. The clathrate is a crystal structure in cold water, in which ice-lattice forms cages that entrap gas molecules. Methane clathrates are stable in cold ocean sediments at depths of about 250 meters. These structures can become destabilized, however, as the result of warming or reduced pressure. MacDonald (1990a) has estimated that some 11,000 GtC is stored in ocean clathrates, and another 400 GtC in permafrost.

The amount of carbon in methane clathrates is thus on the same order of magnitude as that in all coal reserves (7,000 to 14,000 GtC; chapter 2). The release of a significant portion of the methane in clathrates as a consequence of global warming could cause a massive positive feedback that would contribute to still more warming.[25] Revelle (1983a, 257–59) has calculated that, for the warming associated with a doubling of carbon-dioxide-equivalent (e.g., 2°C to 3°C), clathrate destabilization could release enough methane to increase atmospheric concentrations by two-thirds to four-thirds, with a corresponding additional warming effect of 0.65°C to 1.8°C. In view of the scope for much higher global warming over two to three centuries (chapter 2), the amount of induced warming and thus positive feedback from this source could be expected to multiply severalfold.

Another possible source of catastrophe is the disintegration of the West Antarctic ice sheet, which would release some 2 million km³ of ice into the sea before the remainder began to float. This phenomenon could cause mean sea

---

25. Moreover, the greenhouse effect of methane (including its indirectly formed water vapor) is about 20 times as powerful as that of carbon dioxide over a time scale of 100 years and 9 times as powerful on a time scale of 500 years (IPCC 1990b, table 2.8, 64). As the molecular weight of carbon dioxide (CO_2) is 44 atomic units (hydrogen = 1) whereas that of methane (CH_4) is 16, the total potential mass of methane in the clathrate store is approximately one-third that of potential carbon dioxide emissions held in coal resources. The implication is that there is on the order of five (15/3) times as much greenhouse gas potential in methane clathrates as in fossil fuel reserves (which are mainly coal). Note, however, that clathrate destabilization would occur over a much longer time horizon.

level to rise by five to six meters (Revelle 1983b, 442). An increase of this amount would be sufficient to inundate approximately 30 percent of the land area of Florida and Louisiana; 15 percent to 20 percent of Maryland, the District of Columbia, and Delaware; 8 percent to 10 percent of the Carolinas and New Jersey; and as much as 7 percent of Rhode Island and Washington state (Schneider and Chen 1980). Port facilities worldwide would be flooded, as would other low-lying coastal structures. Bentley (as cited in Revelle 1983b, 444) has estimated that disintegration of the West Antarctic ice sheet could occur within 300 to 500 years as a consequence of global warming. Although this prospect is not considered likely under "a typical greenhouse warming scenario" (IPCC 1990b, section 9.4.6), it would presumably become a considerably greater risk with the much larger amount of global warming that could occur over a horizon of some 250 years (see chapter 2 of this study).

Still another potential catastrophic effect is that the melting of ice could change the salinity of the North Atlantic, altering the Pacific-Atlantic salinity differential and disrupting the "deep ocean conveyor" that brings an upwelling of waters from, and the sinking of water into, the deep ocean between Iceland and Greenland. Such an event would completely alter world weather patterns and ocean currents.[26]

Beyond these potential catastrophe scenarios, which have already been the subject of scientific analysis and debate, there could well be serious adverse surprises from global warming from phenomena not yet suspected. The experience of ozone depletion serves as a warning about the risk of adverse surprise. Depletion of stratospheric ozone has occurred much faster than scientists had predicted, largely because their calculations failed to take into account "heterogeneous chemistry"—the influence of particle surfaces on chemical reactions as opposed to processes for homogeneously mixed gases.[27] As a result, governments have been forced to adopt steeper cutbacks of CFCs by earlier target dates.

Unavoidable Warming

Because of the buildup in atmospheric concentrations of carbon dioxide and other greenhouse gases that has already taken place, the earth is already committed to some warming now in the pipeline even if all man-made emissions were to stop virtually immediately. The IPCC estimates that total radiative forcing from 1765 through the year 2000 will have amounted to 2.95 wm^{-2}. Applying

---

26. Rob Coppock of the National Academy of Sciences, speaking at a study group session at the Institute for International Economics, Washington, 29 July 1991.

27. Mack McFarland, speaking at a conference on "Assessing Climate Change Risks," sponsored by Resources for the Future, Washington, 23–24 March 1992.

equation 1.1 above, with the values $R = 2.95$, $\lambda = 0.3$, and $\beta = 1.9$ (as discussed above), the equilibrium amount of warming already committed amounts to about 1.7°C. Moreover, the IPCC estimates that even if an aggressive program of "accelerated policies" were adopted, radiative forcing would reach 4.3 wm^{-2} by the year 2100 (IPCC 1990b, table 2.7). This amount of forcing corresponds to the doubling of carbon-dioxide-equivalent (as discussed above with respect to equation 1.2), so ultimate warming of a central value of 2.5°C seems almost inevitable.

Matters would be worse without aggressive action, however. The IPCC projection for business as usual sets radiative forcing at 9.9 wm^{-2} by the year 2100, corresponding to a commitment to equilibrium warming of 5.6°C, according to equation 1.1 and with climate sensitivity parameter $\Lambda = 2.5$. Moreover, under business as usual the gradient of radiative forcing is still steep by the last quarter of the 21st century (as forcing rises from 8.28 wm^{-2} in 2075). In contrast, the "accelerated policies" manage nearly to halt the further buildup in radiative forcing by that period (as radiative forcing rises only from 4.22 wm^{-2} in 2075 to 4.30 wm^{-2} by 2100).

There is an important message in the "unavoidable warming" analysis: adaptational measures will be required even if aggressive prevention is pursued. However, it is important that the message not be misinterpreted. Some have seemed to argue that policy can only delay global warming, not avoid it (Schmalensee 1991, 74). As the comparison above shows, however, preventive policy can make a major difference in the ultimate amount of warming. Moreover, as developed in chapter 2, the extent of warming over three centuries could far exceed the amount committed by 2100, so the fraction of warming that can be definitively avoided is potentially large.

Geoengineering

The potentially high costs of limiting emissions and the difficulty of mobilizing international cooperation have led some to advocate the use of "geoengineering" to address the greenhouse problem. This approach would use interventions in the atmosphere and biosphere to limit warming—an approach that is equivalent to driving an automobile with one foot on the gas pedal (emissions) and another on the brake (the offsetting geoengineering measures). Scientists have tended to consider many of these proposals dangerous on a global scale, and the geo-engineering approach is conspicuous by its absence in the massive IPCC report (1990a–d).

In 1991, the National Academy of Sciences (NAS) gave geoengineering options a new respectability by urging their scientific study. Nevertheless, the NAS urged caution:

Geoengineering options have the potential to affect greenhouse warming on a substantial scale. However, precisely because they might do so, and because the climate system and its chemistry are poorly understood, these options must be considered extremely carefully. . . . Some of these options are relatively inexpensive to implement, but all have large unknowns concerning possible environmental side-effects. They should not be implemented without careful assessment of their direct and indirect consequences. (NAS 1991a, 59)

The measures listed by the NAS as worthy of close study included the following.

Sunlight Screening

Several alternatives would limit solar radiation reaching the earth (NAS 1991a, 58). A system of 50,000 *space mirrors*, each 100 km^2 in size, would be placed in orbit to reflect sunlight.[28] *Stratospheric dust* would be shot from guns or released by balloons to maintain a dust cloud for reflecting sunlight. *Stratospheric bubbles* in the form of "billions of aluminized, hydrogen-filled balloons" would provide an alternative reflective screen. *Low stratospheric dust* released by airplanes would seek the same objective. *Low stratospheric soot* emitted from reduced-efficiency burning in engines of aircraft flying in the low stratosphere would be another alternative. *Cloud stimulation* (for low clouds over water) by the burning of sulfur in ships or power plants to form sulfate aerosol would seek the same objective.

Other

Ocean biomass stimulation through the fertilization of oceans with iron could stimulate CO_2-absorbing phytoplankton. *Lasers* could be used to break up CFCs in the atmosphere.

Feasibility and Risks

Even the NAS authors imply the infeasibility of space mirrors and CFC-breaking lasers as they tersely note that these are "not included among those recommended for further investigation" (NAS 1991a, 58). They also warn that "there is convincing evidence that the stratospheric particle options contribute to depletion of the ozone layer." They note that cloud stimulation options would require first that "concerns about acid rain . . . be managed through the choice of materials. . . ." (NAS 1991a, 81).

---

28. The summary NAS report provides no details on how a 100-km^2 mirror is constructed, let alone how it is placed into orbit.

As for the option of iron fertilization of the Antarctic ocean to enhance phytoplankton growth, the author of the idea suggests that up to 1 billion tons of carbon might be extracted annually from the atmosphere in this way.[29] Yet this amount would be marginal compared with baseline emissions rising to a range of 20 to 50 GtC annually by 2100–2275 (chapter 2). Moreover, some scientists are concerned that iron fertilization might have as a side effect increased bacterial consumption of phytoplankton fecal pellets at about the depths (1,000 yards) where the eggs of krill (a small crustacean) hatch. The increased bacterial activity could reduce oxygen available for krill, adversely affecting food supply for whales and other sea animals.[30]

In short, it would seem prudent for policymakers, first, to encourage research on the geoengineering options, but second, to place very little weight indeed on these options in the mainstream planning for dealing with the greenhouse problem.

Scientific Research Agenda

The IPCC (1990b, chapter 11) has outlined the priority areas for scientific research. Its list begins with the control of greenhouse gases by natural forces. This subject is imperfectly understood but crucial, because man-made fluxes are typically small relative to natural fluxes and reservoirs. An analysis of the physical and biological processes of carbon dioxide uptake by the ocean is to be carried out by the international Joint Global Ocean Flux Study. Parallel research is in progress on the interaction between atmospheric chemistry and the carbon fluxes of the terrestrial biosphere.

Control of radiation by clouds is another key area for research.[31] Radiation fluxes are influenced by the amount, distribution, and optical properties of water and ice clouds. Satellite measurements of top-of-atmosphere radiation fluxes need to be improved to distinguish between the effects of different types of clouds at different altitudes. The Global Energy and Water Cycle Experiment (GEWEX) seeks to improve the measurement of energy fluxes within the atmosphere, and between air and land and air and sea. Satellite launches for this purpose are expected by 1997.

---

29. John Martin, as cited in "Ideas for Making Ocean Trap Carbon Dioxide Arouse Hope and Fear," *New York Times*, 20 November 1990, C4.

30. Gustav Paffenhofer, as cited in "Ideas for Making Ocean Trap Carbon Dioxide Arouse Hope and Fear," *New York Times*, 20 November 1990, C4.

31. As noted, differing treatment of feedback from clouds accounts for the bulk of the variation in equilibrium warming estimates of alternative GCMs.

Improved analysis of precipitation and evaporation under global warming is important. "Changes in . . . soil moisture and the availability of fresh water resources, are the most serious potential consequences of impending climate change in terms of its effect on man" (IPCC 1990b, 327). The GEWEX program seeks to develop global climatological records of precipitation, including precipitation over oceans. Another need is for field studies of the energy and water budgets of a land area of a size compatible with the grid resolutions of current GCMS (e.g., 10 to 100 km).

The transport and storage of heat by the oceans is another priority area for research. The lag between radiative forcing and warming of the earth's surface is determined by the "largely unknown rate of penetration of heat into the upper 1000 metres" of the ocean (IPCC 1990b, 328). Various satellite observation programs seek to measure ocean dynamics (wave height, surface topography, wind stress).

Improved analysis is needed of the interaction of ecosystems and climate change (e.g., large-scale displacement of particular ecosystems would change surface albedo). Better global observations of vegetation and soils are needed for this purpose.

Improved climate modeling is also a high priority, particularly in the coupling of ocean dynamics with atmospheric changes, as well as in finer spatial resolution. For this purpose, computational resources are important, as well as technological improvements in computing capacity.

In most of these areas, the IPCC foresees important findings by at least the year 2000. This possibility alone suggests the advisability of dividing the policy response into an initial phase for confirmation and a subsequent phase for intensified action.

Another area for scientific confirmation is the use of underwater sonic transmissions to measure ocean warming. The speed of sound through water depends on temperature, and the monitoring of acoustical speed along specific paths could provide statistically reliable evidence of warming in a much shorter period of years than through traditional means of recording temperature (Hansen et al. 1990, MacDonald 1990b).

Hansen et al. (1990) have proposed to expedite scientific measurement of the key climate parameters through a program to launch three relatively small climate satellites. Each would carry the following: instruments for stratospheric aerosol and gas experiments (SAGE); an Earth-Observing Scanning Polarimeter (EOSP) for monitoring tropospheric aerosols and clouds; and instruments for measuring radiative balance (the Earth Radiation Budget Experiment, ERBE). The total cost would amount to $350 million. These three specialized satellites would provide data considerably sooner than the much more ambitious (and less focused) "Mission to Planet Earth" to be launched late in the 1990s, in which the US National Aeronautics and Space Administration (NASA) plans to include the Earth Observing System (EOS).

My own perspective is that there is a crucial area for scientific confirmation that warrants much more attention than it has been given to date, namely, analysis of very-long-term warming, on a time scale of 300 years. As noted above, by far the bulk of the analysis has been of the impact of a doubling of carbon-dioxide-equivalent in the atmosphere. Yet this threshold is expected to arrive as early as 2025, and heat-trapping gases are likely to build up far beyond this level. Because global warming is a cumulative and irreversible process, there is a serious need to explore the much more severe effects that might be expected over a longer horizon. In particular, the calculation of equilibrium warming for scenarios with severalfold carbon-equivalent (e.g., 8 to 16; chapter 2) would add importantly to the ability of policymakers to assess the potential seriousness of the problem. Correspondingly, the development of agricultural crop models to explore the viability of global agriculture under these much more severe, longer-term scenarios should be given a high priority.

Similarly, research is needed on the response of ecological systems to a speed of climate change that is 10 to 50 times as great as experienced historically. Finally, there is an urgent need for more reliable projections of regional and transient (i.e., specific-date) effects, as these are what matter for both impact assessment and adaptation.

Conclusion

The science of the greenhouse effect is persuasive. Global warming has taken place over the last century, and the shortfall from the amount predicted may be largely explained by the effects of sulfate aerosols from urban pollution and by the greater-than-expected stripping of ozone by CFCs. Important elements of confirmation could be available from the schedule of scientific experiments planned over the next decade, although more definitive verification could take much longer. There is a serious need for greater scientific analysis of global warming on a time scale of 250 to 300 years. Because this warming and its associated economic damages would be far greater than what is expected from the conventional (and relatively close) benchmark of a doubling of carbon-dioxide-equivalent, the incorporation of this longer horizon is important for any balanced evaluation of public policy on the greenhouse problem. Chapter 2 turns to an examination of warming in the very long term.

2

Global Warming in the Very Long Term

2

Global Warming in the Very Long Term

An economic analysis of global warming requires an evaluation of the damage to be expected from the greenhouse effect, the corresponding benefits that could be gained by avoiding some or most of the warming, and the costs of adjusting economic activity to limit warming (primarily those imposed by cutbacks in the use of fossil fuels). Several economic models have evaluated the costs of restricting greenhouse gas emissions (chapter 4). One study (Nordhaus 1991a) has examined both the cost and the benefit sides and calculated the optimal reduction in emissions. However, as analyzed in chapter 7 (annex 7A), the Nordhaus analysis is limited by a focus on damage associated with the doubling of carbon-dioxide-equivalent. Similarly, most of the scientific analysis of warming damage has concentrated on this benchmark.

There is a fundamental problem with analyses based on the doubling of carbon dioxide: their horizon is too short. The convention of evaluating effects at this benchmark has provided an important base of comparable estimates by alternative general circulation models (GCMs) and a nascent body of useful economic literature. However, it misses the point that the accumulation of trace gases and consequential global warming is a continuous process that would not stop with the mere doubling of carbon dioxide but, in the absence of policy action, would persist into the indefinite future. Over a much longer horizon there could thus be far greater warming than that associated with benchmark doubling and thus much greater ecological and economic damage. Failure to take this larger damage into account would seriously bias public policy decisions against abatement measures.

The doubling criterion was more plausible when analysts expected this event to be reached no sooner than the second half of the 21st century. However, the Intergovernmental Panel on Climate Change (IPCC) has concluded that the doubling of carbon-dioxide-equivalent of all trace gases will be reached by approximately 2025 (IPCC 1990b, chapter 2, 48). Even though the ultimate actual increase in temperatures corresponding to the "warming commitment" of this event would not occur until decades later because of ocean thermal lag,[1] the revised timing of the carbon-dioxide-doubling benchmark makes it look veritably myopic as a planning horizon.

Schneider (1991, 29) concurs that the principal scientific focus to date has given inadequate attention to the very long term. In his generally favorable review of the IPCC reports, he states:

> The most serious general problem is that the reports—especially their policy aspects—focus too much on climate change up to a fixed date, 2030, instead of giving equal emphasis to the longer-term changes that will result from human actions between now and 2030.

This chapter will advance the following arguments:

- The proper time horizon for policy determination on global warming is on the order of 250 to 300 years, rather than the 35 years until carbon dioxide doubling.

- The extent of commitment to global warming over this more properly defined planning horizon is on the order of 10°C as a central estimate, more than twice the upper bound of the generally accepted range for a doubling of carbon dioxide. The corresponding upper-bound estimate for very-long-term warming would be on the order of 18°C.

- The reason for this much higher range of warming than conventionally considered is that the scope of atmospheric trace gas accumulation is on the order of an eightfold multiple of preindustrial atmospheric concentrations of carbon dioxide, rather than a doubling, and is an even higher effective increase after taking account of other trace gases.

Because the economic stakes in greenhouse damage over this longer-term horizon may dwarf the estimates that have been made to date, the benefit-cost calculus for taking preventive action may be considerably more favorable than suggested by the existing economic studies. Chapters 3 through 7 set forth the elements of such an analysis, based on the estimates of warming in the very long term presented in this chapter.

The analysis that follows is initial, and should ideally be confirmed by additional simulations of GCMs and other scientific investigation of very-long-term warming. However, the outlines would appear sufficiently clear that they should raise serious doubt about the adequacy of the benefit-cost analysis of greenhouse policy to date.

---

1. See chapter 1, note 7, for further detail on ocean thermal lag.

Fossil Fuel Supply

A natural question for economists to ask is whether the greenhouse problem shouldn't simply solve itself through the market process. Specifically, before enough carbon is put into the atmosphere to cause serious damage, will not fossil fuels become so scarce that their high price will suppress further significant atmospheric buildup?[2]

The answer is in the negative. By far the most abundant fossil fuel is coal,[3] and analysis of coal resources alone indicates that the supply is ample to permit atmospheric carbon buildup of severalfold, far beyond doubling. Edmonds and Reilly (1985, 160) estimate that there exist some 5,000 to 18,000 gigatons (Gt) of coal that can be mined at costs of less than $85 per ton (1979 dollars), and 3,800 to 13,000 Gt available at less than $30 per ton.[4] As a working figure, then, it would seem appropriate to estimate that some 10,000 Gt of coal is available at moderate production costs, and perhaps some 20,000 Gt available at production costs considerably below the price levels that recent estimates have suggested are required to suppress demand to levels that would stabilize global carbon emissions.[5]

Nordhaus and Yohe (1983, 116) estimate that one ton of coal contributes 0.7 ton of carbon emissions in the combustion process. On this basis, there should be at least 7,000 gigatons of carbon (GtC) available from coal at moderate prices, and 14,000 GtC available at prices still below levels that hold emissions to low levels.

Primarily because of ocean uptake of carbon dioxide, only part of the carbon emissions from fossil fuel combustion remains in the atmosphere. Estimates by the US Department of Energy and others indicate that in recent years approximately 58 percent of annual carbon emissions have remained in the atmosphere (US Department of Energy as cited in Reilly et al. 1987, 24). As atmospheric concentration increases, there would be reason to expect the atmospheric re-

---

2. As Professor Wilfred Beckerman of Oxford University puts it, perhaps before global warming reaches serious dimensions coal will be so scarce that people will use it for earrings.

3. Resources of oil, oil shale, and gas add only about 10 percent to the carbon stored in coal resources (Sundquist 1990, 202).

4. For comparison, the international price of coal was approximately $44 per ton in 1991 (International Monetary Fund, *International Financial Statistics*, 1992, April 78), or $23 per ton in 1979 dollars (deflating with the US consumer price index; *Economic Report of the President*, February 1992, 361).

5. Manne and Richels estimate that a carbon tax of $250 per ton would be required in the long run to stabilize carbon emissions at 80 percent of the 1990 rate (see chapter 4). In 1979 dollars, and considering the carbon content of coal, this tax would correspond to $118 per metric ton of coal.

tention rate to decline from the standpoint of greater concentration differential between the atmosphere and the ocean and the resulting increased diffusion rate. However, the global warming process could decrease the ocean's ability to absorb carbon dioxide from the atmosphere with respect to that component of absorption related to detritus rain of ocean biota, as biota could be less prolific in a warmer ocean (IPCC 1990b, 10, 12–13). Moreover, warmer sea water would absorb less carbon dioxide, other influences being held constant. For very-long-term analysis, an atmospheric retention ratio of 0.5 would thus seem appropriate as a plausible central estimate.

In short, somewhere between 3,500 and 7,000 GtC (that is, half the carbon content of the relevant range of coal resources) could end up resident in the atmosphere before the market mechanism chokes off further atmospheric buildup through high prices caused by scarcity of a severely depleted resource. The total stock of carbon in the atmosphere at present is 750 GtC (IPCC 1990b, figure 1.1). Thus, the atmospheric concentration of carbon dioxide could multiply fivefold or tenfold before the market process would suppress buildup because of fossil fuel scarcity.

Finally, it must be kept in mind that, from the standpoint of radiative-forcing properties, carbon dioxide itself has accounted for only about 60 percent of the buildup in total trace gases in recent decades. Methane, nitrous oxide, and the chlorofluorocarbons (CFCs) have provided the rest. As discussed below, the share of carbon dioxide in trace-gas buildup is expected to continue at approximately two-thirds. As a result, for a given n-fold multiple of carbon dioxide itself, there is an even larger multiple of total carbon-dioxide-equivalent trace gases above preindustrial levels (when the relative role of the other trace gases was much smaller).[6]

The overall result of these considerations it that a scarce supply of fossil fuel resources, and coal in particular, is unlikely to be an effective constraint to very-long-term warming.

Establishing the Appropriate Time Horizon

It is apparent from the massive reserves of fossil fuels that a time horizon that reaches only to 2025 or perhaps 2050 is far too short for analysis of the greenhouse effect. There are ample reserves to provide for continued fossil fuel burning—and carbon dioxide emissions—until a much more distant future date. Even the IPCC has recognized as much, at least implicitly, as it carries out its explicit analysis as far as the year 2100 (IPCC 1990b).

---

6. This is the reason that the IPCC finds that the effective doubling of carbon dioxide occurs by 2025, even though the atmospheric concentration of carbon dioxide itself by that date would remain below twice the preindustrial level of 280 parts per million by volume.

Figure 2.1 Carbon dioxide production under alternative fossil fuel consumption scenarios

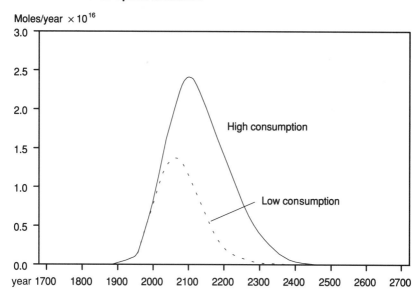

Source: Eric T. Sundquist. 1990. "Long-term Aspects of Future Atmospheric CO_2 and Sea-Level Changes." Reprinted with permission from Roger R. Revelle, et al., *Sea-Level Change,* © 1990 by the National Academy of Sciences. Published by National Academy Press, Washington, DC.

Sundquist (1990) has provided one of the few scientific analyses that examine atmospheric buildup of carbon dioxide over the very long term. Figures 2.1 and 2.2 reproduce Sundquist's analysis. The first shows alternative time paths for fossil fuel consumption and the resulting emissions of carbon dioxide.[7] Sundquist (1990, 201) considers the two alternative scenarios to be "well within the range of fossil fuel resource estimates."[8] As shown in figures 2.1 and 2.2, he estimates

---

7. Figure 2.1 reports emissions in moles $\times$ 10^{16} per year. One mole of carbon dioxide (CO_2) has a weight of 44 grams (the atomic weight of carbon is 12, and that of oxygen of which there are two atoms in one carbon dioxide molecule is 16); 10^{16} moles of carbon dioxide has a mass of 440 Gt (10^{16} moles $\times$ [44 g/mole] $\times$ [10^{-15}Gt/g]). The carbon content is 12/44, or 120 GtC/10^{16} moles of carbon dioxide. Sundquist's maximum emissions of 2.4 $\times$ 10^{16} moles in the year 2100 amount to 288 GtC, about six times the maximum emissions projected here by 2275. Essentially, Sundquist assumes faster burning of fossil fuel reserves, whereas the analysis here anticipates more gradual use, with broadly comparable total consumption over three centuries.

8. The two cases shown in the figures correspond to the addition of 2,500 GtC and 5,000

Figure 2.2 Atmospheric carbon dioxide concentrations under alternative fossil fuel consumption scenarios

Atmospheres × 10^{-3}

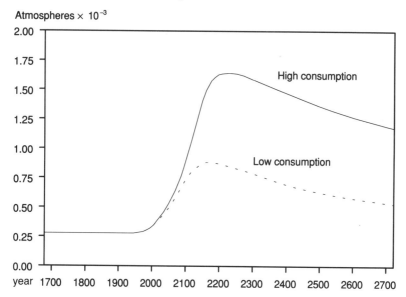

Source: Eric T. Sundquist. 1990. "Long-term Aspects of Future Atmospheric CO_2 and Sea-Level Changes." Reprinted with permission from Roger R. Revelle, et al., *Sea-Level Change,* © 1990 by the National Academy of Sciences. Published by National Academy Press, Washington, DC.

that, under a scenario of high fossil fuel consumption that would exhaust resources over approximately 300 years, the atmospheric concentration of carbon dioxide would rise to over 1,600 parts per million (ppm) after approximately 250 years (nearly six times the preindustrial level) and then drop back gradually to about 1,000 ppm over the following 500 years. The concentration would remain in the range of 700 ppm (somewhat more than twice preindustrial levels) over the period A.D. 4,000–10,000 (Sundquist 1990, 204).[9]

The driving force behind this eventual (but only partial) reversal is the behavior of the deep ocean. Over the first 100 or 200 years, the rate of ocean uptake of carbon dioxide declines because the solubility of carbon dioxide declines as sea water warms, and because of the buildup in the amount of carbon

---

GtC, respectively. The analysis below uses somewhat higher estimates of fossil fuel resources but identifies an essentially similar potential buildup of carbon concentration over a 250-year horizon.

9. Figure 2.2 shows concentrations in parts per thousand, and thus one one-thousandth of the more usual parts per million measure.

dioxide already dissolved in the ocean. However, on time scales of 200 years or more, mixing with the deep ocean begins to dominate, exposing a much more vast reservoir of water to mixing instead of just the upper layers, and thus greatly increasing ocean absorption (Eric Sundquist, US Geological Survey, personal communication, 29 November 1990).

The potential for deep-ocean mixing to begin the reversal process may be seen by a close reading of figures 2.1 and 2.2. Atmospheric concentration begins declining by approximately the year 2225 (figure 2.2). Yet annual global carbon dioxide emissions from fossil fuels in that year are still as high or higher than today (figure 2.1), after having risen far higher in the intervening two centuries. If atmospheric concentration is declining even when annual emissions are as high as today, the implication is that mixing into the deep ocean permits a greater withdrawal of carbon dioxide from the atmosphere (in contrast to the buildup presently associated with current levels of emissions).

An important implication of the Sundquist analysis is that *delay for 250 years is equivalent to avoidance* for the assessment of atmospheric carbon dioxide buildup and global warming. Consider the shift of one ton of carbon from emission in 1990 to emission in 2240. If emitted in 1990, the carbon (or at least about half of it) adds to atmospheric stock. However, if emitted in 2240, it enters the atmosphere just when deep-ocean mixing is removing carbon that entered in 1990, so that rather than making a net addition it merely replaces exiting carbon.

The concept of a 250- to 300-year reversal horizon has important implications for the use of nonrenewable fossil fuels. If used early, they carry a "contamination penalty" because of global warming. However, if stored for use in the very long term, beyond the reversal horizon, their contamination role disappears.[10] Indeed, because they could be used "safely" in the very long term, fossil fuel resources not consumed because of an emissions control program retain a value that, in principle, should be deducted from economic costs in analysis of such programs.[11]

In sum, the Sundquist analysis suggests that the appropriate horizon for greenhouse analysis is on the order of 250 to 300 years. Atmospheric buildup of carbon concentrations can be expected to continue until that period, so that

---

10. This broad-brush interpretation would require closer analysis to take account of the combined influences of the timing of deep-ocean mixing and the extent of withdrawal as a function of the differential between atmospheric and ocean concentrations of carbon dioxide. To some extent the reduction in the latter as the consequence in delay of fossil fuel burning would reduce the removal rate at the 250- to 300-year horizon.

11. The benefit-cost analysis of this study makes no valuation allowance for the remaining inventory of fossil fuel reserves at the end of the 300-year horizon, in part because even with a low discount rate the discounted present value of this stock is sharply reduced after such a long period. The absence of such a valuation is one reason for considering the estimates here to understate the net benefits of restricting global emissions of carbon dioxide.

global warming would reach successively higher levels over a full three centuries. Any analysis that truncates the horizon to just the first 50 or 100 years will understate the eventual extent of warming and thus of greenhouse damage. As discussed below and in chapter 3, there is reason to expect damages to rise nonlinearly with warming. Truncation of the horizon will thus bias the analysis against action, as it will tend to understate the true damages by a greater proportion than it understates the costs of abatement.

Carbon Emissions and Atmospheric Concentration

Carbon emissions over time depend on the interaction of fossil fuel supply and demand. Demand depends on the amount of energy required for economic activity and on the price signals for the shares of fossil and nonfossil fuels in energy supply.

The central projections of three well-known carbon-energy-economic models are presented in table 2.1. The underlying factors driving these models are assumed growth rates for population, labor productivity growth, resulting GDP, energy efficiency, and resulting energy demand and long-term supply schedules for alternative energy sources. As discussed in chapter 4, the models of Edmonds and Reilly (Reilly et al. 1987) and Manne and Richels (1990c) offer considerable detail on alternative energy supply activities.[12]

The baseline projections of the three models through the year 2100 (or, in the case of Edmonds and Reilly, 2075) are extended through the year 2275 as follows. For Nordhaus and Yohe (1983) and Edmonds and Reilly, the rate of growth of fossil fuel emissions in the final 25-year period calculated by the authors is extrapolated over the remainder of the period through 2275. In the case of the Manne-Richels estimates, the absolute linear trend of emissions in the second half of the 21st century is extrapolated through 2275, implying a steadily diminishing growth rate (Alan S. Manne, personal communication, 9 November 1990). For the average of the three models, annual emissions growth in the next century is about 1 percent, well below total GDP growth over the period.

In all three cases, emissions growth rates are low by the 22nd century. Carbon emissions from fossil fuels rise at only 0.54 percent annually after 2100 for Nordhaus-Yohe, and 0.66 percent for Edmonds-Reilly. Evaluating the linear

---

12. For example, Manne and Richels (1990c) incorporate five existing technologies for electric power (hydro, gas, oil, coal, nuclear) and four new sources (advanced gas, coal, and two noncarbon-based sources). They include seven technologies for nonelectric energy supplies (direct-use coal, low- and high-cost oil, low- and high-cost natural gas, synthetic fuels, and nonelectric backstop technology).

extrapolation of Manne-Richels for the period 2150–2200, the annual emissions growth rate is 0.55 percent.

The three models are surprisingly close.[13] Their relatively low rates for long-term emissions growth are driven primarily by the assumption of low population growth.[14] Per capita income continues to grow at moderate rates as incomes in developing countries move closer to those in developed countries, but autonomous growth in energy efficiency and a shift away from fossil fuels toward nuclear, solar, and hydroelectricity in response to price signals cause carbon emissions to rise more slowly than GDP.[15] The principal point for long-term warming analysis, however, is that these energy-economic projections do not assume high growth rates of carbon emissions. On the contrary, long-term growth rates of approximately ½ percent annually appear to be, if anything, biased downward rather than upward.

Nonetheless, the long-term emissions rates are far higher than current levels, partly because of higher growth rates during the first half of the 21st century and partly because of the power of compound growth rates over extremely long periods. Two centuries from today, annual carbon emissions are approximately ten times their current rates, ranging from 47 GtC in the year 2275 based on the Edmonds-Reilly baseline to 71 GtC based on Manne-Richels. In contrast, 1990 fossil fuel emissions amounted to 5.6 GtC (IPCC 1990b).[16]

Given the very-long-term emissions baselines from the three models, table 2.1 then translates the projections into "commitment" to global warming: that is, the equilibrium change in temperature expected after ocean thermal delay. The first step is to estimate the evolution of the atmospheric concentration of carbon dioxide. As discussed above, it is assumed that one-half of annual fossil fuel emissions remain in the atmosphere. On this basis, the cumulative increase in the atmospheric stock of carbon dioxide by the year 2275 is on the order of 3,890 GtC (the average of the three models). This level corresponds to an atmospheric concentration of approximately 2,200 ppm, or almost eight times the preindustrial level of 280 ppm. Even ignoring other trace gases, then, in the

---

13. Note, however, that within the framework of such models it is easy to generate an extremely wide range of emissions projections by varying the assumptions (see, e.g., Nordhaus and Yohe 1983).

14. Thus, Manne and Richels adopt the population projections of Zachariah and Vu (1988), who indicate that world population will plateau by the second half of the 21st century. They calculate that, from 2075 to 2100, world population will rise only from 10.17 billion to 10.42 billion.

15. Thus, in my simulations using the Edmonds-Reilly model, in the baseline projections the share of primary energy supply provided by nuclear, solar, and hydroelectricity combined rises from 10 percent in 1975 to 28 percent by 2075 (Cline 1989).

16. In addition, anthropogenic carbon emissions included an estimated 1.6 GtC from deforestation.

Table 2.1 Global warming in the very long term

	1990[a]	2000	2025	2050	2075	2100	2125	2150	2175	2200	2225	2250	2275
CO_2 emissions (GtC)													
Nordhaus-Yohe	5.6[b]	5.5	10.3	13.3	17.5	20.0	22.9	26.1	29.9	34.1	39.0	44.6	50.9
Reilly-Edmonds	5.6[b]	6.2	8.7	10.7	12.6	14.8	17.5	20.6	24.2	28.5	33.6	39.6	46.6
Manne-Richels	5.6[b]	6.5	10.6	14.3	18.8	26.9	33.2	39.5	45.8	52.1	58.4	64.7	71.0
Cumulative emissions after 1990 (GtC)													
Nordhaus-Yohe	0.0	55.5	253.0	548.0	933.0	1,401.8	1,937.5	2,549.7	3,249.4	4,049.1	4,963.0	6,007.5	7,201.1
Reilly-Edmonds	0.0	62.0	248.3	490.8	782.0	1,125.0	1,528.8	2,004.4	2,564.5	3,223.9	4,000.5	4,915.0	5,991.8
Manne-Richels	0.0	65.0	278.8	590.0	1,003.8	1,575.0	2,326.3	3,235.0	4,301.3	5,525.0	6,906.3	8,445.0	10,141.3
Cumulative addition to atmospheric CO_2 (GtC)													
Nordhaus-Yohe	0.0	27.8	126.5	274.0	466.5	700.9	968.7	1,274.9	1,624.7	2,024.5	2,481.5	3,003.7	3,600.6
Reilly-Edmonds	0.0	31.0	124.1	245.4	391.0	562.5	764.4	1,002.2	1,282.2	1,612.0	2,000.3	2,457.5	2,995.9
Manne-Richels	0.0	32.5	139.4	295.0	501.9	787.5	1,163.1	1,617.5	2,150.6	2,762.5	3,453.1	4,222.5	5,070.6
Atmospheric CO_2 stock (GtC)													
Nordhaus-Yohe	750.0	777.8	876.5	1,024.0	1,216.5	1,450.9	1,718.7	2,024.9	2,374.7	2,774.5	3,231.5	3,753.7	4,350.6
Reilly-Edmonds	750.0	781.0	874.1	995.4	1,141.0	1,312.5	1,514.4	1,752.2	2,032.2	2,362.0	2,750.3	3,207.5	3,745.9
Manne-Richels	750.0	782.5	889.4	1,045.0	1,251.9	1,537.5	1,913.1	2,367.5	2,900.6	3,512.5	4,203.1	4,972.5	5,820.6
Atmospheric CO_2 concentration (ppm)													
Nordhaus-Yohe	353.0	366.1	412.5	482.0	572.6	682.9	808.9	953.0	1,117.7	1,305.9	1,521.0	1,766.8	2,047.7
Reilly-Edmonds	353.0	367.6	411.4	468.5	537.0	617.7	712.8	824.7	956.5	1,111.7	1,294.5	1,509.7	1,763.1
Manne-Richels	353.0	368.3	418.6	491.8	589.2	723.7	900.4	1,114.3	1,365.2	1,653.2	1,978.3	2,340.4	2,739.6
Radiative forcing above preindustrial levels (wm^{-2})													
CO_2[c]													
Nordhaus-Yohe	1.5	1.7	2.5	3.4	4.5	5.6	6.7	7.7	8.7	9.7	10.7	11.6	12.6
Reilly-Edmonds	1.5	1.7	2.4	3.3	4.1	5.0	5.9	6.8	7.8	8.7	9.7	10.6	11.6
Manne-Richels	1.5	1.7	2.6	3.6	4.7	6.0	7.4	8.7	10.0	11.2	12.3	13.4	14.4
All trace gases[d]													
Nordhaus-Yohe	2.5	2.8	4.0	5.5	7.0	8.5	9.8	11.2	12.7	14.1	15.5	16.8	18.2
Reilly-Edmonds	2.5	2.8	3.9	5.2	6.4	7.6	8.8	9.9	11.2	12.6	14.0	15.4	16.8
Manne-Richels	2.5	2.8	4.1	5.6	7.2	8.9	10.7	12.6	14.5	16.2	17.9	19.4	20.8
Commitment to global warming (°C)[e]													
At sensitivity 1.5													
Nordhaus-Yohe	0.9	1.0	1.5	2.0	2.6	3.2	3.7	4.2	4.7	5.3	5.8	6.3	6.8
Reilly-Edmonds	0.9	1.1	1.5	1.9	2.4	2.9	3.3	3.7	4.2	4.7	5.2	5.8	6.3
Manne-Richels	0.9	1.1	1.5	2.1	2.7	3.3	4.0	4.7	5.4	6.1	6.7	7.3	7.8

At sensitivity 2.5													
Nordhaus-Yohe	1.5	1.7	2.5	3.4	4.4	5.3	6.1	7.0	7.9	8.8	9.7	10.5	11.4
Reilly-Edmonds	1.5	1.8	2.5	3.2	4.0	4.8	5.5	6.2	7.0	7.9	8.7	9.6	10.5
Manne-Richels	1.5	1.8	2.6	3.5	4.5	5.6	6.7	7.9	9.0	10.1	11.2	12.1	13.0
At sensitivity 4.5													
Nordhaus-Yohe	2.8	3.1	4.5	6.1	7.9	9.5	11.0	12.6	14.2	15.8	17.4	18.9	20.4
Reilly-Edmonds	2.8	3.2	4.4	5.8	7.2	8.6	9.9	11.1	12.6	14.2	15.7	17.3	18.9
Manne-Richels	2.8	3.2	4.6	6.3	8.1	10.0	12.0	14.2	16.3	18.2	20.1	21.8	23.4

CO_2 = carbon dioxide; GtC = gigatons of carbon; ppm = parts per million; wm^{-2} = watts per square meter.

a. Intergovernmental Panel on Climate Change (IPCC) estimates.

b. IPCC estimates of emissions from fossil fuels only; excludes deforestation.

c. Radiative forcing above preindustrial levels is calculated as $6.3 \ln(C/C_0)$, where C is concentration in the year in question (in ppm) and C_0 is the preindustrial level (279 ppm).

d. For CO_2 forcing up to 6.8 wm^{-2}, estimated by quadratic equation relating total to CO_2 forcing (calculated from IPCC data). At higher levels, calculated as $1.447 \times$ radiative forcing from CO_2 above preindustrial levels.

e. Sensitivity is defined as the amount of warming (in °C) for a doubling of CO_2 above preindustrial levels (radiative forcing = 4 wm^{-2}).

Baselines: J. M. Reilly, J. A. Edmonds, R. H. Gardner, and A. L. Brenkert. 1987. "Uncertainty Analysis of the IEA/ORAU CO_2 Emissions Model." *Energy Journal* 8, no. 3: 1–29; William D. Nordhaus and Gary W. Yohe. 1983. "Future Carbon Dioxide Emissions from Fossil Fuels." In National Research Council, *Changing Climate*, 148. Washington: National Academy Press; Alan S. Manne and Richard G. Richels. 1990. "Global CO_2 Emission Reductions: The Impacts of Rising Energy Costs." Stanford University (mimeographed, February). Emissions growth is estimated at the final estimated period rate after 2075 for Reilly-Edmonds and after 2100 for Nordhaus-Yohe; for Manne-Richels absolute growth after 2100 is based on linear extrapolation of increases from 2050 to 2100 (by personal communication).

absence of special policy action the atmospheric concentration of carbon dioxide is likely to reach eight times its preindustrial level within 200 years.

It is useful to return to the supply discussion to verify the consistency of this outcome with resource availability. The analysis above suggested that coal resources at costs that are not prohibitive are sufficient to provide a five- to tenfold increase in atmospheric carbon dioxide above preindustrial levels. The eightfold increase by the year 2075 identified in table 2.1 is in the midpoint of this range.

Very-Long-Term Warming

The scientific literature of which I am aware is not explicit about the extent of warming that might be expected from such a massive buildup of carbon dioxide (in addition to other trace gases) over two to three centuries. Two references, IPCC (1990b) and Manabe and Bryan (l985), do provide a glimpse of the likely outcome, however, and their findings are described below.

Previous Estimates

Although the principal discussion of the IPCC report focuses on the effects of a doubling of carbon-dioxide-equivalent, the report also states the extent of radiative forcing, actual realized (i.e., "transient") warming, and equilibrium warming commitment that could be expected by the year 2100 under business-as-usual policies. By that date, total radiative forcing would stand at 9.9 watts per square meter (wm^{-2}), of which the contribution of carbon dioxide would amount to 6.84 wm^{-2} (IPCC 1990b, 61). Under the central assumption about the "climate sensitivity" parameter ($\Lambda = 2.5°C$ for a doubling of carbon-dioxide-equivalent), "realized" or "transient" warming would reach 4.2°C, and the commitment to equilibrium global warming would reach 5.7°C. Under the upper-bound value for Λ (4.5°C), realized warming would reach 6.3°C (IPCC 1990b, figure 6.11, 191). By implication, committed equilibrium warming with a higher sensitivity parameter would reach 10.3°C (5.7°C × [4.5/2.5]).

Thus, the IPCC itself projects that, in the absence of policy change, the earth could already be committed to warming of approximately 6°C up to a high of approximately 10°C by the end of the next century. These levels are twice the amounts for a doubling of carbon dioxide, yet they cover only the first third of the relevant very-long-term horizon. Unfortunately, the IPCC authors chose not to highlight even the 2100 estimates. Thus, any intimation of a 6°C warming as a central estimate is completely absent in the policymakers' summary of the report (IPCC 1990a).

In one of the few GCM investigations of the impact of manyfold carbon dioxide increase, Manabe and Bryan (1985) estimate that the surface temperature increase from an eightfold multiple of preindustrial carbon dioxide concentration is 2.3 times as large as that from a doubling of carbon dioxide at a latitude of 50° and 3.7 times as large at a latitude of 30°. On this basis, an eightfold increase in carbon dioxide would cause about three times as much warming as would a doubling of carbon dioxide—just the relationship that would be predicted by the Arrhenius (and Wigley) logarithmic function for radiative forcing.[17] Applying the IPCC's central climate sensitivity parameter of $\Lambda = 2.5$, an eightfold rise of carbon-dioxide-equivalent trace gases would mean a central estimate of 7.5°C for global warming.

Thus, there is at least one GCM simulation that implies very-long-term warming of three times the usual benchmark amount for double carbon dioxide. Moreover, at eight times the preindustrial level of carbon dioxide, the Manabe-Bryan computation still refers to a world with less radiative forcing than envisioned here in the very long term. As just analyzed, fossil fuel emissions alone are sufficient to multiply atmospheric carbon dioxide about eightfold by the late 23rd century. Yet in addition, the further radiative forcing from other trace gases must be incorporated.

New Estimates

It is possible to develop a more explicit estimate of global warming in the very long term by applying the underlying IPCC parameters to projected levels of carbon dioxide concentrations, and adding likely further radiative contributions from other trace gases. Identifying *radiative forcing* is the first step in this analysis.

For carbon dioxide, the Wigley formula for radiative forcing (equation 1.2, chapter 1) may be applied. As noted in chapter 1, the logarithmic relationship of forcing to concentration is likely to hold up even for the much higher concentration levels considered here, because of the rising relative importance of unsaturated bands of the spectrum as previously dominant bands become saturated. The sixth panel of table 2.1 reports the resulting radiative forcing from carbon dioxide (in wm^{-2}), corresponding to the alternative estimates of carbon concentrations in the fifth panel of the table.

The next step in the analysis is to consider the contribution of other trace gases. The IPCC finds that buildup of these gases will continue to provide nearly 40 percent of the increase in warming potential over the next century. IPCC projections for future benchmark years indicate that, under a business-as-usual scenario, radiative forcing for buildup above preindustrial levels amounts to 2.88 wm^{-2} for carbon dioxide by the year 2025 and 4.59 wm^{-2} for all trace gases in that year, for a ratio of 1.59 (that is, approximately 1/0.6; IPCC 1990b,

---

17. That is, $\ln 8 = \ln 2^3 = 3 \ln 2$.

table 2.7, 61).[18] By the year 2100, total radiative forcing is up to 9.9 wm^{-2} in the IPCC projections, of which carbon dioxide contributes 6.84 wm^{-2}. By that time, the ratio of total radiative forcing to carbon dioxide contribution moderates to 1.45.

Incorporation of the future effects of trace gases other than carbon dioxide would ideally be accomplished by a baseline projection of emissions and concentrations of methane, nitrous oxide, CFCs, hydrochlorofluorocarbons (HCFCS), and other greenhouse gases, and corresponding application of radiative forcing formulas. The estimates presented in table 2.1 use a simpler method and merely apply to the carbon concentrations calculated here the ratios of total radiative forcing from all greenhouse gases to that from carbon dioxide reported by the IPCC.[19] Beyond the year 2100 (the most distant date considered by the scientific panel), the ratio of total radiative forcing to that from carbon dioxide is held constant at the level of 2100 in the IPCC projections (1.45:1). The resulting estimates indicate that, by the year 2275, total radiative forcing would be in the range of 19 wm^{-2}, more than four times the amount associated with the conventional doubling-of-carbon-dioxide benchmark (4 wm^{-2}; table 2.1).

The last step in the analysis is to convert radiative forcing projections into estimates of *global warming*, or increases in global mean temperature above preindustrial levels.[20] The final panel of table 2.1 presents three alternative measures, based on alternative climate sensitivity factors (Λ). With the IPCC's "best guess" ($\Lambda = 2.5°C$ for carbon-equivalent doubling), the central estimate of commitment to global mean warming by the year 2275 amounts to a range of 10.5°C to 13.0°C.[21] If the lower extreme is considered (lower-bound $\Lambda =$

---

18. Note that in the IPCC scenario there is moderate success in the curbing of CFCs. See the discussion below for an adjustment to account for recent findings on CFCs.

19. For carbon dioxide concentrations at levels below the IPCC business-as-usual estimate for 2100, the ratio is based on the following equation, estimated from levels in previous years: $RFT = -0.184 + 1.8024\ RFC - 0.0478\ RFC^2$, where RFT is total radiative forcing (in wm^{-2}) and RFC is the amount from carbon dioxide alone.

20. The conversion in table 2.1 applies an approximate value of 4 wm^{-2} for radiative forcing from carbon-dioxide-equivalent doubling, as cited, for example, in the survey of GCMs by Schlesinger and Mitchell (1987, 760). If instead the precise value from the Wigley formula (chapter 1, equation 1.2) is applied, radiative forcing from doubling of carbon-dioxide-equivalent is 4.37 wm^{-2}. Using that alternative benchmark for radiative forcing, the warming estimates of table 2.1 would all be 8.5 percent lower. Alternatively, with the adjustment the climate sensitivity parameter Λ may be thought of as $(4.37/4.0)2.5°C = 2.73°C$. Considering that "masking" by urban pollution and ozone depletion contributed to the shortfall of actual from predicted warming and thus to the relatively low value chosen by the IPCC for the best guess for Λ, this implicit modest increase in Λ would seem to be in the right direction for any change, and perhaps too small for an eventual correction.

21. Note that the span of about one-fourth between the high (Manne-Richels-based) and low (Edmonds-Reilly-based) estimates is smaller than the corresponding variation between baseline cumulative carbon dioxide buildup (69 percent; 5,800 GtC versus 3,600

1.5 combined with the low baseline projection for emissions), the warming commitment by that year would be only 6.3°C. However, in the upper extreme (Λ = 4.5 combined with the high baseline), the commitment to warming by 2275 reaches the striking level of 23.4°C. Even if the lowest emissions baseline is applied, when the climate sensitivity factor is at the upper bound the warming commitment by the year 2275 is 18.9°C.

The method here is meant to provide a central range for very-long-term warming. It should be emphasized that the parameters might change with high atmospheric concentrations of carbon-equivalent. The warming equation ($\Delta T = R \lambda \beta$, chapter 1) could be affected not so much because of a change in the radiative forcing for a given amount of carbon (equation 1.2 in chapter 1), or even because of a change in the ratio of total radiative forcing to that from carbon dioxide. Instead, the principal changes associated with very high concentrations of greenhouse gases would likely be from the feedback parameter (β). The feedbacks are likely to be nonlinear. The overall feedback effect could thus be considerably different from that implied by the alternative values of Λ here; feedback could be either larger (greater warming) or smaller (lesser).[22]

The benefit-cost analysis of chapter 7 draws upon the warming projections of table 2.1. Actual warming (i.e., after allowing for about 25 years of ocean thermal lag) is what matters for economic damage. Accordingly, the benchmark warming for the doubling of carbon-dioxide-equivalent (2.5°C in the central estimate) is scheduled for the year 2050 in the calculations of chapter 7. Very-long-term warming by the year 2275 is placed at 10°C in the central case, 6°C for the lower-bound, and 18°C for the upper-bound. These estimates correspond approximately to the average estimates of table 2.1 for warming commitment by the year 2250.

The central estimate in this study of 10°C warming by 2275 would appear consistent with the IPCC estimate of a 5.7°C warming commitment by the year 2100 (discussed above). Indeed, the estimates here for the year 2100 are somewhat more conservative.[23] Moreover, the pace of warming commitment implied for the period 2100–2275 in the estimates of this study is considerably slower than that estimated by the IPCC for 1990–2100.[24] In short, the very-long-term

---

GtC). This is because of the logarithmic relationship of radiative forcing (and thus warming) to carbon dioxide accumulation.

22. Personal communications with V. Ramanathan, University of California at San Diego, 21 November 1990, and Stephen H. Schneider, National Center for Atmospheric Research, 13 April 1992.

23. For 2100, the average radiative forcing in table 2.1 is 8.3 wm^{-2}, and the average warming commitment 5.2°C. The corresponding IPCC estimates are 9.9 wm^{-2} and 5.7°C, respectively, as discussed above.

24. The IPCC estimates indicate that radiative forcing above preindustrial levels should

projections here would seem to be plausible and perhaps conservative extensions of the IPCC estimates.

The central estimate of 10°C for very-long-term warming is also consistent with potential long-term radiative forcing. As noted above, carbon dioxide concentrations should multiply eight times over this horizon in the absence of policy intervention. With the climate sensitivity parameter of $\Lambda = 2.5$°C, an eightfold multiple causes 7.5°C warming (i.e., three times the amount for doubling, by the logarithmic relationship), even without inclusion of the other trace gases. To reach 10°C, the implicit level of carbon-equivalent would have to reach 16 times preindustrial levels. The seeming large gap between eightfold and 16-fold carbon-equivalent multiplication is explained by the fact that the logarithmic forcing relationship means that the "last eightfold" emission in carbon dioxide contributes relatively little additional forcing (no more than the initial doubling), and thus can be accounted for by the other trace gases.

Figures 2.3 and 2.4 summarize the estimates here. In figure 2.3 the averages of the projections based on the three alternative models are shown for the atmospheric concentration and radiative forcing of carbon dioxide. As the figure shows, although atmospheric concentration rises exponentially, radiative forcing increases only about linearly, as the consequence of the logarithmic relationship of forcing to concentration.[25] Figure 2.4 shows the corresponding estimates for total radiative forcing including that from other greenhouse gases (left scale). This forcing, which is approximately linear over time, translates into the corresponding estimates of global warming *commitment* (right scale). The path of warming commitment is also linear, in view of the linear relationship between equilibrium warming and radiative forcing (chapter 1, equation 1.1).

The approximately linear path of future warming commitment (and thus actual, or transient, warming, which occurs with a lag of two to three decades) is convenient for the subsequent analysis of this study. In particular, the benefits of warming avoidance are related (nonlinearly) to the extent of actual warming. Actual warming in turn may be interpolated linearly between two benchmarks: that for the conventional doubling of carbon-dioxide-equivalent and that for very-long-term warming. These benchmarks are set at 2050 and 2275, respec-

---

rise from 2.45 wm^{-2} in 1990 to 9.9 wm^{-2} by 2100, for an average annual increase of 0.068 wm^{-2}. The projections here, averaging over the three models, show a rise in radiative forcing from 8.3 wm^{-2} in 2100 to 17.2 wm^{-2} by 2250, or an annual increase of 0.059 wm^{-2}. In part, the deceleration is attributable to a slowdown in global population growth and thus the rate of increase in GDP and emissions.

25. That is, if radiative forcing for carbon dioxide, R_c, is of the form $R_c = a \ln (C/C_0)$, where C is atmospheric concentration; C is of the form $C = C_0 e^{gt}$, where concentration grows at the geometric rate g; and warming is of the form $W = bR_c$, we have $W = b(a \ln C_0 e^{gt}/C_0) = bagt = Kt$, where K is a constant (abg). Warming for carbon dioxide is thus linear in time. With the contribution of other trace gases to radiative forcing a constant fraction of that from carbon dioxide, warming from all trace gases is also linear in time.

Figure 2.3   Carbon dioxide concentration and radiative forcing in the very long term

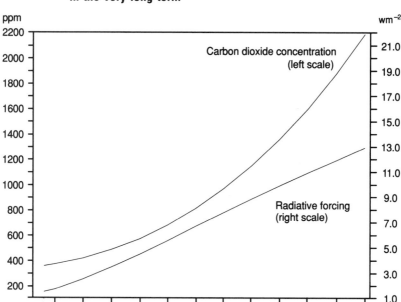

tively, and correspond to the warming commitment dates of 2025 and 2250, respectively.

The Influence of CFCs

The IPCC business-as-usual baseline through 2100, on which the radiative forcing for greenhouse gases other than carbon dioxide is based (as discussed above), assumed that "the Montreal Protocol is implemented albeit with only partial participation" (IPCC 1990b, Appendix I, 349). However, subsequent to the IPCC's estimates, the London extension of this protocol called for a more rapid and comprehensive reduction in CFCs, with elimination of production by the year 2000 (chapter 8). This consideration would suggest that the contribution of CFCs in the warming estimates of table 2.1 is overstated.

Moreover, in late 1991 new scientific evidence indicated that the radiative forcing effect of CFCs had been largely neutralized by the ozone-stripping impact of these gases (as discussed in chapter 1). This evaluation provided an additional argument for making a downward revision in warming estimates to adjust for the overstatement caused by the attribution of radiative forcing to CFCs.

Figure 2.4 Radiative forcing from all greenhouse gases and commitment to equilibrium global mean temperature rise in the very long term

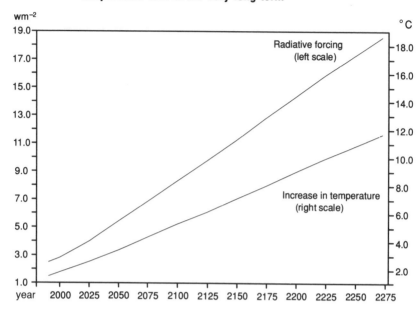

Over the very long term, the net impact of CFC forcing and ozone depletion is ambiguous and, in principle, would depend on the atmospheric residence lifetime of CFCs as opposed to the time lag before the rebuilding of ozone. The IPCC (1990b, table 2.8, 64) estimates the atmospheric lifetime of CFC-11 at 60 years and that of CFC-12 at 120 years. As stratospheric ozone could return to normal levels by the middle of the next century with strict controls on CFCs (Newsweek, 4 November 1991, 49), it may well be that the net impact on a time scale of 50 to 100 years remains one of net positive radiative forcing from CFCs.

Nonetheless, it is informative to consider the effect of complete removal of CFCs from the calculations of very-long-term warming of this chapter. Because this warming is high and the corresponding economic damages considered in chapters 3 and 7 are high, it is important to remove possible upward bias. The IPCC business-as-usual projections place total radiative forcing in the year 2100 at 9.9 wm^{-2}. This total includes a contribution of 0.53 wm^{-2} from CFCs (IPCC 1990b, table 2.7, 61). If this forcing is entirely removed on grounds of the argument of an offset from ozone-stripping, total radiative forcing by 2100 falls to 9.37 wm^{-2}.

As indicated in equation 1.1 of chapter 1, the relationship between global warming and radiative forcing is linear. Therefore, removal of the CFC contribution would reduce the IPCC's estimate of warming *commitment* in the year 2100 from 5.7°C (as discussed above) to 5.4°C (5.7 × [9.37/9.9]). Correspondingly, for the averages of the three alternative emissions projections in table 2.1, complete removal of CFCs would reduce radiative forcing for the year 2250 from 17.2 wm^{-2} to 16.3 wm^{-2}.[26] The year 2250 is approximately the date for the "commitment" of actual warming to be expected by the year 2275 if 25 years is allowed for ocean thermal lag.

Under the central assumption for the climate sensitivity parameter ($\Lambda = 2.5$), adjusted radiative forcing of 16.3 wm^{-2} by 2250 translates into a warming commitment of 10.1°C instead of 10.7°C when the CFC contribution is retained (averages of the three projections, table 2.1). Thus, *even if it is assumed that CFCs make no contribution whatsoever to global warming, the central estimate of actual warming by the year 2275 remains slightly above 10°C.* Therefore, the use of this estimate in the benefit-cost analysis of subsequent chapters would appear robust to consideration of the new evidence on CFCs.

Nor does downgrading of the warming impact of CFCs have much effect on medium-term estimates (which could be important because early effects matter more than later effects in the presence of time discounting). The IPCC scientific committee's new findings translated merely into a delay to 2030 for the warming previously expected by 2025 (*Financial Times*, 18–19 January 1992, 2). Moreover, this delay could be reversed if efforts to reduce urban pollution had the effect of reducing sulfur dioxide emissions and thus the direct albedo and induced cloud effects of sulfate aerosols (as discussed in chapter 1).

Illustrative Regional Extent of Very-Long-Term Warming

It is informative to consider what very-long-term warming of 10°C globally might imply for individual countries and regions. Although GCMs in the past have typically been considered to be too aggregative to provide much guidance for regional effects, three recent high-resolution models provide more detail and fare relatively well in simulating current-day regional climates.[27]

---

26. That is, for the year 2100 the ratio of total radiative forcing to that from carbon dioxide alone is reduced from 1.45 to 1.37 by removal of CFCs. Accordingly, total radiative forcing by 2250 equals the average of the three projections for carbon dioxide forcing (11.9 wm^{-2}) multiplied by this reduced expansion factor (11.9 × 1.37 = 16.3).

27. The models are 1989 versions of models at the Canadian Climate Center, the Geophysical Fluid Dynamics Laboratory, and the United Kingdom Meteorological Office (IPCC 1990b, table 3.2(a); section 5.4, 163–64).

Figures 2.5 through 2.8 show the averages of the three high-resolution models' projections of equilibrium warming from a doubling of atmospheric carbon-dioxide-equivalent. The figures apply the grid resolution of the United Kingdom Meteorological Office (UKMO) model, which has a vertical resolution of 3.75° and a horizontal resolution of 2.5°. They display the results in a two-dimensional matrix with 48 rows and 144 columns, with each matrix cell corresponding to one grid box in the UKMO model.[28] Column 73 is on the prime meridian. It should be noted that the average "sensitivity" factor for the three models is 3.67°C: a doubling of carbon dioxide produces an equilibrium global mean temperature rise of this amount. The high-resolution models have less detail in ocean coupling; whether for this reason or otherwise, they tend to show higher warming than the 2.5°C central estimate of the IPCC.

Figures 2.5 and 2.6 show the regional warming patterns for June, July, and August (summer in the Northern Hemisphere, winter in the Southern); figures 2.7 and 2.8 show the corresponding patterns for December, January, and February (opposite seasons). Each entry in each figure shows the rise in temperature (in degrees Celsius) for the grid area in question.[29] The figures show the tendency toward greater warming at the higher latitudes and lesser warming nearer the equator. It is also evident that, for the land masses excluding the Antarctic, warming tends to be considerably greater in the Northern Hemisphere than in the Southern.

An initial impression of the regional impact of very-long-term warming may be obtained by considering the shift that would occur in summer temperatures at different locations. Tables 2.2 and 2.3 examine this question for the United States and the rest of the world, respectively. For major cities in the United States and abroad, the tables first report the summer average daily maximum

---

28. As developed in Cline (1990e), the earth's surface may be displayed as a (Mercator) projection divided into m grids vertically and n grids horizontally and centered at the prime meridian. Let v be the vertical resolution of the GCM, or degrees latitude covered by each grid, and w be the horizontal resolution, or degrees longitude for each. Then $m = 180/v$ and $n = 360/w$. The $m \times n$ matrix of cells thus generated has the following geographical coordinates for any given grid at its northeast corner (designated as $L_{i,j}$ for location of the ith row and jth column). For the Northern Hemisphere, latitude = $[90 - (1 - i)(v)]$°N; longitude = $[j - (n/2)]w$°E in the Eastern Hemisphere and $[(n/2) - j]w$°W in the Western Hemisphere. For the Southern Hemisphere, latitude = $[i - (m/2) - 1]v$°S; longitude = $[j - (n/2)]w$°E in the Eastern Hemisphere and $[(n/2) - j]w$° W in the Western Hemisphere. For some purposes, the land area of the grid is important. Area may be estimated as $A \approx [\pi R/m]\{[2\pi R \cos(\alpha - v/2)]/n\}$, where R is the earth's radius and $\alpha = [90 - (i - 1)v]$°. Note that this system may be used for management of global data from the GCM and other calculations (e.g., temperature, precipitation, soil moisture) by converting the two-dimensional locational matrix, $L_{m \times n}$, into a three-dimensional matrix $L_{m \times n \times k}$, where each element of the third dimension refers to a data variable.

29. The estimates reported here are derived from IPCC 1990b, figure 5.4.

Figure 2.5 Equilibrium warming for carbon-dioxide-equivalent doubling, Western Hemisphere: June–August[a]

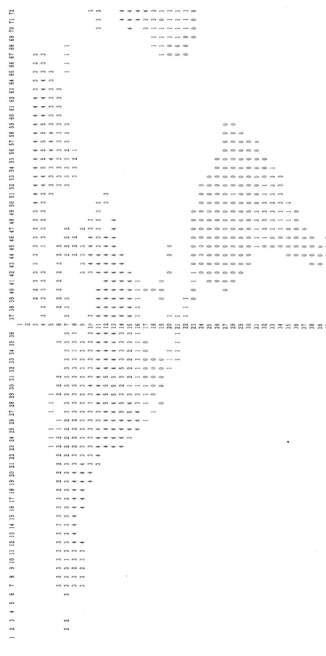

a. Data represent the mean estimates of three general circulation models (CCC, GFDL, UKMO; see text), in degrees Celsius.

Source: Data from Intergovernmental Panel on Climate Change. 1990. *Scientific Assessment of Climate Change: Report Prepared for IPCC by Working Group I.* New York: World Meteorological Organization and United Nations Environment Programme, figure 5.4.

Figure 2.6 Equilibrium warming for carbon-dioxide-equivalent doubling, Eastern Hemisphere: June–August[a]

a. Data represent the mean estimates of three general circulation models (CCC, GFDL, UKMO: see text), in degrees Celsius.

Source: Data from Intergovernmental Panel on Climate Change. 1990. *Scientific Assessment of Climate Change: Report Prepared for IPCC by Working Group I.* New York: World Meteorological Organization and United Nations Environment Programme, figure 5.4.

Figure 2.7 Equilibrium warming for carbon-dioxide-equivalent doubling, Western Hemisphere: December–February[a]

a. Data represent the mean estimates of three general circulation models (CCC, GFDL, UKMO; see text), in degrees Celsius.

Source: Data from Intergovernmental Panel on Climate Change. 1990. *Scientific Assessment of Climate Change: Report Prepared for IPCC by Working Group I.* New York: World Meteorological Organization and United Nations Environment Programme, figure 5.4.

Figure 2.8 Equilibrium warming for carbon-dioxide-equivalent doubling, Eastern Hemisphere: December–February[a]

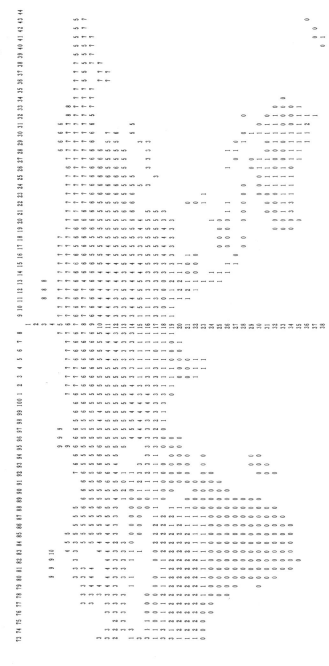

a. Data represent the mean estimates of three general circulation models (CCC, GFDL, UKMO; see text), in degrees Celsius.

Source: Data from Intergovernmental Panel on Climate Change. 1990. *Scientific Assessment of Climate Change: Report Prepared for IPCC by Working Group I.* New York: World Meteorological Organization and United Nations Environment Programme, figure 5.4.

temperature at present. They then indicate the latitude and longitude of each city and its corresponding grid box assignment in the presentation of figures 2.5 through 2.8.

The tables then report the "summer regional warming coefficient" for the relevant grid box. This coefficient is the ratio of the regional summer warming estimate from the three high-resolution models (averaged) to their average global mean warming (3.67°C). Thus, for New York (grid row 14, column 43) the summer regional warming coefficient is 1.09 (4°/3.67°; figure 2.5). The strategy here is to apply these coefficients to the global mean warming for the very long term to obtain regional warming estimates. The assumption that regional changes are proportional to global mean changes in surface temperature is the same as that employed by the IPCC in its estimates of regional changes to the year 2030 (IPCC 1990b, section 5.4.3, 165).

Tables 2.2 and 2.3 report the results of applying the summer regional warming coefficients to a 10°C global mean warming, the benchmark for very-long-term warming. The resulting increase in temperature (e.g., 10.9°C for New York) is then added to the current average daily maximum temperature for July (Northern Hemisphere) or January (Southern Hemisphere) to estimate the level of average daily maximum temperatures in the summer in the very long term (i.e., in the late 23rd century).

These estimates should of course be interpreted as indicative rather than precise. In addition to the possible changes in feedback and other parameters (discussed above), the actual "transient" path of warming could be considerably different regionally from the equilibrium results. Also, individual grid boxes can be considerably in error because of inadequate parameters for land surface. Nonetheless, the estimates provide a glimpse of what regional climates might be like with very-long-term warming.

As may be seen in tables 2.2 and 2.3, such warming at 10°C could be expected to place many prime agricultural areas in jeopardy with respect to crop potential. Consider Iowa. Average maximum daily temperature in the summer would rise from 84°F (the average for Dubuque and Des Moines) to 104°F, or 40°C. As discussed in chapter 3, this increase would be likely to cause extremely severe reductions in yields of wheat, barley, oats, and rye. The warming would also push temperatures toward their ceilings for the production of rice, corn, and sorghum. Even in more northern areas, the impact could be adverse to agriculture. Thus, for Moscow the 10°C rise in global mean temperatures would raise average maximum daily temperature in the summer from 24°C to 33°C, a level at which wheat yields would begin to decline seriously (chapter 3).

Human amenity would also seem subject to serious degradation by such temperature increases. As indicated in table 2.2, at present only 18 out of the 66 US cities examined have July average maximum daily temperatures in excess of 90°F. After very-long-term warming, 62 out of the 66 cities would have

Table 2.2 Increases in July average daily maximum temperature from very-long-term global warming for 66 US cities

City	Location		Grid		Average July daily maximum (°F)	Regional summer warming coefficient[a]	Increment from 10°C global warming (°C)	Average daily July maximum after long-term warming	
	North latitude	West longitude	Row	Column				°F	°C
Albany	42°39'	73°45'	13	43	83	1.09	10.9	102.6	39.2
Albuquerque	35°5'	106°40'	15	30	93	0.27	2.7	97.9	36.6
Amarillo	35°13'	101°49'	15	32	91	0.55	5.5	100.9	38.3
Atlanta	33°45'	84°23'	16	39	88	0.27	2.7	92.9	33.8
Atlantic City	39°22'	74°26'	14	43	84	1.09	10.9	103.6	39.8
Baltimore	39°21'	76°40'	14	42	87	1.09	10.9	106.6	41.5
Bismarck	46°48'	100°47'	12	32	84	1.09	10.9	103.6	39.8
Block Island, RI	41°10'	71°34'	14	44	76	1.09	10.9	95.6	35.3
Boise	43°49'	117°1'	13	26	91	1.09	10.9	110.6	43.7
Boston	42°21'	71°4'	13	44	82	1.09	10.9	101.6	38.7
Burlington	44°29'	73°13'	13	43	81	1.09	10.9	100.6	38.1
Charleston, SC	32°48'	79°57'	16	41	89	0.27	2.7	93.9	34.4
Charlotte	35°14'	80°50'	15	40	88	1.09	10.9	107.6	42.0
Cheyenne	44°40'	101°15'	13	32	83	1.09	10.9	102.6	39.2
Chicago	41°53'	87°38'	13	38	83	1.09	10.9	102.6	39.2
Cincinnati	39°6'	84°31'	14	39	86	1.09	10.9	105.6	40.9
Cleveland	41°30'	81°41'	13	40	82	1.09	10.9	101.6	38.7
Concord, NH	43°12'	71°32'	13	44	83	1.09	10.9	102.6	39.2
Denver	39°43'	105°1'	14	30	88	0.55	5.5	97.9	36.6
Des Moines	41°35'	93°37'	13	35	86	1.09	10.9	105.6	40.9
Detroit	39°37'	90°40'	14	36	83	0.82	8.2	97.8	36.5
Dubuque	42°30'	90°41'	13	36	82	1.09	10.9	101.6	38.7
Galveston	29°18'	94°48'	17	35	87	0	0	87.0	30.6
Harrisburg	40°16'	76°52'	14	42	86	1.09	10.9	105.6	40.9
Hartford	41°46'	72°41'	13	43	85	1.09	10.9	104.6	40.3
Helena	46°36'	112°1'	12	28	84	1.36	13.6	108.5	42.5
Houston	29°46'	95°22'	17	34	94	0	0	94.0	34.4
Huntington, WV	38°25'	82°26'	14	40	86	1.09	10.9	105.6	40.9
Huron, SD	44°22'	98°13'	13	33	87	1.09	10.9	106.6	41.5
Indianapolis	39°46'	86°9'	14	38	85	1.09	10.9	104.6	40.3
Jacksonville	30°20'	81°40'	16	40	91	0.27	2.7	95.9	35.5
Jackson	32°18'	90°12'	16	36	93	0.27	2.7	97.9	36.6
Juneau	58°20'	134°27'	9	19	64	1.09	10.9	83.6	28.7
Key West	24°33'	81°48'	18	40	89	0	0	89.0	31.7
Las Vegas	36°11'	115°8'	15	26	105	1.09	10.9	124.6	51.5

Little Rock	43°16'	96°15'	13	34	93	1.09	10.9	112.6	44.8
Los Angeles	34°3'	118°15'	15	25	84	1.09	10.9	103.6	39.8
Louisville	46°15'	72°57'	12	43	88	1.09	10.9	107.6	42.0
Madison	45°56'	95°55'	12	34	83	1.09	10.9	102.6	39.2
Miami	25°46'	80°12'	18	40	89	0	0	89.0	31.7
Milwaukee	43°2'	87°54'	13	37	80	1.09	10.9	99.6	37.6
Minneapolis	44°59'	93°13'	13	35	83	1.09	10.9	102.6	39.2
Mobile	30°42'	88°5'	16	37	91	0.27	2.7	95.9	35.5
Montgomery	32°23'	86°18'	16	38	92	0.27	2.7	96.9	36.0
Nashville	36°9'	86°48'	15	38	90	1.09	10.9	109.6	43.1
New Orleans	29°58'	90°7'	17	36	91	0	0	91.0	32.8
New York	40°43'	74°1'	14	43	84	1.09	10.9	103.6	39.8
Norfolk	36°40'	76°14'	15	42	90	1.09	10.9	109.6	43.1
Oklahoma City	35°28'	97°32'	15	34	94	0.55	5.5	103.9	39.9
Omaha	41°16'	95°57'	13	34	89	1.09	10.9	108.6	42.6
Philadelphia	39°57'	75°7'	14	42	86	1.09	10.9	105.6	40.9
Phoenix	33°27'	112°5'	16	28	105	0.82	8.2	119.8	48.8
Portland, ME	43°39'	70°17'	13	44	79	1.09	10.9	98.6	37.0
Portland, OR	45°33'	122°36'	12	24	80	1.09	10.9	99.6	37.6
Raleigh	35°47'	78°39'	15	41	88	1.09	10.9	107.6	42.0
Rapid City	44°5'	103°14'	13	31	87	1.36	13.6	111.5	44.2
Roswell, NM	33°24'	104°32'	16	31	94	0.27	2.7	98.9	37.1
Salt Lake City	40°46'	111°53'	14	28	93	1.36	13.6	117.5	47.5
San Francisco	37°48'	122°24'	14	24	71	1.09	10.9	90.6	32.6
San Juan	18°28'	66°7'	20	46	88	0	0	88.0	31.1
Sault Ste-Marie	46°30'	84°21'	12	39	75	1.09	10.9	94.6	34.8
Seattle	47°36'	122°2'	12	24	75	1.09	10.9	94.6	34.8
Spokane	47°44'	118°20'	12	25	84	1.09	10.9	103.6	39.8
St. Louis	38°38'	90°11'	14	36	89	0.82	8.2	103.8	39.9
Washington	38°54'	77°1'	14	42	88	1.09	10.9	107.6	42.0
Wichita	37°41'	97°20'	14	34	93	0.82	8.2	107.8	42.1
Wilmington	39°44'	75°33'	14	42	86	1.09	10.9	105.6	40.9

a. Ratio of June-July-August increase in mean temperature to increase in global mean annual temperature for a doubling of carbon-dioxide-equivalent; average of three high-resolution models (GFDL, UKMO, CCC; see text).

Table 2.3 Increase in mean daily summer maximum temperature from very-long-term global warming in 60 cities worldwide

City	Location		Grid		Average summer daily maximum[a]		Regional summer warming coefficient	Increment from 10°C global (°C)	Average summer daily maximum after long-term warming	
	Latitude	Longitude	Row	Column	°F	°C			°F	°C
Acapulco	16°51'N	99°55'W	20	33	89	32	0.27	2.7	93.9	34.4
Algiers	36°47'N	3°3'E	15	74	83	28	1.09	10.9	102.6	39.2
Amsterdam	52°22'N	4°54'E	11	74	69	21	0.55	5.5	78.9	26.1
Athens	37°58'N	23°43'E	14	82	90	32	1.09	10.9	109.6	43.1
Auckland	36°52'S	174°46'E	34	142	73	23	0	0	73.0	22.8
Bangkok	13°45'N	100°31'E	21	113	90	32	0	0	90.0	32.2
Belgrade	44°50'N	20°30'E	13	81	84	29	1.09	10.9	103.6	39.8
Berlin	52°31'N	13°24'E	10	78	74	23	0.82	8.2	88.8	31.5
Bogota	4.°36'N	74°2'W	23	43	64	18	0	0	64.0	17.8
Bonn	50°44'N	7°5'E	11	75	73	23	0.82	8.2	87.8	31.0
Brussels	50°50'N	4°20'E	11	74	73	23	0.55	5.5	82.9	28.3
Budapest	47°30'N	19°5'E	12	80	82	28	1.09	10.9	101.6	38.7
Buenos Aires	34°36'S	58°27'W	34	49	85	29	0.27	2.7	89.9	32.1
Cairo	30°3'N	31°15'E	16	85	96	36	0.27	2.7	100.9	38.3
Calgary	51°3'N	114°5'W	11	27	76	24	0.82	8.2	90.8	32.6
Caracas	10°30'N	66°56'W	22	46	78	26	0	0	78.0	25.6
Casablanca	33°39'N	7°35'W	16	69	79	26	0.82	8.2	93.8	34.3
Copenhagen	55°40'N	12°35'E	10	78	72	22	0.82	8.2	86.8	30.4
Djakarta	6°10'S	106°48'E	26	115	84	29	0.27	2.7	88.9	31.6
Dublin	53°20'N	6°15'W	10	70	67	19	0.82	8.2	81.8	27.6
Edinburgh	55°57'N	3°13'W	10	71	65	18	0.82	8.2	79.8	26.5
Geneva	46°12'N	6°9'E	12	75	77	25	0.82	8.2	91.8	33.2
Halifax	44°39'N	63°36'W	13	47	74	23	1.09	10.9	93.6	34.2
Helsinki	60°10'N	24°58'E	8	82	71	22	0.82	8.2	85.8	29.9
Hong Kong	22°15'N	114°11'E	19	118	87	31	0	0	87.0	30.6
Istanbul	41°1'N	28°58'E	14	84	81	27	1.09	10.9	100.6	38.1
Johannesburg	26°15'S	28°0'E	32	84	78	26	0.27	2.7	82.9	28.3
Kingston	18°0'N	76°48'W	20	42	90	32	0	0	90.0	32.2
Lagos	6°27'N	3°24'E	23	74	83	28	0	0	83.0	28.3
Lima	12°3'S	77°3'W	28	42	67	19	0	0	67.0	19.4
Lisbon	39°43'N	9°8'W	14	69	79	26	1.09	10.9	98.6	37.0
London	51°30'N	0°10'W	11	72	73	23	0.82	8.2	87.8	31.0
Madrid	40°24'N	3°41'W	14	71	87	31	1.09	10.9	106.6	41.5
Manila	14°35'N	121°0'E	21	121	88	31	0	0	88.0	31.1

Mexico City	19°24′N	99°9′W	19	33	73	23	0	0	73.0	22.8
Milan	45°28′N	9°12′E	12	76	84	29	0.82	8.2	98.8	37.1
Monrovia	6°18′N	10°47′W	23	68	80	27	0	0	80.0	26.7
Montreal	45°31′N	73°34′W	12	43	78	26	1.09	10.9	97.6	36.5
Moscow	55°45′N	37°35′E	10	88	76	24	0.82	8.2	90.8	32.6
Munich	48°8′N	11°34′E	12	77	72	22	0.82	8.2	86.8	30.4
Nairobi	1°17′S	36°49′E	25	87	77	25	0	0	77.0	25.0
Nassau	25°5′N	77°21′W	18	42	88	31	0.55	5.5	88.0	31.1
New Delhi	28°36′N	77°12′E	17	103	96	36	0.82	8.2	105.9	41.1
Nice	43°42′N	7°15′E	13	75	81	27	0.82	8.2	95.8	35.4
Paris	48°52′N	2°20′E	11	73	76	24	0	0	90.8	32.6
Peking	39°55′N	116°25′E	14	119	89	32	1.09	10.9	103.8	39.9
Rio de Janeiro	22°54′S	43°14′W	31	55	84	29	0.82	8.2	84.0	28.9
Riyadh	24°38′N	46°43′E	18	91	107	42	0	0	126.6	52.6
Rome	41°54′N	12°29′E	13	77	88	31	0.82	8.2	102.8	39.3
Santiago	33°27′S	70°40′W	33	44	85	29	0	0	85.0	29.4
Sao Paulo	23°32′S	46°37′W	31	54	81	27	0	0	81.0	27.2
Seoul	37°33′N	126°58′E	14	123	84	29	0.82	8.2	98.8	37.1
Singapore	1°17′N	103°51′E	24	114	88	31	0.27	2.7	92.9	33.8
Stockholm	59°20′N	18°3′E	9	80	70	21	0.82	8.2	84.8	29.3
Sydney	33°52′S	151°13′E	34	133	78	26	0	0	78.0	25.6
Taipei	25°3′N	121°30′E	18	121	92	33	0	0	92.0	33.3
Teheran	35°40′N	51°26′E	15	93	99	37	1.36	13.6	123.5	50.8
Tel Aviv	32°5′N	34°48′E	16	86	87	31	1.09	10.9	106.6	41.5
Tokyo	35°42′N	139°46′E	15	128	83	28	0.27	2.7	87.9	31.0
Toronto	43°39′N	79°23′W	13	41	79	26	1.09	10.9	98.6	37.0
Tripoli	32°54′N	13°11′E	16	78	85	29	0.82	8.2	99.8	37.6
Vancouver	49°16′N	123°7′W	11	23	74	23	1.09	10.9	93.6	34.2
Vienna	48°13′N	16°20′E	12	79	75	24	0.82	8.2	89.8	32.1
Warsaw	52°15′N	21°0′E	11	81	75	24	0.82	8.2	89.8	32.1
Winnipeg	49°53′N	97°9′W	11	34	79	26	1.09	10.9	98.6	37.0

a. For July in the Northern Hemisphere; for January in the Southern Hemisphere.

average daily maximums above this threshold. At present, only 2 of the 66 cities have average daily maximums in July of 100°F or higher. With very-long-term warming, 42 of the 66 cities would exceed this higher benchmark. It is likely that the public would be prepared to pay some amount, and perhaps a great deal, to avoid outdoor temperatures of these levels.

Nonlinear Impact

The largely adverse effects of global warming are outlined briefly in chapter 1 and examined in depth in chapter 3. It is important to recognize from the outset, however, that as a general rule one would expect the economic size of damage from global warming to rise more than linearly with the magnitude of warming. The costs of 10°C warming in the very long term could thus be far more than four times the costs of the 2.5°C benchmark warming for a doubling of carbon-dioxide-equivalent. Consider two areas of potential costs: damage to agriculture, and damage from a sea-level rise.

It seems likely that damage to agriculture would be far worse with a global mean warming of 10°C than it would be with a warming of 2.5°C. As discussed in chapter 3, the effects of carbon dioxide on fertilization are less than linear and contribute little above the first doubling of carbon dioxide. Ceiling temperatures above which crop yields collapse toward zero (in the range of 35°C for fine grains and 45°C for coarse grains) would be likely to be reached in summer for US midlatitudes.

As for sea level, the IPCC estimates that, under business as usual, sea level will rise by 66 centimeters from 1990 to the year 2100, with upper and lower bounds of 110 cm and 31 cm, respectively. This estimate is a "transient" rather than an equilibrium one, from warming commitment by 2100 and the further lag of melting completion behind equilibrium temperature change (IPCC 1990b, 280). A rise of one meter would eliminate 3 percent of the earth's land area and a larger percentage of its crop area (Rosenberg et al. 1989a, 2–3).

The potential damage would be much greater, however, with 10°C warming. The IPCC estimate for 2100 assumes that the Antarctic is a sink for water rather than a source: at temperatures below −12°C, glacier accumulation exceeds ablation as temperature rises (IPCC 1990b, 271), in part because warmer air holds more moisture and delivers more snow. With the much higher warming suggested here for the very long term, it seems highly likely that the Antarctic, which contains 90 percent of the earth's ice, would become a major source for sea-level rise. Hoffman et al. (1986) have projected that, even by the year 2100, the Antarctic could contribute as much as 220 centimeters to sea-level rise, and the total increase could amount to as much as 367 centimeters (IPCC 1990b,

279). On this basis alone, an eventual sea-level rise of at least four meters would seem likely if global mean temperature were to rise by 10°C.

In many other areas as well (for example, water shortages), a greater-than-linear increase of damage with respect to warming would have to be expected. Nonlinearity is thus incorporated into the analysis of the benefits of limiting global warming in chapters 3 and 7.

Avoiding Long-Term Warming

As discussed in chapter 1, some amount of global warming cannot be avoided, in part because there is some warming that is committed and already in the pipeline from past emissions, and in part because it is implausible that the global economy could immediately cut emissions by the 60 percent or so required to stop further atmospheric buildup. The key policy issue thus becomes how much of the prospective warming could be avoided through energetic but feasible action, and at what economic price. For purposes of benefit-cost analysis, it is the benefit associated with *the amount of warming that can be avoided* (rather than total baseline warming) that should be compared against the costs of limiting warming.

Table 2.4 summarizes prospective very-long-term warming with and without measures to restrain the buildup of carbon dioxide and other trace gases. The two alternative baseline estimates are from this study (i.e., table 2.1) and the IPCC (1990b) business-as-usual scenario, as discussed above. The two restraint cases consider policy action scenarios investigated by the IPCC: first, the freeze of emissions at their 1990 levels, and second, a more aggressive program of "accelerated policies." The latter involves the limitation of global emissions (including emissions from deforestation) to an annual level of 5.6 GtC by the year 2000, 5.1 GtC by 2025, and a constant plateau of approximately 3 GtC by 2050 and thereafter (IPCC 1990d, table 8, 29).

The IPCC (1990b, figure A.7, 344) estimates that, under the 1990 plateau scenario, total radiative forcing reaches 5.7 wm^{-2} by the year 2100. Applying the central climate sensitivity factor of $\Lambda = 2.5°C$ for a doubling of carbon dioxide, this forcing corresponds to a warming commitment of 3.3°C.[30] The IPCC does not present more distant estimates. However, if carbon emissions are held constant at the 1990 base of 6 GtC annually during the period 2100–2275, and the fraction retained in the atmosphere is 50 percent, the atmospheric stock of carbon would rise by 525 GtC. The IPCC estimates that atmospheric concentration in the "constant emissions" case would stand at 525 ppm in 2100 (IPCC 1990b,

---

30. As discussed in chapter 1 (equation 1.1), with $\Lambda = 2.5$ we have $\lambda = 0.3$ and $\beta = 1.9$ so that $\Delta T = (0.3 \times 1.9)R = 0.57R°C$.

Table 2.4 Commitment to global warming under alternative scenarios

	2050	2100	2275
Cline baseline (A)			
Radiative forcing (wm^{-2})	5.4	8.3	16.3[b]
Warming commitment[a] (°C)	3.1	4.7	10.1[b]
IPCC business-as-usual (B)			
Radiative forcing (wm^{-2})	6.5	9.9	n.a.
Warming commitment (°C)	3.7	5.7	n.a.
IPCC 1990 emissions plateau (C)			
Radiative forcing (wm^{-2})	4.5	5.7	8.7[b]
Warming commitment (°C)	2.6	3.3	5.0[b]
IPCC accelerated policies (D)			
Radiative forcing (wm^{-2})	4.0	4.3	4.3
Warming commitment (°C)	2.3	2.5	2.5
Warming avoided by policy action			
Emissions freeze (C − A)			
Radiative forcing (wm^{-2})	0.9	2.6	7.6
Warming commitment (°C)	0.5	1.4	5.1
Accelerated policies (D − A)			
Radiative forcing (wm^{-2})	1.4	4.0	12.0
Warming commitment (°C)	0.8	2.2	7.6

n.a. = not available; wm^{-2} = watts per square meter.

a. The warming commitment is specified at a climate sensitivity parameter of 2.5°C for carbon-dioxide-equivalent doubling.

b. See text; excludes chlorofluorocarbons.

Sources: text calculations; Intergovernmental Panel on Climate Change (IPCC). 1990. *Scientific Assessment of Climate Change: Report Prepared for IPCC by Working Group I.* New York: World Meteorological Organization and United Nations Environment Programme, 61 and figure A.7.

figure A.4, 342), for an atmospheric stock of 1,125 GtC. At constant emissions the atmospheric stock would thus reach 1,650 GtC by the year 2275, for a concentration of 770 ppm. Applying the IPCC (Wigley) formula, this carbon concentration would cause radiative forcing of 6.38 wm^{-2}. Applying an expansion factor of 1.37 for all greenhouse gases (the low ratio excluding CFCs, as discussed above), total radiative forcing would reach 8.74 wm^{-2}. This forcing would translate to a central warming estimate of 5.0°C (see note 30).

In the more ambitious "accelerated policies" case, radiative forcing reaches its ceiling by 2100. Table 2.4 thus shows the same radiative forcing and warming commitment for 2275 as for 2100 in this scenario.

The difference between the baseline warming and that under the alternative policy responses may then be determined by deducting the restraint scenario estimates from the baseline estimates. On this basis, in the very-long-term horizon through 2275 the "constant emissions" case would reduce mean global warming from 10°C to 5°C, for a net warming avoidance of 5°C. The "accelerated policies" case would cut mean global warming from 10°C to 2.5°C, for net warming avoidance of about 7.5°C.

The range of estimates has a wide spread around these central values. As noted above, the lower bound identified here for very-long-term warming is 6°C, and the upper bound 18°C. The corresponding lower and upper bounds of warming under the "accelerated policies" scenario would be 1.5°C and 4.5°C, respectively. Thus, the amount of warming avoided in the very long term with aggressive international action might amount to only 4.5°C, but could also reach as high as 13.5°C.

It is apparent from these calculations that if a sufficiently long horizon is considered, very substantial global warming can be effectively avoided rather than merely "delayed" through policy action. Because the terminal date of 2275 is approximately the time when the rapid removal of carbon dioxide by deep-ocean mixing begins to occur, in effect the warming commitment avoided by that time is avoided definitively rather than just delayed.

The Pace of Warming and the Price of Delaying Action

The central estimates of this study are that, without special policy intervention, global warming will amount to 10°C by the year 2275, but that with aggressive action this warming can be limited to 2.5°C. The amount of warming that can be avoided, 7.5°C, amounts to 0.26°C per decade.[31] If the upper-bound estimates are used, the figure is almost 0.5°C per decade.

Delay of an energetic program to limit greenhouse gas emissions has the appeal of giving time for improved scientific certainty before embarking on costly measures. Indeed, the final policy proposal of this study, set forth in chapter 8, opts for a two-stage approach that does apply lesser (but still significant) measures in the first decade but then adopts a more aggressive international regime thereafter if warranted by further scientific corroboration. However, it must be recognized that a price must be paid for delay in action in terms of higher ultimate warming. If no action is taken at all, the price amounts to an expected 0.25°C per decade and perhaps as much as 0.5°C per decade. This rate counsels policy decision sooner rather than later.

---

31. This estimate is approximately the same as the 0.3°C figure used by the IPCC scientific panel, even after revision for the neutral effect of CFCS (*Financial Times*, 18–19 January 1992, 5).

Caveat Lector

It should be clear to the reader, but it warrants reiteration, that the calculation of very-long-term warming presented here is my own and is not a mainstream estimate of the scientific community.[32] Although the projection relies directly on parameters in the report of the IPCC (1990b), that report itself extends no further than to the year 2100. The estimate here has not been confirmed by GCMS or other scientific computations. The closest such calculation, as noted above, is that by Manabe and Bryan (1985).

It should also be recognized, however, that under the upper- bound warming estimates the IPCC warming commitment by the year 2100 is already 10.3°C (as analyzed above). From this standpoint, then, the very-long-term warming figure of 10°C calculated in this chapter may be viewed alternatively as a magnitude of warming that is nearly reached within the confines of the existing scientific estimates and, under upper-bound assumptions, at a much earlier date.

More generally, however, my own view is that there is a great need for further scientific research on very-long-term warming, including GCM runs for the levels of greenhouse gas concentrations and radiative forcing envisioned here. Policy-makers will need such estimates to make a more informed decision on abatement action. The conventional benchmark of warming associated with a doubling of carbon-dioxide-equivalent has so far tended to generate damage estimates on the order of 1 percent to perhaps 2 percent of world GNP (chapter 3; annex 7A).

---

32. In response to my inquiry to the IPCC concerning the calculations here for very-long-term warming, Bruce Callander sent the following reply (4 March 1991): "John Mitchell [United Kingdom Meteorological Office] expressed unwillingness to make any guess as to what GHG [greenhouse gas] concentrations would be in 250 years' time. However, he did point out that, assuming a 2.5K [Kelvin or centigrade]; increase in mean global temperature arises from a doubling of CO_2, then a 10K increase would require an approximate 16-fold increase in CO_2-equivalent. Available reserves of carbon are thought to be sufficient only for a 4- to 8-fold increase in CO_2, so such a large rise seems unlikely even in the long term."

However, as discussed above, an eightfold increase in carbon dioxide concentration should arise solely from carbon dioxide emissions over the 250- to 300-year horizon examined; in addition, the inclusion of other trace gases has the effect of raising the carbon-dioxide-*equivalent* increase to approximately the 16-fold indicated by Mitchell. The ratio of total radiative forcing to that from carbon dioxide alone is conservatively placed at 1.37, based on IPCC parameters, as discussed above. The Wigley formula for eightfold carbon dioxide generates $R = 6.3 \ln 8$ wm^{-2} = 13 wm^{-2}. Expansion for other trace gases yields total radiative forcing equal to $13 \times 1.37 = 17.8$ wm^{-2}. We may invert the Wigley formula to identify the level of carbon-dioxide-equivalent that corresponds to this total radiative forcing: $\ln Z = 17.8/6.3$; $Z = 16.9$, where Z is the carbon-dioxide-*equivalent* multiple of preindustrial levels. Thus, Mitchell's 16-fold requirement for carbon-dioxide-equivalent would be approximately the central estimate based on the analysis here for the very long term. As noted above, the surprise arises simply because, by the time there is eightfold carbon dioxide, the decay of its marginal radiative forcing power (following the logarithmic function) implies that the increment contributed by non-carbon-dioxide greenhouse gases is extremely high when expressed in terms of still further carbon dioxide.

As the estimates of the costs of severe limitation of warming tend to be on the order of 2 percent to 3 percent of GDP (chapters 4 and 7), an economic analysis that omits very-long-term warming is likely to conclude that avoiding global warming is not cost-effective.

Within the more conventional framework of analyzing only the doubling of carbon-dioxide-equivalent, the case for aggressive limitation of emissions is thus likely to have to stand solely on appeal to essentially noneconomic standards, such as a scientific apprehension that warming at historically unprecedented rates is inherently dangerous, or the view that the species loss, sea-level rise, and other effects associated with conventional benchmark warming are unacceptable even without placing an explicit valuation on them. In some fundamental sense such views may be valid as value judgments, and indeed the ballot box offers the test for their validity in a democratic society. The point here is simply that if the weight of economic benefit-cost analysis is to be added more definitively to the case for aggressive action to limit global warming, it would seem inevitable that further scientific work will be required concerning the very-long-term implications. Examination of very-long-term warming is thus one of the priority items on the agenda for scientific research set forth in chapter 1.

3

The Economic Benefits of Limiting Global Warming

3

The Economic Benefits of Limiting Global Warming

For purposes of public policy, it is desirable to determine the range of economic damage that may be expected from global warming.[1] If these damages are far smaller than the costs of reducing emissions from fossil fuels, deforestation, and other sources, then the case for preventive action is weak on grounds of traditional economic policy formation and must stand solely on ecological concern. If instead the economic damages equal or exceed the costs of limiting global warming, preventive action is warranted on economic grounds alone, reinforcing the case for action on the basis of concern about ecological risk.

For a time in the late 1980s, it appeared that policy action on the greenhouse problem would be based simply on the scientific view that global warming would take place. The international scientific review by the Intergovernmental Panel on Climate Change (IPCC, discussed in chapter 1) seemed to be the vehicle for resolving the issue. However, by 1990–91 it had become apparent that the scientific determinations were just the first step in the policy process. Policymakers were beginning to emphasize the need to weigh the costs of preventive action against the prospective damages that might be expected from global warming. For US officials at least, this calculus still found the case for action unconvincing, in part because of remaining scientific uncertainty (chapter 8).

The sole economic analysis that had attempted to place a valuation on the prospective damages from global warming had identified only a small economic impact and correspondingly counseled extremely modest action (Nordhaus 1990a, 1991a; see chapter 7, annex 7A, of this study). The striking implication of that study was that, even if the scientific predictions were entirely correct, the greenhouse effect would simply be too moderate in economic terms to warrant much preventive effort. Although that conclusion might have been alarming to those

---

1. An earlier version of this chapter appears in Cline (1992b).

in the scientific community and general public who felt that the expected eco-logical effects would be unacceptable, the implication was that policy action beyond a bare minimum would have to be justified on noneconomic grounds. Other estimates of the damages of global warming tended to be only qualitative or to be confined to individual effects rather than a comprehensive evaluation (IPCC 1990c; Environmental Protection Agency 1989a).

At the same time, as reviewed in chapter 4, several quantitative studies emerged on the cost side of the issue.[2] Typically based on energy-economic models, these calculations began to provide what appeared to be a relatively robust range of estimates of the price that economies would have to pay to limit emissions of greenhouse gases. This price was placed relatively high in the range of 2 percent to 3 percent of GDP on an ongoing basis (chapter 4). As the international com-munity negotiated toward a convention on climate change in preparation for the United Nations Conference on Environment and Development in June 1992 (chapter 8), there was considerable risk that the seeming concreteness of cost estimates for preventive action, set against the only fragmentary measurements of the benefits of limiting global warming, would bias the policy process toward inaction.

This chapter seeks to provide an evaluation of the benefits of limiting global warming that is more comprehensive and satisfactory than those previously available. The estimates here first attempt to identify more thoroughly than before the economic damages to be expected from warming associated with a doubling of carbon-dioxide-equivalent, the conventional benchmark. However, what more distinctly sets the analysis apart from previous calculations is the incorporation of the dimension of rising economic damage from the much higher warming over the very long term of 250 to 300 years (chapter 2). It should be emphasized that the estimates must be seen as broad approximations rather than precise measurements, especially for the more intangible ecological effects (e.g., species loss). Nonetheless, the findings here seem sufficiently clear to suggest that previous examinations have tended to understate the scope of economic damage that may be expected from global warming. This conclusion applies especially to damages over the very long term.

Analytical Framework

Ideally, the measurement of economic benefits to be obtained from the limiting of global warming should include the following elements.

---

2. In particular, Manne and Richels (1990a), Edmonds and Barns (1990), Jorgenson and Wilcoxen (1990b), Congressional Budget Office (1990), and Nordhaus (1990a). For sur-veys, see Hoeller et al. (1990), Edmonds and Barns (1991), and Darmstadter and Plantinga (1991).

First, estimates should be prepared for each major actor in the international bargaining that will be required for action, as global warming will affect each country differently and in varying intensity. The countries and groups relevant for this purpose include at least the United States, the European Community, the Commonwealth of Independent States (former Soviet Union), Japan, and Canada, because of their large roles in global economic activity and emissions.[3] In addition, other key actors include China, because of its large coal reserves; Brazil and Indonesia, because of their large emissions from deforestation; Eastern Europe, where industrial emissions have been unusually high; Bangladesh, Egypt, and certain island nations, where severe damage from sea-level rise may be expected; and the Sahel and other developing regions already facing vulnerability of water supply.[4]

The high-resolution general circulation models (GCMS) have sufficient area detail to provide these geographical estimates.[5] The IPCC (1990b, 163–65) does warn that "confidence is low" for the regional (as opposed to global) calculations of the GCMS, especially with respect to precipitation and soil moisture. Nonetheless, as noted in chapter 2, the high-resolution GCMS have been relatively successful in simulating current-day regional climates and would seem to be the appropriate point of departure for analysis for individual countries and regions.

The estimates of this chapter attempt to distinguish effects among certain countries, especially in agriculture. However, much of the analysis here is oriented toward the United States, in part because of the use of underlying analysis by the US Environmental Protection Agency (EPA) but also because of the sheer scope of the research task involved. Future research would usefully extend the calculations more fully to other geographical areas, especially the key actors just listed. In lieu of geographically more comprehensive estimates, the benefit-cost analysis of chapter 7 below draws implicitly on the results found for the United States as an initial pattern for global effects.

Second, greenhouse damages should be identified by category of effect. Chapter 1 summarized the principal aspects of expected damage from global warming. Anticipating the empirical estimates of this chapter, table 3.4 in the overview

---

3. Some regional detail on at least the United States, the European Community, and Russia would also seem desirable, as their geographical expanses include areas likely to face significantly different impacts.

4. See table 8.1 for country-specific estimates of carbon dioxide emissions from the burning of fossil fuels and deforestation.

5. Thus, the UK Meteorological Office model, with resolution of 2.5° horizontal and 3.75° vertical, divides the earth's surface into 6,912 grids. At the equator, each grid has a north-south distance of 417 km and an east-west distance of 278 km; at higher latitudes the east-west distance is smaller (Cline 1990e).

section at the end of this chapter distinguishes 16 broad categories of economic effects of global warming.

Third, the damages from global warming need to be specified for different points in time. In practice, the approach of this chapter is to identify two temporal benchmarks: equilibrium warming from the doubling of carbon-dioxide-equivalent, and that from very-long-term warming. As noted in chapter 2, the corresponding dates for actual realized warming are set at 2050 and 2275, respectively. As developed in chapter 7 below, actual warming at intermediate periods may be estimated by linear interpolation. The corresponding damage associated with warming in intermediate years applies a geometric (i.e., exponential) relationship between damage and warming, providing what amounts to geometric interpolation between the two benchmarks (chapter 7, equations 7.5 and 7.6).

Fourth, the analysis should take account of adaptation.[6] Efforts to adapt reduce the damages of global warming and thus the benefits of limiting warming. However, adaptation also reduces the costs attributable to prevention measures, because these costs must be calculated on a net basis and therefore should appropriately deduct adaptation costs if estimated prevention benefits are correspondingly being reduced because of adaptation.

With regard to technological change more generally, it is true that unanticipated improvements in technology could reduce the extent of damages from global warming (e.g., through the development of miracle seed varieties resistant to drought). However, as argued in chapter 8, there is no reason to expect unforeseen technological breakthroughs to reduce greenhouse damages and the corresponding benefits of abatement policy action by more (or less) than they reduce the costs of action. There is therefore no presumption that the inability to fully incorporate future technical change biases the benefit-cost ratio for policy action either upward or downward.

Fifth, the benefits from preventive action must take account of the extent of the remaining warming not avoided by the policy measures in question. It is necessary to estimate a projection of both the warming damages under the baseline of no policy intervention and those still present under the policy scenario in question. The "benefit" of the policy is then the difference between the two projections over time, not the full amount of the baseline damage projection.

Sixth, analysis of benefits over time requires discounting to permit comparison of effects at different time periods (discussed in chapter 6).

Seventh, it is necessary to scale the estimated benefits. The variable used here (and in chapter 7) for scaling is gross domestic product (GDP). Absolute magnitudes of damage are first estimated against today's economic scale, and then

---

6. Thus, Schelling (1983, 453) calls attention to adaptation and technical change by warning that analysis of the greenhouse effect should not make the mistake of "superimposing a climate change that would occur gradually in the distant future on life as we know it today."

the resulting percentage of GDP is applied to future GDP levels. In reality some damages are likely to rise less than proportionately with GDP, and others more than proportionately. Agricultural effects would tend to rise less than GDP because of Engel's law (demand for food is income-inelastic). Such effects as electricity requirements for air conditioning might be expected to rise proportionately, or more than proportionately, with GDP, as they are likely to have unitary or above-unitary elasticity of demand with respect to per capita income. Still other effects, such as valuation on human life and the value of species loss, could be expected to rise more than proportionately with GDP. Human life valuation will reflect lifetime earnings capacity, which rises with per capita GDP; valuation of species and other ecological intangibles may be expected to be income-elastic, because economies have greater scope for allocating resources to these concerns as income rises further above subsistence levels. Overall, scaling by GDP would seem to be an appropriate approximation.[7]

Eighth, welfare weights might appropriately be applied to make policy comparisons across countries and regions. Thus, losses to a poor country such as Bangladesh might receive greater weight in global calculations than would be indicated solely on the basis of that country's measured GDP, because of the greater "marginal disutility" of losses at living standards close to subsistence levels.

Ninth, it is appropriate to include some form of weighting to take account of policymaker risk aversion. If policymakers are cautious, there should be relatively more weight attributed to the high-damage variants than to the low-damage variants flanking the central-case estimates.

Of these various dimensions, the analysis of this chapter concentrates on economic categories of damage, time horizon, and (to a lesser extent) geographical location and adaptation. The discussion of chapter 2 considers the component of damage that can be avoided through policy action. Chapter 6 examines time discounting; and chapter 7 synthesizes the elements of the analysis into an overall benefit-cost evaluation that incorporates risk aversion.[8]

---

7. Some stress that GDP itself is a misleading measure because it does not take account of environmental damage, the value of leisure time, and other important aspects of economic welfare. Although undoubtedly true to some extent, this critique is irrelevant to the question of gauging the impact of greenhouse damage against the GDP yardstick. Both the benefits of avoiding damage through abatement and the costs of abatement are expressed as percentages of GDP; therefore, any modification of GDP for factors such as those just mentioned would enter into both the numerator and the denominator of the benefit-cost ratio and thus wash out. In any event, such corrections seem unlikely to reduce measured GDP by more than, say, 10 percent to 15 percent; in this case, greenhouse damages would be 2.2 percent of "true" GDP rather than 2.0 percent (for example), with no major change in the qualitative interpretation. In sum, distaste for GDP is essentially a red herring if used as a critique against scaling greenhouse damages and abatement costs by this conventional measure.

8. Note that Cline (1992b) develops (but does not estimate) the following summary

Inherent Damage Limits?

Before turning to the specific estimates of this chapter, it is important to scrutinize an argument that stems solely from the "economic categories" dimension. Nordhaus (1991a) and Schelling (1991) have argued that, at least for industrial countries, the potential damage from global warming is greatly limited by the small share of climate-sensitive sectors in GDP. For example, in countries where agriculture accounts for less than 3 percent of GDP (according to the argument), even sharp reductions in agricultural output would represent relatively small percentages of GDP. There is some merit in this point, as one might expect a developing economy with a far higher share of agriculture to be more vulnerable than an industrial economy. However, the argument tends to understate potential damages generally and for industrial economies in particular.

Of the 16 categories identified in table 3.4 and analyzed below, only four are related to outdoor activity and thus directly affected by climate (agriculture, forestry, leisure, and construction). Eleven of the categories are not even tied to a specific production sector. Some of the effects are more likely to show a higher impact in an industrial economy than in a developing economy. Human life is one such effect, if standard approaches based on lifetime earnings (for example) are the criterion. Coastal defenses are likely to be another: the prospective investment in defending New York or Amsterdam is likely to exceed that of defending Recife, Brazil (abstracting from the different physical situations), because of higher structural buildup and property valuation in the countries that are more highly developed. The same may be said of the "pollution spillover" category.

Even in agriculture, the "inherent limitation" argument ignores the diamond-water paradox. Agriculture is only 3 percent of US GDP because agricultural production is abundant and prices are low. With serious cutbacks in agricultural

---

measure of benefits from greenhouse policy:

$$PVGB = \sum_i \sum_j \sum_t \lambda_j \left[w^l \, b' \, (i,j)^l_{p,t} + w^c \, b'(i,j)^c_{p,t} + w^u \, b' \, (i,j)^u_{p,t} \right] / (1 + \rho)^t$$

where PVGB is the discounted present value of benefits, b' is the entry in a matrix of benefits net of adaptation effects, i is the economic category of damage, j is the country or region, t is the year, ρ is the discount rate, w is the risk weight, l is the low-damage case, c is the central damage case, u is the upper-bound damage case, p is the policy scenario in question, and λ is the equity weight. For its part, $b'(i,j)$ is the ijth cell in the matrix:

$$B_{p\,'\,\text{\textit{ti}}} = D_{b,t} - D_{p,t} + C_{a,t} - (-\Delta D_{a,t})$$

where matrix D refers to damages, subscript b denotes the baseline, matrix C_a refers to the costs of implementing adaptation measures, and matrix ΔD_a is a matrix of changes in damages resulting from adaptation.

production, and given price-inelastic demand, ex post prices would be much higher. Proper evaluation of the loss of consumer surplus would mean a much larger damage potential than might be suspected from the small share of agriculture in present GDP.[9] In sum, it is misleading to cite the low shares of climate-sensitive sectors in the existing structure of production as prima facie evidence that the benefits of global warming abatement are likely to be small.

Agriculture

The specific estimates of the impact of the greenhouse effect may appropriately begin with the agricultural sector.

General Considerations

Global warming is likely to damage agriculture in many areas but aid it in others. The principal damage will arise from heat stress and decreased soil moisture. Warmer temperatures cause the growing cycle of the plant to accelerate, allowing less time for plant development before maturity. Thus, even under irrigation, corn yields are estimated to decline by as much as 50 percent in the Great Lakes region with temperature increases from a doubling of carbon dioxide as estimated with the Geophysical Fluid Dynamics Laboratory (GFDL) general circulation model (Ritchie et al. 1989, 1-1). Moreover, the continental interiors are expected to become drier with global warming. The principal offsets would be longer growing seasons in cold, northern climates and the fertilization effect of greater atmospheric carbon dioxide. Kane et al. (1989, 3) provide the following overview:

> The warming and increased precipitation in the northern latitudes [near 70°N] would improve the agricultural prospects in Canada, northern Europe, and the USSR. . . . The increases in temperature and drying of interiors of continents in the mid-latitudes [near 40°N and S] is expected to lead to reductions in agricultural productivity in the United States and western Europe. Projected coastal inundation of rice growing regions in parts of Southeast Asia, such as Bangladesh, combined with the projected movement of the Asian monsoon away from the Indian sub-continent could lead to reduced agricultural production.

On the basis of EPA studies and studies by the International Institute for Applied Systems Analysis and the United Nations Environment Programme, the three

---

9. The point may be seen by considering the extreme: if world agricultural production fell to zero, so would world population. The economic loss would equal the entirety of GDP, not just the ex ante share attributable to agriculture.

authors estimate that global warming from carbon-dioxide-equivalent doubling would reduce average yields by 20 percent in the United States and the European Community and by 18 percent in Canada, but increase yields by 15 percent in northern Europe and Australia, 10 percent in the former Soviet Union, and 4 percent in Japan.

Despite such estimates, it is an emerging stylized fact that the damage to agriculture from global warming will be moderate:

> because most farmers are not dumb, but rather are accustomed to continually adapting . . . [and] the projected impacts of climate are small in comparison with impacts associated with government subsidies, international trade, and other economic factors or . . . technological progress. (Ausubel 1990, 14)

In his review of the benefits of abatement, Nordhaus (1991a) places greenhouse damage (from a doubling of carbon-dioxide-equivalent) to US agriculture within a range of $-\$9.7$ billion to $+\$10.6$ billion annually (1982 prices), and thus a mean value of nearly zero, based on EPA estimates (discussed below).

For its part, the IPCC (1990c, 12) concludes:

> Negative impacts could be felt at the regional level as a result of changes in weather, diseases, pests and weeds associated with climate change. . . . There may be severe effects in some regions, particularly in regions of high present-day vulnerability that are least able to adjust technologically to such effects. There is a possibility that potential productivity of high and mid-latitudes may increase because of a prolonged growing season, but it is not likely to open up large new areas for production, and will be largely confined to the Northern Hemisphere. On balance, the evidence is that in the face of estimated changes of climate, food production at the global level can be maintained at essentially the same level as would have occurred without climate change; but the cost of achieving this is unclear. Nonetheless, climate changes may intensify difficulties in coping with rapid population growth.

Thus, the IPCC essentially adopts the benign interpretation, but with caution and recognition of likely damage to vulnerable regions.

There are several reasons to suspect that the benign view is too optimistic. Most important, it fails to consider effects over the very long term. As analyzed below, with eventual global warming on the order of 10°C, agricultural damage would be likely to rise nonlinearly. However, even for the standard benchmark of carbon-dioxide-equivalent doubling, there are grounds for skepticism. First, recent work on drought has concluded that the incidence of severe droughts would be greatly multiplied (Rind et al. 1990). Second, the moderate impact projections usually are premised on an important boost from carbon dioxide fertilization. Yet it is unclear that this phenomenon will prove as effective in the field—in farms around the world—as in the laboratory. Moreover, the amount of carbon dioxide buildup is considerably less than twofold for the doubling of carbon-dioxide-*equivalent* of all trace gases.

Consider drought. Rind et al. use results of the Goddard Institute for Space Studies (GISS) general circulation model to calculate that the incidence of severe droughts (measured by the Palmer index), which currently occur only 5 percent of the time, would rise to 50 percent frequency by the 2050s. Their finding is based on the difference between precipitation and potential evapotranspiration (E_p). They find that:

> E_p increases most where the temperature is highest, at low- to mid-latitudes, while precipitation increases most where the air is coolest and easiest to saturate by the additional moisture, at higher latitudes. . . . Higher temperatures increase the atmospheric water-holding capacity . . . of the order of 33% . . . and thus the ability of the atmosphere to draw moisture from the surface. (Rind et al. 1990, 9983).

The GISS GCM calculates E_p as a function of the difference between the specific humidity at ground level and that at a height of 30 meters (as well as wind velocity and turbulence). E_p rises strongly with ground temperature. Actual evaporation equals potential multiplied by an efficiency factor ($ET = \beta E_p$). The authors argue that the GCMs tend to understate the efficiency factor (at estimates of $\beta \approx 0.2$, versus the observed US range of 0.6 to 0.9), in part because of the absence of a vegetative canopy in the models. The overall thrust of the analysis by Rind et al. is that the GCMs understate the decline in soil moisture in projections of warmer climates. The implication is that agricultural estimates based on the GCM projections may understate the damage from global warming.

Similarly, Gleick (1987) uses GCM climate projections and a water-balance model for the Sacramento basin in California to calculate that summer soil moisture would fall by 8 percent to 44 percent under carbon-dioxide-equivalent doubling.

So far, however, the crop models have not explicitly incorporated the influence of drought in evaluating the impact of global warming on yields. In particular, the models typically begin each year afresh, with no model "memory" of water depletion in a preceding year. Yet, as shown by the experience of California in the late 1980s, it is the successive accumulation of back-to-back drought years that eventually has the most devastating impact. The economic losses from drought can be large. In the 1988 US drought alone, losses (primarily agricultural) amounted to $40 billion (Wilhite 1990).

The second area that may warrant skepticism is the heavy reliance on carbon dioxide fertilization in the benign assessments. Photosynthesis is the transformation of carbon dioxide and water into plant matter (carbohydrates) and oxygen.[10] The so-called C_3 crops (wheat, rice, soybeans, fine grains, legumes, root crops, most trees) have relatively inefficient photosynthesis (because of loss from induced respiration) and benefit substantially from increased exposure to carbon dioxide. The C_4 crops (maize, millet, sorghum, sugarcane) are more efficient and obtain relatively smaller photosynthesis gains from more carbon dioxide. In addition, both types experience stomatal (pore) closure from increased carbon dioxide, with the result that less water is lost to transpiration and the plants become more efficient in water use. The overall result is that a doubling of carbon dioxide (from 330 to 660 ppm) raises yields in greenhouse experiments by an average 34 percent for C_3 and 14 percent for C_4 crops (Schneider and Rosenberg 1989, 27–28).

However, these effects have not been documented under normal open-field farm conditions. The EPA (1989a, 110) suggests:

> Few studies have examined the interactive effects of CO_2, water, nutrients, light, temperature, pollutants, and sensitivity to daylight on photosynthesis and transpiration . . . [or] growth and development of the whole plant. Therefore, considerable uncertainty exists concerning the extent to which the beneficial effects of increasing CO_2 will be seen in crops growing in the field under normal farming conditions with climate change.

More recently, experiments by Bazzaz and Fajer (1992) have cast doubt on the carbon-fertilization benefits of the greenhouse effect:

> [A]ssumptions about the benefits of a world replete with CO_2 may be overstated. Studies have shown that an isolated case of a plant's positive response to increased CO_2 levels does not necessarily translate into increased growth for entire plant communities. . . . [P]hotosynthetic rates are not always greater in CO_2–rich environments. Often plants growing under such conditions initially show increased photosynthesis, but over time this rate falls and approaches that of plants growing under today's carbon dioxide levels. . . . When nutrient, water or light levels are low, many plants show only a slight CO_2 fertilization effect.
>
> Competitive interference and limited nutrients will influence not only natural ecosystems such as meadows and forests but also man-made ecosystems such as farms. *For this reason, we do not expect that agricultural yields will necessarily improve in a CO_2 rich future* [emphasis added]. Again, at first glance, harvests do seem to benefit from such an atmosphere: Bruce A. Kimball of the U.S. Department of Agriculture reviewed more than 700 agronomic studies and found that, on average, grain production increased 34 percent in high CO_2 conditions. But on closer examination, it becomes clear that such yields were dependent on the presence of fertilizers and water—resources often well supplied only on farms in the developed world. . . . Large quantities of fertilizers, biocides and water must be added to crops for them to be productive in a CO_2–rich environment. But of course today water

---

10. The photosynthesis reaction is $6CO_2 + 6H_2O \rightarrow C_6H_{12}O_6 + 6O_2$. The reverse direction is respiration.

is a limited and expensive resource. We fear that the costs of these inputs, in dollars and in environmental quality, may be too great. (Bazzaz and Fajer 1992, 68–71)

The authors' warning concerning the need for ample water to enable plants to respond to carbon fertilization is especially relevant in view of the likelihood of increased water scarcity as a consequence of global warming, as discussed below.

Other experts have also emphasized caution on whether open-field carbon fertilization (under changed temperature and rainfall conditions) would be as substantial as the laboratory experiments suggest (Parry 1990, 40–41; NAS 1991a, 37). Nonetheless, the majority view has stressed the large body of evidence supporting at least the laboratory results (Kimball and Rosenberg 1990), and some experts note that selected open-field experiments are beginning to confirm those findings.[11] Overall, it would seem risky to count on agriculture in general experiencing the same degree of benefits from carbon fertilization as has been observed in the laboratory experiments, especially in developing countries where the complementary water and fertilizers may be lacking.

A different type of limitation of assumed carbon fertilization is that it is ex-pected to increase plant mass relative to nutritional content. The nitrogen content of plants would decrease as the carbon content increases, "implying reduced protein levels and reduced nutritional levels for livestock and humans" (Parry 1990, 41). The "effective yields" in nutritional terms could thus rise by less than weight yields. Bazzaz and Fajer (1992, 72) further point out that this same effect would be likely to induce greater crop consumption by insects, as grasshoppers and caterpillars would seek to compensate for lower nutritional quality through greater leaf consumption.

In addition, CO_2 fertilization tapers off relatively quickly with rising atmos-pheric concentration. Parry (1990, 38) estimates that for maize there is no further enhancement at concentrations above 550 ppm. For wheat, the rate of pho-tosynthesis rises from about 50 mg CO_2 dm^{-2}h^{-1} at 350 ppm (approximately current concentration) to 62.5 mg at 550 ppm; the rate rises only to 68 mg at 750 ppm and rises no further than a 70-mg ceiling for 850 ppm and higher.[12] As discussed below, the exhaustion of direct carbon dioxide enrichment in the face of above-linear increases in crop damage from heat stress and soil moisture decline mean that agricultural losses under very-long-term warming would be expected to far exceed those for the usual carbon-doubling benchmark.

---

11. US Department of Agriculture experiments in Arizona found that cotton grown in open-air fields with enhanced carbon dioxide levels showed large increases in yields (Norman J. Rosenberg, Resources for the Future, personal communication, June 1991).

12. The photosynthesis rates refer to milligrams of carbon dioxide per square decimeter per hour.

Another difficulty with interpretation of the typical agricultural results is the tendency to mistakenly link double carbon dioxide content (and its attendant enrichment) with the *warming* associated with carbon-dioxide-*equivalent* doubling. Because of other trace gases, there would be considerably less than double carbon dioxide at double total trace gas equivalent.[13] Specifically, the IPCC projects in its business-as-usual case that by the year 2025 the radiative forcing from all trace gases would be slightly higher than the equivalent of a doubling of carbon dioxide above preindustrial levels. At that time, atmospheric concentration of carbon dioxide would be enough to generate 2.88 watts per meter squared (wm^{-2}) radiative forcing. Using the IPCC–Wigley formula ($R = 6.3 \ln C/C_0$, where R is radiative forcing, C is carbon concentration, and $C_0 = 280$ ppm, the preindustrial level), we may calculate that the IPCC expects only 442 ppm carbon dioxide concentration at the equivalent-doubling benchmark.[14] Most of the agricultural studies use 330 ppm as the base level for atmospheric concentration and 660 ppm for the "doubled amount" in calculating yield impacts (EPA 1989a, 100). So *actual atmospheric carbon concentration is only expected by the IPCC to rise by about one-third the amount typically assumed in the agricultural estimates that incorporate "carbon dioxide doubling" enrichment.*

In sum, there are several reasons to be concerned that the present estimates of the agricultural effects of global warming are too optimistic and that, even for the modest benchmark of a doubling of carbon-dioxide-equivalent, agricultural damages would be larger, and gains smaller, than in the current mainstream calculations.

Damage Estimates: The United States

The EPA presented the following summary estimates of agricultural damage in its 1989 report to Congress. Combined producer and consumer economic effects of global warming at benchmark carbon-dioxide-equivalent doubling would range from − $5.9 billion annually (GISS model) to − $33.6 billion (GFDL model)

---

13. Nor is the force of this argument much affected by recent findings that chlorofluorocarbons may have little net warming effect because of their influence in stripping ozone, another greenhouse gas (chapter 1). As noted in chapter 2, by the year 2100 the exclusion of CFCs makes only minimal difference to the IPCC's projected radiative forcing, because a large substitution to HCFCs was already assumed. As for the date 2025, the time for benchmark carbon-dioxide-equivalent doubling, the IPCC projection had included only 0.11 wm^{-2} radiative forcing from the CFCs out of 1.71 wm^{-2} for trace gases other than carbon dioxide and a total of 4.59 wm^{-2} including carbon dioxide (IPCC 1990b, table 2.7).

14. This calculation remains almost unchanged if account is taken of a faster phaseout of CFCs. If the CFC-HCFC radiative forcing in the IPCC report is taken from the "accelerated policies" rather than "business as usual" scenario, total radiative forcing by 2025 drops only from 4.59 wm^{-2} to 4.50 wm^{-2} (IPCC 1990b, table 2.7, 61).

at 1982 prices, before taking account of carbon fertilization. After including the effect of carbon fertilization at an increase from 330 ppm to 660 ppm, the estimates were + $10.6 billion for GISS and − $9.7 billion for GFDL (EPA 1989a, 104).[15] These are the estimates Nordhaus (1991a, 932) uses.

The EPA text, but not its summary table, cautions that the estimates incorporating carbon fertilization may be too optimistic because they assume *double carbon dioxide (from 330 ppm to 660 ppm)* even though the weather scenarios are for equilibrium $2 \times CO_2$ *equivalent* warming. It acknowledges that the concentration of carbon dioxide will be only about 450 ppm in 2030 when the doubling benchmark arrives, and it warns that, although the "carbon fertilization" variants apply 660 ppm, actual concentration would still be only 555 ppm in 2060, when the equilibrium warming effects of the 2030 radiative forcing are felt (after three decades for ocean thermal delay; EPA 1989a, 100).

Actually, the potential bias is even greater, because the concept under investigation is the *equilibrium* effect of the $2 \times CO_2$ equivalent benchmark. Whereas the 2060 climate in the EPA calculations (GISS Transient Scenario A) is relatively close in terms of temperature and precipitation to the IPCC's equilibrium climate for doubling carbon-dioxide-equivalent (as might be expected from the fact that the two diverge in time by about the amount required for ocean thermal lag), the transient EPA benchmark has considerably higher carbon concentration than the IPCC's corresponding value for equilibrium under "doubling" of carbon-dioxide-equivalent. It would be inappropriate to count even 555 ppm carbon as available for fertilization at the equivalent-doubling benchmark, because if carbon dioxide trends continue along the path that would take concentration to 555 ppm by 2060, then the warming commitment would have been increased substantially beyond the equivalent-doubling mark. Essentially, to combine even 555 ppm carbon concentration with the GCM warming projections is to mix a transient concept (concentration) with an equilibrium concept (equivalent doubling).

A proper interpretation of the EPA estimates thus requires a careful weighting of the two alternative sets: with carbon fertilization, and without. For measurement of the equilibrium effects of carbon-dioxide-equivalent doubling, the proper amount of carbon fertilization to accept corresponds to the IPCC's 440 ppm, not 660 or even 555 ppm. On this basis, it is appropriate to give a weight

---

15. The corresponding breakdown between consumers and producers was as follows. Without carbon fertilization: consumers − $7.3 billion to − $37.5 billion, producers $1.5 billion to $3.9 billion. With carbon fertilization: consumers − $10.3 billion to + $9.4 billion, producers $0.6 billion to $1.3 billion. In each case the GFDL model shows the less favorable results. The two models show comparable average temperature increase (GISS 4.5°C, GFDL 5°C) but GFDL shows serious reductions in precipitation, whereas GISS shows moderate increases in most of the five broad regions considered (EPA 1989b, volume 1, vi–vii).

of two-thirds to the estimates without carbon fertilization and one-third to the estimates with fertilization. That is, the actual increase in carbon concentration, from 330 ppm to 440 ppm, is only one-third of the way to the 660 ppm used in the carbon-enriched calculation. Even this calculation gives the benefit of the doubt to the carbon fertilization effect because it makes no allowance for the possibility (some would say likelihood) that open-field results will be less favorable than those in the laboratory, nor for possible lesser nutritional content per plant mass.[16]

It should be recognized that this adjustment by linear interpolation may give different results from those that would be obtained by rerunning the crop models with a $2 \times CO_2$ climate (temperature, rainfall, soil moisture) and a 440-ppm carbon dioxide concentration. The interactions of climate and carbon fertilization can be nonlinear. Nonetheless, linear interpolation is the best available shorthand method for adjusting the crop estimates so that they represent an equilibrium rather than a transient concept. The resulting central estimate for the United States is that benchmark warming from carbon-dioxide-equivalent doubling would impose total (consumer and producer) damages of $13 billion annually at 1982 prices,[17] or $17.5 billion annually at 1990 prices.[18]

An alternative central estimate based on drought incidence might be formulated as follows. Suppose the Rind et al. estimate of increase in incidence of severe drought from 5 percent to 50 percent is accepted. Suppose the $40 billion figure for the 1988 drought is applied as the cost of severe drought. On this basis, the expected annual damage from benchmark warming would be (50 percent − 5 percent) × $40 billion = $18 billion annually. This alternative approach gives an almost identical estimate to that of the appropriately adjusted

---

16. Note also that the carbon-equivalent "doubling" represented by the approach here is above the preindustrial level (280 ppm) used by the IPCC rather than the 1958 level (330 ppm) used by the EPA.

17. This amount equals $(2/3)[(-5.9 - 33.6)/2] + (1/3)[(10.6 - 9.7)/2]$.

18. Note that there is no further adjustment for the fact that the underlying GCMs have higher climate sensitivity parameters than the IPCC's "best guess" ($\Lambda = 2.5°C$). The IPCC (1990b, 64, table 5.1) estimates that central North America (35–50°N, 80–105°W) would experience 2.8°C actual mean annual warming by 2030 with $\Lambda = 2.5°C$ and global mean realized (transient) warming of 1.8°C, for a regional warming coefficient of 1.56 (= 2.8/1.8). With this coefficient applied to $\Lambda = 2.5°C$, equilibrium warming for the United States would be 3.9°C for carbon-dioxide-equivalent doubling. In contrast, the simulation runs of the EPA models applied (GISS, GFDL) have an average US mean equilibrium warming (for 48 states) of 4.7°C for the same benchmark (EPA 1989b, vi). The EPA estimates might thus be seen as overstating damage by some 20 percent (or somewhat more considering nonlinearity). Nonetheless, influences omitted in the calculations seem likely to cause offsetting understatement of damages. These include lesser carbon fertilization in the open field than in the laboratory, and omission in the crop models of the effects of weeds and pests, heat damage to pollination (e.g., for maize), and the impact of sequential drought years.

EPA figure, although the concept is very different because the damage under the drought-probability approach is an expected average reflecting good and bad years, whereas the EPA figure is for a median year.

In other important recent work, Resources for the Future has attempted to do an in-depth calculation for the Missouri-Iowa-Nebraska-Kansas (MINK) area (Rosenberg and Crosson 1991). The study is unique in that it seeks not only to incorporate carbon dioxide fertilization but also to take account of farmer adaptation (earlier planting, use of longer season varieties, changes in tillage to conserve water). The study uses the actual climate conditions of the 1930s as an analog for a 2030s climate.

The MINK results find that if climate change alone is considered, warming by 2030 cuts agricultural production in the area by 17.1 percent. If carbon fertilization (specified at 100 ppm, from 350 ppm today to 450 ppm) is incorporated, the production loss is only 8.4 percent. With on-farm adaptations but without carbon fertilization, the production loss is 12.1 percent. With on-farm adaptations and carbon fertilization, production declines by only 3.3 percent (Rosenberg and Crosson 1991, 11–12).[19] Equilibrium long-term losses in the region's forests are 20 percent to 50 percent even with carbon fertilization, and stream flows decline by 28 percent in the Missouri and Upper Mississippi basins and 7 percent in the Arkansas basin, suggesting that forestry and water supply may be areas of relatively greater damage.

The results of the MINK study, which is among the most careful of all the agricultural studies, might seem at first glance to imply that, with carbon fertilization and farmer adaptation taken into account, agricultural damages in the United States as a result of global warming would be limited. A second look suggests otherwise. The 1930s climate was only 0.9°C warmer than that of the 1951–80 base period (Rosenberg et al. 1991, table 3.2). In contrast, the warming associated with benchmark carbon-dioxide-equivalent doubling for the MINK area would be 5°C for the average of three high-resolution GCMS (IPCC 1990a, figure 5.4, summer and winter average, as shown in figures 2.5 and 2.7, chapter 2, of the present study). This warming would be 3.4°C if scaled down by the ratio of the IPCC's best-guess climate sensitivity parameter, $\Lambda = 2.5$°C, to the average Λ for these three models ($\Lambda = 3.7$°C; IPCC 1990b, 87, table 3.2). Benchmark equilibrium warming is thus more than three times that assumed by the MINK authors. Moreover, the MINK estimates may be favorably biased by using for carbon dioxide enrichment the concentration (450 ppm) that would be associated with benchmark trace-gas-equivalent doubling, even though the warming considered in the study is less than half that standard. Considering these factors, and even without allowance for nonlinearity in the damages, one

---

19. The estimates do not appear to incorporate valuation changes on consumer surplus.

would expect the damage associated with the normal warming benchmark to be at least three times the MINK estimate. On this basis, *even with carbon fertilization and farm adaptation included, the MINK estimates imply agricultural losses of about 10 percent from equilibrium warming of carbon-dioxide-equivalent doubling.*

The adjusted MINK agricultural losses are even higher if the study's alternative estimate taking account of indirect effects on livestock production is considered. The estimates just reviewed refer to a narrow "export" concept for grains use. However, the study also provides estimates in which grains are instead considered as inputs into regional livestock. In this variant, induced losses in animal production and meat packing raise total losses to 5.7 percent of crop and animal output value, even when the beneficial effects of carbon fertilization and adaptation are taken into account (Rosenberg and Crosson 1990, 16). Applying the threefold expansion just suggested to translate the MINK results to an equilibrium climate with $2 \times CO_2$–equivalent, the resulting losses amount to about 17 percent of agricultural production. Moreover, because the livestock industry could not count on easily importing grain inputs from outside the region in such a world (because of comparable losses elsewhere), the regionally integrated estimates may be more relevant than the "export" estimates.

US agricultural production amounted to an estimated $93 billion in 1990 (*Economic Report of the President,* February 1991). Although there would tend to be gains from warming in Minnesota, Wisconsin, and the Dakotas, the agricultural losses in the South and West would tend to be considerably larger proportionately than those in the MINK states (EPA 1989a, 101; EPA 1989b, volume 1, section 5). For the United States as a whole, losses would thus conservatively be on the order of $10 billion to $17 billion annually, reformulating the MINK results for compatibility with the usual warming benchmark and applying the range of 10 percent to 17 percent loss just identified. This estimate ranges from about two-thirds to about the same as that obtained here after adjusting the EPA central estimate, even though the MINK study incorporates farm adaptation.

Explicit treatment of loss of consumer surplus could raise all the estimates further. In a simple model of agricultural supply and demand, annex 3A below suggests that as an approximation the total consumer and producer surplus lost from lower output is at least as large as the yield decrease multiplied by the initial value base. That result obtains for the horizontal supply curve. With the geometrically rising supply curve implied by the Ricardian concept of declining fertility of marginal land, combined producer and consumer surplus losses would tend to be higher, and perhaps much higher (annex 3A).

To recapitulate, for the United States the agricultural damages from benchmark CO_2–equivalent global warming would amount to some $18 billion annually (both the adjusted EPA basis and the Rind et al. drought approach), with a floor of perhaps $10 billion (MINK-adjusted, low "export" variant).

International Yield Estimates

For other countries, estimates tend to be in the form of calculated changes in yields rather than value-based estimates. However, by combining yield impacts with the estimated value base, it is possible to obtain a minimum estimate of producer and consumer losses (under the proposition just stated). For Canada, Parry (1990) estimates that spring wheat yields will fall by 15 percent to 37 percent, although winter wheat should improve. Drought frequency would multiply 13-fold in Saskatchewan. Maize and soybean yields would fall in Ontario. The IPCC places spring wheat yield reductions at 18 percent (IPCC 1990c, 2–15), based on estimates by G. D. V. Williams and by B. Smit.

It is expected that in southern Europe there will be a large decline in summer soil moisture and a major reduction in agricultural potential (Parry 1990). In the former Soviet Union, production could improve in Siberia, but soils there are relatively unproductive (Flavin 1989). Studies in the former Soviet Union suggest that decreased soil fertility, increased salinity, and increased soil erosion would more than offset prospective warming benefits, and that in the Leningrad and Perm areas yields of winter rye and spring wheat would decline because of premature ripening of crops (S. E. Pitovranov, as cited in Parry and Carter 1989).

For northern Japan, yields of rice, corn, and soybeans have been predicted to rise by some analysts (M. Yoshino et al., as cited in Parry 1990, 121). However, as noted below, preliminary estimates by an international team assembled by the EPA find negative yield effects.

The Scandinavian countries are seen as standing to gain the most from global warming effects on agriculture (IPCC 1990c, 2–16). For China, the IPCC cites mixed results, with a stronger summer monsoon threatening greater flooding in southern China; possible increases in rice, maize, and wheat yields nationally; but maize decreases in the eastern and central regions (IPCC 1990c, 2–19).

Most analysts see Central America as vulnerable to decreases in soil moisture (Parry 1990; *New York Times*, 17 October 1990). In the Sahel, an increase in evapotranspiration is expected to exceed the increase in precipitation and therefore to reduce soil moisture (Parry 1990). Drier soils are expected to reduce yields in Northwest and West Africa, the Horn of Africa, and southern Africa (*New York Times*, 17 October 1990). The Middle East is similarly considered vulnerable.

Cline (1992b, annex table A-1) provides a summary of prospective agricultural effects as identified by Working Group II of the IPCC. More specific estimates are available from the underlying studies consulted by the IPCC and from more recent studies. Table 3.1 presents an overview of the available yield estimates. Most are drawn from the summary provided by Kane et al. (1989). For Australia, China, and Japan, the estimates are identified merely as "negative," based on

Table 3.1 Estimates of agricultural yield changes from global warming, various countries

Country	Crop	Yield change (percentages)
Australia[a]	Various	Negative
Belgium	Wheat, spelt	7
Canada (Saskatchewan)	Spring wheat	−18
China[a]	Maize	Negative
Denmark	Wheat, spelt	10
European Community	Various	−20
Finland		
Helsinki	Spring wheat	10
	Barley	9
	Oats	18
Oulu	Spring wheat	20
	Barley	14
	Oats	13
France	Wheat, spelt	−11
Germany	Wheat, spelt	−5
Iceland	Hay	64
	Pasture	48
Italy	Wheat, spelt	−1
Japan[a]	Rice	Negative
Netherlands	Wheat, spelt	1
Soviet Union		
Leningrad	Rye	−13
Cherdyn	Spring wheat	−3
Saratov	Spring wheat	13

a. See text for further details.

Source: Sally Kane, John Reilly, and Rhonda Bucklin. 1989. "Implications of the Greenhouse Effect for World Agricultural Commodity Markets." Washington: US Department of Agriculture (June).

preliminary results of an international team conducting research under EPA auspices (EPA 1990). If confirmed, these initial findings will represent important reversals for China and Japan in comparison with the previous IPCC surveys.

Table 3.2 applies the estimates of table 3.1 to the value of the agricultural base in each country in question to obtain an impression of agricultural effects globally.[20] The final two columns apply the central percentage yield change to the initial agricultural GDP base with a multiple ranging from $\alpha\beta = 0.75$ to $\alpha\beta = 1.25$, where α is the ratio of the output reduction after incorporation of low-cost adaptational changes to the initial yield reduction; and β is the ratio of total change in consumer and producer surplus to the reduction in output

---

20. For the United States, the table entries are based on the agricultural loss estimated above, expressed as a percentage of base output. For Australia, China, and Japan, the magnitudes are simply postulated, pending final results of the EPA international study. Note that the negative impact in these preliminary EPA results is based on my interpretation that only 440 ppm carbon fertilization should be incorporated for purposes of analyzing equilibrium carbon-dioxide-equivalent warming.

Table 3.2 Rough estimate of the impact of carbon-dioxide-equivalent doubling on agriculture, selected countries

Country	GDP, 1988 (billions of dollars) Total	GDP, 1988 (billions of dollars) Agriculture	Yield change (percentages)	Implied value change $\alpha\beta = 0.75$	Implied value change $\alpha\beta = 1.25$
Australia	205	8.2	−10.0[a]	−0.6	−1.0
Belgium	145	3.0	7.0	0.2	0.3
Canada	440	17.6	−18.0	−2.4	−4.0
China	360	120.8	−10.0[a]	−9.1	−15.2
Denmark	95	4.1	10.0	0.3	0.5
Finland	90	5.2	15.0	0.6	1.0
France	900	30.8	−11.0	−2.5	−4.2
Germany	1,130	16.5	−5.0	−0.6	−1.0
Iceland	5	2.0[b]	50.0	0.8	1.3
Italy[b]	765	31.1	−10.0	−2.3	−3.8
Japan	2,850	65.4	−5.0[a]	−2.5	−4.2
Netherlands	215	8.5	1.0	0.1	0.2
Soviet Union	1,000[c]	200.0[c]	0.0	0.0	0.0
United States[d]	4,885	89.8	−20.0	−13.1	−21.9
Total	12,815	603.0	−6.9	−31.1	−52.0

α = ratio of net output effect at a given product price after adaptation to the initial effect; β = ratio of total producer and consumer surplus change to net output effect evaluated at the base price.

Note: the estimates do not take into account importer versus exporter status.

a. Postulated; see text for details.

b. Based on Parry (1990, 87).

c. Rough estimate.

d. Based on text estimate of $17.5 billion for 1990.

Sources: Table 3.1, this volume; World Bank, *World Development Report 1990*; International Monetary Fund, *International Financial Statistics, Yearbook 1990*. World Bank and International Monetary Fund data reprinted with permission.

volume at base-period prices. As suggested above, β is likely to be substantially greater than unity. It should be noted that the estimates of table 3.2 do not take account of trade patterns and essentially treat all consumer and producer surplus effects as proportionate to the production base, whereas the presence of international trade means that consumer surplus losses would tend to be relatively greater for food importers, and producer surplus effects relatively greater for food exporters. Nonetheless, the estimates provide a first approximation of international effects.

The estimates of table 3.2 suggest that, worldwide, the central expectation would be for net agricultural losses from benchmark greenhouse warming. This result is less optimistic than the IPCC suggestion that world agricultural output (or costs) could change by ±10 percent, depending on climate, soil moisture, and carbon dioxide enrichment effects (IPCC 1990c, 2–24). One reason appears to be the reliance of the IPCC on favorable effects for China in the rough global estimate.

The central estimate of table 3.2, in contrast, is that the adverse effect of $2 \times CO_2$–equivalent warming amounts to a loss of some 7 percent of world agricultural production (or about $40 billion annually for the countries considered, midpoint of the two variants). The loss is largest in both absolute and relative terms in the United States. The large proportionate gains in northern countries operate on a sufficiently small base that they do not compensate for losses in the United States, China, Canada, Italy, and Japan.

Agriculture Under Very-Long-Term Warming

The central estimate for US agricultural losses from benchmark $2 \times CO_2$ warming is set at approximately $18 billion annually (1990 US economic scale). For very-long-term warming, losses could be expected to be much greater. Most agricultural experts confronted with a 10°C warming scenario indicate that agricultural losses would be devastating.[21]

The crop models used in many of the estimates of table 3.1 could ideally be tailored to examine the impact of global warming of 10°C for very-long-term warming. If they were, it seems likely that the results would show extremely severe reductions in crop yields. Crops typically cannot grow at temperatures above 35°C to 45°C; wheat, barley, oats, and rye, for example, cannot grow above 35°C, while corn, rice, and sorghum cannot grow above 45°C (Office of Management and Budget and US Department of Agriculture 1989). Yet these ranges could be reached in summertime in a wide range of US agricultural areas under very-long-term warming (chapter 2). As noted above, the carbon dioxide fertilization effect is exhausted at about 800 ppm (and earlier for maize). Evapotranspiration tends to rise more than linearly with temperature and thus outstrips precipitation increases, so that soil moisture under very-long-term warming would be likely to be dramatically reduced.

The broad expectation would be that agricultural losses would be more than linear with respect to temperature rise. Suppose the relationship were only mildly nonlinear and less than quadratic, for example, that $D = k(\Delta t)^{1.2}$, where D is damage, k a constant, and Δt is the change in temperature. Then if $\Delta t = 10$°C instead of 2.5°C, the damage would be $(10/2.5)^{1.2} = 5.3$ times as large. The initial benchmark world agricultural loss of 7 percent would rise to 37 percent. Under these conditions, the consumer surplus losses could rise dramatically as agricultural output became scarce in the face of inelastic demand.

---

21. For example, Paul Waggoner, of the Connecticut Agricultural Experiment Station, commented to this effect at a Resources for the Future conference on greenhouse non-linearities held in Washington, 23–24 March 1992. However, he was skeptical that 10°C warming could occur.

In short, with a central estimate for agricultural losses on the order of $18 billion annually for the United States and $40 billion worldwide for the normal benchmark of $2 \times CO_2$-equivalent warming (2.5°C), the corresponding estimates for very-long-term warming would be in the range of $95 billion and $212 billion, respectively, even before allowing for greater proportionate consumer welfare losses (and without scaling to future economic size).[22]

Forests

Global warming is expected to cause a poleward migration of forests and a change in their composition. Sedjo and Solomon (1989) use the Holdridge Life Zone classification system together with GCM projections of changed climate by grid area to calculate global forest changes from $2 \times CO_2$ warming. They find that boreal forests would decline by 40 percent and temperate forests by 1.3 percent, whereas tropical forests would rise by 12 percent (measured by biomass; area figures are comparable). The net change would amount to a decline of 3.7 percent globally in biomass and 5.8 percent in area.

However, these estimates are equilibrium measures after enough time has passed for complete migrational adjustment to the new climate. The potential northern range of forest species in the United States is expected to shift northward by 600 to 700 km over the next century from global warming, and the southern boundary could move north by 1,000 km. However, the actual migration pace could be as low as 100 km over the same period because of slow migration capacity (EPA 1989a, 71). The implied result would be a "temporary" decline in forested area for some three centuries or more (because of tree death on the southern boundary in excess of additional growth on the northern boundary) and thus much larger forest loss than after eventual equilibrium is reached.

Studies cited by EPA (1989a, 83–84) indicate that over the next 100 years US forests could lose 23 percent to 54 percent of standing biomass in the Great Lakes region and 40 percent in western forests. On this basis, it might be esti-

---

22. The estimates of agricultural impact in this study place no weight on the view that global warming will have little impact on agriculture because it will come primarily at night. Although new data indicate that warming in this century has been greater at nighttime than during the daytime, the likely explanation is that increased urban pollution has provided an offset (Beardsley 1992). Reflection of solar radiation from sulfate aerosols and additional clouds from pollution would tend to reduce the daytime warming otherwise expected. However, it is implausible in the extreme that, over the long term, nations would increase their urban pollution apace with increased carbon emissions; on the contrary, most nations have begun major programs to reduce pollution. Moreover, the sulfate aerosol effect is regional and may be expected to have diminishing returns with increasing sulfur dioxide concentration.

mated that global warming from the doubling of carbon-dioxide-equivalent could cause a loss of 40 percent of US forests. Some portion of this loss could be avoided by increased planting to locate the replacement species in the areas of in-migration sooner than they would naturally arrive. But the EPA (1989a, 86), expressing doubts about this response, points out that "seedlings that would appear to be favored on some northern sites several decades in the future may not survive there now because of constraints imposed by temperatures, day length, or soil conditions."

In 1989, the US logging industry produced $13 billion in gross output (*U.S. Industrial Outlook* 1990, 6–2). The wage bill for 92,000 employees amounted to $1.7 billion. If, as in most US industries, the ratio of wages to capital services was at least two to one, total factor inputs cost approximately $2.6 billion. The value of the wood extracted was thus approximately $10 billion. In view of the prospective 40 percent forest loss, these estimates would imply greenhouse warming damages on the order of $4 billion annually for the United States just for the commercial portion of forests. It is unlikely that these losses would be offset by higher cutting rates, as the current rates of extraction already reflect optimum considerations.[23]

Neither the EPA nor other authors appear to have placed quantitative estimates on forest loss.[24] The EPA does suggest that, despite doubts about successful anticipatory planting for migrating species, US reforestation efforts would need to double or triple above their current rate of 0.4 percent of forest area annually at a cost of $400 million annually (EPA 1989a, 89). On this basis, some $600 million in additional reforestation costs could be expected. If the increased reforestation limited the potential forest loss by one-third, the net annual loss would amount to (2/3 × $4 billion) + $600 million, or a total of $3.3 billion.[25]

The estimates here, based on the EPA results, do not incorporate possible beneficial effects on forests from carbon fertilization.[26] The EPA authors argue that higher carbon dioxide concentrations "may not significantly affect forest

---

23. Similarly, one does not expect a major reduction in a livestock herd to call forth higher slaughter rates; the calculus of the slaughter (extraction) rate remains, as before, a function of the interest rate and the ratio of present to future price. Over the time horizon here, future prices would not fall very fast, so the extraction rate would be unlikely to rise.

24. Thus, Nordhaus (1990b) merely refers to such losses as "small."

25. The resulting extent of forest product loss (2/3 × 40 percent = 26 percent) would be approximately the same as identified by Binkley (1987), who estimates that global warming would cause income from timber sales to decline by 20 percent in the East and 26 percent in the West by 2030 (cited in Regens et al. 1989, 308).

26. As noted, most trees are C_3 plants and thus should benefit from carbon fertilization.

productivity" because of the limiting factors of water, nutrients, and light under the canopy (EPA 1989a, 81). Bazzaz and Fajer (1992, 71) indicate that competition among trees for such "scarce resources" may account for the findings in experiments in two deciduous temperate forests and one Mexican rain forest, which showed that "tree seedling communities were not more productive in a CO_2–rich atmosphere when different species were grown together."

Similarly, although the estimates here do make some allowance for limitation of losses through forest management, it may be asked whether a higher fraction of the losses could be avoided than the one-third assumed here. Intensively managed plantation systems could increase water and nutrients to take greater advantage of potential carbon fertilization. However, in the United States such managed plantations account for only a small part of forested area.[27]

The estimate of forest loss developed here could be understated from two other standpoints. First, as noted, the estimate makes no allowance for public valuation of forested area for its own sake (esthetic or for camping and hiking use), but focuses instead on a narrow valuation of lumber loss. Second, the underlying EPA estimates do not incorporate losses from "possible increases in fires, pests, disease outbreaks, wind damage, and air pollution" (EPA 1989a, 71).

In the very long term, two factors would work in opposite directions on the value of forest losses. Eventual completion of migration would potentially reverse the major loss associated with the difference between potential and actual migration rates. However, in the absence of policy changes, warming could be expected to increase without interruption over the next 250 to 300 years, so there would be a continual lag of forest migration behind that of potential boundaries. Thus, little could be expected from achieving a new equilibrium (because over the time frame none would be attained). At the same time, much higher temperatures and drier conditions would be likely to cause additional damage to the forests. A plausible conclusion is that under business as usual there would be no reduction in the annual losses even over the very long term, and that instead there would be further increases. In the absence of more formal analysis, something on the order of twice the loss associated with $2 \times CO_2$-equivalent might be appropriate for the very-long-term loss.

Internationally, the shift toward tropical, and away from boreal and temperate, forests suggests that most developing countries would experience relatively less forest loss than would the mid- to high-latitude countries. In this important

---

27. Smith (1991) indicates the following breakdown of US forests (in millions of hectares): unmanaged natural, 120; managed natural, 190; suburban, 80; urban, 40; intensively managed plantation, 20.

instance, the pattern of relative gains from global warming by such northern areas as Scandinavia would thus be likely to be reversed.[28]

Research in progress for the EPA finds that globally approximately half of all land area would show a shift in the vegetation life zone as a consequence of benchmark carbon-dioxide-equivalent doubling. Tundra and desert area would decline by approximately 40 percent and 20 percent, respectively, whereas dry forest would increase by about one-third and wet forest would show little change (positive for some GCMs, negative in others; Thomas M. Smith et al., in EPA 1990). Although the expansion of forest at the expense of desert would be felicitous, the estimates are equilibrium changes. Thus, major forest loss over the period of perhaps two to three centuries would still mean damages over the relevant horizon.

Species Loss

Analyses of the extent of species loss from global warming are sparse, and so far quantification in the corresponding economic valuation remains non-existent. Yet some argue that overall biosphere viability depends on biodiversity because of lessened ability to respond to shock with a narrower biological range.

The EPA (1989a) has noted in general terms the risk of increased species extinction because of changes in habitat and predator-prey relationships as well as physiological changes. The EPA indicates major reductions in population, but not species loss, for shellfish, fish, and waterfowl as sea-level rise causes saltwater intrusion into wetlands. The study cites estimates that human activity is already reducing the some 10 million species by a rate at least 1,000 times as fast as would occur from natural forces (EPA 1989a, 152). It cites the poleward migration of forests as a major reason to expect stress on species, especially in view of natural and man-made barriers to animal migration.[29] Coral reefs could be expected to suffer coral death from warmer waters, with extinction of some coral species (as suggested by trends in recent years, including the effect of El Niño warming; Glynn and de Weerdt 1991).

Economists have identified the economic value of species as being of three types: use, option, and existence. Direct use is the most obvious and would include, for example, the use of certain species in the production of medicines.

---

28. Moreover, in some northern countries, such as Finland, the value of forestry production considerably exceeds that of agriculture, so that forestry losses could dominate agricultural gains.

29. One interesting response might be government purchase of land to establish migratory corridors (Peters, as cited in Goklany 1989).

Option value refers to the economic value of preserving a species to retain the option that it may be of economic use in the future. Existence value is a benefit inherent in the existence of the species, like the value society places on the existence of a particular great work of art. Much of the concern with biological diversity seems to derive from existence value (Elliott Sober, as cited in Batie and Shugart 1989).

The yew tree provides a good example of the option value of a species. In 1991, medical researchers found that the drug taxol, derived from the bark of the relatively rare Pacific yew tree, showed impressive effects in causing remission of ovarian and breast cancer.[30] Society could be well advised to pay a fee to avoid the extinction of species (i.e., purchase an "option" to retain them) because some, like the yew tree, might eventually be found to have medicinal or agricultural value. Indeed, plant and animal species already used in traditional and modern medicine number over 5,000 in China, 2,000 in the Amazon Basin, and 2,500 in the former Soviet Union; in the United States, one-fourth of all prescriptions contain ingredients from plants, and over 3,000 antibiotics are derived from microorganisms (Reid et al. 1992, 1–3). Similarly, natural plant varieties are important for enriching agricultural varieties.

Weitzman (1991) has proposed an elegant approach to conceptualizing the value of biodiversity. His method depicts the evolution of a genealogical tree of different species from a common ancestor. He defines biodiversity as, essentially, the total length of all branches on this family tree. If a species must be sacrificed, the greatest possible biodiversity will be maintained by choosing to give up that species that is the shortest final branch of the tree and is thus most closely related to another species on the tree. The caveat is that if the remaining closely related species is unique and thus on a long branch separate from the other species derived from the same ancestor, and is thus extremely distant from them (and hence valuable for biodiversity), the probability that this remaining close relative may itself be lost must be taken into account. This line of reasoning leads to the implication that it is better to concentrate scarce environmental resources on assuring survival of such species rather than dispersing these resources in an attempt to save a larger number of species that are only slightly differentiated by type.

Weitzman's analysis is potentially rich, but it would seem to require extension in some dimensions. First, some weight might be given to the "salience" of species. Public willingness to pay for a species' preservation is likely to be influenced by its perceived importance. For example, the bald eagle would likely be considered more worth saving than, say, a variety of earthworm. The scientific assessment could differ (e.g., because of the role of the earthworm in soil fer-

---

30. Sedjo (1992); *Journal of Commerce*, 20 December 1991; "Trees That Yield a Drug for Cancer Are Wasted," *New York Times*, 19 January 1992, 1.

tility). Second, some weight might appropriately be given to species close to humans (primates) in the expectation that their option value is high because of their genetic similarity to humans and therefore prospective utility in medicine. Third, there may be "keystone" species whose extinction would threaten the collapse of entire related species structures.

Society is already incurring certain costs that may provide an initial idea of the value of species preservation. As a recent major example, the US government declared in 1991 that 11.6 million acres of timberland in the Northwest would be put off limits to logging to preserve the habitat of the spotted owl (*Wall Street Journal*, 29 April 1991). This area corresponds to 1.6 percent of total forest land in the United States (738 million acres; EPA 1989a, 72). As developed above, a working estimate for the commercial value of forest resources is $10 billion annually. Therefore the land set aside for the spotted owl represents an opportunity cost of $160 million annually.[31]

Many species are already endangered or threatened in the United States (including the bald eagle, the grizzly bear, the Florida panther, the whooping crane, and numerous other fauna and flora; Council on Environmental Quality 1991, 138). An extremely conservative estimate might be that the incremental endangerment of these and all other species from benchmark $2 \times CO_2$ warming amounts to, say, 25 times the present endangerment of the spotted owl alone. On this basis, the public might be prepared to pay at least 25 times as much toward species preservation under the species-threatening conditions of a doubling of carbon-dioxide-equivalent as for the present case of the spotted owl. If so, the annual value of the prospective species damage from benchmark warming would amount to 25 × $160 million = $4 billion. However, the appropriate value could just as easily be an order of magnitude larger, or $40 billion annually. The central estimates here use the more conservative figure, but accompany it by some explicit additional but unmeasured value (Δ_s in table 3.4). For very-long-term warming with temperature increases four times as great, a simple linear extrapolation would once again be a conservative estimate, because species loss would probably rise nonlinearly.

Before more satisfactory estimates of the benefits of avoiding species loss can be made, it will be necessary to obtain a better idea of the prospective extent of loss, ideally with numerous concrete illustrations. With such estimates in hand, it might be possible to use the "contingent evaluation" survey technique for evaluating a public good (see, e.g., Brookshire et al. 1982).

---

31. The illustration is complicated by the fact that, for many, the motive in saving the spotted owl is primarily to preserve its habitat—forests that include trees centuries or even thousands of years old. US environmental law protects species but not ancient forests, yet many in the public set an "existence" value on such forests. The problem is essentially one of externality: such value (which may or may not be large) is not taken into account when the ancient tree is sold for lumber in the private market.

Sea-Level Rise

Global warming should raise the level of the seas, as a result of thermal expansion of water and melting of land-based glaciers and ice sheets.[32] The IPCC has estimated that, under "business as usual," actual global warming would amount to 4.2°C by the year 2100 (and warming "commitment" even more). The group's central estimate for corresponding sea-level rise is 66 cm (IPCC 1990b, figure 9.6).

US Estimates

James Titus of the EPA and his coauthors note that the IPCC estimate was lower than those of most previous studies and was based on the assumption that the Antarctic would accumulate more ice rather than be a source of melting over the next century—a view not universally accepted by glaciologists (Titus et al. 1992). The EPA thus continues to use a sea-level increase of one meter by the year 2100 as its central estimate.

It should be noted that a point estimate for 2100 is not an equilibrium estimate, because the melting continues over lengthy periods. Titus et al. note that, in the last interglacial period 100,000 years ago, when temperatures were 1°C warmer, the sea level was approximately six meters higher than it is today. The vast disparity between six meters for 1°C of warming and one meter for 4°C suggests that the ultimate sea-level increase would be much higher than the point estimate at 2100. Unfortunately, neither the IPCC nor the EPA appears to have specified the very-long-term sea-level rise associated with a specific equilibrium temperature change. Ideally, one would identify the time path of sea level over, say, the next 300 years as the consequence of no warming, benchmark $2 \times CO_2$ warming ($= 2.5°C$), and very-long-term warming (e.g., 10°C).

In its 1989 report to Congress, the EPA estimated that, for the United States, a one-meter rise in sea level by the year 2100 would require $73 billion to $111 billion in cumulative capital costs to protect developed areas through the building of bulkheads and levees, the pumping of sand, and the raising of barrier islands (EPA 1989a, 123). It estimated that in addition there would be a loss of dry land of 4,000 to 9,000 square miles.

The agency has recently updated its estimates to incorporate the economic value of the land lost. Morgenstern (1991) indicates that the revised estimates place the economic losses associated with a one-meter sea-level rise at $10.6 billion annually.[33]

---

32. The melting of sea ice would have no influence, as the volume of its submerged portion is equal to that of its water equivalence.

33. He notes that this figure is twice the amount used by Nordhaus (1990b), which was based on the earlier EPA estimates.

Titus et al. (1992, 8–11) summarize the damages as follows.

A rise in sea level would inundate wetlands and lowlands, accelerate coastal erosion, exacerbate coastal flooding, threaten coastal structures, raise water tables, and increase the salinity of rivers, bays, and aquifers. . . . Coastal marshes and swamps . . . collect sediment and produce peat upon which they can build [so that] most wetlands have been able to keep pace with the past rate of sea-level rise [but would be unable to do so] if sea level rose too rapidly. . . . Moreover, [where] people have built bulkheads just above the marsh . . . the wetlands would be squeezed between the estuary and the bulkhead. . . . Such a loss would reduce available habitat for birds and juvenile fish. . . . [For barrier islands t]ypically . . . the bay side is less than a meter above high water. Thus, even a one meter rise in sea level would threaten much of this valuable land with inundation. . . . a one meter rise in sea level would generally cause beaches to erode 50/100 meters from the Northeast to Maryland; 200 meters along the Carolinas; 100/1000 meters along the Florida coast; and 200/400 meters along the California coast. . . . [Yet] most US recreational beaches are less than 30 meters . . . wide at high tide. . . . [A] one meter rise in sea level would . . . enable a 15-year storm to flood many areas that today are only flooded by a 100-year storm. . . . [A] rise in sea level would enable saltwater to penetrate farther inland and upstream in rivers, bays, wetlands, and aquifers, which would be harmful to some aquatic plants and animals, and would threaten human uses of water.

The authors estimate that if the shoreline retreats naturally, a one-meter sea-level rise would inundate 7,700 square miles of dry land (an area the size of Massachusetts). Seventy percent of the losses would be in the Southeast (Florida, Louisiana, North Carolina). The eastern shores of the Chesapeake and Delaware bays would also lose sizable areas.

The updated EPA analysis by Titus et al. reaches the following costs of a one-meter sea-level rise for the United States if developed areas are protected. Dry land amounting to 6,650 square miles would be lost, and 49 percent of today's wetlands would be lost. The value of land lost would be $17 billion to $128 billion for wetlands, $21 billion to $71 billion for undeveloped dry land, and $14 billion to $48 billion for land for dikes. Coastal defenses would cost $27 billion to $146 billion for sand, $62 billion to $170 billion to elevate structures, and $11 billion to $33 billion to construct dikes. The total costs would reach $270 billion to $475 billion. The amount would be $128 billion to $232 billion for a 50-cm rise and $576 billion to $880 million for a rise of two meters (Titus et al. 1992, table 9).

The central estimate from the updated EPA estimates is thus a capital cost of $370 billion for a one-meter sea-level rise. Morgenstern's translation of this cost into an annual cost of $10.6 billion implies a discount rate of 2.9 percent. There are important conceptual questions in obtaining the annualized damage value. Essentially the costs of sea-level rise divide into two types: capital costs of protective constructions, and the recurrent annual cost of forgone land services.

The capital costs would be spread over a 100-year period. The land "rent" values would also phase in over the same period. But because the rental opportunity cost is likely to be set at a higher market interest rate than that appropriate for evaluation of the capital costs, the two components should probably be treated individually.

Of the $370 billion total, $224 billion is capital costs for sand, structure elevation, and dike construction. An appropriate way to evaluate this portion is to consider the present value of a 100-year stream of a $2.24 billion capital outlay annually. Discounting at 1.5 percent (the social rate of time preference suggested in chapter 6), the average annual capital outlay for construction amounts to $1.2 billion. Essentially, the entire capital outlay is not made at the outset, so the annual economic cost is considerably smaller than implied by application of even a 3 percent interest rate to the principal.

In contrast, the economic costs associated with land loss can be higher. With a base of 13,000 square miles of wetlands, the 49 percent loss amounts to 6,440 square miles. Titus et al. note that wetland preservation programs typically cost $30,000 per acre. Using a more conservative $10,000 per acre value for wetland, and a real land rental rate of 10 percent, each acre of wetland lost costs $1,000 annually. The loss of 6,440 square miles thus generates $4.1 billion in annual losses.[34] For dry land, the median price in US coastal states is approximately $2,000 per acre (US Department of Agriculture 1990). Allowing twice the median for greater value near the coast, a conservative valuation would be $4,000 per acre (still lower than the minimum $6,000 in the Titus et al. study). With a land rental opportunity cost of 10 percent real, this land typically contributes $400 annually to economic activity. The annual cost of the 6,650 square miles of dry land loss (midpoint) thus amounts to $1.7 billion.

Overall, this alternative approach yields US damage from sea-level rise at $7 billion annually. This estimate is of the same order of magnitude as Morgenstern's $10.6 billion, but it takes explicit account of the long phase-in of the capital expenditures. An important implication is that the composition of the total costs resulting from sea-level rise would be much more heavily weighted toward the loss of annual economic services of the land than toward capital costs of coastal defense construction than is implied in the capital values approach of Titus et al. and Morgenstern.[35]

Over the very long term, damage from sea-level rise could be far greater. As noted in chapter 1, over 300 to 500 years the West Antarctic ice sheet could disintegrate, raising sea level six meters—an event not considered likely with

---

34. 6,440 sq mi × 640 acres per square mile × $1,000 per acre.

35. In the Titus approach, wetland and dryland loss accounts for 40 percent of damage costs, and coastal defense amounts to 60 percent. In the approach here, the composition is 75 percent and 25 percent, respectively.

just benchmark warming of 2.5°C but perhaps considerably more likely with very-long-term warming of 10°C. Even without such a catastrophe, the damage would be likely to rise more than linearly with warming, suggesting much larger losses with very-long-term warming. One reason is that higher warming would be expected to push the Antarctic from a zone where increased snow buildup from more moist, warmer air offsets increased melting (temperature below − 12°C; IPCC 1990b, 271) to a range where the Antarctic could become a large source of water. In addition, not only would the extent of sea-level rise be larger, but the economic damage from a given increment of sea-level rise would increase, imposing further nonlinearity. Thus, Yohe (1992, table II.1) estimates that a doubling of sea-level rise causes approximately a tripling of economic damage. In view of nonlinearity, the estimate in table 3.4 sets US losses from sea-level rise associated with very-long-term warming at $35 billion, a conservative five times the amount for benchmark carbon dioxide doubling.

Other Countries

As noted in chapter 2, Rosenberg et al. (1989a) estimate that a one-meter rise in sea level would cause a loss of approximately 3 percent of the world's land area. The IPCC (1990c) provides a useful review of the impact of sea-level rise by major country affected. The study cites estimates that a one-meter rise would inundate 12 percent to 15 percent of Egypt's arable land and 17 percent of Bangladesh. It notes that in flat deltaic areas, such a rise would cause shores to retreat several kilometers, displacing populations. The most vulnerable deltas include the Nile in Egypt; the Ganges in Bangladesh; the Yangtze and Hwang Ho in China; the Mekong in Vietnam; the Irrawaddy in Burma; the Indus in Pakistan; the Niger in Nigeria; the Parana, Magdalena, Orinoco, and Amazon in South America; the Mississippi in the United States; and the Po in Italy (IPCC 1990c, 6–3, 6–4).

A study prepared by Delft Hydraulics Laboratory for the IPCC estimated the costs of coastal protection shown in table 3.3. These costs do not include the value of lost land (although they may overstate dike construction and other defense costs because they assume that any area with a population density of 10 per km² or more would be defended). It is evident from the table that the most severe costs of shoreline defense would be in numerous island nations, with the highest proportionate costs in the Maldives. Thus it is not surprising that many of these nations have formed the Alliance of Small Island States to press for international agreements limiting emissions (*New York Times*, 5 February 1991). Also according to the Delft study, other countries with coastal defense costs of at least 0.5 percent of GDP annually would include Argentina,

Table 3.3 Costs associated with a one-meter rise in sea level, selected countries and territories

Country or territory	Annual cost (percentages of GNP)[a]	Length low coast (km)	Beach length (km)
Maldives	34.33	1	25
Kiribati	18.79	0	0
Tuvalu	14.14	0	0
Tokelau	11.11	0	0
Anguilla	10.31	30	5
Guinea-Bissau	8.15	1,240	0
Turks and Caicos	8.10	80	5
Marshalls	7.24	0	0
Cocos (Keeling) Island	5.82	1	0
Seychelles	5.51	1	25
Falklands	4.75	1	0
French Guiana	2.96	540	0
Belize	2.93	500	0
Papua New Guinea	2.78	6,400	0
The Bahamas	2.67	400	200
Liberia	2.66	2,200	0
The Gambia	2.64	400	0
Mozambique	2.48	10,015	25
St. Kitts and Nevis	2.33	40	10
Nieu	2.18	6	0
Guyana	2.12	1,040	0
Suriname	1.94	2,800	0
Sierra Leone	1.86	1,835	0
Aruba	1.85	1	15
Pitcairn Island	1.71	0	0
Fiji	1.53	11	25
São Tome and Principe	1.46	3	5
Nauru	1.25	3	0
British Virgin Islands	1.24	1	10
Tonga	1.14	4	0
Cayman Islands	1.04	1	25
Cook Islands	1.03	0	0
Equatorial Guinea	1.02	7	0
Antigua and Barbuda	1.01	50	10
Sri Lanka	0.89	9,770	30
Togo	0.87	300	20
St. Lucia	0.82	25	10
Burma	0.77	7,470	0
Benin	0.74	485	10
Micronesia, Fed. St.	0.73	0	0
New Zealand	0.70	14,900	100
Palau	0.69	7	0
Grenada	0.67	6	5
Netherlands Antilles	0.66	25	30
Senegal	0.65	1,345	0
Ghana	0.64	2,400	20
Somalia	0.62	700	0
Western Samoa	0.59	11	0
Madagascar	0.56	1,190	0
St. Vincent and Grenadines	0.55	7	5

a. This estimate does not represent the total cost of sea-level rise, only the cost of erecting shore protection structures.

Source: Intergovernmental Panel on Climate Change. 1990. *Potential Impacts of Climate Change: Report Prepared for IPCC by Working Group III.* World Meteorological Organization and United Nations Environment Programme (June).

Bangladesh, Mozambique, and Vietnam (*Change,* The Hague, Netherlands, April 1990).

Work in progress in the EPA's international studies program indicates that, in China, a one-meter rise in sea level could displace over 72 million people in the absence of measures to hold back the sea (Han, Hou, and Wu, in EPA 1990). The losses would be concentrated in the Lower Liao River Delta, the North China Coastal Plain, the East China Coastal Plain, and the Pearl River Deltaic Plain. Shanghai and other major and ancient cities would be completely submerged, and over 125,000 km^2 of agricultural land would be lost. Another study in the same series estimates that, for Egypt, a one-meter rise would eliminate one-fourth of the agricultural land on the Nile delta and displace 8 million people (El-Raey, in EPA 1990).

Other nations at high risk include Thailand and Indonesia (*New York Times,* 5 February 1991). Among the developed countries, the United States would appear to be the most affected by sea-level rise (and it has the highest absolute costs in the Delft study, in view of its long and highly developed coastline; *Change,* The Hague, Netherlands, April 1990). In Europe, beaches along the Mediterranean (Greece, Yugoslavia, Italy, Turkey) would be adversely affected, along with tourism. Venice, which has already experienced a fourfold rise in floods over the last century, would be subjected to increased flooding. The low-lying portion of Poland's coast along the Baltic would be seriously threatened, along with a population of nearly half a million people. In Australia, the Great Barrier Reef would be threatened, as would hundreds of deltas, bays, estuaries, and islands (IPCC 1990c, 6–14, 6–15).

Elsewhere in Europe, the costs of sea-level rise would appear to be relatively moderate. Rosenberg et al. (1989a, 6) point out:

> Along the coast from France to Denmark sea walls and dikes already stand at least 16 meters above mean sea level . . . to reduce the probability of exceedance to less than 1 in 10,000 years. A 1 m SLR [one-meter sea-level rise] will not be particularly difficult to contend with where such structures already exist.

Similarly, the costs for the former Soviet Union would appear relatively limited.

Space Cooling and Heating

The EPA (1989a, chapter 10) has estimated the increased demand for electricity for space cooling (air conditioning), net of reduced demand for heating to be expected as a consequence of global warming. The estimates assume the GISS scenarios, indicating 1.2°C warming in the United States by 2010 and 3.7°C by 2055. The EPA estimated that the resulting increase in electricity demand above baseline would amount to $4.5 billion in "annual costs for capital, fuel, and operation and maintenance" by 2010 and $53 billion by 2055 (midpoint estimates, 1986 dollars; EPA 1989a, 192). In addition, there would be cumulative capital cost increases of $36 billion by 2010 and $224 billion by 2055 (midpoints). The EPA study identified the largest increases in demand for electricity to be in the South and midcontinent (20 percent to 30 percent above 2055 baseline) and predicted intermediate increases in California and the mid-Atlantic states (10 percent to 20 percent), more moderate increases in the mountain and north central states (0 percent to 10 percent), and net reductions in the demand for electricity in four northwestern states and the three northeasternmost states (0 percent to − 10 percent; EPA 1989a, 193).[36]

As indicated in the methodological section above, it is useful to state damages against an initial base-year GDP size and then deal separately with scaling for future years. Against a 1990-scale economy (rather than the future baseline), expected warming would increase operating expenses for electricity by $3.6 billion by the year 2010 and $18.6 billion by 2055; the corresponding increases in cumulative capital costs would be $29 billion and $89 billion (at 1990 prices; Cline 1990a).

Considering ocean thermal lag, the EPA-GISS estimates for 2055 would approximately correspond to equilibrium estimates for $2 \times CO_2$ equivalent. However, the GISS model yields somewhat higher warming than the IPCC's $\Lambda = 2.5°$ (with GISS, $\Lambda = 4.2°$; IPCC 1990b, table 3-2a). Scaling back to the IPCC's standard, adjusted estimates (at the 1990 economic scale and prices) for the year 2055 would stand at $11.2 billion for annual operating and capital costs (i.e., 60 percent of the amount before adjustment), with cumulative capital costs placed at $53 billion.[37] The annual damage of $11.2 billion would constitute one of the largest impacts of benchmark $2 \times CO_2$ warming, larger than the damage from sea-level rise and about two-thirds the size of agricultural losses (table 3.4).

The EPA estimates, even after scaling back to 1990 economic size, indicate significant nonlinearity. The operating costs mushroom from $4.5 billion for 1.2°C warming to $18.6 billion for 3.7°C warming. If we apply the form $D = k(\Delta t)^\gamma$ and estimate from the two "observations" just mentioned, then

---

36. A further review of the EPA estimates is presented in Cline (1990a).

37. This central estimate is several times the Nordhaus (1990b) estimate of $1.65 billion annual cost at 1981 prices, even though the Nordhaus study is based on the draft version of the same EPA study used here. Considering that the lowest figures in the EPA table are $3 billion to $6 billion "annual costs" for 2010 at 1986 prices, there is no evident way the Nordhaus estimate could be so low, unless perhaps the annual costs were misinterpreted as capital costs. If this occurred, and the $36 billion midpoint capital costs for 2010 are added and a 6 percent discount rate is applied (the Nordhaus rate), and prices are converted to 1981 levels, the result would be $2.0 billion—annually close to the Nordhaus range. However, this approach, besides confusing capital and annual costs, would have applied a 2010 benchmark rather than the more appropriate 2055 level.

$\gamma = 1.26$. On this basis, in the case of 10°C very-long-term warming with Δt four times as large as for $2 \times CO_2$ equivalent warming, additional US annual space-cooling costs (operating expenses) would amount to $11.2 billion $\times 4^{1.26}$ = $64 billion (at the 1990 economic scale and prices).

The EPA electricity estimates are already net of savings on space heating. However, these savings do not include those for oil and natural gas heating. Nordhaus (1990b) has estimated savings on heating costs at $1.16 billion annually (1981 prices), on the assumption that heating costs would decline by 1 percent. However, he apparently includes electricity savings in the estimate, whereas the EPA estimates of the demand for electricity are already net of savings on heating. Estimates by the Energy Information Administration (EIA) of the US Department of Energy (1990a, 30) place nonelectric energy consumption for heating (residential and commercial) at 7.3 quadrillion Btus for 1990. At an average price of $2.60 per million Btus for natural gas, residual oil, and distillate oil in 1982 dollars (US Department of Energy, EIA 1990a, 233), or $3.50 at 1990 prices, each quad costs $3.5 billion. Nonelectric heating thus amounted to some $25.6 billion in 1990. If it is assumed that benchmark warming would reduce heating costs by an optimistic 5 percent, the annual savings would amount to $1.3 billion.[38]

Internationally, the IPCC summarizes energy demand effects as follows. For the United States (based on the EPA study), the capacity for electricity would need to rise 14 percent to 23 percent above baseline by 2055. For Japan, 3°C warming would cause a 5 percent to 10 percent rise in electricity demand above baseline. In contrast, for Germany a 1°C warming is calculated to reduce energy consumption (apparently including nonelectric consumption) by 13 percent for older single-family homes and up to 45 percent for new homes, while increasing

---

38. Howard Gruenspecht (then of the Council of Economic Advisers, personal communication, 29 April 1991) has questioned the result here that increased space-cooling costs far exceed reduced heating costs from global warming. He argues that, for major US cities, some warming would move the population-weighted average closer to, rather than farther from, the ideal indoor temperature. However, this observation is not inconsistent with the results here, if two considerations are taken into account. First, the extent of temperature increase even for a doubling of carbon-dioxide-equivalent seems likely to go beyond the slight amount of warming that might move temperatures closer to an ideal comfort level. This consideration is of course dramatically reinforced if the analysis is extended to very-long-term warming. Second, air conditioning is by electricity, which has large efficiency losses, whereas heating is primarily by gas and oil. In this regard, James Titus (EPA, personal communication, 14 May 1991) has made the following observations. Efficiency losses are large in the conversion of oil and gas into electric power through generation and transmission—on the order of 60 percent to 70 percent. For a given change in the number of Btus, the cost is thus far higher for an increase in electric air conditioning than is the saving from a decrease in gas or oil heating. Moreover, the greater the temperature differential, the less efficient the air conditioner. In addition, air conditioning in automobiles would increase with warming, whereas automobile heating requires no additional fuel because the engine must be cooled in any event.

energy consumption for air conditioning by 12 percent to 38 percent. The result is a net decrease in energy demand for space heating and cooling by 12 percent in 2010. Similarly, for the former Soviet Union a 1°C warming is expected to generate larger savings in heating costs than increases in air conditioning costs. However, whereas this milder warming might move these countries toward, rather than away from, optimal comfort temperatures, warming from benchmark carbon dioxide doubling could go well beyond that point and turn net savings into net losses.

The international group noted that a smaller percentage of electricity consumption is devoted to residential and commercial use in developing countries than in industrial countries (28 percent versus 55 percent for Japan, for example). It thus conjectured that incremental electricity needs from global warming would be less than 10 percent in developing countries (IPCC 1990c, 5–19, 5–20).

Human Amenity

Personal comfort could conceivably improve from very mild global warming; indeed, in the United States internal migration has been toward the warmer states in recent decades. However, it would seem likely that personal amenity from outdoor comfort would begin to deteriorate as warming moved closer to the 2.5°C central estimate for benchmark carbon-dioxide-equivalent doubling, and would undergo severe deterioration from the very-long-term warming suggested above. As noted in chapter 2, with very-long-term warming on the order of a 10°C global mean increase, of the 66 largest US cities the number with average maximum daily temperatures above 90°F in July would rise from 18 to 62, and the number with average daily maximums above 100°F in July would rise from 2 to 42.

Mearns et al. (1984) use statistical distributions of current temperatures to explore the impact of global warming on extreme temperature events for the United States. In their base case, they increase mean temperature by 3°F (1.7°C) and hold the variance and autocorrelation of daily temperatures constant. Under these assumptions, they calculate that the frequency of heat waves (defined as five consecutive days with maximum temperature at least 95°F) would multiply threefold (estimated for Des Moines, Iowa). Again, there is reason to believe that people would be willing to pay something to avoid a threefold increase in heat waves.

Global warming could reduce the disamenity of severe winters in colder areas, providing some offset to the increased disamenity of heat waves and generally hotter summers. One way to approach estimation would be the survey technique (contingent evaluation), with questions formulated to elicit a meaningful evaluation of what the respondent would be prepared to pay to avoid the change (or, for more clement winters, what he or she would be prepared to pay to enjoy the change). In the absence of such estimates, valuation of human disamenity from global warming remains unestimated for the central calculations here, but with the presumption that this damage valuation could be extremely large in the case of very-long-term warming. For purposes of establishing an order of magnitude, if people were willing to pay just 0.25 percent of personal income to avoid the sharp increase in heat waves and other effects of a benchmark $2 \times CO_2$ warming in outdoor comfort, the damage of such disamenity would stand at some $10 billion annually for the United States.

Disamenity damages in other countries would depend on location and income level. For high-latitude countries, the effect would probably be favorable (i.e., negative disamenity damage). For mid- and low-latitude countries, disamenity effects might dominate, and almost certainly would do so under very-long-term warming. Valuation would tend to be higher for higher income countries, even relative to GDP, under the assumption that amenity is an income-elastic service.

Life and Morbidity

In the United States, an estimated 1.1 million of the 1.7 million deaths annually are from diseases that are potentially sensitive to weather (cerebrovascular, pulmonary, diabetes, heart, pneumonia and influenza; EPA 1989a, 221). Heat waves as well as very cold weather increase the incidence of stroke and heart attacks. Air pollution increases the occurrence of respiratory diseases (emphysema and asthma), and longer, warmer summers are expected to increase the severity of air pollution (as discussed below).

As cited in EPA (1989a, 224), Kalkstein has carried out a statistical analysis relating deaths to weather variables (including temperature and humidity). He has then applied changed weather conditions under carbon-dioxide-equivalent doubling to calculate the change in number of deaths for 15 major US cities. The estimates assume one case with no acclimatization and another case with full acclimatization, the latter estimated on the basis of corresponding mortality statistics for a control city with climate conditions comparable to those in the warmer future for the city in question. The estimates with acclimatization yield some anomalies (i.e., higher deaths with than without acclimatization to the new climate, or lower deaths after acclimatization than at present). However, the majority of estimates are in the directions expected. Moreover, increased summer deaths substantially exceed decreased winter deaths. For the unweighted sample, summer deaths rise from 1,156 at present to 7,402 under warming without acclimatization and 2,198 with acclimatization. Winter deaths fall from 243 at present to 52 without acclimatization and 159 with acclimatization (the latter result is spurious, because in winter the population should be able to do at least as well with acclimatization as without).

The Kalkstein estimates may be reinterpreted by enforcing as the postwarming summer deaths the *minimum* of the following: present level, postwarming without acclimatization, and postwarming with acclimatization. Similarly, postwarming winter deaths may be set as the *maximum* of present, future with acclimatization, and future without acclimatization. When this screening is performed, and when the resulting net death rates per 1,000 population of the individual cities are weighted proportionately to city population, the overall result is that benchmark warming would increase mortality by 0.0397 person per 1,000 population. Applied to the present US population base, this result indicates that global warming under carbon-dioxide- equivalent doubling would cause some 9,800 additional deaths annually.

Life valuation methods for public policy often take as a point of departure the lifetime earnings of an individual, under the assumption that earnings are what the society is willing to pay the individual (and thus the person's "marginal product"). Average nonagricultural wages in the United States amounted to $17,994 in 1990 (*Economic Report of the President,* February 1991, 336). If a working life span is set at 45 years and a 1.5 percent discount rate is applied, the value of average lifetime wages is $595,000. If this rate is applied to the estimated increase in deaths, annual mortality costs from global warming would amount to $5.8 billion for the United States.

The value of damage could be much greater on the basis of some of the higher life-valuation estimates in the literature (Cropper and Oates 1990). On the basis of the statistical relationship of wages to risk of death by occupation and industry, estimates of the "value of a statistical life" have been placed in the range of $2 million and even up to $6 million. Contingent valuation studies that ask workers what wage differentials would be required for more dangerous work generate results in the same range ($2 million to $3 million). On the other hand, studies that measure actual behavior in hazard avoidance (e.g., the purchase of smoke detectors) place the value of a statistical life at a much lower range of $500,000 to $600,000. Moreover, for environmental risks that are longer term and have a lower probability of death (e.g., exposure to hazardous waste), the value of a statistical life is even lower ($200,000 to $400,000), in part because the risk is some 20 years or more in the future.

One issue in valuing a life in the range of $2 million to $3 million is that the implied value of the entire US population would be more than 100 times the size of GDP. Since each worker's productive life is only some 45 years, this implied aggregate amount would be at least twice what American society could afford to pay for its own survival. This seeming anomaly can be resolved, however, if it is considered that for events that would only cause the death of a small fraction of the population, people might well be prepared to pay a higher per-death insurance cost than implied by the budget constraint of per capita life span GDP, given risk aversion and the opportunity for risk pooling.

The incidence of increased deaths would tend to be disproportionately among the elderly. It might be argued that the lifetime earnings approach would consequently apply a substantial reduction to this estimate. However, in other areas of health policy the US public has shown no inclination to value the lives of the elderly at any less than (for example) those in the 20- to 30-year age group. Accordingly, no reduction is applied here for the age distribution of the incremental deaths.

A related issue is that increased deaths from warming might primarily be instances in which the date of death is "merely" advanced by a few years. There might be some grounds for reducing the estimate from this standpoint. However, from another perspective the estimate is already low, as it uses the average wage rather than total income per capita and implicitly excludes the deceased's human and financial capital income from lifetime valuation. Use of GDP per capita would increase the loss estimate by about one-fourth.

On balance, the rate used here is probably an understatement of the value of a life saved, compared with most of the estimates in the literature. However, there is a more fundamental question about the estimates of global warming effects. Many in the medical profession are reportedly skeptical about the statistical estimates relating death to temperature and tend to doubt that there would be any major mortality consequences from warming; instead, they tend to be more concerned about morbidity effects (Rob Coppock, National Academy of Sciences, personal communication, 26 March 1991). It is unclear, for example, whether the statistical tests have adequately controlled for the tendency of older people to live in warmer cities in retirement. In lieu of more concrete analysis of the medical basis for mortality effects, the estimates here may be seen as compensating for a possible overstatement of mortality effects by applying a conservative per-life valuation.

Morbidity could increase in the area of "vector borne diseases," where the vectors are such carriers as ticks and mosquitoes and the diseases include Rocky Mountain spotted fever, Lyme disease, malaria, and dengue fever. Simulations for the United States on a possible increase of malaria under warming are inconclusive (EPA 1989a, 230). However, there would be a general migration of the vectors (carriers) from low to middle latitudes.

Placing a value on health effects is difficult, and no estimate of health losses is included in the central damage calculations reported in table 3.4. However, US health expenditures are so large (12 percent of GDP, or some $700 billion) that even a small increment could imply substantial costs. For example, an increase in medical expenses by just ½ percent would impose annual costs of over $3 billion.

Migration

Those who approach the greenhouse issue primarily from the standpoint of adaptation rather than abatement often stress migration as a means of response (see, e.g., Schelling 1983, 455–56). This raises two types of costs: utility sacrificed by the migrant, and cost imposed on the target host country.

In the abstract, it seems curious indeed that migration cost would be construed implicitly as minimal or even negative by some in the adaptation school. To state the issue starkly, peoples have often fought wars to avoid being forced to leave their homelands against their will. There is little reason to suppose that, when the cause is climate change rather than an invading army, they will instead be indifferent between staying and moving. There is also a question of the ultimate feasibility of the migration response. As the amount and quality of land "opened up" by warming becomes smaller relative to the land closed off, the migration option becomes progressively less viable. Only so many people will fit onto Iceland.

Long before people move en masse toward more favorable regions, however, they will confront political obstacles to cross-border migration. This raises the second type of migration cost: that imposed on, or at least perceived by, the target country. For migration from developing to industrial countries, neoclassical economic analysis from a global standpoint might attribute a gain rather than a cost for each additional immigrant. Labor would be reallocated away from countries where the marginal product of labor is low to countries where it is high.[39] However, in terms of political economy, revealed behavior indicates that the perception of imposed costs from increased immigration dominates; otherwise the borders of industrial countries would be completely open. Moreover, as the rise in immigration would stem solely from an adverse "push" on source nations, it is also impossible to argue that citizens of those nations would benefit from increased migration associated with global warming.

For the United States, it is not difficult to envision increased pressure of legal and illegal immigration from global warming. Increased hurricane damage and sea-level rise could intensify the push of immigration from the Caribbean. Increased drought could do the same for immigration from Mexico.

Present-day stocks and flows of immigrants provide a rough basis for a sense of the costs that might be imposed by warming-induced migration. Approximately 1.8 million illegal immigrants, 70 percent of them from Mexico, applied for legalization under the 1986 Immigration Reform and Control Act. In the period 1975–80, an estimated 130,000 undocumented aliens from the Western Hemisphere entered the United States each year (Goering 1990). The annual

---

39. Such a gain would abstract from the distributional effects between capital and labor.

flow of legal immigrants has been approximately 640,000 (*Statistical Abstract of the United States*, 1991, 9). The base of legal and illegal immigrants is thus approximately 800,000 annually.

Suppose that benchmark warming ($2 \times CO_2$) increases illegal immigration by 25 percent and legal immigration by 10 percent. Suppose that, on a base of 800,000 immigrants, the share of illegals is 20 percent. Then warming would increase annual immigration by about 100,000. Infrastructure spending (education, roads, police, sanitation) in the United States is primarily at the state and local level. State and local government spending in 1989 amounted to $762 billion (*Economic Report of the President*, February 1991, 383), or approximately $3,000 per capita. Suppose that an immigrant only begins to pay taxes that cover his incremental social infrastructure costs after a period of 18 months (for illegals the period could be longer). Then each additional immigrant imposes a cost of $4,500 on the United States.[40] On this basis, an extra 100,000 immigrants annually would represent a cost of $450 million as an adverse effect of benchmark warming for the United States.

Outside the United States, there are indications that concern about increased immigration induced by global warming is especially high in Europe, where immigration problems already have intensified in the past decade as the consequence of political change in Eastern Europe and North Africa. As semiarid African states are among those expected to be seriously affected by global warming, such concern would appear well founded.

Hurricane Damage

Emanuel (1987, 485) argues that tropical cyclones, or hurricanes, are "particularly sensitive to sea surface temperature as the latent heat content of air at fixed relative humidity is a strongly exponential function of temperature, approximately doubling for each 10°C increment of temperature above 0°C." He calculates that for a rise of 3°C in sea surface temperature, there is a 30 percent to 40 percent rise in the maximum drop of barometric pressure. Wind velocity rises as the square root of the drop in barometric pressure. Wind pressure against obstructions rises with the square of wind speed. Applying a 2.3°C-to-4.8°C range of GCM estimates for increased August temperatures in the tropics under

---

40. This calculation makes no allowance for the possibility that subsequently the taxes paid by the immigrant would exceed his share of infrastructure costs. Precisely because higher-skilled immigrants are likely to have high incomes and above average taxes, immigration quotas tend to favor them over low-skilled applicants. For illegal immigrants, however, skills (and earning potential) tend to be lower, and evasion of formal taxation tends to be higher. For both reasons, the taxes they pay might never come to equal their share in infrastructure costs.

$2 \times CO_2$, Emanuel estimates that the destructive potential of hurricanes would rise by 40 percent to 50 percent.

Similarly, Hansen et al. (1989, 70–71) find in $2 \times CO_2$ simulations with the GISS model that moist static energy (the sum of sensible heat, latent heat, and geopotential energy) rises by 10 kJ/kg at the earth's surface and 8 kJ/kg at the upper troposphere (approximately 40,000 feet). Because of the increase in this gradient, and thus greater vertical penetration of moist convection (as well as increased evaporation and higher temperatures at low levels), they conclude that global warming would bring "increased intensity" of "both ordinary thunderstorms and mesoscale tropical storms."

Wendland (1977) has provided empirical support for the relationship of hurricanes to ocean surface temperatures. From monthly data for 1971–81, the frequency of hurricanes is closely related to the size of ocean area with a temperature over 26.8°C, and the relationship is exponential.

For its part, the IPCC (1990b, section 5.3.3, 162) surveys these and other studies and concludes: "There is some evidence from model simulations and empirical considerations that the frequency per year, intensity and area of occurrence of tropical disturbances may increase, though it is not yet compelling." In part, this tentativeness is attributable to the fact that, except for the high-resolution models, the GCMs have grid areas too large to capture "smaller scale disturbances such as hurricanes."[41]

The Emanuel study provides a basis for the quantification of prospective damages. Over the last 40 years, US hurricanes have caused an annual average of $1.5 billion in damages at 1989 prices (Cline 1990b). For the United States the most costly storm on record was Hurricane Hugo in 1989 ($7 billion). On the basis of the 50 percent increase suggested by Emanuel, the increased damage to be expected from benchmark warming would be $750 million annually. Hurricanes also cause loss of life, typically a total of 50 to 100 lives annually.

For other countries, especially island states, hurricane damage from global warming could be more severe. In 1970, tides from a cyclone killed hundreds of thousands in what is now Bangladesh. Hurricane Fifi in 1974 killed some 5,000 in Central America. Hurricane Gilbert caused $8 billion in damage in Jamaica alone in 1988 (IPCC 1990c, 5–10).

---

41. The IPCC (1990b, section 5.3.3, 161) also noted, however, that climate models tend to show a "reduction in day-to-day and interannual variability in the mid-latitude storm tracks in winter" (i.e., *not* hurricanes), because of "the reduction in the equator-to-pole temperature gradient." Nonetheless, if this judgment is meant to imply lesser storm intensity, it would not appear to take account of the other gradient—the vertical one just noted (Hansen et al. 1989). Thus, the IPCC reports one GCM result indicating that the temperature at an altitude of 22 km would fall by 4°C and the temperature at an altitude of 0 to 10 km rise by 4°C at latitude 40°N under $2 \times CO^2$ (IPCC 1990b, figure 5.2). The increase in vertical temperature gradient would seem likely to increase storm intensity.

The exponential relationship of latent heat content of air (at fixed relative humidity) to temperature, and the threshold effect whereby ocean surfaces above 26.8°C become subject to hurricane conditions, suggest that increased hurricane damage from global warming would be more than linear in relation to temperature rise. Thus, damages under very-long-term warming could be far greater proportionately than the corresponding ratio of temperature increase to that under benchmark $2 \times CO_2$ warming.

The Construction Sector

It is often assumed that global warming would benefit the construction sector because "lengthening of the construction season" would be "likely to increase productivity" (Nordhaus 1990b). However, the increased incidence of heat waves (discussed above) would seem likely to eliminate some summer construction days. More important, although construction is adversely affected by frost, it is also inhibited by rainfall (Jones 1964 and Russo 1966, as cited in Solomou 1990). For example, gravel digging has to stop under conditions of heavy rain.

Solomou (1990) has examined data on UK construction and rainfall in the period 1856–1913 and found a close negative correlation between the two. The GCMs typically predict an increase in global mean precipitation by about 8 percent as the consequence of benchmark $2 \times CO_2$ warming, and the estimates range as high as 13 percent to 15 percent (IPCC 1990b, table 3-2, 87). As noted above, there would be increased precipitation in winter in midlatitudes and year-round in the high latitudes and tropics. The IPCC similarly notes an adverse effect of rainfall on industry more generally and cites Parry and Read to the effect that "rainfall is responsible for more delays than any other climatic variable" for UK industry (IPCC 1990c, 5–34).

More work is required before a judgment can be offered on whether the adverse effects of increased rainfall on construction (and other industries) would be greater or smaller than the beneficial effects of warming on construction (and other activities) during winter months.

Leisure Activities

Studies for Canada cited by the IPCC indicate that the ski industry would lose 40 percent to 70 percent of skiable days as a consequence of warming from carbon dioxide doubling, even after taking account of the availability of snow-making machinery (IPCC 1990c, 5–35). Losses would presumably be larger in relative terms in US ski areas, where the temperature base is already higher. Other outdoor leisure activities would be much less affected. For example, golf might benefit in cold areas but be adversely affected in warm regions because of high temperatures and along heavily populated coastal areas where rainfall would tend to increase. Increased camping is sometimes cited as a benefit of warming, but it is unclear whether those who hold this view have taken into account the impact of forest loss and increases in precipitation.

Tourism could also be affected in areas where coral reefs are attractions. Coral bleaching and coral death were observed in the Pacific after the 1982–83 El Niño and in the Caribbean after unusually high water temperatures in the summer of 1987 (EPA 1989a, 157; *In Depth: Consumer Reviews for Sports Divers,* Austin, TX, September 1990). Glynn and de Weerdt (1991) indicate that the 1982–83 event may have brought extinction to two coral species (out of 12) along the Pacific coast of Panama. Coral bleaching results from the expulsion of symbiotic algae under environmental stress. As the algae are the primary source of food for the coral, the result can be coral death. Stress on coral reefs is expected to occur under global warming, in part because of higher temperatures but also because vertical accretion of reef flats may be unable to keep up with sea-level rise.

Placing a dollar value on impacts in leisure activities is difficult. However, as a point of departure, the US ski industry accounted for an estimated $5.6 billion in economic activity in 1988, when there were 53 million skier visits to ski areas (Waters 1990). If we suppose that global warming of 2.5°C would reduce ski activity by 60 percent in the United States, and it is assumed that half of the gross loss is offset by the difference between the value of released labor and other variable factors of production on the one hand and the loss of consumer surplus on the other, then the net loss would be on the order of $1.7 billion annually. This estimate makes no allowance for tourism losses associated with coral reef death. As noted, there is no clear case for attributing offsetting net gains in other leisure activities.

Water Supply

Warming is expected to put stress on water supply. A smaller share of precipitation in the form of snow, combined with earlier snowmelt, would mean higher runoff in the winter. Runoff in the spring and summer would correspondingly be reduced. In those areas or periods where precipitation declines, the combination of higher evaporation (from warmer temperatures) and lower precipitation would reduce soil moisture and water levels and flows. At the same time, the demand for water would tend to rise with warming, because of increased needs for irrigation and for cooling in electric power production (EPA 1989a, 165–70).

Average precipitation in the United States is 4,200 billion gallons per day (bgd). Of this amount, 2,765 bgd evaporates, 338 is withdrawn for use, and 1,435 bgd goes to surface and groundwater flows. Of the withdrawals, 140 bgd is for irrigation, 131 for thermoelectric power, 36 for domestic use, and 31 for industry and mining. Each of these sectors returns a portion of the flows, so that the shares of net consumption are different: 76 bgd for irrigation, 4 for electric power, 7 for domestic use, and 5 for industry and mining (EPA 1989a, 166).

Using a water balance model for the Sacramento basin, Gleick (1987) estimates that a 4°C increase in temperature would decrease summer runoff by 55 percent even if there were a 10 percent rise in precipitation. If there were a 10 percent decline in precipitation in the region, the reduction in summer runoff would amount to 65 percent. Winter runoff would increase in both cases (but would decrease if precipitation fell 20 percent).

The EPA estimates that warming from a doubling of carbon-dioxide-equivalent would reduce annual water deliveries in California's central valley basin by 200,000 to 400,000 acre-feet, or by 7 percent to 16 percent, even as demand for water rises by some 1.4 million acre-feet by as early as 2010 (EPA 1989a, 251). The price of water in California in a normal year is approximately $250 per acre-foot (*New York Times*, 6 March 1991). In this one instance, then, the costs of increased water scarcity would amount to $75 million annually (300,000 acre-feet × $250).

Nationwide withdrawals of water amount to 0.378 billion acre-feet annually.[42] Assuming $250 per acre-foot for domestic and industrial use (59 percent) and $100 for irrigation (41 percent), the annual value of water withdrawals is on the order of $70 billion annually. If water availability were to decline just 10 percent with climate change (based on the Gleick and especially the EPA–California estimates), the annual cost would amount to $7 billion.

Inefficient water allocation could make the costs higher. After five years of drought, in early 1991 California authorities cut off irrigation water to a wide range of agricultural producers. The first desalinization plant for residential water supply in the United States is now planned for Catalina Island in Southern California. Other communities are considering turning to salinization plants. Costs are expected to amount to $1,000 per acre-foot (*New York Times*, 6 March 1991). If such sources represent the marginal cost of water, the estimate just suggested could substantially understate the value of water lost to climate change.

---

42. 338 bgd × 365 days = 123,370 bgd = 123.4 × 10^{12} gallons. One acre-foot = 326,000 gallons. Annual withdrawals = (123.4/326) × 10^{12-3} gallons = 0.378 × 10^9 gallons.

One way to ease prospective shortages would be to reform pricing practices so that agricultural uses pay a price closer to that for residential and commercial use. In the past, politics has prevented this outcome. Moreover, as discussed above in the analysis of agriculture, the demand for irrigation is highly likely to rise from global warming, especially if the projections of sharply higher drought incidence are accurate.

The IPCC reports on various methods for estimating the impact of global warming on water supply. The group stresses that river basin runoff is very sensitive to small variations in climatic conditions, largely because runoff is a residual between precipitation and soil absorption or evaporation, and small changes in any of the underlying variables can cause a much larger proportionate impact on this residual. For the United States, water basin simulation models show that in a warmer, drier climate (+ 2°C, − 10 percent precipitation), water supply in 18 major water regions (covering the bulk of national supply) would decline by approximately one-third (calculated from IPCC 1990c, figure 4.2). Under the same conditions, annual river runoff in regions with relatively low precipitation would decline by 70 percent (IPCC 1990c, 4–7). These estimates suggest that the 10 percent decline applied above is conservative.

For Canada, several studies based on GCM estimates for global warming indicate that, in the Great Lakes region, runoff to the lakes could decline by 8 percent to 11 percent (for warming of 3.1°C to 4.8°C and a precipitation change of − 3 percent to +8 percent). Farther to the north, in the James Bay region the studies show increased runoff because of much higher precipitation (+ 15 percent to + 17.5 percent); and for the Canadian prairie (Saskatchewan River), estimates diverge (IPCC 1990c, 4–6).

For Europe, several studies based on water balance models and GCM projections suggest that there would be reduced precipitation and runoff in the south (Spain, Portugal, Greece), possible decreases in runoff in the central region, and significant increases in the north (the United Kingdom, the Netherlands, and Belgium; IPCC 1990c, 4–11, 4–12).

For the former Soviet Union, studies in part based on paleoclimatic analogues have suggested that global warming would tend to increase water resources, as a 2°C global warming would increase annual runoff by 10 percent to 20 percent on all the large rivers. An important exception is that in the south of the forest zones of the European part of the former Soviet Union and in western Siberia annual runoff could fall by 80 percent or more (IPCC 1990c, 4–15, 4–16).

The IPCC reports that, for Japan, normal GCM projections are especially inadequate because they do not provide information on typhoons. Japanese experts anticipate that with global warming there would tend to be longer periods of drought, interrupted by intense precipitation. Water shortages could become more prevalent.

Detailed studies in New Zealand conclude that with global warming there would be a large increase in annual runoff through most of the country but a large decrease along the eastern shores of the two islands. The studies indicate a sharp increase in flooding (IPCC 1990c, 4–19; figure 4-5).

The broad picture that emerges is that, as Gleick (1987) suggests, stress on water supply may be one of the most important consequences of global warming. The principal exception would be in the high latitudes and tropics, where increased precipitation would be concentrated (chapter 1; Rind et al. 1990). The prospective decrease in supply in many areas (especially the United States) would confront an increase in demand that could pose severe price increases. Rosenberg et al. (1989a) recall that as early as the 1960s there were discussions in the United States of large-scale water transfers from Alaska and northern Canada to the Southwest and high plains of the United States, and in the Soviet Union there was even consideration of reversing the northerly flow of some major rivers (until the large economic and environmental costs became more apparent). Water shortages could revive some of these proposals (at least for the United States), with the certain effect of stirring political conflicts over water transfers between regions and among sectors (especially away from agriculture).

If global benchmark warming of 2.5°C would cause problems for water supply, very-long-term warming in the range of 10°C would seem likely to cause much more dramatic difficulties. It is useful to recall the point made by Rind et al.: with a warmer atmosphere, more water is in the atmosphere in the form of water vapor and less is left in the surface land, lakes, and rivers (i.e., not all of the water transferred to the atmosphere comes from the oceans). As Rind et al. note, "from the Claussius-Clapeyron equation, an incremental increase in temperature produces a greater increase in atmospheric moisture-holding capacity when the temperature is warmer" (1990, 9983). One would thus expect evapotranspiration to rise more than linearly with temperature, causing a nonlinear rise in water availability problems.

Nonlinearity is confirmed in the simulations of Gleick (1987). He finds that summer runoff decreases by 12 percent when temperature rises by 2°C and precipitation rises by 10 percent. Summer runoff decreases by 49 percent when temperature rises by 4°C and precipitation rises by 20 percent (Gleick 1987, 146). Thus, a doubling of both the temperature and the precipitation increases leads to a quadrupling of the percentage cutback in summer runoff. Yet there is reason to believe that the result would be even worse, because, as noted above, summertime precipitation would be unlikely to rise in midlatitudes.

In sum, a damage estimate on the order of $7 billion annually might be appropriate and perhaps conservative for the United States for water supply under global warming with the doubling of carbon-dioxide-equivalent. Water supply thus ranks as another of the preeminent categories of economic damage from global warming, in the same range as sea-level rise (table 3.4). For warming four times as large over the very long term, damage would be likely to be much more than four times as high. In the formulation $D = k(\Delta t)^\gamma$, one might expect $\gamma = 1.5$ (for example). In that case, the very-long-term damage would amount to \$7 billion $\times$ $4^{1.5}$ = \$56 billion (against the 1990 economic scale).

Urban Infrastructure

The EPA has examined the impact of global warming on urban infrastructure costs. For coastal cities, sea-level rise or more frequent droughts would increase the salinity of coastal aquifers and tidal surface waters, requiring a response where these are the sources of water. New Orleans illustrates the point. In the drought of 1988, when the Mississippi River was far below normal levels, it was necessary to build a temporary nine-meter silt wall to halt the upriver advance of saltwater that threatened the city's water supply. In the Philadelphia-Wilmington-Trenton area, a sea-level rise of just 0.3 meters could require a 12 percent increase in reservoir capacity to prevent saltwater from advancing past water intakes on the Delaware River (EPA 1989a, 239). In addition, more frequent and intense storms would likely overload existing storm sewer systems. Flooding and the release of untreated waste into watercourses from storm and wastewater systems could require new sewer systems.

A study for New York City found that, with benchmark warming, increased water use for cooling large buildings and for lawn watering could increase annual water demand by 5 percent, while increased evaporation of water in reservoirs could cut supply by 10 percent to 24 percent. Saltwater infiltration from rising sea level could place some intakes below the salt line during the summers with mild droughts, reducing supply further. The EPA summary of various studies for New York estimated that, for water supply adjustments alone, the city would need to invest an additional \$3 billion as a consequence of $2 \times CO_2$ warming (EPA 1989a, 243).

In Miami, apart from costs for levees to deal with rising sea level (considered separately above), capital outlays for canal control, drainage, and raising streets (otherwise subject to collapse from water table infiltration of their base, for about one-third of the streets) would amount to some \$580 million. In contrast, for Cleveland the savings on snow and ice control and municipal heating would offset higher air-conditioning costs, and additional dredging and water supply costs would be negligible (EPA 1989a, 241–42).

Urban infrastructure investments, primarily those related to adjustments in water supply, sewer, and drainage systems, might amount to something on the order of \$10 billion, based on the New York and Miami estimates. Divided over

75 years[43] and discounted, a $10 billion capital cost amounts to approximately $100 million annually.

Pollution

The benefits of action to reduce global warming would include two types of gains that stem from the interrelationship of global warming to more traditional problems of pollution. First, there would be a direct "damage avoidance" similar conceptually to the avoidance of damage to agriculture (for example). This effect would arise because a warmer climate could aggravate the problem of air pollution, as discussed below. Second, there would be a spillover benefit from the action undertaken to reduce global warming to the extent that the action involved a cutback in the burning of fossil fuels that presently contribute to air pollution. For example, if the use of coal is reduced as a consequence of policy action on global warming, there is a spillover benefit in the form of reduced pollution associated with coal burning (for example, emissions of sulfur dioxide and resulting acid rain). The discussion that follows will focus on the first of these two concepts, but the second is also important.

A warmer climate would aggravate urban pollution. One piece of evidence is that in the hot summer of 1988 the extended stagnation periods and high temperatures caused 76 cities in the United States to exceed the national ambient air quality standard (NAAQS) for low-level (tropospheric) ozone pollution by 25 percent or more (EPA 1989a, 200).

Air pollution involves total suspended particulates (TSP), sulfur dioxide, carbon monoxide, nitrous oxide, ozone, and lead. Of these, the most severe problem in terms of the number of persons living in areas with air quality indexes that exceed (violate) the NAAQS is that of ozone (75 million in 1986); TSP and carbon monoxide also remain leading problems (41 million each). Ozone has proven the most difficult to reduce. Its concentrations declined only 13 percent from 1979 to 1986, compared with reductions of 23 percent for TSP and 37 percent for sulfur dioxide (EPA 1989a, 201–2).

Numerous studies confirm that ozone concentrations rise with temperature (see, e.g., IPCC 1990c, 5–46, 5–47). Models estimated by Morris indicate that a 4°C rise in temperature (approximately the $2 \times CO_2$ benchmark for the United States) would increase the number of person-hours of exposure to ozone in excess of the NAAQS ceiling of 120 ppb from 661,000 to 2.1 million in central California and from 29.8 million to 47.5 million in the Midwest and Southeast

---

43. Some of the effects here are for carbon-dioxide-equivalent doubling, and thus within a time horizon of 50 years for effective warming. Others refer to one-meter sea-level rise, whose occurrence is on a 100-year time scale.

(EPA 1989a, 214). The EPA has summarized the various estimates with the conclusion that a 4°C rise in temperature could cause an increase in peak ozone concentrations by 10 percent. The result would be to double the number of cities exceeding the standards from 68 to 136, causing most midsize and some small cities in the Midwest, South, and East to be added to the list of those presently in violation.

The EPA has applied its past models relating ozone concentrations to emissions of volatile organic compounds (VOC) to estimate that, to offset benchmark $2 \times CO_2$ warming, it would be necessary to reduce VOC in the United States by 700,000 tons from a base of 6 million tons expected for the year 2000. At an estimated cost of $5,000 per ton, the agency calculates that the resulting costs would amount to $3.5 billion annually (EPA 1989a, 215).

Warming could affect other parts of the pollution problem as well. At higher temperatures, there is a greater concentration of hydrogen peroxide, the agent in the conversion of atmospheric sulfur dioxide into sulfuric acid (acid rain). Higher demand for electricity for air conditioning (discussed above) would mean greater pollution from power plants. A 10 percent rise in electric power demand would mean a 30 percent rise in sulfur dioxide emissions (IPCC 1990c, 5–47). If total cloud cover declined with global warming (chapter 1), there would be a greater incidence of sunlight available to cause greater ozone production. The rise in water vapor associated with warming would accelerate the reaction rates of VOCs and increase production rates of ozone, hydrogen peroxide, and sulfates (EPA 1989a, 207).

One way to pursue a quantitative grasp of the issue is to consider the amount being spent to abate pollution already. The EPA has estimated that, in 1990, the US economy spent $115 billion in pollution abatement, the vast bulk of it in the private sector (Roberts 1991a). Of this total, 29 percent was for air pollution abatement. Therefore something like $33 billion annually was already being spent in the United States to combat air pollution. The Clean Air Act of 1990 was expected to increase annual expenses by at least $25 billion. For example, lower emissions required for automobiles were likely to cost some $500 per vehicle (about $5 billion annually), and reduction of sulfur dioxide emissions in power plants was expected to cost an additional $2 billion to $4 billion annually (*New York Times*, 23 October 1990). The relevant base for environmental spending on air pollution is thus in the range of some $60 billion annually.

The potential impact of global warming policy on these costs may then be visualized by asking by what percentage these costs would be changed. On the side of direct damage avoidance, if a warmer climate raised total abatement costs by Y percent to hold air quality standards constant, then the "benefit" of avoiding the warming amounts to $60 billion $\times$ Y percent. On the side of spillover benefits of greenhouse action, if lower fossil fuel burning (for example) cut the size of the air pollution problem by Z percent, there would be a $60 billion $\times$ Z percent benefit from the action.[44] Thus, just a 10 percent reduction in urban pollution as a side effect of a shift away from fossil fuels would contribute a benefit of $6 billion annually. Although not included in the central estimates here, this illustrative estimate suggests that favorable side effects in reducing pollution from a program of emissions abatement could be in the same general range as, say, benefits from limiting sea-level rise or water losses (as reviewed above). Indeed, aggressive cutbacks in fossil fuel emissions might reduce existing air pollution by much more than 10 percent, suggesting a beneficial side effect on the order of tens of billions of dollars annually rather than $6 billion.

The IPCC "impacts" report (IPCC 1990c) has only two pages on air pollution, out of a volume of over 300 pages, suggesting that relatively little is known about this area. It reports very little on the impacts outside the United States. However, in view of the severe pollution problems of Eastern Europe, the former Soviet Union, and some cities in developing countries (e.g., Mexico City and São Paulo), there could be relatively wide geographical participation in any benefits in air pollution avoidance (and reduction) associated with policy action to abate global warming.

For much higher warming over the very long term, the effects in the area of air pollution are likely to be nonlinear (i.e., they would rise more than proportionately with temperature). For example, although the underlying relationship of ozone concentration to temperature is approximately linear (EPA 1989a, 205), the problem involves thresholds, so that increased concentrations can push cities over the acceptable ceilings and require action where none was necessary before (i.e., an infinite percentage increase in expense from a zero base).

Overview

Table 3.4 presents a summary of the damage estimates developed in this study for the case of the United States. For the very-long-term estimates, the term γ

---

44. There is an interaction term that must be handled carefully. The policy action would reduce the base for the pollution problem, thereby reducing the benefit by Y percent $\times$ $60 billion. In the extreme, if the greenhouse policy action eliminated all air pollution problems, the base of $60 billion would shrink to zero. The second, spillover benefit would equal Z percent $\times$ $60 billion = 100 percent $\times$ $60 billion = $60 billion, but it would be double-counting at that point to attribute an additional X $\times$ $60 billion for the further damage avoided.

Table 3.4 Estimates of annual damage from global warming to the US economy at 1990 scale (billions of 1990 dollars)

	2xCO$_2$ (2.5°C)	Very-long-term warming (10°C)
Agriculture	17.5	95.0
Forest loss	3.3	7.0
Species loss	4.0 + Δ_s	16.0 + Δ'_s
Sea-level rise		35.0
Construction of dikes, levees	1.2	
Wetlands loss	4.1	
Drylands loss	1.7	
Electricity requirements	11.2	64.1
Nonelectric heating	-1.3	-4.0
Human amenity	X_a	Y_a
Human life	5.8	33.0[a]
Human morbidity	X_m	Y_m
Migration	0.5	2.8[a]
Hurricanes	0.8	6.4[b]
Construction	$\pm X_c$	$\pm Y_c$
Leisure activities	1.7	4.0
Water supply	7.0	56.0
Urban infrastructure	0.1	0.6[a]
Air pollution		
Tropospheric ozone	3.5	19.8[a]
Other	X_o	Y_o
Total	61.6	335.7
	$+X_a+X_m+X_o+\Delta_s\pm X_c$	$+Y_a+Y_m+Y_o+\Delta'_s\pm Y_c$

a. $\gamma = 1.25$.

b. $\gamma = 1.5$.

refers to the exponential pace of the expansion of damage as temperature rises $(D = k[\Delta t]^\gamma)$, where specific text estimates are not made.[45]

The estimates here indicate that, even for benchmark warming of $2 \times CO_2$-equivalent, damages for the United States could be relatively large. The $61 billion estimate is approximately 1.1 percent of GDP.[46] Moreover, it excludes several of the unestimated effects, and the potentially important species loss may be underestimated. The table's estimates for damage from very-long-term warming are more striking and, on average, are approximately 5½ times the estimates for $2 \times CO_2$-equivalent.

The very-long-term damages require appropriate scaling. Most of the effects would rise proportionately with GDP, and some would rise more than proportionately (e.g., species loss, if existence value to society is an income-elastic service). The long-term damages are thus on the order of at least 6 percent of GDP.

The central damage estimates of this study, based on estimates for the United States, are that warming associated with benchmark doubling of carbon-dioxide-equivalent (2.5°C) would impose losses of at least 1 percent of GDP and that very-long-term warming of 10°C would cause damage amounting to at least 6 percent of GDP. As indicted in table 3.4, numerous damages are excluded in these central figures. Incorporation of some of the "softest" estimates could substantially raise calculated losses.

Thus, as noted above, the annual value of species loss for benchmark doubling might well be $40 billion rather than $4 billion; annual human amenity costs might amount to $10 billion, health damages $3 billion, and the side benefits of pollution reduction from emissions abatement at least $6 billion. If these estimates are included, the total damages from permitting unabated global warming reach $117 billion annually for benchmark doubling, or 2 percent of GDP.

The benefit-cost analysis below accordingly uses a range of 1 percent to 2 percent of GDP for damages from benchmark warming (the doubling of carbon-dioxide-equivalent, with warming at 2.5°C). As it turns out, this is the same range proposed by Nordhaus (1991a). Although his direct calculations reach only ¼ percent of GDP, he suggests the range of 1 percent to 2 percent of GDP to take account of effects he does not measure.

Even the range of 1 percent to 2 percent of GDP for carbon-dioxide-equivalent doubling, and correspondingly 6 percent to 12 percent of GDP for very-long-

---

45. Note, however, that the estimate for leisure activity rises less than linearly in the long-term estimate, because the ski industry is already cut by more than half in the $2 \times CO_2$ scenario.

46. This estimate is approximately seven times the direct estimate of Nordhaus (1990b), which is $6.6 billion at 1981 prices. However, it is consistent with his "medium damage" estimate, placed at 1 percent of GDP to allow for unmeasured effects in his direct estimate.

term warming, does not reflect the damage associated with upper-bound warming (climate sensitivity parameter Λ = 4.5°C). With a damage function exponent of γ = 1.3, damage for upper-bound warming would reach levels 2.15 times as high (= $[4.5/2.5]^{1.3}$). Thus, with upper-bound warming, damage would be expected to reach 2.1 percent to 4.3 percent of GDP for carbon-dioxide-equivalent doubling, and 13 percent to 26 percent of GDP for very-long-term warming. On this basis, even for $2 \times CO_2$, the high-damage case considered here has approximately twice the highest damage considered by Nordhaus (1991a).

Conversion of the damages in table 3.4 into avoidance benefits requires a sense of the portion of damage that could be avoided with an aggressive anti-greenhouse policy. As analyzed in chapter 2, over the very long term it is likely that as much as 2.5°C out of a total 10°C potential warming (central estimate) cannot be avoided even with aggressive action. The 2.5°C minimum is equivalent to $2 \times CO_2$-benchmark warming. On this basis, the amount of long-term damage that can be avoided through energetic policy measures should equal the difference between the first and second columns of table 3.4 (stated, in both cases, against a 1990-scale US economy). This difference, which amounts to 5 percent of GDP, is the basis for the (somewhat more conservative) "avoidance proportion" applied in the benefit-cost analysis of chapter 7.

This analysis has the sobering implication that much of the damage usually considered is already unavoidable. It also emphatically underscores the importance of the very-long-term analysis. If all that were in store were the damages typically associated with benchmark $2 \times CO_2$-warming, there would be some basis for largely abandoning attempts at abatement on the grounds that a large portion of the damage is unavoidable (although the slower speed of the warming with abatement might still warrant action on ecological grounds). Attention would then more appropriately focus on adaptation. But if the much larger stakes in the very long term are valid, there are correspondingly much stronger grounds for abatement policy action.

Annex 3A

The Welfare Effects of Agricultural Yield Reductions Resulting from Global Warming

Global warming is expected to reduce agricultural yields in many regions, even after allowance is made for the fertilization effect of higher atmospheric carbon dioxide and for partially offsetting changes in agricultural practices. To translate yield reductions into estimates of economic damage, however, it is generally insufficient merely to apply the percentage yield changes to the prospective baseline value of agricultural output. This note sets forth a simple methodology for calculating the welfare effects, taking account of consumer and producer surplus on the basis of underlying supply and demand curves.

The Case of Infinitely Elastic Supply

It is useful to begin with a special case: land is completely homogeneous and the supply curve horizontal, with constant unit cost. Let λ be the ratio of post-warming yields to original yields ($\lambda < 1$). Then, as shown in figure 3A.1, the horizontal supply curve will shift upward from the original price P_0 to $P_1 = P_0(1/\lambda)$. That is, each hectare will produce only λ much as before at the same capital and labor costs, so the price per bushel will have to be $1/\lambda$ times as high for the sales to cover the same costs as before.

In this special case, the welfare effect of lower yield approximates what might intuitively be expected: for a given percentage cut in yields, the welfare change is approximately equal to this percentage multiplied by the original value of production. Consider figure 3A.1. The welfare change equals the change in consumer surplus plus the change in producer surplus. With a horizontal supply curve, there is no producer surplus, either before or after the yield decrease. For its part, consumer surplus declines by the area $a + b$. If the demand curve is steep in the relevant region, this area will approximate $(P_1 - P_0)Q_0 = [(1/\lambda) - 1]P_0Q_0$. This amount equals the percentage decline in yield multiplied by the original value of output.

A Generalized Ricardian Supply Curve

In practice, land is not wholly homogeneous, and the supply curve is more likely to be upward sloping than horizontal. The following analysis will demonstrate that, under production conditions of a classical Ricardian agricultural

Figure 3A.1 Welfare effects of lower agricultural yields under constant costs

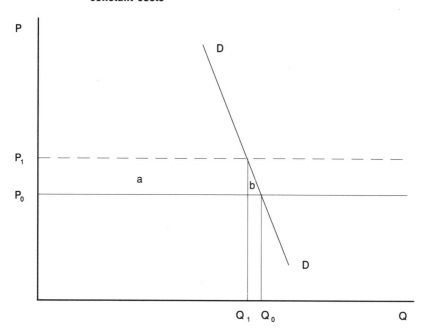

model, and with a plausible demand function, the welfare losses from yield reduction are likely to be larger than the percentage yield reduction times the initial value of production.

Consider a Ricardian agricultural supply function, based on the declining productivity of land incorporated at the margin. Let the amount of labor and capital required per hectare be fixed (for the moment) at L and K, respectively. Then variable costs per hectare are:

(3A.1) $c = wL + rK$

where w is the wage rate and r the rental cost of capital. Let n denote the nth hectare (or million-hectare block) brought into production. Let q denote yield per hectare (e.g., bushels) and P price (e.g., dollars per bushel). Then profit earned on the nth hectare is:

(3A.2) $\pi_n = Pq_n - c.$

Define P_n as the price required to call forth production on n hectares. This price will be such that profit just falls to zero on the marginal hectare, so that:

(3A.3) $\pi_n = 0 = P_n q_n - c; P_n = c/q_n.$

Let yield on the marginal hectare be a declining function of the number of hectares brought into production. Then:

(3A.4) $\quad q_n = q_0 - \alpha n \, ; \, n < q_0/\alpha.$

Total production equals the number of hectares times the average yield over all qualities of land in production, or:

(3A.5) $\quad Q_n = 0.5 \, n \, [q_0 + q_n]$
$\qquad\quad = 0.5 \, n \, [2q_0 - \alpha n]$
$\qquad\quad = nq_0 - 0.5 \, \alpha n^2.$

From equations 3A.3 and 3A.4, the supply price may be rewritten as:

(3A.6) $\quad P_n = c/[q_0 - \alpha n].$

To find the supply of hectares as a function of the price, we may write:

(3A.7) $\qquad\qquad q_n = c/P_n;$
$\qquad\quad q_0 - \alpha n = c/P_n;$
$\qquad\qquad\quad n = [1/\alpha][q_0 - (c/P_n)].$

Agricultural output supply as a function of price, in turn, is (from equations 3A.7 and 3A.5):

(3A.8) $\quad Q = [1/\alpha][q_0 - (c/P_n)]q_0 - 0.5\alpha\{[1/\alpha][q_0 - (c/P_n)]\}^2$
$\qquad\quad = a - bP_n^{-2}$

where a is $0.5q_0^2/\alpha$ and b is $0.5c^2/\alpha$.

The Impact of Changes in Yields

Now consider the effect of multiplying all yields by λ ($\lambda < 1$). Denoting the new situation by primes, we have:

(3A.9) $\quad q_n' = \lambda q_n$
(3A.10) $\quad P_n' = c/[\lambda q_n] = [1/\lambda]P_n.$

That is, the price required to call forth n hectares into production will now be $1/\lambda$ times as high as before.

Total production becomes (from equation 3A.8):

(3A.11) $\quad Q = 0.5[\lambda q_0]^2/\alpha - [0.5c^2/\alpha][(1/\lambda)P_n]^{-2}$
$\qquad\quad = \lambda^2 a - \lambda^2 b \, P_n^{-2}$
$\qquad\quad = \lambda^2 Q$

The result of the yield multiplication by λ is thus to shift the supply curve to the left at any given price by the multiple λ^2.

Figure 3A.2 Welfare effects of lower agricultural yields with diminishing returns

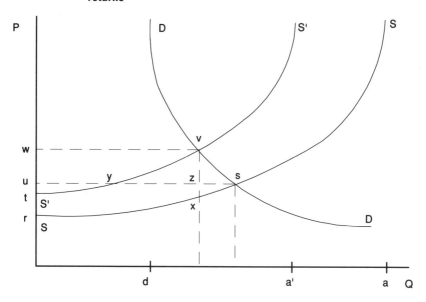

Figure 3A.2 shows the original and shifted supply curves. As indicated by equations 3A.8 and 3A.11, they turn vertical at a and a' (which is equal to $\lambda^2 a$), respectively, as the final term involving the inverse of the square of the price vanishes when the price rises to infinity. Essentially, the supply curve turns vertical when the full amount of productive land is exhausted, that is, where $n = q_0/\alpha$ (and $q_n = 0$).

It is immediately evident from the comparison of the original supply curve, SS, and the new curve after yield decrease, $S'S'$, that the price may potentially rise by more than $[(1/\lambda) - 1]$, the increment when the supply curve is horizontal. Indeed, if there were an attempt to hold production at fractionally below a', the new price would have to approximate infinity and thus would be infinitely times as high as the original price rather than just $1/\lambda$ times as high.

In fact, the bare minimum that the price may rise is by the multiple $1/\lambda$. Consider the intercept on the price axis (r in the initial supply curve and t in the shifted curve). This is the farmers' reservation price for bringing the first hectare into production. With yield λ times as high as before, the initial reservation price will be $1/\lambda$ times as high ($t = r/\lambda$). So the revised supply curve lies along a path on which the price turns infinitely higher than before at quantity a' and is at least $1/\lambda$ times as high as before when quantity is nearly zero. At all intermediate points, the price along the new curve will be more than $1/\lambda$ times the price on the original curve for the same output.

Equilibrium and Welfare Loss

The actual market equilibrium will depend on the demand curve. For ease of solution, it is helpful to specify demand also as a function of the inverse of the square of price:

(3A.12) $D = d + e P^{-2}$.

In this curve, an infinite price makes the second term vanish, and demand, d, remains at the absolute minimum (for example, the amount of food needed to avoid starvation). At lower prices, the second term takes effect, and if the price goes to zero the second term becomes infinitely large.

Equilibrium under the original conditions occurs at:

(3A.13) $D = Q = d + eP^{-2} = a - bP^{-2}$; $P^* = \sqrt{[e + b]/[a - d]}$.

Correspondingly, the equilibrium after a decrease in yield occurs at:

(3A.14) $P_1 = \sqrt{[e + \lambda^2 b]/ [\lambda^2 a - d]}$

and the ratio of the new equilibrium price to the old price is:

(3A.15) $P'/P^* = \sqrt{\dfrac{ea + \lambda^2 ba - ed - \lambda^2 bd}{\lambda^2 ea + \lambda^2 ba - ed - bd}}$.

It is evident from equation 3A.15 that the price has risen ($P'/P^* > 1$), because the first term in the numerator is larger than the first in the denominator, the second and third terms are identical, and the fourth term in the numerator is negative and smaller than that in the denominator, so that the numerator is strictly larger than the denominator. How much larger depends on the supply and demand parameters (a, b, d, and e) as well as the yield multiple (λ).

The welfare effects of the yield decrease as shown in figure 3A.2 are as follows. Consumer surplus declines by the area *usvw*. Producer surplus changes from *rsu* to *tvw*. Net welfare change is thus:

(3A.16) $\Delta W = tvw - rsu - usvw$.

As suggested in the diagram, the loss of original producer surplus (*rsu*) may approximate the gain in new producer surplus (*tvw*), leaving the bulk of the consumer surplus loss (*usvw*) as net welfare loss (deadweight loss). As suggested above, this loss is likely to exceed the percentage of yield reduction multiplied by original output value.

4

Economic Models of Carbon Reduction Costs: An Analytical Survey

4

Economic Models of Carbon Reduction Costs: An Analytical Survey

Economic research on the greenhouse problem has progressed much further on the costs of abatement than on the benefits. This chapter presents a summary of the leading model-based studies. Together with engineering estimates, they provide an emerging consensus view of the range of economic costs that can be expected if carbon dioxide emissions are cut to levels compatible with much slower buildup of atmospheric concentration.

Important surveys of "top-down" economic models of abatement costs already exist (Hoeller et al. 1991, Darmstadter and Plantinga 1991, Boero et al. 1991, Edmonds and Barns 1990). This chapter seeks to provide further perspective on the conceptual framework of each of the major models, identify critical limitations of some of the existing studies, and add the results of more recent models. Chapter 5 then surveys the more important recent "bottom-up" engineering-economic studies and studies of forestry options.

The analysis begins with a general statement of the economic effects that may be expected from carbon emissions reductions. I will argue that, although the range of estimates has been large, the more reliable ones tend to congregate in the vicinity of 2 percent to 3 percent of GNP as the permanent, recurring cost that would be imposed by the reduction and then stabilization of global carbon emissions. The initial discussion suggests that this range is consistent with what might be expected from general principles.

Analytical Framework

Economists tend to analyze the costs of reducing greenhouse gas emissions through the use of top-down models that employ a production function approach, in which goods and services are produced by labor, capital, and energy. Cutbacks in carbon emissions require some reduction in energy availability.

141

With less energy to cooperate in the production process with the available labor and capital, output declines. This reduction in output is the economic cost imposed by curtailing carbon dioxide emissions.

Substitutability

The reduction of carbon emissions can be accomplished by any of the following means:

- substitution of more polluting fossil fuels (e.g., coal) by less polluting ones (e.g., natural gas), or intrafossil fuel substitution (IFFS)

- substitution of nonfossil fuels (e.g., nuclear, solar) for fossil fuels (nonfossil fuel substitution, or NFFS)

- substitution of energy by labor and capital in the production process (other factor–energy substitution, or OFES)

- substitution of energy-intensive products by non-energy-intensive products in the consumption mix (product substitution, or PS)

- reducing deforestation or increasing afforestation.

Carbon reduction imposes economic costs not only because of the resulting decline in production as less energy becomes available to cooperate with labor and capital, but also because of valuation changes associated with the shift to a less desired composition of products in consumption. Typically the models measure the "GNP" cost associated with the reduced volume of production. Conceptually, the Hicksian "equivalent variation" (the increase in income that would be required to leave the consumer at unchanged welfare) is a more meaningful measure, as it incorporates the loss of producer and consumer surplus from the changes in both the volume and the composition of production.

The greater the scope for substitution away from carbon pollution in each of the above dimensions, the lower will be the production costs. In broad terms, the substitution possibilities are as follows.

Coal generates approximately 26 kg of carbon emissions per million British thermal units (mmBtu), oil 20.4 kg per mmBtu, and natural gas 14.5 kg per mmBtu.[1] Thus, the same energy output can be achieved from gas with a savings of almost one-half in carbon emissions compared with coal. An example of

---

1. Calculated from Office of Technology Assessment (1991, 7). Note that the discussion here is in terms of carbon-equivalent. The weight in terms of carbon dioxide is 3.67 times as large, reflecting the total atomic weight of a molecule of carbon dioxide (44) relative to that of a molecule of carbon (12, on a scale with oxygen = 16).

substitution toward natural gas is the replacement of coal- and oil-fired thermal plants by gas turbine combined-cycle systems based on high-efficiency turbines derived from jet engine technology (Williams 1989).

In the next few decades there should be considerable scope for carbon reduction from IFFS. We may obtain a sense of the maximum scope for IFFS by considering the current contribution of each fossil fuel to global carbon emissions. In 1985, coal accounted for 2.2 gigatons of carbon (GtC), oil 2.1 GtC, and gas 0.7 GtC (IPCC 1990a, 71, figure ES-1). On this basis, if coal were entirely replaced by natural gas, the present level of fossil fuel carbon emissions would decline by about 20 percent (i.e., a one-half cut in carbon intensity on two-fifths of fossil fuel emissions). Over the long term, however, the supply of natural gas and oil is only a small fraction of coal supply, so the long-run scope for IFFS is limited.[2]

Substitution of fossil by nonfossil fuels (NFFS) offers the most important opportunities for emissions reductions. A serious and sustained attack on global warming means a largely nonfossil fuel economy for the long-term future. Biomass energy is one crucial substitute, because as much carbon is absorbed from the atmosphere during the growth of biomass as is released by burning it. This closed cycle generates no net emissions. Nuclear power is another substitute for fossil fuels, although improved (e.g., inherently safe) design and resolution of the waste disposal issue must be addressed if heavy reliance is to be placed on this alternative. Solar energy is another substitute, and there have been important cost reductions in solar thermal and photovoltaic energy (Ogden and Williams 1989). Hydroelectricity and wind-generated energy are additional potential alternatives. The National Academy of Sciences (1991a, 56–57) estimates that such renewable sources of energy could provide up to 18 quadrillion Btu (quads), equivalent to about two-thirds of present US electrical capacity.[3] In general, substitution for fossil fuels is expected to be easier in electricity generation, and more difficult in transportation, where liquid fuels have important advantages. As will be seen, the cost of a noncarbon "backstop technology" plays a pivotal role in the economic cost estimates of carbon emissions abatement.

Finally, product substitution in final demand may provide some scope for reduction of energy and/or carbon emissions. As discussed below, only one of the leading models (Jorgenson and Wilcoxen 1990b) explicitly takes this dimension of substitution into account.

---

2. Thus, Sundquist (1990, 202) reports World Energy Congress estimates that ultimately recoverable resources of coal amount to 6,743 GtC, whereas these resources are only 253 GtC for crude oil, 133 GtC for natural gas, 288 GtC for oil shale, and 97 GtC for oil sands.

3. The National Academy of Sciences estimates (in quads) are as follows: hydroelectric, 2; geothermal, 3.5; biomass, 2.4; solar photovoltaics, 2.5; solar thermal, 2.6; wind, 5.3.

The oil shock of the 1970s and early 1980s provided a laboratory experiment demonstrating the possibility of these various forms of substitution. Because of the oil price shock, US carbon emissions were no higher in 1987 than they had been in 1972, despite a 46 percent rise in real GDP (Jorgenson and Wilcoxen 1990a; *Economic Report of the President*, February 1992, 300).

In the top-down economic models, the four dimensions of substitutability enumerated here are typically captured by the application of "elasticities," or parameters that tell the percentage change in the dependent variable (e.g., the labor-energy ratio) for a given percentage change in the independent variable (the corresponding price ratio).[4] In the "bottom-up" engineering approaches, the scope for substitution tends to be identified from absolute shifts in energy requirements through changes in technology (e.g., replacement of conventional by compact-fluorescent light bulbs), and is frequently alleged to be available at cost savings rather than increases (in which case the elasticity between the old and the new technology is undefined—the shift should not require any price change at all).

Economic Cost

It is useful to place a broad magnitude on the likely economic cost of carbon emissions abatement by appealing to economic theory and taking into account the present size of the energy sector. From standard (neoclassical) theory, the share of a factor of production in total output tells the elasticity, or responsiveness, of production to changes in inputs of the factor.[5] In industrial economies,

---

4. More specifically, the elasticity of substitution between x and y equals: $(\%\Delta[x/y])/(\%\Delta[p_x/p_y])$, where $\%\Delta$ is the percentage change.

5. The necessary assumptions are that each factor is paid its marginal product, and that overall there are constant returns to scale (otherwise marginal product payment overexhausts output when returns are increasing and underexhausts it when they are decreasing). The elasticity of output with respect to the factor is the percentage change in output caused by a 1 percent change in the amount of the factor. Suppose the production function is $Q = f(E,H)$ where Q is output, f is a function, E is the amount of energy, and H is the amount of all other factors. Then the marginal product of energy is $\delta Q/\delta E$. The percentage change of output relative to the percentage change in energy is $e = [\delta Q/Q]/[\delta E/E]$. The proposition that this elasticity equals the share of energy in the economy may be demonstrated as follows. Energy is paid $E[\delta Q/\delta E]$, or the factor amount times the factor marginal product (unit payment). Total output is Q. Dividing the former by the latter gives the factor share in the economy, or $(E[\delta Q/\delta E])/Q$. This final expression may be rearranged to equal the previous expression, e. The identity between factor share and output elasticity of the factor holds for any neoclassical production function (with constant returns to scale). In the specific Cobb-Douglas form ($Q = \alpha E^\beta H^{1-\beta}$), it is additionally true that the factor share and the output elasticity are constant (and equal to the exponent,

the share of energy in GNP is in the range of 5 percent to 7 percent.[6] On the basis of standard theory, then, one would expect GNP to fall by some 0.06 times the percentage reduction in energy availability.

The proportionate decline in energy, in turn, depends on the required proportionate reduction in carbon, and on the extent to which energy must be cut back for a given reduction in carbon. Typical baselines for global carbon emissions place the total in the range of 20 GtC annually by the year 2100 (chapter 2). With current annual emissions at 6 to 7 GtC, the average over the next century is on the order of 13 GtC annually. If increases in carbon dioxide concentration are to be held to minimal levels, emissions must be cut to 4 GtC annually or perhaps less. For the 21st century on average, then, carbon reductions sufficient to stabilize atmospheric concentration would amount to some 70 percent from baseline.

Carbon reductions through IFFS and NFFS do not reduce energy availability, but instead only reduce its carbon intensity. As will be developed in the survey below, a central estimate is that these two sources of adjustment should be able to limit the required percentage cutback in energy to about half the desired percentage reduction in carbon emissions. On this basis, a 70 percent cut in carbon emissions would require only a 35 percent cut in energy used. Substitution through replacement by other factors (OFES) and shifts in the composition of demand (PS) then must absorb this remaining cutback in energy. These shifts will require some reduction in production. The amount of the output reduction is indicated by the output elasticity of the energy factor. If this elasticity is, say, 0.06 as just suggested, then the 35 percent cutback in energy will require a reduction of approximately 2 percent in GNP. If substitution possibilities in IFFS and NFFS are lower, so that the cutback in energy is greater, or if the substitution possibilities in OFES and PS are lower than revealed by the current energy factor share, then the output loss may be somewhat higher.[7]

---

or β for energy and $1 - \beta$ for the composite other factor). In the less restrictive "constant elasticity of substitution" (CES) function ($Q = \alpha[E^\rho + H^\rho]^{1/\rho}$), neither the factor share nor the output elasticity is constant, but at any particular point the two are equal.

6. Boero et al. (1991, 15) place the energy share at 4 percent. For the United States, in 1988 total expenditure on energy amounted to $406 billion, or 8.3 percent of GNP. However, this figure is a mixture of wholesale and retail concepts. Spending on energy in the residential sector ($146 billion, at an average price of $10.87 per mmBtu) is mainly retail. The commercial sector ($72 billion at $10.87 per mmBtu) and the transportation sector ($141 billion, $6.55 per mmBtu) are mixtures of wholesale and retail. The industrial sector ($90 billion, $4.46 per mmBtu) is wholesale. If the average of industrial and transportation are used to measure wholesale prices and the sectoral estimates are adjusted accordingly, at the wholesale level spending in 1988 amounted to $321 billion, or 6.6 percent of GNP (US Department of Energy, Energy Information Administration 1990b, v-vi; *Economic Report of the President*, February 1991, 286).

7. Although the required carbon cutback rises with time, the percentage output loss would

In short, from first principles and from data on the current size of the energy sector in GNP, one may arrive at output losses from carbon cutbacks that are close to the range of estimates generated by the growing body of energy-economic models, as reviewed below. To some extent this similarity reflects the construction of these models around the basic economic principles just outlined. Nonetheless, in view of the diversity of approaches of the models, the type of calculation set forth here provides a useful reality check on the estimated effects.

An additional word is in order concerning the factor shares approach. Several economists have suggested that the damages from global warming are likely to be limited for industrial countries because of the small share of agriculture and other climate-sensitive sectors in their GNP. However, none of these authors seems to have focused on the corresponding point on the cost side: with the energy factor input claiming a relatively limited share of production, there should be relatively small costs from reductions in energy availability. Of course, the diamond-water paradox must be kept in mind on both sides. As cutbacks become larger, induced price increases (for food, for example, in the one case, or energy in the other) can raise the sector's share to levels considerably higher than at the outset.[8]

Carbon Taxes

The economic models typically include an estimate of the carbon tax required to reduce emissions to a target level. Thus, as discussed below, Manne and Richels (1990a) identify $250 per ton of carbon as the tax required to reduce long-run US carbon emissions to 20 percent below their present absolute level; other studies tend to identify rising carbon taxes over time to restrain emissions to a fixed target. In process activity models such as that of Manne-Richels, the tax derives from the difference between the unit cost of the carbon-free backstop technology and that of the carbon-based backstop. In elasticity-oriented models, the tax derives from the proportionate increase in price required to drive down the quantities of energy and carbon demanded.

Carbon taxes of $100 to $400 per ton (numbers that arise in the various models) have a certain shock value, particularly when compared to the price of coal; however, they are more moderate compared with prices of other fossil fuels. Thus, the Congressional Budget Office (CBO 1990, 20–21) calculates that a tax of $100 per ton of carbon amounts to $60 per (short) ton of coal, $1.63 per thousand cubic feet of natural gas, $13 per barrel of oil,

---

not necessarily be greater in the second half of the 21st century than in the first once the influence of new technological alternatives is taken into account.

8. This occurs if the price elasticity of demand (for food) or the elasticity of substitution (for energy in production) is low.

and 30 cents per gallon of gasoline. Relative to estimated year-2000 prices at the producer level (in 1988 dollars), a tax of $100 per ton of carbon amounts to 256 percent for coal, but a much lower 53 percent for natural gas and 49 percent for oil.

The Manne-Richels long-run tax of $250 per ton of carbon is equivalent to 75 cents per gallon of gasoline or $30 per barrel of oil. It is illuminating to consider the following thought experiment. Suppose that OPEC had successfully held prices in the early 1980s, and that the price projections for oil at that time had been realized. By today the price of oil would have been perhaps in the range of $50 per barrel.[9] So the carbon tax under consideration would have the effect of boosting oil prices to the level that many had expected they would reach solely from market developments before the mid-1980s collapse in oil prices. Of course, in that scenario other carbon fuels (especially coal) would have been relatively cheaper than under the carbon tax scenario. Nonetheless, the experiment does suggest that carbon taxes required to arrest global warming may not be so dramatically removed from experience.

It is important to recognize that the carbon tax level does not directly translate into economic loss. The corresponding reduction in GNP (or better, equivalent variation) will depend on the substitution elasticities (or demand elasticities) of the particular model. Thus, sticker shock on carbon taxes should not be interpreted as direct evidence of enormous output loss.

The total output impact and thus the economic cost associated with a given carbon ceiling may be estimated in various ways, all in principle equivalent. In "programming" models, which optimize among various activities subject to constraints, the output sacrifice is measured by the differential between total activity in the absence of the carbon constraint and the lower activity level achievable when the carbon limit is imposed. In production function models (for example, CES) the reduction in output is similarly measured by application of the lower level of the energy factor into the production equation. In models without an explicit production structure, the output impact can still be inferred. In such models, the response of carbon and energy to a carbon tax is typically derived from a price elasticity of demand. This price elasticity in turn should reflect the production opportunity cost of energy. It is possible to integrate across marginal taxes to infer the production cost of the carbon constraint. In all three methods, however, the level of the marginal tax will not necessarily be a good guide to the total economic cost (as in the Manne-Richels model reviewed below).

---

9. In fact, in real terms the 1980 price of some $34 per barrel would amount to $44 per barrel today even without further increases (inflating by the US wholesale price index; International Monetary Fund, *International Financial Statistics*, June 1982, 58; *Yearbook* 1990, 731; April 1991, 553).

Figure 4.1   Carbon taxes, revenues, and economic cost

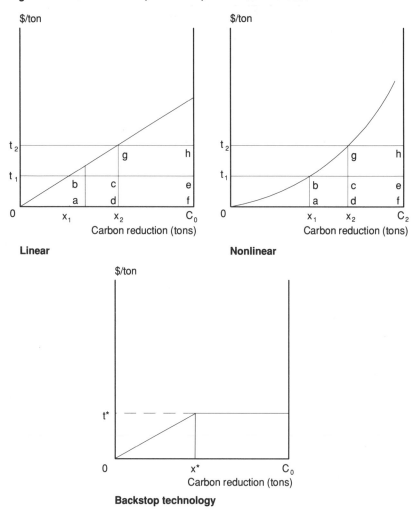

Linear

Nonlinear

Backstop technology

Figure 4.1 illustrates the usual relationship between the carbon tax and its economic cost. The horizontal axis shows the number of tons of carbon (x) cut back from the baseline level (up to a maximum of the entire initial carbon level, C_0). The vertical axis shows the tax (in dollars per ton of carbon) required to achieve the cutback in question. A tax of t_1 will induce a cutback of x_1 tons; a tax of t_2, x_2 tons.

Because firms and consumers will be prepared to part with an extra ton of carbon (and its associated energy) only if the marginal tax equals the opportunity cost of the carbon, in principle the required tax rate should tell the "marginal product" of the extra carbon (energy) at the given level of availability. Thus, at point x_1 the vertical distance t_1 should tell the reduction in GNP that will occur when a single ton of carbon is removed. By summing up, or integrating, all of these vertical slices from the origin to x_1, it is possible to measure the total economic loss caused by the carbon tax. At the same time, it is possible to measure the tax revenue that will be collected: this is equal to the tax rate times the number of tons of carbon that remain in use ($t_1 [C_0 - x_1]$).

In the first panel of figure 4.1, the tax curve is linear. As the tax rate is doubled from t_1 to t_2, the carbon cutback doubles from x_1 to x_2 tons. The economic cost of the tax rises from triangle $0ab$ to triangle $0dg$. Because the triangles are similar, the height and base of triangle $0dg$ are twice the height and base of triangle $0ab$. As a result, the area of the larger triangle is four times that of the smaller triangle. This result is the well-known quadratic relationship of a welfare cost to a tax or tariff distortion.[10] Nordhaus (1990b) strongly emphasizes this nonlinearity of the economic cost of carbon cutbacks to argue that some abatement can be purchased "on the cheap" but that reductions on the scale implied by several of the internationally discussed targets (such as a reduction by 20 percent and subsequent freeze) could be disproportionately expensive relative to the value of the greenhouse damage avoided.

The relationship of the economic cost to the tax revenue may also be seen in figure 4.1. At modest levels of carbon reduction, the economic cost may be only a small fraction of the tax revenue. Thus, for cutback x_1 the economic cost triangle $0ab$ is much smaller than the revenue rectangle $abef$, which is equal to the remaining carbon in use ($C_0 - x_1$) times the tax rate (t_1). However, the economic cost rises with the square of the tax whereas the revenue rises less than proportionately with the tax rate (in the linear case, and eventually begins to decline), so the economic cost becomes progressively larger relative to the tax revenue.

Figure 4.1 also shows two other cases. In the second panel, the tax curve is nonlinear. The less the substitutability between energy and other factors of production, the more steeply nonlinear the tax curve will have to be. It is shown in annex 4A that, even in the case of relative ease of substitutability, with elasticity of substitution equal to unity in the Cobb-Douglas production function, the tax curve (which also equals the marginal product of carbon curve) is nonlinear. In this case the required tax rises more than proportionately with

---

10. See, e.g., Harberger (1974). More generally, if μ is the price elasticity of demand for carbon, the tax t will cause a reduction of $\Delta C = x = (t/p_0)\mu C_0$, where p_0 is the baseline price so that t/p_0 is the percentage price increase. The area of the economic cost triangle (the "welfare cost") is $W = \frac{1}{2}(t \Delta C) = \frac{1}{2} tx = \frac{1}{2}(t)([t/p_0]\mu C_0)$. This expression generates a term that is quadratic in t: $W = \frac{1}{2} t^2 \mu C_0/p_0$. Thus, in the linear tax curve the economic cost rises as the square of the tax rate.

the target cutback in carbon. As in the linear tax curve, the economic cost rises more than proportionately with the tax rate (although in this case the economic cost rises less than quadratically with the tax rate).[11]

The third panel of figure 4.1 shows a wholly different energy-economic structure. In this case there are two backstop technologies at high but constant price, one carbon based and the other carbon free. In the long term the economy must turn to one backstop or the other. Once the tax rises to a level equal to the difference between their two costs, carbon may be cut further in unlimited amounts at no further tax increase. The tax curve turns horizontal (at t^*). In this case, economic cost (the area under the tax curve) rises quadratically with the carbon cutback and tax rate up to the threshold x^* (if the tax curve is linear to that point), but less than quadratically thereafter (and if x^* is small relative to C_0, the relationship is broadly linear—the area of a rectangle as its base increases). In this case, then, the monotonic relationship of the required tax to the target reduction is broken, and so is the generally expected near-quadratic relationship of the economic (welfare) cost to the tax rate or target carbon cutback. Essentially, the technological divorce between carbon cutback and energy cutback permits much smaller relative economic costs for carbon reduction.[12]

As developed in chapter 7, the summary carbon tax function used in the benefit-cost analysis, based on the models surveyed in this chapter, is a linear relationship whereby the long-term carbon tax must be an additional $5 per ton for each extra percentage-point cutback of emissions from baseline, up to a maximum of $250 per ton (based on the Manne-Richels backstop technology discussed below). Because an initial tranche of cutbacks through a move to improved practices may be largely costless (chapter 5), the tax may arguably be necessary only for reductions

---

11. Consider a nonlinear tax curve of the form $t = ax + bx^2$. The economic cost is the integral:

$W = \int (ax + bx^2)\, dx$ from 0 to x, or:

$W = c + a/2\, x^2 + b/3\, x^3$

where c is the constant of integration. Economic cost will thus vary as somewhere between the square and the cube of cutback x. However, the required tax t varies as between x and the square of x. Treating x as the corresponding inverse function (so that x varies as between the 1/1 and the 1/2 power of t), the mapping of W on t will vary as the power (2 to 3)/(1 to 2) with t, and thus less than quadratically but more than linearly.

12. Thus, in the Manne-Richels model examined below, the economic cost of carbon restraints in the United States is 3 percent of GDP in the year 2020 at a carbon tax of $400 per ton and a carbon cutback of 40 percent from baseline; yet the economic loss is still only 3 percent of GDP in the year 2100, when availability of the backstop technology means that the carbon tax need be only $250 per ton, and the cutback is as high as 75 percent from baseline carbon emissions.

beyond that threshold.[13] However, there will be greater assurance that the proper signal is being sent to achieve the initial cost-free cutbacks if it is assumed instead that they too require the presence of the carbon tax. Under the latter interpretation, a reduction of carbon emissions by, for example, 10 percent from the long-term baseline would require a carbon tax of $50 per ton.[14]

Fiscal Effects and Trading

The revenue from a carbon tax would be potentially so large as to have macroeconomic consequences. Consider a tax of $100 per ton, higher than the Jorgenson-Wilcoxen model indicates is necessary for major carbon restraint but lower than the Manne-Richels model estimate. This tax rate would raise revenues on the order of $500 billion annually at the global level, and about $130 billion for the United States (about 2 percent of GDP).

In most cases, it would be desirable to recycle these tax revenues to avoid contractionary pressure on aggregate demand and thus recession.[15] In the case of the United States and other nations with severe fiscal gaps (including many developing countries), it could be appropriate to retain a larger portion of carbon tax revenue in treasury coffers to help in budgetary adjustment. Moreover, where taxation faces ideological opposition, the rationale for carbon taxes as a "user fee" to internalize global externalities could help overcome fiscal impasse.

For that portion of carbon tax revenue recycled to the economy, there would be an efficiency gain. Fiscal systems in industrial countries tend to have a high incidence of deadweight loss, because income, capital, and other taxes discourage effort or risk-taking or otherwise distort incentives (e.g., Whalley and Wigle 1990).[16] The revenue from taxes levied for purposes of carbon abatement could be used to replace the most inefficient existing taxes, in which case there

---

13. In chapter 7, a tax efficiency benefit is attributed to tax revenue. As the calculation seeks to be conservative by not overstating these benefits, it assumes that the tax is not necessary to generate the initial tranche of engineering efficiency gains.

14. The alternative assumption, that the initial cost-free tranche of efficiency gains requires no tax, would generate a carbon emissions cutback of some 30 percent from baseline for a $50 per ton tax, if the costless gains amount to 20 percent of emissions.

15. This contractionary pressure is the chief reason the Congressional Budget Office (1990) estimated that a phase-in of a $100 carbon tax over 10 years for the United States would cause a loss of 2 percent of GDP annually by the second five years. Such estimates reflect primarily the demand-depressing effect of any tax, rather than the production possibility effects of curtailing energy (and carbon-intensive energy in particular). However, for long-term analysis it seems preferable to exclude short-term macroeconomic effects. Keynesian demand reduction overstates the damage, because collected revenue can be returned to the economy.

16. The carbon tax also imposes a burden, but the burden is already accounted for in the calculation of costs of carbon reduction.

could be a supply-side effect of increased investment and labor effort that would cause output gains offsetting a portion of the microefficiency losses from energy curtailment. Jorgenson and Yun (1990) estimate that, for the United States, the marginal efficiency loss from an extra dollar of tax revenue amounts to 38 cents. On this basis, the reduction of other taxes made possible by revenue from the carbon tax would provide an economic benefit on the order of one-third of carbon tax revenue, providing a moderate offset to the costs of carbon reduction.

Similarly, the issue of tradeability can have a powerful impact on the cost estimates. Several of the leading models are country-specific and provide only limited insight into the prospects for cost limitation through trading of emissions quotas among countries. As discussed below, the GREEN model prepared at the Organization for Economic Cooperation and Development (OECD) explicitly allows for trading and finds substantial cost reductions from this additional degree of flexibility.

Afforestation

An alternative to curtailment of carbon emissions is the sequestering of carbon through afforestation. In a long-term perspective, afforestation is only a temporary solution, because net carbon uptake continues only as long as the forest is expanding. Once it is mature, carbon released by dying trees offsets that sequestered by new trees. This option also requires the diversion of considerable land areas. Nonetheless, reduced deforestation and increased afforestation can make an important, low-cost contribution to a strategy of limiting global warming for at least the initial decades, as set forth in chapters 5 and 7. Afforestation can make an even greater contribution over the long term if the resulting forest resources can eventually be put to use as biomass fuel to replace fossil fuel.

Principal Models

Manne and Richels

Alan S. Manne and Richard G. Richels (1990a–d) have provided one of the most influential models of the impact of reductions in carbon emissions. Their model combines process analysis of major individual energy sources with a production function approach and uses nonlinear programming to maximize the discounted value of consumption utility over time subject to specified carbon restraints. The economy is forward looking so that firms and consumers take account of the future in today's decisions.

The model applies a nested production function in which there is unitary elasticity of substitution (Cobb-Douglas function) between capital and labor and between electric and nonelectric energy, and a constant, nonunitary elasticity of substitution between each of these two separate clusters of inputs (i.e., the nonenergy and energy factors).[17] Although the production function form chosen permits output even with energy completely absent, the particular substitution parameters chosen tend to generate a substantial cut in output for a given reduction in energy (as discussed below).

Manne and Richels identify five existing technologies for electric energy (hydro, gas, oil, coal, and nuclear) and four future technologies (advanced combined-cycle gas, new coal-fired, advanced noncarbon high cost, and advanced noncarbon-low cost). For nonelectric energy there are six existing technologies (internationally traded oil, domestic oil at low cost, domestic oil at high cost, coal, gas at low cost, and gas at high cost) and two future technologies (coal-based synthetics and a noncarbon, nonelectric backstop).

The authors do not commit themselves to a specific most likely candidate for the all-important future backstop technologies, noting that they could include "solar, nuclear, biomass, clean coal technologies with CO_2 removal, etc." (Manne and Richels 1990b, 10). They do, however, assign crucial benchmark costs to energy from each source. They place the cost of coal- (or shale-) based synthetics at $10 per mmBtu, thereby capping carbon-based fuel costs at an equivalent of $60 per barrel of oil. Their nonelectric, noncarbon backstop is set at $20 per mmBtu in 1988 dollars, twice as high as the carbon fossil backstop and 10 times as high as the $2 per mmBtu for coal. Of the four types of adjustment outlined at the outset, the Manne-Richels (MR) model gives greatest attention to substitution among energy forms (IFFS and NFFS). Its production function also explicitly models the effect of other factor–energy substitution (OFES). However, the model operates at an aggregate level, and so does not directly measure the fourth type of adjustment, namely, changes in composition of final demand (product substitution, or PS). At best this last influence is implicit in the degree of substitutability assumed between energy and other factors.

For their baseline, Manne and Richels have GDP growth slowing from 2 percent to 1 percent annually by the mid–21st century for the advanced areas of the world—the United States, other OECD (OOECD), and the Soviet Union and Eastern Europe (SUEE) and from 4 percent to 2½ percent over the same period for the rest of the world (ROW, mainly developing countries), with China treated separately and experiencing considerably faster growth initially. The slowdowns are meant to reflect the expected near-stabilization of world population in the

---

17. Specifically, $Y = (a[K^\alpha L^{1-\alpha}]^\rho + b[E^\beta N^{1-\beta}]^\rho)^{1/\rho}$, where Y is real GDP, K is capital, L labor, E electric energy, N nonelectric energy, and the parameter ρ is related to the elasticity of substitution (σ) as follows: $\rho = (\sigma - 1)/\sigma$.

middle of the 21st century. The authors assume that the rate of autonomous energy efficiency improvement (AEEI) is 0.5 percent annually in the United States and OOECD; only 0.25 percent in SUEE because these areas will be "further industrializing before moving toward a service-based economy;" but 1.0 percent in China because of its "enormous potential for efficiency improvements" (Manne and Richels 1990c, 7).[18] The resulting baseline emissions rise from 5.7 GtC annually to 26.9 GtC in the year 2100. The respective shares of the five regions just enumerated (USA, OOECD, SUEE, ROW, China) shift from 22, 23, 26, 18, and 11 percent in 1990 to 15, 16, 12, 35, and 22 percent in 2100. Thus, the combined emissions shares of the developing countries and China rise from 29 percent to 57 percent of the global total.

The authors then set carbon emission ceilings at 1990 levels through the year 2000, and at 20 percent below these levels by the year 2020, for the three advanced regions. They set ceilings at twice the 1990 levels for ROW and China. The overall effect is to permit global emissions to rise to 15 percent above 1990 absolute levels by 2030, and then stabilize at a total of 6.6 GtC annually (versus the 4 GtC or less annually that might be compatible with avoidance of further major atmospheric buildup of carbon dioxide).

To achieve even these limitations requires carbon taxes that gradually rise to quite steep levels before tapering off to a long-term plateau at a uniform global $250 per ton of carbon, equivalent to $30 per barrel of oil or 75 cents per gallon of gasoline. This tax equals the difference between the cost of the carbon-based and the carbon-free backstop technologies, as it is this wedge that must be neutralized for firms and consumers to be willing to adopt the latter alternative. For the United States, the tax reaches even higher levels initially and peaks at $400 per ton in 2020; it then declines as the new technologies come on stream. The highest tax occurs in the Soviet Union and Eastern Europe (some $650 per ton during 2020–2060). The reasons are that the region is assumed to have lesser substitutability in consumption and production (the elasticity of substitution between energy and nonenergy factors is set at 0.4 in the United States and OOECD but only 0.3 elsewhere) and lesser availability of alternative energy sources (oil, gas, nuclear) than in the OECD. In contrast, the tax never exceeds the long-run $250 for China.

The economic cost of carbon limits rises gradually to a plateau of 3 percent of GDP for the United States and holds at about this level for 2030–2100. For the rest of the OECD a parallel plateau holds at about 2 percent of GDP; the plateau is lower because of relatively larger undiscovered oil and gas resources as well as a larger nuclear power industry. GDP losses reach over 4 percent in 2030–2040 in SUEE before stabilizing at 3 percent (for the same reasons noted for the

---

18. Note that the influence of rising technical efficiency is incorporated through a shift over time in the parameter b in the production function reported above.

high tax). Losses are low for ROW through 2030 (with abundant oil permitting avoidance of coal, and with more generous carbon ceilings) but reach 5 percent of GDP by 2100.

The largest losses occur in China, reaching 8 percent of GDP by 2040 and rising to 10 percent by 2100. The high cost arises because "China's fossil fuel resource base is dominated by coal [and] it will be costly to accept any constraints on carbon emissions." The authors leave unexplained why the costs are so much higher for China but the required taxes are not; however, this divergence confirms the point made above that there is no automatic mapping between the two. In alternative simulations, the authors find that, if China is permitted to quadruple its emissions, its GDP costs can be held close to zero through the mid-21st century but still reach 8 percent of GDP by 2100. In that scenario, however, world emissions reach 7.9 GtC instead of 6.6 GtC.

An important limitation of the MR model is its lack of modeling of trade, either in production or in energy resources (except for exogenously specified "bounds on the willingness of each region to import or export oil," Manne and Richels 1990c, 3) which have the anomalous effect of causing a price divergence between imported and domestic oil. Each region essentially maximizes using its own resources. In principle the option of trade would permit achievement of the same targets at lower world output cost. Similarly, the model does not incorporate terms of trade. Thus, it may understate the costs to ROW (which includes OPEC) if adjustment occurs through consumption taxes imposed in the OECD.

A key element in the MR cost estimates is the AEEI. At a global average of only 0.4 percent (weighting by base-year world carbon shares), this parameter means that the baseline emissions would be expected to reach considerably higher levels than if the AEEI were set at, for example, 1 percent annually, as in most applications of the Edmonds-Reilly model (discussed below).[19] With a higher baseline, there is a greater and more costly task involved in reducing carbon emissions to the target level.

Perhaps the most important assumption of the model, however, is the cost of the carbon and noncarbon backstop technologies. A first point to recognize about the backstop cost is that it is essentially arbitrary, as is hinted by the fact

---

19. Unfortunately, the comparisons are not quite this simple. Thus, in contrast to the MR global emissions of 14.6 GtC in 2050, the Edmonds-Reilly model generates 7.7 to 10.7 GtC for that year if "median" parameters are used, but 15.4 to 18.7 GtC if "mean" parameters are applied even though in both cases the AEEI is 1 percent annually in all regions (Reilly et al. 1987, 16). Similarly, in the Edmonds-Barns version of the model, reviewed below, global emissions in 2050 stand at 14.2 GtC, almost the same level as in the MR results. Note that these comparisons cast doubt on a tentative conclusion voiced in recent sessions of the Stanford-based Energy Modeling Forum: that the differences in the two models' baselines derive mainly from differences in the AEEI. This inference may apply to the United States, but it does not hold for the global estimates.

that the authors do not single out a specific technology that they expect will fulfill this task. A second point is that the backstop cost is inherently open to critique. Thus, Darmstadter (1991) suggests that the figure of $20 per mmBtu is too high,[20] whereas Jae Edmonds (personal communication) has noted that the MR model may be relatively optimistic by postulating any backstop at fixed cost.

A third important feature of this approach is that it sets an absolute limit on the carbon tax required. Without the backstop, the tax would tend to continue rising over time to close the ever-widening gap between the unlimited and the limited emissions levels.

Additional detail in the MR model for the United States provides a further feel for the workings of the model. In a pessimistic variant with AEEI = 0, the US model shows that by 2030 the carbon restraint would cause a 43 percent reduction in electric energy and a 21 percent reduction in nonelectric energy from baseline (Manne and Richels 1990a, figure 5). Even these levels of energy output could only be achieved with major intrafossil and nonfossil fuel substitution. Thus, in the absence of carbon limits, by 2030 electric energy would be almost wholly from coal (except for a small fraction from hydro). Under the limits, only about one-third would be from coal; one-third would come from "advanced high cost" sources (e.g., photovoltaic), and about one-fifth from natural gas. In the case of nonelectric energy, in 2030 about two-fifths would come from oil (mainly imported) with or without carbon limits. However, the remainder would come primarily from carbon-based synthetics in the absence of limits, but instead would come largely from the nonelectric backstop under the carbon constraints.

Thus, the model relies modestly on IFFS and heavily on NFFS to limit the carbon content of energy. It also achieves a considerable part of the adjustment through OFES—the reduction of energy relative to other factors. The illustration just given involves a cut in all energy by about one-third, at a cost of a 5 percent reduction in production (pessimistic variant). The implied elasticity of output with respect to energy is one-sixth. As this implicit parameter is more than twice the factor share of energy in the US economy, one suspects that the output effect in the MR model is if anything biased toward overstatement of the adverse effect. That

---

20. As does R. H. Williams, cited in Boero et al. (1991, 92). Williams argues that the relevant comparison for noncarbon versus carbon backstop for nonelectric energy is not between synthetic oil and gas versus biomass and hydrogen, as assumed by Manne and Richels (at $10 per mmBtu versus $20 per mmBtu, respectively), but methanol from coal versus methanol from biomass. Williams estimates the latter costs at $11.40 per mmBtu and $16.20 per mmBtu, respectively, even with current technology, so that the opportunity cost of enforcing the noncarbon backstop is only $4.80 per mmBtu, or less than half the MR figure. The corresponding implication is that the long-term carbon tax need be only about $120 rather than $250.

is, as set forth above, the output elasticity of a factor (energy) is usually expected to equal its share in output. Application of energy's income share (6 percent) to the projected cutback in energy (about 30 percent) would imply a GDP loss of about 2 percent rather than the model's estimated 3 percent (central variant).

Similarly, in terms of the model itself, the use of a substitution elasticity of 0.4 between energy and other factors may tend to be downward biased. As the authors note, conceptually this elasticity is approximately the absolute value of the price elasticity of demand for energy. For the long term one might have thought that this price elasticity would be close to unity rather than as low as 0.4. Considering that the model when applied internationally uses an even lower substitution elasticity (0.3), the relatively high output costs estimated for non–OECD areas may be especially overstated.

Edmonds-Reilly et al.

Another highly influential model is that originally prepared by Edmonds and Reilly (1983a, 1983b, 1986; Reilly et al. 1987). The ER model is essentially an energy-carbon accounting framework that tells the amount of emissions by major world region at 25-year intervals from 1975 to 2100.

The model is unique in that its original development was directly focused on the issue of carbon emissions. In contrast, most of the other major models were originally designed to examine the impact of energy availability and policy on the economy. These divergent origins help explain the relative strength of the ER model on the energy carbon emissions side and its lesser robustness on the side of impact on the economy.

The model divides the world into nine regions: United States, other OECD west, other OECD Asia, centrally planned Europe, centrally planned Asia, Middle East, Africa, Latin America, and South and East Asia. Energy is divided into nine types: conventional oil, conventional gas, unconventional (synthetic) oil, unconventional gas, coal, biomass, solar electricity, nuclear electricity, and hydroelectricity. The model applies iterative price adjustments to achieve equilibrium between supply and demand for each fuel market in each region. Carbon emissions arise from the equilibrium annual uses of oil, gas, coal, and shale oil.[21] The impact of annual emissions on the atmospheric stock of carbon dioxide depends on the assumed "atmospheric retention ratio," placed at 58 percent in the base case.

For resource-constrained energy sources, supply is determined by a logistics curve that identifies the cumulative fraction of total resource endowment ex-

---

21. The authors' carbon coefficients are, respectively, 19.2, 13.7, 23.8, and 27.9 teragrams per megajoule (1983a, 76; 1986, 170). The relative carbon intensities are close to those identified by the Office of Technology Assessment as noted above.

hausted by a given date. Annual production equals the change in this cumulative fraction multiplied by the total (original) resource stock. Supply for the resource-constrained technologies (conventional gas and oil) does not respond to price, but instead proceeds at a given extrapolative rate over time. Middle Eastern oil is an exception, as OPEC production is specified exogenously.

Each of the other seven energy types is treated as a backstop technology (including coal because of its essentially unlimited supply) with a family of horizontal long-run supply curves at successively higher price levels associated with respective grades, and with an upward sloping short-term supply curve that assesses a cost penalty if output is forced to rise faster than a "normal" rate. Technical change is incorporated in a shift of the long-run cost curve over time.

For each region the price of each energy type depends on world price (and thus on production cost), the transport cost to the region in question, and the tax or subsidy applicable in the region. Only fossil fuels are traded across regions, however. Demand by energy type depends on population, per capita income, income elasticity of demand, price, and price elasticity of demand.

The model includes a feedback parameter to capture the influence of changes in energy *prices* on GDP. The general notion is apparently that an increase in price causes an adverse impact on economic activity. However, this relationship is not explicitly modeled as a production function process, and it implicitly appears to have more the nature of a Keynesian demand effect. The original purpose of this parameter appears to have been primarily to ensure accurate measurement of energy use and carbon emissions rather than quantification of output effects, and the authors state that:

> Even the magnitude of the first order effects are in question, though for most values of expected energy prices, magnitudes of r_y [the GDP feedback elasticity] are expected to be relatively small. (Edmonds and Reilly 1983a, 84)

In their initial analysis, Edmonds and Reilly identified a baseline value of 26.3 GtC for carbon emissions by the year 2050. They estimated that atmospheric doubling (to 580 parts per million for carbon dioxide) would occur by the period 2049–2067. They then simulated the impact of global carbon taxes by applying a tax of 100 percent on coal and lesser taxes commensurate with carbon content for oil (78 percent) and gas (56 percent). Their conclusion was relatively pessimistic: such taxes would only delay the period of concentration doubling by a decade (Edmonds and Reilly 1983b). One reason was the induced supply-demand effect of a carbon tax: the resulting depression of the world price meant some offsetting rise in consumption. Another was that the tax was mild; with coal at the minehead priced at some $25 per ton and containing 0.6 ton of carbon (Congressional Budget Office 1990, 20), a 100 percent tax would amount to only about $65 per ton of carbon even if applied at the consumption level (as in the ER model), far below the MR $250 carbon tax.

In a subsequent study, Edmonds and Reilly conducted sensitivity analyses and found with their median parameters that the baseline for global carbon emissions would be considerably lower, at only 7.7 to 10.7 GtC in the year 2050 (Reilly et al. 1987, 16). However, the subsequent study did not conduct the tax experiment to analyze the scope for delaying atmospheric carbon doubling.

Conveniently available in personal computer form (Edmonds and Reilly 1986), the ER model has attracted a flock of users, each obtaining different results. Applying a heavy "environmental tax" in specific rather than ad valorem form and assuming an optimistic 1½ percent AEEI, Mintzer (1987) concluded that carbon emissions could be cut to some 2 GtC annually through most of the next century, thereby avoiding the bulk of global warming. In contrast, Darmstadter and Edmonds (1989) subsequently concluded that it would be an ambitious task just to freeze emissions at about 5 GtC annually, in part because they considered Mintzer's assumptions about AEEI too high and about per capita income growth too low. However, Darmstadter and Edmonds did not explore the impact of a carbon tax.

I have conducted simulations with the ER model, applying the mean parameters from the authors' 1987 sensitivity study. I estimated that, in the baseline, global emissions would reach 9.6 GtC by 2050 and 11.7 GtC by 2075. However, with taxes set at 150 percent on coal, 100 percent on oil, and 50 percent on gas (consumption level), emissions could be held to under 4 GtC through 2075, thereby delaying the date of atmospheric doubling from 2065 to 2150 (Cline 1989, 41–42).[22] The Congressional Budget Office has also used the ER model to estimate that a carbon tax of $100 per ton imposed multilaterally would delay the date of atmospheric carbon dioxide doubling from 2060 to 2080, and that a tax of $100 rising to $300 could delay the doubling date to 2100 or after (Congressional Budget Office 1990, 63).

About all that can be asked of these uses of the ER model is that they generate a menu of alternative percentage cutbacks in emissions for specified alternative carbon taxes. Even this task is complicated by differing parameter assumptions used by the different authors. As for the corresponding question of the economic cost of alternative emissions reductions, I will argue below that at least the past estimates using the ER model must be interpreted with extreme caution.

The most recent (and presumably most authoritative) estimates of the ER model appear in Edmonds and Barns (1990). The authors examine emissions through the year 2050. Their world population rises from 6.2 billion in 2000

---

22. Also see my 1989 study for more detail on the comparison between Darmstadter-Edmonds and Mintzer.

to 8.6 billion in 2050, following the IPCC assumptions. In their reference case, labor productivity grows at 1.7 percent annually in industrial countries and 2.5 percent annually in developing countries. AEEI is set at 1 percent annually, and energy consumption rises at about 2 percent annually. In the base case, carbon emissions rise from 4.7 GtC per year in 1975 to 14.2 GtC in 2050.

The authors then apply carbon taxes ranging up to $500 per ton of carbon. The taxes are applied at the producer level and are uniform across all regions. Emissions in 2050 fall to 9 GtC with a tax of $100 and to 7 GtC with a tax of $170; they then fall with a gentler slope to 5 GtC with a tax as high as $500 per ton (in 1989 dollars; Edmonds and Barns 1990, figure 4). The authors emphasize that the kink in the response curve indicates substantial sensitivity to tax increases below $170 per ton of carbon, but relative lack of sensitivity at higher tax rates. The reason is that the $170 threshold is sufficient to drive coal out of use, and further carbon savings become more difficult to obtain. They find that a tax of $250 per ton of carbon would stabilize emissions at 6.25 GtC annually by 2050.

The coincidence of the Edmonds-Barns estimates with those of Manne and Richels is noteworthy and to some extent deceptive. Both find that a marginal tax of $250 per ton will stabilize world carbon emissions at about 6½ GtC by the mid-21st century. However, because the ER model has no definitive non-carbon backstop, the tax must keep rising if emissions are to be held constant thereafter. In contrast, the long-term tax in the MR estimates suffices to hold emissions to the specified ceiling even in subsequent decades.

Edmonds and Barns introduce an important improvement in the ER model. They provide an alternative method for estimation of the economic cost of emissions restrictions. In the original model, the only clue to this cost is the change in world GDP calculated by application of the GDP feedback elasticity to the rise in energy prices. However, that method is unsatisfactory. These feedback elasticities (set at -0.1 for industrial countries and -0.2 for developing countries) are at best a stylized representation of the experience of the 1970s and 1980s. But during that period, the energy shocks had primarily short-term Keynesian effects in causing recession. These contractionary demand shocks caused much greater GDP losses than would be the case with wholly anticipated increases in energy prices over the very long term, especially as any energy taxes could (and probably would) be rebated to the system to avoid siphoning off demand. Instead, it is the summation over all microeconomic, production function impacts of higher energy prices that is relevant for long-term analysis. For these reasons it is probably best to discard outright the previous GDP cost estimates made with the ER model.[23]

---

23. Including my own earlier calculation that the carbon tax scenario (150 percent on

The new, alternative method presented in Edmonds and Barns interprets the carbon tax as the marginal cost at any given level of carbon emissions cutback. Thus, a small tax generates a small cutback, and a larger tax a larger cutback. The authors reason that the integral of the area under this "marginal cost curve" provides a valid estimate of the aggregate economic cost of any specified carbon tax emissions cutback scenario—the same logic as set forth in the tax curve analysis above. When they integrate the marginal taxes in their scenario freezing world emissions at 6.2 GtC, they find that total economic cost amounts to $0.1 trillion at 1989 prices by 2025, and $0.7 trillion by 2050. It may be calculated from their assumptions that world GDP stands at $42 trillion in 2025 (at 1989 prices) and at $76 trillion in 2050, so these cost estimates translate into 0.24 percent of GDP in 2025 and 0.93 percent in 2050.[24] Thus, in the best Edmonds-Barns estimates, the emissions freeze scenario imposes economic costs of less than 1 percent of GDP through the first half of the 21st century.[25]

Edmonds and Barns present a highly informative decomposition of the total cutback in emissions into its component parts, similar to the individual substitution effects proposed here. They note the identity:

$$CO_2 = (CO_2/FF) \times (FF/CF) \times (CF/E) \times (E/GNP) \times GNP$$

where FF is fossil fuels, CF is carbonaceous fuel (fossil plus biomass), and E is energy. They then show for alternative tax rates the composition of the reduction in emissions. For example, with a tax rate of $233 per ton of carbon, 23 percent of the cutback is obtained through a reduction in the CO_2/FF ratio; 30 percent from a reduction in FF/CF as the result of massive expansion of biomass (for which net carbon emissions are zero, as noted above); 21 percent from a reduction in CF/E as noncarbon sources of energy replace carbon sources; 21

---

coal, 100 percent on oil, 50 percent on gas) would cost 7.4 percent of world GDP (Cline 1989). My 1989 study already noted skepticism about this estimate and contrasted it with the lower estimate that might be expected on the basis of the energy factor share in GDP. Note that Jorgenson and Wilcoxen (1990b) state simply that "it is impossible to use the [ER] model for analyzing the impact of restrictions on greenhouse gas emissions on US growth."

24. On the basis of data in World Bank, *World Development Report 1989*, and Collins and Rodrik (1991), world GDP in 1989 was $12.2 billion for the Western industrial countries, $2.5 billion for the Soviet Union and Eastern Europe, and $4.2 trillion for developing countries, for a total of $18.9 trillion. The Edmonds-Barns baseline assumes 1.85 percent GDP growth in the first two areas and 3.3 percent growth in the developing countries, yielding the text figures for GDP.

25. The authors also present the alternative cost estimates based on the GDP feedback elasticity, which amount to $1 trillion for 2025 and $4 trillion for 2050, or 2.4 percent and 5.3 percent of GDP, respectively. They present an appendix arguing that, if the elasticity parameters are correct, the two alternative methods should give identical results. For the reasons noted here, however, the marginal tax integration method seems valid, whereas the simple GDP feedback elasticity would appear inappropriate for long-term analysis.

percent from reduction in E/GNP; and 5 percent from an outright cut in GNP (based on the feedback parameter). The first factor (CO_2/FF) corresponds to IFFS as used in this study; the second (FF/CF) and third (CF/E) correspond to NFFS; and the fourth (E/GNP) and fifth (GNP) factors correspond to the effect of OFES.

An implication of the Edmonds-Barns decomposition is that only about one-fifth of the adjustment need come from the suppression of the energy input. The rest can come from reducing the carbon content of energy, with a major contribution from biomass.[26] If the energy compression measure is used as a check on economic cost, and if an output elasticity of 0.06 is applied for energy based on its factor share, then the one-fifth cut in energy should generate a 1.2 percent loss in GNP. This is almost the same as what Edmonds and Barns calculate (0.9 percent GNP loss for 2050) when they use their improved marginal-tax-integration method.

Jorgenson and Wilcoxen

Dale Jorgenson and Peter Wilcoxen (1990b) have provided a third major model of the economic effects of carbon reductions. Their model is only for the United States. However, it has considerable sectoral detail and is well regarded for its consistency with underlying economic theory (Kopp 1991). The principal limitation of the model in its applications so far appears to be the questionable realism of its low baseline projections of economic activity and carbon emissions, and thus its modest estimates of required carbon reductions.

The JW model is a dynamic computable general equilibrium model. Its parameters are econometrically estimated from 1947−85 data, rather than calibrated from a single year as is often the case for such models. There are 35 industrial sectors. For each, the econometrically estimated production function includes an endogenous specification for productivity growth. In general, productivity growth is found to be negatively related to energy prices, so that carbon taxes could slow the rate of technical change.

There are 672 household types. Each household reaches consumption-saving equilibrium by optimizing its "full consumption" (including leisure) over time. Capital is the cumulation of past investment. Labor and capital are completely mobile, so that there is a single wage and a single rate of return across all sectors, and there is no loss of fixed capital when the composition of demand suddenly changes. Substitution in the production process occurs between each pair of

---

26. Note that the percentage share of biomass in carbon reduction rises significantly as the total amount of cutback and the carbon tax rise. Thus, at a tax of $31 per ton of carbon the shift to biomass provides only about 17 percent of the cutback, whereas the share reaches 45 percent of the total reduction at a tax of $498 per ton of carbon (Edmonds and Barns 1990, figure 20).

four factors: labor, capital, energy, and materials. Energy is most easily substituted by materials (substitution elasticity = −1.16), has intermediate substitutability with labor (−0.64), and is least substitutable with capital (−0.15). Intraenergy substitution is relatively high, with the substitution elasticity against coal set at −2.8 for crude oil, −2.1 for refined oil, −2.5 for electricity,[27] and −1.5 for gas utilities.

Unlike most models, that of Jorgenson and Wilcoxen does not project an exogenous baseline for GNP. Instead, GNP is endogenous. The authors project all exogenous variables to 2050 and then freeze these variables so that by 2100 there has been sufficient time for the model to adjust endogenous variables fully. Population is a crucial exogenous variable, and the authors expect US population to reach its peak by 2050. The endowment of skills is also important, and they expect that the average education of the labor force will stabilize by about 2030. Capital is a key endogenous determinant of GNP, and the rate of capital formation depends on initial wealth: if this is low, there is a tendency toward saving and capital accumulation; if high, there can be dissaving.

The net effect of the exogenous population and endogenous capital assumptions is apparently that GNP grows relatively little over the first half of the 21st century. Primarily for this reason, by 2050 the baseline amount of carbon emissions stands at only 1.67 GtC (up from 1.34 GtC in 1990; calculated from Jorgenson and Wilcoxen 1990b, 300), or about 60 percent of the MR baseline level for 2050. Although the study reports estimates for 2100, by its construction the model's meaningful terminus occurs at 2050 (when the freeze to accommodate a forward-looking solution takes place).

The authors conduct three main experiments: a freeze of emissions at the 1990 level; a cut in emissions by the year 2005 to only 80 percent of the 1990 level; and a freeze of emissions at the year-2000 level. The respective carbon taxes required are $15 per ton (equivalent to $9.75 per ton of coal and $2.05 per barrel of oil), $42 per ton, and a mere $6 per ton. The corresponding GNP losses are 0.5 percent, 1.1 percent, and 0.2 percent.

These cost estimates are substantially toward the low end of the field of those obtained from the top-down models. The low estimates are particularly surprising in view of the earlier critique by Hogan and Jorgenson (1991) that the MR estimates were overly optimistic because of failure to take account of the adverse effect of higher energy prices on factor productivity growth. Some have critically attributed the low estimates to an unrealistic assumption of complete

---

27. This specification would appear vulnerable to misleading results, as it raises the question of what fuels will be used to produce "electricity," and the authors do not intend the substitution to be fully (for example) nuclear for coal-based plants. However, in practice this relationship plays little role in the estimates, according to the authors (Peter Wilcoxen, personal communication, 30 April 1991).

capital mobility (Kopp 1991), but that assumption is not unreasonable for an analysis that extends over 50 years. Instead, the primary reason for the low cost estimates appears to be the low baseline for carbon emissions, as discussed above. In the most severe cutback examined, emissions must decline by only 36 percent, from 1.67 GtC in 2100 (also in 2050) to 1.07 GtC (80 percent of the 1990 level). In contrast, in the MR model the percentage cutback from baseline to meet essentially the same target is 63 percent (see table 4.2).

When reexamined in light of the relatively modest cutback, the JW results begin to look more expensive than at first glance. Thus, the ratio of the percentage loss of GNP to the percentage cutback in emissions from baseline in the JW model (1.1/36 = 0.031) is about two-thirds as large as that in the MR model (3.0/63 = 0.048), closer than might be suspected from the size of the GNP effect (one-third as large).

The details of the JW results also provide some surprises. In the most extreme experiment, the 36 percent cut in carbon is accomplished largely by a 31 percent reduction in energy (as measured in Btus). This impact is relatively severe and suggests little scope for IFFS and NFFS in the model despite the seemingly high intraenergy substitution elasticities. Thus, the ratio of the energy cut to the carbon reduction is far higher in the JW model (31/36 = 0.86) than in the ER model (where, as outlined above, the cutback in energy accounts for only 21 percent of the carbon reduction). The implied ease of maintaining output without energy is greater than might be suspected from the factor-energy substitution elasticities reported by the authors. Indeed, in the JW case, the decline in output is only about half as large as would be expected by applying the percentage reduction in energy to the factor share of energy in GNP (31 percent × 0.06 = 1.86 percent).

Product substitution also appears to play little role in the JW results, suggesting that its omission in other models may not make much difference. In the most severe experiment, the only sectors that show major changes are the ones directly involved in energy: coal (− 60 percent change in output), crude oil and natural gas production (− 8 percent), oil refining (− 5 percent), and gas utilities (− 4 percent; Jorgenson and Wilcoxen 1990b, 304). Otherwise the changes are all limited. The only increases occur in agriculture (1 percent), food (3 percent), tobacco (2 percent), and "other services" (½ percent). All other sectors show small reductions (the largest being a decline of 2 percent in chemicals).[28]

---

28. Note that the JW sectoral results cast doubt on the those estimated earlier by the Congressional Budget Office using the same JW model. In that study, it was estimated (for example) that a $100 tax on carbon would increase production of apparel, textiles, leather, and paper by about 10 percent (Congressional Budget Office 1990, 41). Considering the important role of petroleum feedstocks in textile fiber production, these earlier results were curious in their own right.

Finally, Jorgenson and Wilcoxen also conduct experiments applying an energy tax (on Btu) and an ad valorem tax rather than a carbon tax. As would be expected, both alternatives require greater reductions in GNP to meet carbon reduction targets than does the more targeted carbon tax. To cut long-run carbon emissions by 19.6 percent requires a loss of 0.5 percent of GNP. To achieve the same cutback requires a GNP sacrifice of 0.6 percent using the Btu tax, and 1.0 percent of GNP using the ad valorem energy tax.

The efficiency difference appears small for the Btu versus the carbon tax and warrants further investigation in view of the possibility that political pressures from coal mining interests in particular (and arguments for "fairness") might impede the implementation of a carbon tax.[29] The relatively close results from the carbon and Btu taxes (as opposed to the greater costs of the ad valorem tax on energy) would seem to stem from the limited scope in the JW model for substitution to non-carbon-emitting sources of energy and the resulting close adherence of energy use to carbon emissions. In contrast, the ER model with its large scope for switching to biomass and other non-carbon-emitting energy sources would be likely to show a greater cost penalty from the use of a Btu tax than from a direct carbon tax for the purpose of reducing carbon emissions.

In a sense, the most profound implication of the JW study is that the greenhouse problem is one that calls for painful solutions primarily for the developing countries. In the JW world, economic growth and increases in carbon emissions will be so modest in the industrial countries that these nations will not have to cut emissions by much; the massive cutbacks from baselines will need to occur only where those baselines will be much higher in the future than today—that is, in the developing countries. However, most projections have higher baselines for the United States (and other industrial countries), making the problem one that is shared more fully by both North and South.

Nordhaus

William D. Nordhaus has provided a series of analyses of the economics of greenhouse policy over more than a decade (Nordhaus 1976, 1979, 1990a, 1990b; Nordhaus and Yohe 1983). His recent, highly influential approach has stressed that all greenhouse gases must be considered jointly, and that by far

---

29. The US coal mining industry employs 163,000 workers (*U.S. Industrial Outlook*, 1990). This figure is much closer to the 70,000 employed in footwear, which has been unable to secure protection against imports, than to the 1.8 million employed in textiles and apparel, which have successfully obtained protection (but not as much as representatives of the two industries would like). It is thus not evident that coal interests could successfully block a carbon tax if there were a broad public perception that such a measure had a high environmental priority.

the least costly reduction in these gases should come from the already-planned phaseout of chlorofluorocarbons (CFCs).[30] Nordhaus is the one analyst who has also attempted to complete the benefits side of the calculus by considering the prospective greenhouse damages avoided. His findings (1991a) point to a minimal course of action limited largely to CFC elimination, on the grounds that his estimate of damage from global warming is small and warrants little cost for preventive measures.

Nordhaus's early work (1976) examined least-cost reduction of carbon dioxide emissions using a multicountry mathematical programming model. Subsequently Nordhaus and Yohe (1983) examined sensitivity to alternative assumptions. The relatively aggregative model version designed for this purpose (in view of computational limits) considers the world as a whole, with two types of energy: carbon and noncarbon. There are two productive factors: energy and labor. Overall productivity rises over time through the combined influences of technical change and implicit capital deepening. Carbon emissions are based on weighted averages from present and future expected composition of fossil fuels (with rising emissions relative to Btu because of a prospective shift toward coal and shale). The output effect of reducing carbon emissions is traced by a production function with an elasticity of substitution of -0.7 for energy versus labor (equal as well to the price elasticity of demand for energy), and -1.2 for carbon versus noncarbon energy (central estimates).[31]

The baseline price of noncarbon energy depends on technical change and is drawn from existing energy studies. The price of carbon-based energy depends

---

30. The findings of the IPCC (1990a) should give one pause about the scope for mitigating the greenhouse problem through the fortuitous coincidence that nations have agreed to eliminate CFCs for other reasons (namely, to halt stratospheric ozone depletion). The IPCC estimates show that, under business as usual (incorporating partial fulfillment of the earlier Montreal Protocol calling for a 50 percent cut in CFCs), with total radiative forcing rising from 2.95 wm^{-2} in 2000 to 9.9 wm^{-2} in 2100, the contribution of CFCs is an increase from 0.25 wm^{-2} to 0.53 wm^{-2}, or only 4 percent of the total increment (IPCC 1990a, table 2.7). The complete phaseout of CFCs (in accordance with the subsequent London Protocol) would at most provide approximately a 5 percent cut in baseline greenhouse gas radiative forcing (0.53/9.9), less than half the 11 percent cut estimated by Nordhaus (1990b, 33). The CFC solution is even less promising if account is taken of the 1991 scientific findings that CFCs may be neutral for warming because of their side effect of stripping ozone, another greenhouse gas (see chapter 1 of this study).

31. The production function is:

$$Q = A L^d [bC^r + (1 - b)N^r]^{(1 - d)/r}$$

where Q is output, A incorporates technical change and capital, L is labor, C is fossil fuel energy, N is nonfossil energy, d is the share of labor (including capital) in GNP, $1 - d$ is the share of energy in GNP, and b is the fraction of energy supplied by fossil sources. The terms A and d evolve over time (Nordhaus and Yohe 1983, 102). Note that the authors also apply higher and lower elasticities.

on technical change and resource depletion, and in addition contains a term for taxation. The impact of a carbon tax arises through the resulting rise in the ratio of carbon to noncarbon energy prices, the induced shift from the former source to the latter, the resulting reduction in the overall energy input, and the consequent decline in output as less energy is available to work with labor (and capital).

In the base case projections, world population grows at 1.7 percent annually through 2000, 1.1 percent from 2000 to 2025, and 0.3 percent thereafter. Labor productivity rises at 2.3 percent, 1.6 percent, and 1 percent annually in these respective periods, and noncarbon energy prices rise at 0.6 percent, 0 percent, and 0 percent annually in the same periods. The central projections show global carbon emissions rising from 5.5 GtC in 2000 (a figure now outdated) to 13.3 GtC in 2050 and 20 GtC by 2100. Nordhaus and Yohe show, however, that a wide range of outcomes is possible as the result of changing assumptions about parameters or exogenous variable growth rates. The authors simulate the impact of alternative carbon taxes, and in their highest tax scenario ($68 per ton of coal-equivalent in 2040 and $90 by 2060 and after, or $97 and $129, respectively, per ton of carbon-equivalent), carbon emissions fall 41 percent from baseline in 2050 and 30 percent from baseline in 2100 (table 4.2).

The Nordhaus-Yohe (NY) estimates of required taxes per percentage-point reduction in emissions from baseline are higher than those of Jorgenson and Wilcoxen, but lower than the corresponding MR and Edmonds-Barns estimates. Thus, for 2050, the marginal tax per ton of carbon per percentage-point cutback from baseline amounts to $5.9 in the MR model (world), $4.9 in the ER model, $2.8 in the NY model, and $1.2 in the JW model (calculated from table 4.2).

In Nordhaus's more recent work (1990b), he has extended the analysis to incorporate global output costs, other greenhouse gases, and the "benefits" side of the policy equation (greenhouse damage avoided). As a central part of this analysis, Nordhaus first provides a synthesis of the carbon tax estimates by several existing models, including three of his own, the MR model, the ER model, studies for the Netherlands, and studies by Robert Williams. Nordhaus provides a scatter diagram suggesting relatively close adherence of these various sources to a central curve showing marginal carbon taxes (horizontal axis) against percentage cutback of emissions from baseline (vertical axis). The curve is substantially nonlinear; thus, the tax must rise by only $25 per ton of carbon to obtain an extra 10 percent cutback in emissions when starting at a 20 percent cutback; but an extra $75 tax per ton of carbon is required for the same result when starting already at a 70 percent cutback (see table 4.2). Nordhaus stresses that, when the marginal cost is considered, even the process-engineering studies (that for the Netherlands and the Williams estimates) show comparable costs (i.e., they lie close to the central curve) despite their much lower average costs for initial emissions reductions.

Table 4.1   Nordhaus cost function for greenhouse gas reduction

Carbon dioxide		All greenhouse gases, CO$_2$ equivalent		
Percentage reduction	Carbon tax (dollars per ton)	Percentage reduction	Percentage CO$_2$ cut	Cost (percentages of GNP)
6	13			
10	20	10	n.a.	n.a.
		17	6	0.03
20	45	20	n.a.	0.05
30	67	30	n.a.	0.25
40	98	40	n.a.	0.5
50	131	50	≈50	1.0
60	170	60	≈60	1.7
70	225	70	≈70	2.5
80	300	80	≈80	3.9
90	448	90	≈90	n.a.

n.a. = not available; CO$_2$ = carbon dioxide.

Source: William D. Nordhaus. 1990. "To Slow or Not to Slow: The Economics of the Greenhouse Effect." New Haven: Yale University (mimeographed, 5 February).

Table 4.1 reports the Nordhaus synthesis in the first two columns. Thus, to achieve a 50 percent reduction in carbon emissions from baseline, a tax of $131 per ton of carbon (in 1989 dollars) is required.[32] Note that the cost curve has no time dimension, whereas costs might be expected to fall over time with a widening menu of technological alternatives (as examined below). Note also that the Manne-Richels "observations" on the cost curve are somewhat misleading. As the MR model has a constant long-term marginal tax for carbon cutbacks at $250 per ton, its observations should plot a vertical line at $250, rather than adhering to the Nordhaus summary curve (abstracting from the temporary bulge in the MR taxes before backstop technology becomes available).

Nordhaus then integrates the carbon dioxide analysis with consideration of other trace gases. For this purpose, he adopts a time-discounted equivalence of carbon dioxide with other trace gases, taking account of atmospheric residency as well as radiative forcing (infrared blocking) power.[33] As analyzed in detail in annex 7A of this study, Nordhaus then estimates the benefits of avoiding damage from global warming, and identifies the optimal amount of cutback in emissions of greenhouse gases, where marginal benefits equal marginal costs.

---

32. The schedule shown by the first two columns of table 4.2 generates the following least-squares regression line:

$\ln (1 - y) = -0.00338 - 0.00528\ T$

where T is the carbon tax per ton and y is the proportionate reduction in emissions.

33. Nordhaus's finding is that carbon dioxide accounts for about 95 percent of total trace gas equivalence when analyzed in this manner. This share is considerably higher than that subsequently identified by the IPCC, which shows carbon dioxide contributing a steady two-thirds of radiative forcing through the 21st century (IPCC 1990a, table 2.7, 61).

It is possible to derive from the Nordhaus cost estimates a schedule of percentage cutbacks in carbon emissions and corresponding economic costs in percentages of GNP. The last three columns of table 4.1 summarize these estimates. For high values of greenhouse gas cutback, the percentage reduction in carbon dioxide is approximately equal to that for greenhouse gases overall. It is in these ranges that one finds the cutbacks conceptually comparable to those in the MR and ER studies for stabilization in global emissions.

Thus, for the year 2050 it would require a 49 percent cut from the Nordhaus baseline to limit carbon emissions to the 6½-GtC range examined both by Manne and Richels and by Edmonds and Reilly. As this cut would be approximately equal to a 50 percent greenhouse gas cut in the Nordhaus efficient strategy, his estimated output cost amounts to 1.0 percent of world GNP (table 4.1). If 2100 is considered, a cut of carbon emissions from baseline to this same ceiling would require a 68 percent reduction. Interpolating from table 4.1, the resulting cost in output would amount to 2.3 percent of global GNP.

The Nordhaus cost estimates are thus modestly lower than those of Manne and Richels for the same cutbacks. They appear to be extremely close to those of Edmonds and Barns (tax integration method) for 2050. Like Edmonds and Barns (and unlike Manne and Richels), the Nordhaus method yields rising percentage of GNP costs for a rising percentage cutback from baseline, and if the Edmonds-Barns estimates extended to 2100 they might find something like the 2.3 percent of GNP cost estimate implied by the Nordhaus estimates for a freeze in the vicinity of 6½ GtC annual emissions. Both Edmonds and Barns and Nordhaus thus imply that holding a constant absolute carbon emissions level over the distant future as world GNP rises will require costs that are a rising rather than constant percentage of global GNP.[34]

From a broader perspective, the Nordhaus cost estimates fit comfortably into the general parameters discussed above. The NY production model has the same framework as set forth here: the impact of reducing energy will be determined by the initial factor share of energy, which tells the elasticity of output with respect to the energy factor. Indeed, the moderate Nordhaus estimates are somewhat surprising in view of the lack of IFFS in this version of his model.[35] As will be examined below, however, the central point about the Nordhaus analysis is that it counsels very limited action on the greenhouse problem not primarily

---

34. This point is immediately implicit from the Nordhaus carbon tax–percentage cutback synthesis curve. Because the percentage cutback in emissions from baseline must rise over time when an absolute emissions ceiling is sought in the face of growing world GNP and emissions, the marginal tax is also rising if this curve is valid (but note again the MR exception to the curve).

35. However, this influence may be counteracted by the relative ease of substitution between labor and energy in the NY production function, which is Cobb-Douglas and has unitary elasticity of substitution.

because it identifies unusually high costs of abatement, but because it arrives at small estimates of the benefits of abatement that do not warrant much disruption of the economy.

Whalley and Wigle

Few of the models of economic effects of carbon limits investigate the implications of alternative forms of the carbon tax, and most models make little explicit provision for international trade effects. Whalley and Wigle (1990) use a computable general equilibrium model to incorporate both of these aspects. They emphasize the finding that carbon tax revenues are potentially enormous, as are the distributive implications of alternative tax designs.

The Whalley-Wigle (WW) model divides the world into six regions: European Community, North America, Japan, other OECD, oil exporters, and rest of world (ROW, which includes the centrally planned economies). Each area has endowments of four resources: carbon energy resources, noncarbon energy resources, sector-specific factors in energy-intensive manufactures, and other primary factors. There are five "products": carbon energy, noncarbon energy, composite energy, energy-intensive goods, and other goods. The model uses CES production functions at each of three stages of output: production of carbon or noncarbon energy from primary factors and respective energy resources; production of composite energy from carbon and noncarbon energy; and production of energy-intensive goods (primary metals, glass, ceramics, and other basic manufactures) and other goods from primary factors, energy, and sector-specific factors. The highly aggregative model treats all carbon energy as uniform, thereby ruling out IFFS. Its noncarbon energy is limited to relatively small amounts of hydroelectric, nuclear, and solar, thereby probably understating NFFS from such potentially important future sources as biomass.

Whalley and Wigle specify a supply elasticity of 0.5 for carbon energy and 0.3 for noncarbon. Their elasticity of substitution between the two in production of composite energy is 1.0. The elasticity of substitution in final demand between composite energy and the energy-intensive and "other" goods is set at 0.5.

The authors conduct their analysis using discounted present values (at a 5 percent annual real rate) over the 40-year period from 1990 to 2030. Their baseline projects annual GNP growth at 2.7 percent in ROW, 2.5 percent in the oil-exporting area, and 2.3 percent elsewhere. The discounted global GNP cumulated over the period is approximately $450 trillion. Whalley and Wigle estimate the corresponding discounted value of the carbon energy base at $43 trillion. This base of 10 percent of GNP for carbon energy appears somewhat on the high side, considering the GNP share of only 6 percent for all sources of energy suggested above. If so, the economic costs of cutbacks are likely to be overstated.

Whalley and Wigle conduct three main experiments, each designed to reduce carbon emissions by 50 percent from baseline over the full 40-year period: a producer tax, a consumer tax, and an internationally levied tax with revenues redistributed in proportion to population. In all three cases, the tax required to achieve the 50 percent emissions cut is an average of about $440 per ton of carbon. Global economic costs are approximately the same in all three alternatives. Under either a production or a consumption tax, the cost is 4.4 percent of world GNP. Under a globally (rather than nationally) collected tax, losses are 4.2 percent of GNP.

Whalley and Wigle emphasize the distributional implications of their findings, which depend crucially on the tax mode implemented. Thus, in the consumption tax variant it is the oil-producing countries that suffer disproportionately (18.7 percent of GNP loss). Conversely, these countries experience large gains when the modality is a production tax (4.5 percent of GNP), as they are able to levy the tax on foreign consumers of their exported oil. North America experiences the largest loss under the global tax variant (9.8 percent of GNP), as revenue is redistributed toward other (primarily developing) countries. Importantly, this loss stems not from forgone production but from the outright income transfer involved in the large carbon tax revenue reallocated abroad. In the aggregate, the potential international transfers associated with the carbon tax reach as high as 10 percent of global GNP. This powerful redistributive base permits the income of the developing countries to rise by 1.8 percent in the global tax case, even though global income falls 4.2 percent.

Among the three alternatives, global political feasibility would seem by far the greatest for the consumption tax. Legislatures imposing a carbon tax are likely to want to control and use its proceeds for their own countries. A global tax imposed by an international agency and redistributed by population shares is highly improbable, especially in view of past unwillingness of industrial countries to provide large concessional flows. As for the production tax variant, it would require strong discipline on the part of OPEC, as individual members would have a temptation to cut the tax and gain market share. Nonetheless, some combination of the producer and the consumer tax may be required for an arrangement acceptable to all parties; otherwise one group would tend to end up making major transfers to the other.

For purposes of this survey, the Whalley-Wigle (WW) estimates of global cost are of the most direct interest. The model yields cost estimates that are on the high side, approximately twice the 2 percent of GNP figure suggested at the outset. The high cost would appear to stem primarily from the absence of intrafossil fuel substitution (IFFS) and the very limited scope for nonfossil fuel substitution (NFFS) as the consequence of the low supply elasticity for noncarbon energy and its low initial share. As a result of this lack of flexibility, the 50 percent cut in carbon emissions requires a 47 percent reduction in total energy. The WW model is thus extremely pessimistic on the scope for addressing the problem through reducing the carbon content of energy rather than energy itself. Whereas Whalley and Wigle calculate that 94 percent (47/50) of carbon reduction must come from energy reduction, Edmonds and Barns place this fraction at only 21 percent (as discussed above). It is no surprise that the much greater relative cutbacks required in energy yield a larger relative impact on production and economic cost.[36]

The WW results are also on the high side for the carbon tax, almost twice as high as the MR long-term tax of $250 per ton. The authors calculate that their tax of $440 per ton is equivalent to a "gross" tax of more than 85 percent, such that a dollar spent on a ton of carbon contains more than 85 cents of tax (on a net tax basis, the rate is over 500 percent, or 85/15). One explanation for the high rate is the model's rigidity in providing low- or noncarbon sources of energy. However, an additional reason may be the model's treatment of shifting of the tax burden. The incidence depends on the elasticity of supply of the carbon resource. If supply is highly inelastic, the principal effect of the tax is to seize rent from fossil fuel producers, rather than to raise prices to consumers and cut back the use of carbon fuels. If instead the supply elasticity is high, it is consumers that primarily bear the tax through higher prices, with a correspondingly larger effect in reducing carbon emissions. One suspects that the use of an intermediate supply elasticity means that relatively high taxes must be imposed because a substantial portion of their effect is being neutralized by rent redistribution away from producers.

The WW model also shows changes in trade patterns under a carbon tax. The oil-exporting region stops importing energy-intensive manufactures and starts exporting them, whereas Europe and Japan do the reverse. The implication is that the relative scarcity of energy rises in Europe and Japan after the imposition of carbon taxes, although the authors provide little explanation of this outcome. Nor do they simulate the model prohibiting changes in interregional trade to permit identification of the extent to which trade in goods facilitates achievement of carbon reductions.

Whalley and Wigle include a final simulation in which carbon emissions per capita must be equalized in achieving the 50 percent cutback. This variant imposes drastic losses on industrial countries (18.6 percent of GNP in the United States) and globally (8.5 percent), although it does limit the losses of the de-

---

36. Note also, however, that the economic cost concept used by Whalley and Wigle is Hicksian equivalent variation. This welfare measure takes account of changing relative scarcities and relative prices, and tends to give larger proportionate reductions than does GDP, which is an index of the volume of production at constant relative prices.

veloping countries (to 1.2 percent of GNP versus 6.8 percent in the consumption tax case). The global tax with reallocation by population would be better for both developing and industrial countries than a regime requiring per capita emissions equalization.

In sum, the WW results tend to flank the other models on the high side with respect to global average output effects; they suggest that taxes may need to be higher than indicated in most models when tax burden shifting is taken into account; and they provide dramatic estimates of the potential redistributive effects of a carbon tax, thereby calling attention to the importance of the design and modality of the tax.

OECD-GREEN

Analysts at the OECD have completed preliminary work on a dynamic general equilibrium model called GREEN (Burniaux et al. 1991a; technical details in Burniaux et al. 1991b). The model analyzes the period up through 2020. It divides the world into seven regions: North America, OECD-Europe, OECD-Pacific, the Soviet Union, China, energy-exporting less developed countries (EELDCS), and rest of world). The model has five energy sectors (coal, natural gas, crude oil, refined petroleum, and electricity—the only noncarbon energy source) and three nonenergy product sectors (agriculture, energy-intensive manufactures, and other goods and services). Households allocate their income between consumption in four goods (food, fuel, transport and communication, other goods and services) and saving. Primary factors include labor, agricultural land, new capital, sector-specific old capital, and sector-specific fixed factors for each of the fuel sectors.

The individual energy sectors produce composite energy through a CES production function.[37] There is a composite "factor" from a CES combination of capital and sector-specific factors. These two composites merge (CES) for a next-tier composite of capital and energy, which in turn merges again (CES) with labor at a subsequent tier to form a composite input. At the final tier of production, the composite input produces output subject to a (Leontief) input-output structure that takes account of intermediate materials.

Coal has an almost infinite supply elasticity in the model. Oil and gas have finite resources, but the resource base has some response to price. The noncarbon energy source (electricity) has a relatively low supply elasticity (0.2). Interregional trade is modeled with imperfect substitution between goods from different

---

37. The elasticity of substitution among alternative energy types is a crucial parameter in determining the level of carbon emissions in GREEN. In the model version examined here, there is no allowance for the potential of backstop technologies in curbing emissions, although these were to be included in a subsequent version of the model.

areas (the "Armington assumption"), except for crude oil, which is homogeneous. The EELDCS are assumed to set the world oil price, and other regions behave as price-takers.

The OECD authors project a baseline carbon emissions growth of 2 percent annually, under assumed energy efficiency growth (AEEI) of 1 percent annually in all regions. World emissions thus reach 10 GtC by 2020. The model's benchmark data (which refer to 1985) provide illuminating facts such as heavy reliance on coal in China (87 percent of emissions) and ROW (mainly India and Eastern Europe, 70 percent of emissions) but lesser reliance elsewhere (34 percent in North America, 42 percent worldwide). The data identify major interregional divergences in existing prices of fossil fuels, which range from 22 in the Soviet Union and 49 in China to 132 in Europe and 144 in OECD-Pacific, on an index in which the North American price equals 100. These price distortions play an important role in determining the levels of the carbon taxes across regions.

Burniaux et al. then simulate the effect of a carbon constraint that requires the OECD countries and the Soviet Union to cut emissions to 80 percent of 1990 levels by 2010 and freeze their level thereafter, and similarly imposes a post-2010 freeze after permitting a 50 percent increase in the EELDCS and China (ROW is not modeled). The aggregate effect is to freeze global emissions at the 1990 level through 2020. In each region, the carbon tax is computed on a basis of the equilibrium price of carbon that achieves the required emissions constraint.[38]

The carbon taxes rise persistently over time because of the widening gap to be closed between unrestrained and restrained emissions. For the year 2020, the global average carbon tax amounts to $215 per ton of carbon (1985 dollars), in the same range as the long-run MR tax. The tax stands at about $210 per ton in North America, Europe, and the EELDCS, but reaches as high as $955 per ton in OECD-Pacific. For the OECD on average the tax is $308 per ton, or $30 per barrel of oil. In contrast, the tax is only $63 per ton in China and $101 per ton in the Soviet Union.[39]

Carbon tax revenues in 2020 amount to 3.7 percent of GDP in North America, 4.9 percent in Europe, 5.6 percent in OECD-Pacific, 4.6 percent in the EELDCS, 4.2 percent in China, and 6.6 percent in the Soviet Union. These preliminary estimates confirm the point made by Whalley and Wigle that carbon tax revenues could be enormous.[40]

---

38. This price is the shadow price obtained in dynamic programming optimization subject to the carbon constraint. The carbon tax is applied at the level of consumers of *primary* fuels, thereby avoiding distortions between domestic and imported fuels.

39. The authors stress that the carbon tax estimates are likely to be very sensitive to model specification and parameterization (personal communication, 6 June 1991).

40. However, the GREEN revenue estimates are less than half the 10 percent of world GNP calculated by the WW model, even though the average GREEN carbon tax is 0.7 times as

The GREEN model's estimate of real income effects includes both deadweight losses on production and consumption and terms-of-trade effects. Because the OECD regions import less energy under a carbon restraint, their terms of trade improve and the resulting income gain partially offsets the deadweight losses.[41] Global GDP loss in 2020 is 1.8 percent, although because of losses of consumer and producer surplus the corresponding welfare loss (Hicksian equivalent variation) is larger, at 2.2 percent of household real income. Real income loss by 2020 amounts to 0.8 percent in North America, 0.9 percent in Europe, and 2.4 percent in OECD-Pacific, representing an aggregate real income loss of 1.2 percent for the OECD (weighting by GDP shares). The real income losses amount to 2.3 percent of GDP in China, 0.6 percent in the Soviet Union, and 7.5 percent in the EELDCS, where terms-of-trade losses double the underlying GDP loss. In return, these economic costs purchase a cutback in global carbon emissions that amounts to 43 percent from baseline by 2020.

The high carbon tax in the OECD-Pacific is attributed to relatively high baseline growth of emissions in the region and to the fact that the area already has the highest energy prices, especially for coal. At the other extreme, the low carbon tax in China stems from the country's large coal endowment and the extremely low relative price of coal. China has a comparative advantage in reducing emissions because it otherwise relies heavily on this cheap, high-emissions fuel.

This view of the carbon tax might be thought of as the "fat-cutting" school: the more profligate the country's carbon performance in the baseline, the cheaper will be achievement of the carbon reductions. One wonders, however, whether this analytical framework is consistent with the "opportunity cost" approach implied by the MR carbon tax. In the MR model, it is the differential between the carbon- and the noncarbon backstop technologies that determines the carbon tax. But if the country's alternative fuel is cheap, high-emissions coal, by the MR approach one would expect a higher rather than a lower carbon tax would be required to dissuade use of this source.

The resolution of this apparent paradox is as follows. In an elasticity-based model such as GREEN, the absolute tax required to obtain a given percentage cutback in emissions will tend to be lower for a country with a low initial price of the carbon fuel. The constant elasticity will generate a similar percentage price increase for a similar percentage emissions reduction, so the absolute price

---

high as the WW tax. The divergence again suggests that Whalley and Wigle may overestimate the value base of carbon energy.

41. The model fixes the current account at its benchmark year value. When the carbon tax reduces the demand for imported energy in the OECD areas, the resulting reduction in the energy trade deficit must be balanced by a corresponding reduction in the surplus on nonenergy trade. Given that interregional trade flows are modeled by an Armington specification, this adjustment is achieved through a rise in relative export prices, and thus a terms-of-trade gain.

increase (and thus the absolute tax) will be lower in the country with the low initial price. But the underlying assumption is that there is a smooth envelope of fuel choices. In contrast, in a linear-process model with discontinuous choices among alternative fuels each operating at a different cost plateau (as in the MR model), the percentage increase in price required to induce a specified percentage cut in emissions may be very different between the country with low-cost fuel and that with high-cost fuel. In the extreme in which the low-cost country switches directly to the long-term backstop, the tax will have to be higher in this country because the gap between its initial cost and the backstop cost is wider. However, even in a linear process model the tax need not be higher for the low-cost, high-carbon country if there are intermediate technologies (e.g., natural gas) that provide sufficient scope for the target carbon cutback without the need for the country to resort to the higher-cost backstop adopted by the country with higher initial cost (and lower initial carbon) technology.

Like Edmonds and Barns, Burniaux et al. find pronounced diminishing returns to carbon reductions once coal is eliminated. Thereafter, further cuts in carbon become much more expensive. Coal accordingly features prominently in the results. By 2020 the price of coal multiplies sixfold from baseline levels in North America, OECD-Pacific, and the EELDCS, and threefold in China, whereas the price increase is much smaller for crude oil and natural gas. Globally the production of coal falls by two-thirds from baseline, but oil output declines by only 15 percent (all in the EELDCS). The production of energy-intensive manufactures is little affected in North America, but substantially reduced in OECD-Pacific where the carbon tax is much higher. The severe reductions estimated for coal output lead the authors to note the implications for international negotiations, as world coal reserves are concentrated in just a few countries (primarily the United States, the Soviet Union, and China; World Resources Institute, *World Resources 1990–91*, 320–21).

The existence of wide divergences in carbon taxes generates ample opportunity for profitable trading of carbon emissions rights. Burniaux et al. run the model with trading in emissions rights and find that the same carbon restraint target may be achieved at only half the global welfare cost: a loss of only 1 percent of world real income from its baseline level in 2020. North America and Europe remain essentially outside the emissions trade. China, the Soviet Union, and the EELDCS export carbon rights, and OECD-Pacific imports them. China gains the most from emissions rights trade, as it is able to achieve a 2½ percent real income *gain* against baseline (instead of a comparable loss without this trading). In return for emissions rights sales that generate the equivalent of 5 percent of its GNP, China cuts back its emissions by 70 percent from baseline. Similarly, the Soviet Union is able to achieve trading rights gains sufficient to offset fully its baseline economic costs (0.6 percent of GNP in each case). The OECD-Pacific is able to reduce its real income costs from 2.4 percent of GDP to 2 percent through purchasing emission rights.

Burniaux et al. have undertaken some limited sensitivity analysis with two key parameters: the elasticity of intrafuel substitution and the AEEI. If the former is raised from 1.2 to 2.0, the global cost of meeting the emissions ceiling is cut by half, to 1 percent of GNP. On the other hand, if AEEI is set at 0.5 percent annually instead of 1.0 percent, global emissions rise at 2.5 percent rather than 2 percent in the baseline, and the larger required cutback imposes larger costs. Finally, the authors include a calculation of the cost to the OECD countries if they attempt to achieve the global carbon reduction target by themselves. In this case their carbon tax must reach $2,200 per ton of carbon, and their real income losses escalate to 7 percent of GNP, or more than five times the loss when other countries cooperate with the OECD in cutting back global emissions.

Several major implications emerge from the preliminary OECD study. First, the costs of reducing carbon emissions are squarely within the 2 percent to 3 percent of annual GNP suggested at the outset. Carbon emissions can be cut by 45 percent from baseline by 2020 at a global welfare cost of 2.2 percent of GNP. Second, these costs can be reduced by half through international trading in emissions rights. Third, China's losses are about average (rather than three times the world average as in the MR results—although to a considerable extent the divergence between the two studies stems from the longer MR time horizon).[42] Fourth, China could actually gain rather than lose from carbon restrictions under a regime with international trading in emission rights. Fifth, the incorporation of international trade in fuels and other goods importantly influences the analysis, because it allows for terms-of-trade effects that tend to moderate OECD losses and amplify those of the EELDCS.

Overall, the GREEN model is an important extension of detailed general equilibrium modeling on a global scale. The principal limitations of the version of the model examined here include its reliance on stylized elasticities for energy sources rather than the more detailed process information of the type contained in the MR and ER models, and its extension in time no further than 2020.[43]

---

42. Thus, in the MR results, China's losses are still only 2 percent of GNP by 2020, when the additional emissions allowed to LDCs mean the restraints have not yet begun to bite much.

43. In particular, the use of "electricity" as the sole noncarbon energy sector raises questions. Manne and Richels find that the most important influence among the energy sectors is the backstop noncarbon technology for nonelectric energy. Note that a revised version of GREEN scheduled for release in 1992 was to include an extension of the time horizon to 2050, incorporation of backstop technologies, a change to 12 regions, a revised production structure ("putty/semi-putty"), and endogenization of the oil price. However, the overall costs of carbon targets would seem unlikely to change much (although further

Blitzer et al.

One of the few models available for a developing country is provided by Blitzer, Eckaus, Lahiri, and Meeraus (1991), or BELM, who have estimated a dynamic general equilibrium model for Egypt. Their model applies a 100-year horizon beginning in 1987, although because of distortions associated with terminal conditions (i.e., investment requirements to sustain growth in the postmodel period), they report results only through 2052. The model has four energy sectors: crude oil, natural gas, petroleum products, and electricity. Electricity is produced by a limited amount of hydroelectric resources and by gas and oil; Egypt has virtually no coal. In runs that permit backstop technologies, electricity may also be produced by cogeneration, nuclear power, or a composite of "renewable" sources: solar, wind, and biomass. Gas-powered transportation is an additional backstop technology.

There are six other product sectors (agriculture, manufacturing, construction, transportation, services, and noncompeting imports). The model maximizes the discounted sum of consumer utility over the planning horizon. [44] Production is subject to the normal intermediate input (interindustry) material balances requirements. [45] There are alternative technology choices in the production of each product, employing different combinations of the productive factors: fuel, electricity, capital, and labor.

For each alternative technology there is a fixed coefficient of fuel input to production (Btus per unit of output), although fuel may be provided either by oil or by natural gas. The authors suggest that the scope for fuel substitution by other factors is better identified by enumerating alternative technologies than by application of a more aggregate (CES) production function between energy and other factors (as in several other models); this is a reasonable position so long as a sufficiently wide scope of technology alternatives has been considered. Carbon emissions arise in fixed proportions to fuel use by technology and sector.

Capital is specific to each sector and technology. Although the authors do not report typical capital life, their horizon is sufficiently long that this structure appears to impose high adjustment costs only in runs that involve an early reduction in carbon emissions. [46] The model assumes annual labor productivity

---

regional detail could reveal divergences), and the addition of backstop alternatives should if anything reduce the cost estimates by putting an upper limit on the cost of noncarbon alternatives.

44. The rate used for the results reviewed here was 7 percent per year (Richard S. Eckaus, personal communication, 5 March 1992).

45. "Production" is of adjusted value added including payment to energy (in contrast to the usual treatment of energy as an intermediate input excluded from value added).

46. That is, a longer adjustment period reduces, but does not eliminate, adjustment cost,

growth of 1 percent but (unlike the MR and ER models) no automatic energy efficiency increase (AEEI). The implication is that any natural tendency for energy efficiency to rise would have to be the consequence of the appearance of new technologies over time; in practice the model apparently introduces only the backstop technologies with a time delay.

The BELM baseline optimizes discounted consumption utility over time and includes initial adjustments to correct for underpricing of fuels. The baseline does not explicitly identify the expected path of carbon emissions.[47] GDP growth averages about 4 percent through 2025 and about 5 percent thereafter. A curious feature of the model is that manufacturing rises from 32 percent of GDP to 57 percent by 2052, far above the share in past experience of developed countries. Limited agricultural land and scarce agricultural labor drive this result. However, as manufacturing is energy intensive, this unusually high projected share of manufacturing in the economy may overstate the emissions baseline. The model does allow for an initial correction of underpricing of electricity in the Egyptian economy.

BELM conduct two sets of experiments. In the first, carbon emissions are cut by alternative specified percentages from baseline in alternative future years. In the second, the model is allowed to choose when to cut emissions subject to a cumulative total percentage cut from baseline. The authors find that, under the first approach, cuts imposed immediately cause discounted full-horizon welfare losses of 4.3 percent for a 20 percent cut, 9.5 percent for a 30 percent cut, and 22 percent for a 40 percent cut from baseline. A cushion of time reduces adjustment costs: a delay of a decade in emissions cutbacks (e.g., to 1997) reduces welfare losses by 40 percent; of two decades, to over 66 percent; and of three decades, to almost 80 percent. In all cases, emissions reductions induce a product composition shift away from manufacturing, transport, and electricity toward agriculture and services. Essentially, carbon emissions are being "exported" through the shift toward obtaining manufactures from abroad. Although rational for the individual country, this response raises obvious questions of summing up at the global level.

The BELM estimates of output loss would appear to be on the high side, although the discounting procedure tends to disguise this result. For a 30 percent cut from the emissions baseline imposed in 1997, GDP falls by 15 percent initially, by as much as 27 percent from baseline by 2007, and by 10 percent to 15 percent in the period 2025–50 (Blitzer et al. 1991, chart 3A). Overall the average BELM

---

because a larger fraction of capital may be used through its productive lifetime rather than being turned prematurely obsolete from the imposition of constraints on carbon emissions.

47. However, in a private communication (5 March 1992), Eckaus has indicated that emissions grow from 17.4 million tons of carbon in 1987 to 37.0 million tons in 2017 and 245 million tons by 2052. The slower initial growth rate reflects efficiency improvements.

reduction is about 15 percent. Yet, as developed below, in view of the elasticity of output with respect to energy (as revealed by energy's factor share in the economy) and the likely elasticity of energy availability with respect to carbon changes, one might more generally expect a 30 percent cut in carbon from baseline to cause a reduction of only about 1 percent in GDP (30 percent $\times$ 0.06 $\times$ 0.5; see discussion below). On this basis, the BELM output estimates are as much as an order of magnitude larger than the central values in most of the other models. The limited translation of these losses into discounted welfare effects (e.g., a 4.3 percent loss rather than 15 percent) apparently stems from the use of a relatively high discount rate (7 percent) combined with delay of the cutbacks for an initial decade (implementation in 1997 in a model that begins in 1987).

The second set of experiments tends to delay all emissions cuts until late in the planning horizon, thereby sharply reducing the discounted value of welfare loss.[48] However, these calculations raise both a political question and an economic question. The political question is whether a politician who has inherited a large backlog of emissions cutbacks will honor the commitment. The economic question is whether the discount rate used is so high that it may understate the value of distant future welfare losses. At 7 percent per year, the rate would seem excessive in view of the analysis of the social rate of time preference in chapter 6 of this study.

The third and fourth sets of experiments repeat the simulations but introduce the option of using nonconventional backstop technologies by the year 2002. The availability of the backstop technologies makes little difference in the scenarios that permit carbon cuts to be postponed to the distant future subject to a cumulative total, again reflecting the power of discounting. However, when percentage cuts from baseline are imposed early, the savings from backstop availability are large.[49]

The authors interpret their central findings to indicate that:

The welfare losses due to the imposition of annual restrictions on the rate of carbon emissions are quite substantial, ranging from 4.5 [percent] for a 20 percent reduction in annual carbon emissions to 22 percent for a 40 percent reduction in emissions. (Blitzer et al. 1991, 70)

---

48. For example, a 20 percent cut in cumulative emissions without regard to timing causes a loss of only about one-third of one percent in discounted welfare; the corresponding cut from baseline beginning in 1987 causes a loss of 6 percent in welfare.

49. Thus, the 20 percent cut from baseline imposed in 1987 causes a welfare loss of 4.3 percent without the backstop, but the loss falls to just 1 percent merely from the addition of the cogeneration backstop.

However, an alternative interpretation is that the study shows that carbon limitations could have relatively limited costs for countries in Egypt's situation. Shah and Larsen (1991) estimate that just the elimination of subsidies to energy use in Egypt would bring a 25 percent cut in the country's carbon emissions. The BELM model assumes that a first tranche of "efficient" emissions reductions is already undertaken in the (optimal) baseline, but this assumption implicitly means that the country would receive no international "credit" against carbon targets for the efficiency-improving cuts. Surely just the opposite is the case; indeed, elimination of inefficient carbon emissions through the elimination of subsidies is an integral part of any future global strategy for developing-country response to the greenhouse problem (see chapter 8).

Quite apart from the subsidy efficient baseline issue, it is useful to consider which of the BELM scenarios is closest to what might be regarded as a norm for developing countries in a global action plan. Manne and Richels (1990c) use the standard of a doubling of emissions and then a freeze at this plateau. As discussed in chapter 8, a doubling of the absolute level of developing-country carbon emissions is compatible with deep percentage cutbacks from baseline by late in the 21st century, and with an aggressive program of international abatement action.

The principal BELM cutback is a specified percentage from baseline in all periods. In the MR approach, there is no cutback in the first few decades for developing countries, but an absolute ceiling after emissions double. By implication, percentage cutbacks from baseline rise successively thereafter. Imposition of such a profile on the BELM baseline causes a 63 percent total cutback, without discounting.[50] If the emissions are discounted at the BELM rate of 7 percent, the cumulative discounted reduction to meet the MR restriction is only 19 percent— because by far the largest absolute emissions occur late in the horizon when shrinkage by discounting is large. Discounted at 2 percent (more in keeping with the rates suggested in chapter 6), the cutback is 52 percent.[51] On this basis, a rough equivalence to the pattern of double-and-freeze would appear to be approximately a 35 percent cutback from the BELM baseline (i.e., an average between the two discounted reductions just cited).

---

50. That is, when the levels cited in note 47 are subjected to a ceiling of double the initial level, or 34.8 million tons annually, the cumulative sum of emissions through 2052 falls by 63 percent.

51. The procedure here examines discounted emissions as a proxy for rerunning the model with the constrained emissions profile. A full simulation along these lines would force emissions to adhere to the new profile and optimize discounted consumption utility. The implicit assumption in the shorthand calculation here is that there is a linear relationship between emissions and consumption in a given year, so that discounted emissions provide an approximation of effects on discounted consumption utility. Without discounting, the "percentage cut in emissions" is exaggerated, because the very high emissions occur late in the horizon.

Considering that a 25 percent cut in emissions might be expected from elimination of subsidies, and that international credit would likely be given for this cutback, the net reduction further imposed by a greenhouse policy of the MR profile would amount to some 10 percent (i.e., the 35 percent cut just indicated less the 25 percent provided by the Shah-Larsen subsidy removal). This reduction should cause welfare losses smaller than the 20 percent cutback examined by BELM. The average production (GDP) loss from baseline under that scenario is approximately 5 percent.[52] With half the cutback the production losses should be half this amount or less. On this basis, Egypt's economic loss from an MR type of limit would be in a range close to that found for emissions cuts of 50 percent to 60 percent from baseline by industrial countries in the middle of the next century (i.e., about 2 percent to 3 percent of GDP).[53]

Short-Term Costs: The CBO-DRI Model

The Congressional Budget Office has applied the Data Resources Model of the US economy to examine the costs of a phase-in of carbon taxes over the first decade (CBO 1990). The authors specify a tax of $100 per ton of carbon, with an equally phased implementation in increments of $10 per year. As a standard macroeconomic model, the DRI model captures both the contractionary and the inflationary effects of higher energy prices. It estimates that the CBO scenario would cause a sacrifice from baseline of 1 percent of GNP by 1993 and a steady 2 percent of GNP in the period 1995–2000. The price index (GNP deflator) would stand 2 percent above baseline in 1995–97 and 1 percent above baseline in 2000 (CBO 1990, 35).

The calculations assume that one-half of carbon tax revenue is recycled and the other half used for deficit reduction. Alternative model runs indicate that the GNP loss is little affected by full rather than half use of the revenue for deficit reduction. However, the CBO authors did not run the model with complete rebate of tax revenue. As the standard macroeconomic models are driven by Keynesian demand influences, this alternative would almost certainly have resulted in smaller GNP losses, because it would have avoided the contractionary demand effect of higher tax revenue. Complete rebate is the proper policy scenario to consider, as it is important to examine global warming policy separately from fiscal policy. Alternative simulations show that, if a $100 tax were implemented immediately (i.e., without phase-in), "the economy could enter a period

---

52. The output loss is zero in the first 5 years, rises to a peak of 15 percent by 2007, and is back to an average of zero by 2032–52 (Blitzer et al. 1991, chart 3A).

53. This is despite a possible tendency in the model toward insufficient scope allowed for substitution (e.g., because of the fixed Btu output coefficient for each technology).

of stagnation for several years, with little GNP growth and sharp rises in unemployment." These results are sensible and underscore the importance of avoiding macroeconomic shocks by providing the greatest possible advance warning of any program of carbon taxes, to maximize anticipation and smooth adjustment.

In sum, the CBO simulations with the DRI model place income losses in the first decade at 1 percent of GNP in the first five years and 2 percent of GNP in the second five. When it is considered that this outcome is almost certainly an overstatement because it fails to permit complete rebate of tax revenue, the results are compatible with the concept of a moderate early transition path to the type of longer-term estimates primarily considered here. As noted above, the CBO authors also apply the ER and JW models, but for purposes of this survey the more definitive statements of the results of these models are those discussed above.

US Department of Energy

In the autumn of 1991 the US Department of Energy (DOE) submitted an extensive report to Congress in response to the latter's request to evaluate the impact of "a 20-percent reduction in domestic CO_2 emissions in the short run (5 to 10 years) and a 50-percent emissions reduction in the long run (15 to 20 years)" (US Department of Energy 1991, v). The study used the Department's "Fossil2" model to project US energy supply, demand, and prices through the year 2030. It applied these projections to the ER model and the DRI model as the starting point for estimating the impact of emissions cutbacks.

The DOE study found that to cut carbon dioxide emissions by 20 percent below 1990 levels by the year 2000 would require a carbon tax of $500 per metric ton of carbon and impose an economic cost of $95 billion annually by that year (US Department of Energy 1991, vii). Considering that US GDP should be on the order of $7 trillion by 2000 (in 1991 dollars), this cost would amount to about 1.3 percent of GDP. The study further found that if an approach reducing all greenhouse gases based on their equivalent global warming potential (GWP) were pursued rather than cuts limited to carbon dioxide, a 20 percent cutback from 1990 levels could be achieved much more cheaply, at a tax of $30 to $40 per ton of carbon-equivalent and an annual economic loss of only $6 billion to $13 billion by 2000 (US Department of Energy 1991, ix).

The DOE results are generally in line with those of the models surveyed above. The $500 per ton tax is consistent with the initially high taxes in the MR model, if the earlier date for the 20 percent cutback from 1990 levels is taken into account. The corresponding costs for the economy in the DOE estimates are in fact relatively low. In terms of figure 4.2, addition of a DOE "observation" at 20 percent on the horizontal axis and 1.3 percent on the vertical axis would leave

Figure 4.2 Alternative estimates of the output costs of reducing carbon emissions

Percentage reduction in GNP

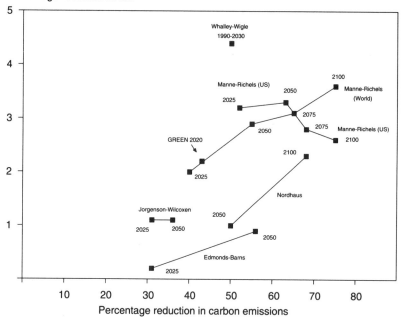

Percentage reduction in carbon emissions

Sources: for GREEN: J. M. Burniaux et al. 1991. "GREEN—A Multi-Region Dynamic General Equilibrium Model for Quantifying the Costs of Curbing CO$_2$ Emissions: A Technical Manual." Paris: Economics and Statistics Department, Organization for Economic Co-operation and Development. For Jorgenson-Wilcoxen: Dale W. Jorgenson and Peter J. Wilcoxen. 1990. "The Cost of Controlling US Carbon Dioxide Emissions." Cambridge, MA: Harvard University (mimeographed, September). For Manne-Richels: Alan S. Manne and Richard G. Richels. 1990. "CO$_2$ Emission Limits: An Economic Cost Analysis for the USA. *The Energy Journal* (forthcoming); Alan S. Manne and Richard G. Richels. 1990. "Global CO$_2$ Emission Reductions—the Impacts of Rising Energy Costs." Stanford, CA: Stanford University (mimeographed). For Whalley-Wigle: John Whalley and Randall Wigle. 1990. "The International Incidence of Carbon Taxes." Paper presented at a conference on "Economic Policy Responses to Global Warming" sponsored by the Instituto Bancario San Paolo di Torino, Rome (September). For Nordhaus: see text.

the overall relationship between depth of cut and economic cost in the scatter diagram broadly unchanged (especially in view of the early year).[54]

---

54. Moreover, a 20 percent cut from 1990 levels means an even larger percentage cut from the 2000 baseline, placing the DOE "observation" further to the right on the diagram and even closer to the main trend.

The DOE study also found that a target of 50 percent cutback in carbon dioxide from 1990 levels by the year 2010 was not possible even with a $750 tax per ton of carbon. However, it recognized that the models probably understated sensitivity to such extreme taxes (US Department of Energy 1991, xiii). Note that the models surveyed here do not examine such extreme cuts over such a short time horizon (the larger percentage cuts considered here are *from baseline* and thus not as deep as the 50 percent cut from 1990 levels, and occur later when technological alternatives have widened).

The DOE analysis did not take account of an initial tranche of low- or zero-cost carbon emissions cutbacks (reviewed in chapter 5). However, it usefully calculated the sharp reductions in costs possible through incorporating a reforestation strategy, a conclusion supported by the analysis in chapter 5. Thus, whereas a 20 percent cut from 1990 levels of total greenhouse gas GWP would require a carbon tax of $150 per ton of carbon-equivalent, "the addition of a reforestation program could reduce the tax rate to between $15 and $30" per ton of carbon-equivalent (US Department of Energy 1991, xxi).

In sum, the DOE results would appear broadly consistent with those of the models surveyed here and the reforestation analysis below. The principal exception is that low-cost efficiency gains from a move to best practices are incorporated in the analysis of chapters 5 and 7, but omitted in the DOE study (and, for that matter, from the economic models reviewed in this chapter).

Synthesis of Findings

Table 4.2 presents a summary of the estimates of the leading models. The table first reports baseline emissions.[55] As indicated, the MR, Edmonds-Barns, and NY models all envision relatively similar emission paths ($13\frac{1}{2}$ to $14\frac{1}{2}$ GtC by 2050). Similarity of the baseline is important, because otherwise a seemingly high economic cost to meet a carbon restraint target may stem from a high baseline and large required cutback rather than a greater cost per unit percentage cutback. The principal divergence in baselines occurs for the United States, between the MR results on the one hand and the JW results on the other. It is fair to say that in this regard the JW model is the outlier, and most models would show US emissions growth closer to that indicated by the MR model.

---

55. Note that the "world" aggregates for the MR model apply evolving regional carbon emissions shares to obtain average carbon tax, and regional income shares to estimate global output loss. The former are linear interpolations between the 1990 and 2100 results. The latter are based on the MR regional growth rates, as applied to the following base-year income shares: US + OOECD + SUEE = 77.7 percent; China = 1.6 percent; ROW = 20.6 percent. Note that the year 2100 income shares stand at 49.2 percent, 5.7 percent, and 45.1 percent, respectively. (See note 24 for income data sources.)

Table 4.2 Alternative cost estimates for reductions in carbon emissions, 1990–2100

Study	Area	1990	2000	2025	2050	2075	2100
Baseline emissions (GtC)							
Manne-Richels	World	5.7	6.2	10.4	14.6	18.8	26.9
Manne-Richels	US	1.3	1.4	2.1	2.7	3.1	4.0
Edmonds-Barns	World	5.6	6.2	9.0	14.2	n.a.	n.a.
Jorgenson-Wilcoxen	US	1.3	1.5	1.6	1.7	n.a.	n.a.
Nordhaus-Yohe	World	n.a.	5.5	10.3	13.3	17.5	20.0
Whalley-Wigle	World	n.a.	n.a.	n.a.	n.a.	n.a.	n.a.
OECD-GREEN	World	5.7	6.9	10.0[a]	n.a.	n.a.	n.a.
Emissions under constrained scenario (GtC)							
Manne-Richels	World	5.7	5.9	6.2	6.5	6.6	6.6
Manne-Richels	US	1.3	1.3	1	1	1	1
Edmonds-Barns	World	5.6	6.2	6.2	6.2	6.2	6.2
Jorgenson-Wilcoxen	US	1.3	1.1[b]	1.1	1.1	n.a.	n.a.
Nordhaus-Yohe	World	n.a.	5.5	8.4	7.9	10.7	13.9
Whalley-Wigle	World	n.a.	n.a.	n.a.	n.a.	n.a.	n.a.
OECD-GREEN	World	5.7	5.7	5.7[a]	n.a.	n.a.	n.a.
Percentage reduction from baseline							
Manne-Richels	World	0	−5	−40	−55	−65	−75
Manne-Richels	US	0	−7	−52	−63	−68	−75
Edmonds-Barns	World	0	0	−31	−56	n.a.	n.a.
Jorgenson-Wilcoxen	US	0	−27[b]	−31	−36	n.a.	n.a.
Nordhaus-Yohe	World	0	0	−18	−41	−39	−30
Whalley-Wigle	World	0	n.a.	−50[c]	n.a.	n.a.	n.a.
OECD-GREEN	World	0	−17	−43[a]	n.a.	n.a.	n.a.
Carbon tax associated with emissions reduction (dollars per ton)							
Manne-Richels	World[d]	0	0	292	326	279	250
Manne-Richels	US	0	0	375	250	250	250
Edmonds-Barns	World	0	0	100	280	n.a.	n.a.
Jorgenson-Wilcoxen	US	0	37[b]	43	42	n.a.	n.a.
Nordhaus-Yohe	World	0	0	33	113	129	129
Whalley-Wigle	World	0	n.a.	445[c]	n.a.	n.a.	n.a.
OECD-GREEN	World	0	21	215[a]	n.a.	n.a.	n.a.

GDP loss associated with emissions reduction (percentages)

Model	Region						
Manne-Richels	US	0	0.5	3.2	3.3	2.8	2.6
	Other OECD	0	0.1	1.2	1.6	1.8	1.8
	SUEE	0	0.5	4.2	3.7	2.6	2.9
	Rest of world	0	0	0.8	2.8	3.5	4.2
	China	0	0.1	3.4	8.4	9.2	10.5
	World	0	0.2	2.0	2.9	3.1	3.6
	World exc. China	0	0	1.9	2.6	2.8	3.2
Edmonds-Barns	World[e]	0	1.0[b]	0.2	0.9	n.a.	n.a.
Jorgenson-Wilcoxen	US	0	n.a.	1.1	1.1	n.a.	n.a.
Nordhaus-Yohe	World	0	n.a.	n.a.	n.a.	n.a.	n.a.
Whalley-Wigle	World	0	n.a.	4.4[c]	n.a.	n.a.	n.a.
OECD-GREEN	World	0	0.1	2.2[a]	n.a.	n.a.	n.a.

n.a. = not available; GtC = gigatons of carbon; OECD = Organization for Economic Cooperation and Development; SUEE = Soviet Union and Eastern Europe.

a. In year 2020.

b. In year 2005.

c. 1990–2030; estimate centered on 2010.

d. Weighted by regional shares in constrained carbon emissions.

e. Tax integration method.

Source: See text.

The constrained emissions paths and corresponding percentage cutbacks from baseline appear next in the table. The MR and Edmonds-Barns experiments are close in specification, and both are in the spirit of the Toronto (World Conference on the Changing Atmosphere, June 1988) target of a 20 percent cutback by 2005 and 50 percent cutbacks over the longer term. The NY policy scenario is less ambitious.

The final two sections of the table report the carbon tax and the percentage reduction in GNP from baseline associated with each of the respective reduction scenarios. The carbon taxes generally lie within the range of $100 to $300 per ton. However, it would have been desirable to learn the tax levels the Edmonds-Barns analysis would have projected for 2075 and 2100, because their tax path requires ongoing increases to stabilize emissions whereas the MR long-term tax rate is flat at $250 per ton.

Figure 4.2 provides a scatter diagram of the percentage cut in GNP against the percentage cut in carbon emissions (both from baseline). The figure also identifies the source and time frame of each estimate. The observations are those shown in table 4.2, with the addition of two points from the Nordhaus synthesis cost line reported in table 4.1 (the implicit 2050 and 2100 estimates discussed above). However, both table 4.2 and figure 4.2 omit the Blitzer et al. estimates for Egypt, because of the ambiguities raised above. Unless otherwise indicated, the data refer to global cost and emissions estimates.

Two major patterns are apparent in figure 4.2. First, almost all of the estimates are in the range of 1 percent to $3\frac{1}{2}$ percent of GNP. Second, there is a tendency toward higher GNP cost for larger percentage cutbacks in carbon emissions, with the notable exception of the MR model for the United States.

It is possible to identify the influences on GNP cost by estimating a simple regression:

$$(4.1) \quad \%Y = -1.25 + 0.09\ \%C - 0.024t + 0.263U + 1.625W;\ R^2 = 0.74$$
$$(0.69) \quad (0.02) \qquad (0.0126)\ (0.37) \qquad (0.88)$$

where $\%Y$ is the percentage reduction in GNP, $\%C$ is the percentage cutback in carbon emissions from baseline, t is time (number of years from 1990), U is a dummy variable for the United States, and W is a dummy variable for Whalley and Wigle. Standard errors are in parentheses. The US dummy variable is not significant and may be omitted. The WW variable is statistically significant at almost the 95 percent level, indicating that the WW model is a statistical outlier. As it contributes only one observation, it adds no information on the slope of the line, and the overall relationship may thus appropriately be reestimated omitting this observation.

The reestimated equation becomes:

(4.1') $\%Y = -1.16 + 0.091\ \%C - 0.0246\ t;\ R^2 = 0.75$
        $(0.68)\quad(0.024)\qquad(0.012)$

In the reestimated equation the two independent variables are statistically significant at the 95 percent level, and the intercept is significant at the 90 percent level. The estimates indicate that, for a given point in time, escalating the desired cutback in carbon emissions by 10 percentage points will cost an extra 0.9 percent of GNP. However, there is an important negative time factor, so that if the cutback occurs further in the future the output loss is less severe. This phenomenon reflects in particular the MR model in which backstop technologies only become available after 2030 or so. The final right-hand-side term means that a given cut in emissions implemented 10 years later will be less costly by 0.25 percent of GNP.

Equation (4.1') may be applied to investigate the "consensus" cost of implementing a strong program of carbon emissions abatement. For purposes of the baseline, we may take the simple average of the MR, Edmonds-Barns, and NY projections (table 4.2). This average yields emissions of 9.9 GtC in 2025, 14.1 GtC in 2050, 18.1 GtC in 2075, and 23.4 GtC in 2100.[56] If the objective is set at freezing global emissions at their 1990 level, target emissions are limited to 5.7 GtC throughout the next century. The resulting percentage cutbacks from baseline in the four quarter-century benchmark years are 42.4 percent, 59.6 percent, 68.5 percent, and 75.6 percent, respectively.

Application of equation (4.1') to these target cutbacks yields the following percentage reductions in GNP from baseline: 1.8 percent in 2025, 2.8 percent in 2050, 3.0 percent in 2075, and 3.0 percent in 2100. By the second half of the century, the greater ease in cutback that comes with greater passage of time approximately neutralizes the more severe percentage cutback against baseline.

For purposes of analytical understanding of these results, it is useful to return to the concept of the factor share and output elasticity of energy. The figure and regression analysis represent a "reduced form" relationship between the percentage loss of GNP and the percentage cut in carbon emissions. However, this summary relationship reflects two more meaningful economic components: the sensitivity of output to the energy production factor, and the sensitivity of the energy input to the carbon restraint.

Abstracting from the shift associated with time, it is possible to formulate the output effect of carbon restraints as follows:

(4.2) $\%Y = \epsilon_{QE}\ \epsilon_{EC}\ \%C$

---

56. The estimate for 2100 here is modestly higher than in table 2.1, where a figure for that year based on the ER model is included and is at a lower level than the MR and NY estimates.

Table 4.3 Stylized parameters for carbon reduction costs (percentages except for elasticities)

Study	Carbon reduction	Cut in energy	ϵ_{EC}	GNP loss	ϵ_{QE}	ϵ_{QC}
Manne-Richels	55	24[a]	0.43[a]	2.9	0.121[a]	0.053
Edmonds-Barns	57	12	0.21	0.9	0.075	0.016
Jorgenson-Wilcoxen	36	31	0.86	1.1	0.035	0.030
Nordhaus	60	n.a.	n.a.	1.7	n.a.	0.028
Whalley-Wigle	50	47	0.94	4.4	0.094	0.088
GREEN	43	n.a.	n.a	2.2	n.a.	0.051
Synthesis	50	25	0.51[b]	2.0[c]	0.08	0.040

n.a. = not available; ϵ_{EC} = elasticity of energy availability with respect to carbon; ϵ_{QE} = elasticity of output with respect to energy; ϵ_{QC} = elasticity of output with respect to carbon.

a. Imputed based on US pessimistic case. See text.

b. Two-thirds weight is applied to Manne-Richels and Edmonds-Barns; one-third to Jorgenson-Wilcoxen and Whalley-Wigle.

c. Estimated from regression equation evaluated at a 50 percent cut in 2050. See text.

where $\%Y$ is the percentage reduction in GNP, ϵ_{QE} is the elasticity of output with respect to energy, ϵ_{EC} is the elasticity of energy availability with respect to carbon emissions, and $\%C$ is the target reduction in carbon emissions.

Table 4.3 presents the decomposition of the output effect into these two components based on central estimates from the principal models considered here. The Edmonds-Barns, JW, and WW results all give sufficient information to identify both the percentage cut in energy and the percentage reduction in emissions. The MR world model does not report the percentage cutback in energy. However, in the MR USA model (Manne and Richels 1990a), the results reported for the most pessimistic case indicate that a 70 percent reduction in carbon is associated with approximately a 30 percent reduction in energy (as discussed above). On this basis, ϵ_{EC} is 30/70 = 0.43. That leaves the remainder of the overall output-carbon elasticity for the second component (energy elasticity with respect to carbon).

The final row in table 4.3 offers a set of stylized parameters based on the models reported. To obtain ϵ_{EC} it applies a weight of two-thirds to the MR and Edmonds-Barns results, as these are the two models with the most impressive energy process detail, and a weight of one-third to the JW and WW results. This parameter is approximately 0.5. As a result, the summary relationship indicates that a 50 percent cut in carbon requires a 25 percent reduction in energy. GNP loss is then estimated by applying the regression reported above to a 50 percent carbon reduction in 2050, yielding a 2 percent output loss. The output elasticity of energy, ϵ_{QE}, is then derived from the change in GNP relative to the change in energy, or 2/25 = 0.08. As it turns out, the stylized output elasticity with respect to energy is just about what was predicted at the outset:

the share of energy in GNP (which would be 0.06). That the output elasticity is moderately higher (0.08) reflects less-than-unitary elasticity of substitution between energy and other factors, such that as energy is reduced its factor share rises. Finally, the synthesis parameters indicate a reduced-form elasticity of output with respect to carbon ($\epsilon_{QC} = \epsilon_{QE} \epsilon_{EC}$) of 0.04. At the most summary level, then, a carbon reduction of x percent will require a reduction of GNP by $0.04x$ percent, caused by an energy reduction of $0.5x$ percent in combination with an output elasticity of energy of 0.08.

Conclusion

Overall, these estimates imply that a global freeze on carbon emissions would cost about 1½ percent to 2½ percent of world GNP in the first half of the 21st century and about 3 percent of GNP in the second half. There is an important reason to believe that, if anything, this range is too high. None of the models incorporates a response of technical change to the price of carbon-based energy. Yet it would seem likely that some additional technical change would be induced toward noncarbon energy sources if there were a large and permanent incentive in the form of a carbon tax. Moreover, the range of 1½ percent to 3 percent of GNP over the next century needs to be adjusted to incorporate any "free" carbon reductions that might be available in light of existing engineering information (but with prudent interpretation about feasibility), and to take account of any low-cost emissions reductions that might be achievable through afforestation and reduced deforestation. As developed in chapter 5, once these adjustments are made, the cost range identified here can serve as a point of departure for benefit-cost analysis of abatement measures in policy formation on global warming.

Annex 4A

Nonlinearity of the Carbon Tax Curve

Suppose that a unit reduction in carbon emissions (e.g., by one ton) requires a given amount of reduction in energy (e.g., by 38.5 million Btu; this is the actual ratio for coal). Suppose also that the economy's production function is Cobb-Douglas:

$$(4A.1) \quad Q = \alpha E^{\beta} H^{1-\beta}$$

where Q is output, E is energy (in Btu), and H is all other factors of production. If intrafossil fuel and nonfossil fuel substitution are ruled out, E varies proportionately with carbon, so that we may speak of carbon as the factor input, and of a marginal product of carbon that varies proportionately with the marginal product of energy. If units are redefined, the factor E may be considered as equal to tons of carbon.

Under these conditions, what will be the shape of the carbon tax curve? At any given level of energy (carbon) input, the opportunity cost of a unit of energy (carbon) is its marginal product, and this is the level of the tax that must be levied to induce firms and consumers to give up one unit of energy (carbon). Figure 4A.1 shows an illustrative marginal product curve for carbon. When the full baseline amount of carbon is applied in the production process (C_0), its marginal product stands at q_0. If carbon (energy) is cut back by 50 percent from baseline to C_1, the marginal product rises to q_1. Conversely, the marginal product of carbon is lower (q_0) when the amount available is larger (C_0), reflecting diminishing returns to the variable factor when other factors (H, land and labor) are held constant. Under these assumptions, the tax curve of text figure 4.1 is merely the mirror image of the marginal product curve of figure 4A.1. That is, a large cutback such as that to C_2, toward the left end of figure 4A.1, generates a high marginal product (q_2); the corresponding point on the tax curve of text figure 4.1 will be toward the right end (and thus toward complete cutback of carbon, C_0) and will similarly show a high carbon tax required.

The lower the degree of substitutability between energy and other factors, the more nonlinear will be the marginal product curve of energy, and the higher will be the tax required for relatively large cutbacks in energy. The Cobb-Douglas function has unitary elasticity of substitution between energy and other factors, and thus relative ease of substitution. Thus, a 1 percent rise in the price of energy relative to that of other factors causes a 1 percent reduction in the ratio of the energy input to other factor inputs in this function. In the alternative CES production function, there is lesser substitutability (e.g., the absolute value of the elasticity of substitution is less than unity), implying a more sharply nonlinear marginal product curve for energy. If it can be shown that even for the Cobb-Douglas function the

Figure 4A.1   The marginal product of carbon

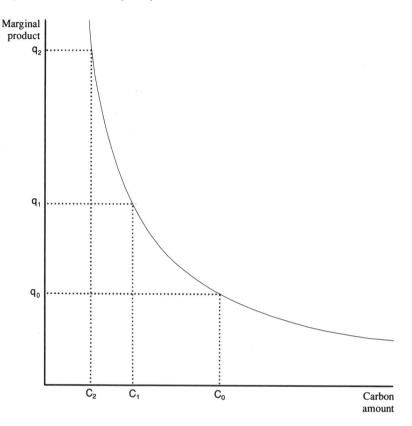

marginal product curve (and thus the tax curve) is nonlinear, then the same conclusion should hold for the full class of production functions usually considered meaningful (i.e., those with unitary or lower elasticity of substitution).

Consider a cutback of the energy input from level E_0 to level E_1, where $E_1 = \lambda E_0$. Then, from equation 4A.1, the respective marginal products of energy will be:

(4A.2) $\delta Q / \delta E_0 = \beta \alpha E_0^{\beta-1} H^{1-\beta}$

and

(4A.2') $\delta Q / \delta E_1 = \beta \alpha E_1^{\beta-1} H^{1-\beta} = \beta \alpha [\lambda E_0]^{\beta-1} H^{1-\beta}$
$\qquad\qquad = \lambda^{\beta-1} \delta Q / \delta E_0$

Thus, the marginal product of energy varies with the exponential function $(\beta - 1)$ of the ratio of the energy input to the initial level of energy. For example, if energy is cut in half, $\lambda = 0.5$, and the marginal product of energy is $\lambda^{\beta - 1}$ times as large as before.

As discussed in the text of this chapter, we expect the exponent 0.5 in the production function, which is the output elasticity with respect to energy, to equal energy's share in GDP, or about 0.06. Thus, the term $(\beta - 1)$ has a value of -0.94, or close to negative unity. Under these conditions, the term $\lambda^{\beta - 1}$ approximates (λ^{-1}) or $1/\lambda$. As an approximation, then, when the energy input falls to a ratio equal to λ times its initial level, its marginal product rises to a magnitude equal to $1/\lambda$ times its original level. In the example of $\lambda = 0.5$, for a halving of energy, the marginal product will almost double.

The resulting shape of the marginal product of energy curve turns out to be close to a rectangular hyperbola. That is, because the marginal product varies almost inversely with the amount of energy, the product of the two is nearly constant, so the area of any rectangle with corners at the origin and on the marginal product curve is close to a constant value. This curve's shape is non-linear, of the type shown in figure 4A.1. This outcome confirms the proposition that the marginal product curve and thus the tax curve are nonlinear even for the Cobb-Douglas case with relative ease of factor substitution. It follows that, for the full class of probable production functions, the tax curve should be nonlinear.

5

Carbon Abatement Costs: Engineering Estimates and Forestry Options

Carbon Abatement Costs: Engineering Estimates and Forestry Options

Two broad approaches have been used to examine the cost of abatement of greenhouse warming: "top-down" economic models and "bottom-up" engineering estimates. Chapter 4 provided an analytical survey of the leading top-down models. This chapter reviews the engineering estimates. In addition, it considers the alternative analyses of the cost of addressing the greenhouse problem through afforestation and reduced deforestation. The discussion then seeks to draw an overall synthesis on the prospective costs of global warming abatement.

A prominent difference between the two approaches has been that the engineering estimates tend to suggest that there is a range of energy efficiency improvements (and carbon reductions) available at zero or negative cost. In contrast, the economic models typically estimate that there will be an economic cost associated with any reduction in carbon emissions. The engineering-based analysts often respond that an array of market failures prevents adoption of efficiency measures that would actually save rather than cost money. The discussion below reviews these arguments, as well as the related issue of whether financial incentives or mandated controls should be used to achieve improved efficiency.

For policy purposes, the objective of this chapter is to derive further information from the engineering and forestry studies to obtain an appropriate central view about the shape of the cost curve for greenhouse gas abatement. Figure 5.1 shows the conceptual nature of this exercise. Most economic model–based analyses will show rising costs (expressed as percentages of GDP; vertical axis) for higher targeted percentage reductions of carbon dioxide emissions or total greenhouse gases (horizontal axis). The first panel shows a simple, linear relationship. Although the law of diminishing returns might imply a nonlinear curve (becoming steeper at higher percentages of carbon reduction), the model

Figure 5.1 Hypothetical carbon reduction cost curves

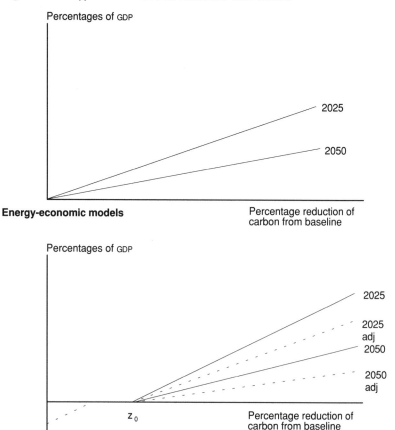

results surveyed in chapter 4 suggest that the relationship is merely linear. Those results indicate, moreover, that the further into the future the percentage of reduction is delayed, the lower the cost will be (because of a wider array of technical alternatives), and thus the first panel shows a more gently sloped cost curve for a later target date.

The engineering and forestry information should provide the basis for two alterations in the overall cost curve (second panel of figure 5.1). First, to the extent that negative- or zero-cost options do exist for reducing emissions, their effect is to dislocate the origin of the cost curve toward the right, so that the first z_0 percent of reductions may be obtained at zero or negative cost.[1] Second, the engineering and forestry information may provide a basis for concluding that the slope of the cost curve is gentler than implied by the economic models. If so, the curve will shift to the two broken lines shown in the second panel.

The engineering estimates additionally serve the purpose of providing flesh for the skeletons on which the economic model estimates are based, typically using assumed or statistically estimated "elasticities" showing the response of energy and carbon to carbon taxes. In this sense they serve as reassurance that physical options for reducing emissions exist on the engineer's drawing board as well as on the economist's spreadsheet.

Attainable Efficiency Gains and Carbon Reductions: Illustrations

Energy-engineering-economic analysts have long maintained that major improvements in efficiency remain possible at low cost. Recently, two studies have added an aura of authority to this view: a study by the National Academy of Sciences (NAS 1991a) on possibilities for mitigating greenhouses gases, and a parallel study by the congressional Office of Technology Assessment (OTA 1991).

Buildings

Perhaps the most popular example of available energy savings is the compact fluorescent bulb. Lovins and Lovins (1991, 2) note that a 15-watt compact fluorescent bulb emits the same amount of light as a 75-watt incandescent bulb and lasts 13 times as long; they maintain that over its lifetime it can save enough coal-fired electricity to reduce carbon emissions by one ton, and at a net savings. The NAS (1991a, 54) reaches the striking conclusion that the replacement of an average of just 2.5 heavily used interior incandescent bulbs and one exterior bulb by compact fluorescent lights would reduce average household lighting energy requirements by 50 percent. Reasons why the compact fluorescent bulb has not already been widely adopted may include its relatively high initial cost and the different color of its light (discussion at the Center for Environmental Information, conference on Global Climate Change: The Economic Costs of Mitigation and Adaptation, Washington, 4–5 December 1990).

---

1. In fact, the intercept in the statistical regression line for the cost curve in chapter 4 is negative, indicating that even the top-down models are consistent with an initial range of negative-cost carbon reductions. However, because there are no negative-cost observations, this pattern is also consistent with an initial nonlinear range with positive but low cost.

Table 5.1 Energy consumption in the United States, by type, 1988 (exajoules)

Energy type	Industry	Buildings	Transportation	Total
Coal	3.0	0.2	0.0	19.8
Oil	9.2	2.8	21.9	35.8
Natural gas	8.1	7.9	0.5	19.6
Electricity	10.4	19.7	0.0	30.2[a]
Total	30.7	30.7	23.1	84.3[b]

a. Electric power is not additive with total.

b. Numbers may not sum to total because of independent rounding.

Source: Roger S. Carlsmith, William U. Chandler, James E. McMahon, and Danilo J. Santini. 1990. "Energy Efficiency: How Far Can We Go?" ORNL/TM-11441. Washington: US Department of Energy, Energy Information Administration, *Annual Energy Review 1988,* May 1989.

Window glazing, weather stripping, better insulation in building shells, and increased use of heat pumps and solar heating can reduce energy requirements for space heating and cooling. The OTA finds that with "moderate shell efficiency measures, such as thicker insulation and better windows, new homes will require an estimated 50 percent less heat and 25 percent less air conditioning than today's average new home" (OTA 1991, 17). More efficient and better insulated tanks and improved showerheads and other low-flow devices can reduce water heating costs. Citing a study by Rosenthal prepared for the NAS, Lovins and Lovins (1991, 12) estimate that, overall, presently available technologies could save 45 percent of the electricity and 50 percent of the direct fuel used in US residential and commercial buildings, and could do so at large net savings rather than increased cost. Carlsmith et al. (1990, 195) estimate that 36 percent of US energy consumption is in commercial and residential buildings; industry accounts for another 36 percent and transportation for the remaining 28 percent (table 5.1). Building improvements (primarily lighting conversion and insulation) could thus have a major impact on overall energy consumption and carbon emissions.

Transportation

One-fourth of total US energy consumption and two-thirds of oil consumption are in the area of transportation (table 5.1). US automobiles and light trucks alone account for 15 percent of the world's oil consumption (OTA 1991, 20). This energy use could be reduced by higher vehicle efficiency and reduced driving. The OTA anticipates that the average efficiency of new light vehicles, already up from 13 miles per gallon (mpg) in 1973 to 24 mpg in 1985, will rise to 37 mpg by the year 2010.[2] The group judges that this rate could be increased to 55 mpg or higher by 2010 under conscious policies to reduce carbon emissions (OTA 1991, 21, 153, 161). The OTA also notes that, despite the frequent criticism that higher fuel efficiency means lesser safety because of smaller car size, fatalities have declined since the mid-1970s even as average car size has declined (OTA 1991, 159). For the future, changes in design and devices such as airbags can help maintain safety.

The NAS (1991a, 55) less ambitiously considers that, with no change in fleet, automobile efficiency could rise to 32.5 mpg (CAFE) and that with fleet downsizing the measure could reach 46.8 mpg. More optimistically, Lovins and Lovins estimate that readily available technological improvements could increase US automobile efficiency to 33.7 mpg on the road (about 45 mpg CAFE) with no change in fleet new-car size and performance; the authors cite prototype vehicles with performance of well over 100 mpg.[3]

Increased fuel efficiency can be supplemented by savings from transportation management, including increased mass transit, car pooling, introduction of high-speed rail travel to replace short-distance air travel, improved maintenance (including proper tire inflation), and other measures. Important gains in fuel efficiency also appear to be available for heavy trucks, aircraft, and ships.

Industry

Engineering estimates suggest substantial scope for energy savings in industry. There have already been important gains, as US industry's use of energy fell from 33.8 exajoules (EJ) in 1973 to 30.6 EJ in 1988, despite an increase of more than one-third in industrial output over the same period (an exajoule is 10^{18} joules, or 0.95 quadrillion British thermal units). Within-industry gains in efficiency saved over 10 EJ, and shifts in the composition of product demand another 5 EJ (Carlsmith et al. 1990, 201).

The OTA (1991, 23) estimates that four sectors—paper, chemicals, petroleum, and primary metals—account for three-fourths of energy use in manufacturing. It notes that energy savings could be large if these industries maintain their 1980–85 rates of efficiency gains (2.3 percent to 4.3 percent annually). More broadly, the cogeneration of electricity as a byproduct of industrial heat is one major area for gains. Others include motor efficiency and (for carbon reduction) shifting from coal- to gas-fired operations.

---

2. The Environmental Protection Agency's (EPA) corporate average fuel economy (CAFE) measure. On-the-road efficiency is about one-fourth lower.

3. They cite "crushable-metal-foam bodies . . . series-hybrid drives, switched-reluctance motors integrated into the axles at zero marginal weight, power-electronic regenerative braking" and other innovations (Lovins and Lovins 1991, 8).

Energy savings in industrial processes are important. Thus, Carlsmith et al. (1990, 208–10) note that electric arc furnaces using scrap are much more energy efficient for steel production than are traditional techniques and could increase their share of output from 36 percent to 60 percent. Other innovations include direct reduction or smelting of ore for making iron. The authors estimate that, overall, energy requirements in steelmaking could be reduced by 42 percent by 2010 at a cost below that of the energy saved. In the aluminum sector, improved design of electrolytic reduction cells, recycling, and direct casting can increase energy efficiency. Other examples of improvements in industrial processes include new techniques for making polyethylene (Unipol), low-pressure oxidation in industrial solvents, changes in paper-drying techniques (as well as paper recycling), and shifting from the wet to the dry process in cement making.

Electricity and Renewables

The replacement of high-carbon (coal) by low- or no-carbon electricity (gas, nuclear) is the other major area for reduction of carbon emissions, as 85 percent of carbon dioxide emissions by electric utilities in the United States are from coal-burning plants (OTA 1991, 92). One attractive alternative is the replacement of coal- and oil-fired thermal plants by gas turbine combined-cycle systems, especially new high-efficiency turbines derived largely from advances in jet engines (intercooled steam-injected gas turbines and chemically recuperated gas turbines; Williams 1989).

As for nuclear energy, political obstacles caused by concern about catastrophic failure and the disposal of nuclear waste could limit expansion;[4] moreover, costs tend to be higher than for fossil fuels. Nevertheless, higher operation rates of existing nuclear plants (at the 70 percent rates typical of Europe and Japan) could provide modest carbon savings, and more ambitious gains might be possible through new plants with improved designs, expected to be available after 2005 (OTA 1991, 25, 92).

Several renewable sources of electric energy show promise. The NAS estimates the following potential for additional US power generation from these sources (in quadrillion Btu, or quads): hydroelectric, 2; geothermal, 3.5; biomass, 2.4; solar photovoltaics, 2.5; solar thermal, 2.6; wind, 5.3 (NAS 1991a, 56–57). The total of 18.3 quads amounts to almost two-thirds of present US electrical ca-

---

4. The United States is still without a permanent disposal site for nuclear waste. The tentatively selected Yucca Mountain site in Nevada faces political opposition within that state, has not yet been finally endorsed scientifically for safety, and would not be ready before 2005 in any event (*Washington Post*, 28 April 1991).

pacity.[5] However, the NAS summary report indicates neither the expected cost levels for renewable energy sources nor their availability dates.

Lovins and Lovins (1991) find the speed of progress encouraging, and they maintain that renewable energy has already become close to competitive with fossil fuels. The authors note that integrating different types of renewable systems helps to alleviate problems such as storage (a problem for solar energy) and that even relatively costly sources of energy (e.g., photovoltaics) can already be competitive in remote areas. Citing research by the five national laboratories in the United States, the authors indicate that renewable electric and nonelectric energy could provide 44 EJ by the year 2030 at competitive costs (6 cents per kilowatt-hour of baseload, in 1988 dollars), or half of present total US energy demand (Lovins and Lovins 1991, 19).

Renewable sources for vehicle fuel could include methanol, compressed natural gas, ethanol from corn, synthetic natural gas from woody biomass, and even hydrogen (for which technology is the least developed). Methanol would provide little reduction in greenhouse gases if made from natural gas and would tend to increase them if made from coal. Compressed natural gas would have potential leaks of methane, a powerful greenhouse gas, that could largely offset the lesser carbon content of natural gas as opposed to oil. The OTA notes that ethanol from corn could aggravate greenhouse gases if coal were used for process heat. Among biomass fuels, the OTA finds that synthetic natural gas from woody biomass or methanol from the same source would have the largest potential for reducing greenhouse gas (a reduction of 60 percent to 70 percent from that emitted by vehicle fuels used at present), so long as the feedstock were offset with replacement biomass growth (OTA 1991, 159–60).

An Overview of Potential Carbon Reductions

Table 5.2 presents a summary of recent findings on the potential for energy savings and carbon emissions reductions by category. The studies in question are those of the OTA, the NAS, and Lovins and Lovins. The effects are grouped by three classes of adjustment: greater energy efficiency (the first two groups); lesser use of carbon to produce energy (the next two); and forestry measures to reduce emissions (the final category).

For the OTA estimates, the first column refers to cutbacks attainable by 2015 with "moderate" measures; the second, the larger reductions that would be possible with "tough" measures (implementation is discussed below). The estimates are stated as percentages of total (not individual-sector) US carbon

---

5. US electricity consumption stood at 30.2 EJ in 1988 (Carlsmith et al. 1990, 195), or 28.7 quads.

Table 5.2 Alternative estimates of the scope for energy savings and carbon reduction in the United States

Category	Office of Technology Assessment: 2015 reductions as percentage of total 1987 emissions		National Academy of Sciences: percentage reduction		Lovins and Lovins: energy savings possible	
	Moderate	Tough	Low	High	Twh	Percentage of total oil use
Stationary energy efficiency	20.1	38.45				
Lighting						
Residential	0.6	0.8	50	50		
Commercial	2.6	3.5	30	60		
Industrial	0.6	0.95				
Total	3.8	5.25			560	
Space cooling and heating						
Residential	2.2	3.4	40	60	—[a]	—[a]
Heating						
Cooling						
Commercial	4.1	6.35				
Heating			20	30	256[b]	
Cooling			30	70	392[b]	
Total	6.3	9.75			648	2.7–4.9
Water heating						
Residential	1.2[c]	1.9[c]	28[d]	41[d]		
Commercial	0.1	0.1	28[d]	38[d]		
Total	1.3	2.0			80–125	
Residential appliances	—[e]	—[e]	9[d]	23[d]	15[f]	
Office equipment	1.6	2.1				
Industrial processes	4.99	10.29			6.0	1.6
Industrial motors	1.2	3.85	23[d]	23[d]	300	
Industrial and commercial cogeneration	1.0	7.4	—[h]	—[h]		
Transportation energy efficiency	3.8	15.95				
Light vehicles						
Automobiles	0.8	3.65	32.5 mpg[i]	46.8 mpg[i]		37.2[j]
Trucks	0.5	2.6				
Total	1.3	7.25				
Trucks, buses, trains						
Trucks	0.7	2.8	40.3 mpg[i]	40.3 mpg[i]		
Total	0.7	2.8				6.6[k]

Measure					
Nonhighway		17[d]	17[d]		3.2[m]
Aircraft					3.8[n]
Transport management					
Public	0.2	3.5			
Speed limits	1.2	1.4			
Carpooling	0.4	1.0			
Total	1.8	5.9			
Carbon replacement, electric power					
Nuclear	4.6	11.85		2.4 quads	
Biomass	4.1	4.1		2.0 quads	
Hydro	0.0	1.2			
Other nonfossil	0.5	0.5			
Geothermal				3.5 quads	
Photovoltaic				2.5 quads	
Solar thermal				2.1 quads	
Wind				5.3 quads	
Total				13.9 quads	
Total	0.0	2.35		70.0	
Gas substitution	0.0	3.7	60		10.9
Other carbon replacement	0.0	2.55			
Industrial switch to gas	0.0	2.55			
Forestry					
Conservation	0.2	6.3			
Afforestation	0.2	0.2			
Urban	0.0	0.7			
Other	0.0	2.3			
Total	0.2	3.0		—[b]	
Timber productivity	0.0	3.1			
Other[a]	2.1	0.9		75[f]	
Total	31.3	77.2		1,783.0	64.4–66.6

twh = trillion watt-hours; mpg = miles per gallon.

a. Included in commercial.

b. Includes residential.

table continued next page

Table 5.2 Alternative estimates of the scope for energy savings and carbon reduction in the United States continued

Category	Office of Technology Assessment: 2015 reductions as percentage of total 1987 emissions		National Academy of Sciences: percentage reduction		Lovins and Lovins: energy savings possible	
	Moderate	Tough	Low	High	Twh	Percentage of total oil use

c. Includes appliances.

d. Calculated from corresponding "increase in efficiency."

e. Included in water heating.

f. Electronics.

g. Includes "housekeeping."

h. 25,000 Mwh.

i. Efficiency attainable, corporate average fuel economy (CAFE) measurement.

j. Assumes 71 mpg average mileage.

k. Saving of 40 percent.

m. Saving of 27 percent in existing aircraft (1.6), 40 percent in new (1.6).

n. Saving of 50 percent.

p. Assumes reforestation of 28.7 million hectares.

q. Includes fossil fuel efficiency and electricity carbon standards.

r. Residential process heat.

Sources: Office of Technology Assessment. 1991. *Changing by Degrees: Steps to Reduce Greenhouse Gases.* Washington: OTA, 11; National Academy of Sciences. 1991. *Policy Implications of Greenhouse Warming.* Washington: National Academy Press, 54–57; Amory B. Lovins and L. Hunter Lovins. 1991. "Least-cost Climatic Stabilization." Old Snowmass, CO: Rocky Mountain Institute (March).

emissions in 1987 (1.3 gigatons of carbon [GtC]); the corresponding percentages projected for the year 2015 are 0.7 times as large (i.e., the OTA expects carbon emissions to rise to 1.9 GtC by 2015 in the baseline).

The OTA calculates that moderate measures would suffice to reduce US carbon emissions in the year 2015 by 31.3 percent of 1987 levels, or by 21.9 percent of baseline levels for 2015. "Tough" measures could achieve reductions of 77.2 percent of 1987 levels, or 54 percent of 2015 levels. The OTA study calculates that the moderate measures could be implemented with net savings, although the reduction of some 15 percent in energy expenditures would be partially offset by higher costs of appliances, cars, and houses. It states a wide cost range for the "tough" measures, from a "savings of a few tenths of a percent to a cost up to 1.8 percent of Gross National Product (GNP) projected for 2015" (OTA 1991, 10). If "a few tenths" is set at -0.3, then the midpoint cost in the "tough" scenario amounts to 1.5/2, or 0.75 percent of GNP.

In terms of figure 5.1, the OTA estimates thus suggest that, for the United States, the point z_0 for cost-free or net-benefit carbon reductions would stand at about 20 percent of 2015 emissions. Moreover, for a point equal to 54 percent carbon emissions reduction, the cost would amount to a midpoint of only 0.75 percent of GNP. Considering that in chapter 4 a summary regression of cost model estimates would place a 54 percent cutback in carbon emissions from baseline in 2015 at a cost of 3 percent of GNP,[6] the OTA estimates imply not only a dislocation of the origin (to point z_0) but also a substantially lower slope of the cost curve (i.e., a shift to the broken line in figure 5.1).[7] Even if the upper bound of the OTA estimate is adopted, at 1.8 percent of GNP for a 54 percent emissions reduction it is considerably lower than what is typically found in the "top-down" models.

As indicated in table 5.2, a large share of the potential cutback (two-thirds in the moderate case, one-half in the "tough" case) arises in improved efficiency in stationary uses. In this subgroup, about one-third of potential reduction is in space cooling and heating; about one-half is in industrial energy use, especially industrial processes and (in the "tough" case) gains through cogeneration. The second subgroup for increased energy efficiency transportation provides only about one-sixth to one-fifth of potential carbon savings. The next broad category, replacement of high-carbon by low- or no-carbon energy, provides comparable savings, primarily in the generation of electricity. Finally, forestry measures

---

6. From equation 4.1': $-1.16 + 0.091(54) - 0.0246(2015 - 1990) = 3.1$ percent.

7. A linear cost curve passing through zero at 20 percent cutback, and 0.75 percent of GNP at 54 percent cutback, has the following form: $\%Y = -0.44 + 0.022 \%C$, where $\%Y$ is cost as a percentage of GNP and $\%C$ is the percentage cut in carbon emissions from baseline. This slope is less than one-fourth that found in the regression from economic model estimates.

provide little contribution in the moderate case and less than one-tenth of the cutback in the "tough" case.

The columns in table 5.2 for the NAS estimates also show relatively large potential energy and carbon reductions. Potential energy savings in stationary uses average about 30 percent in the low case and 45 percent in the high case. The NAS review foresees a one-third increase in light-vehicle efficiency to 32.5 mpg (CAFE) with no change in average car size necessary; with downsizing and other fleet changes, efficiency could approximately double (with implicit fuel savings of 25 percent and nearly 50 percent, respectively). Fuel savings of more than one-sixth are also attainable in aircraft. The NAS estimates of relatively large additional electricity potential from renewable sources are discussed above.

Table 5.2 also reports estimates by Lovins and Lovins (1991), derived from their "cost curves" for energy savings.[8] The authors estimate that 450 trillion watt-hours (twh) can be saved at a *negative* cost of 1.4 cents per kwh through improved lighting, as reduced maintenance costs exceed installation costs. Other major sources of low-cost electricity savings include "drivepower" (300 twh at a cost of 0.3 cent per kwh), cooling (392 twh at 1.0 cent per kwh), and space heating (256 twh at 3.0 cents per kwh). Overall, the authors estimate that 1,350 twh can be saved at a unit cost of 1.0 cent per kwh or less, and 1,730 twh at a unit cost below 3½ cents per kwh (in 1986 dollars). Compared with the average US price of 6 to 7 cents per kwh,[9] this estimate implies that nearly three-fourths of US consumption of electricity (2,306 twh in 1986) could be eliminated at a net savings through efficiency gains. Such estimates would appear much more optimistic than the OTA and NAS calculations, however.

Similarly, the cost curve suggested by Lovins and Lovins for improved efficiency in US oil use attributes massive savings potential to improved vehicle

---

8. These curves are typical of the methodology in the engineering approach. They are based on an array of various energy-saving measures, ordered from least cost (e.g., per kilowatt-hour) to highest cost. For each entry there is an estimate of the amount of energy that can be saved (e.g., in kilowatt-hours). A cost curve is then drawn, with the unit cost on the vertical axis and the amount of energy saved on the horizontal axis. The curve is a step function, or a rising series of horizontal lines with each connected to its successor by a vertical line. Each horizontal line segment tells the unit cost (height) and the amount of energy that can be saved (width). Note that this methodology differs from the typical economic-elasticity approaches in an important way. It assigns a strict sequential ordering of each of the alternative measures, a step that is possible only because of the assumption that *all* of the adjustments for the particular category (e.g., automobile fuel efficiency) occur at a standard unit cost. In contrast, the elasticity approaches implicitly assume that adjustment takes place simultaneously across the whole front of categories and that there are low-cost and higher-cost adjustments along a continuum within each.

9. In February 1991, average electricity prices stood at 7.6 cents per kwh for residential use, 7.3 cents per kwh for commercial use, and 4.7 cents per kwh for industrial use (US Department of Energy, Energy Information Administration, *Monthly Energy Review*, February 1991).

Table 5.3 Alternative estimates of US emissions reductions resulting from National Academy of Sciences moderate-cost measures
(millions of metric tons of carbon-equivalent)

	Reduction from 1990 levels (maximum impact)	Cost	OTA 2015 scaled to 1990 levels[a]	
			Moderate	Tough
Building energy efficiency	245	B	114	183
Vehicle efficiency	82	B	15	79
Industrial energy management	136	B–L	73	210
Transportation system management	14	B–L	24	68
Power plant heat rate	14	B–L		
Landfill gas collection	54	L		
Halocarbon-CFC reduction	381	L		
Agriculture	54	L		
Reforestation	54	L–M	2	68
Electricity supply	272	L–M	60	109
Total	1,306			
Total for six comparable categories	817		291	717

B = net benefit; L = low cost (up to $36 per ton of carbon); M = moderate cost (from $37 to $367 per ton of carbon); CFC = chlorofluorocarbon; OTA = Office of Technology Assessment.

a. Total US greenhouse gas emissions in 1990 were equivalent to 8 billion tons of carbon dioxide, or 2.2 billion tons of carbon. Of the total, 1.3 billion tons of carbon were from carbon dioxide; the remainder includes methane, CFCs, and nitrous oxide. Calculated from National Academy of Sciences (1991a, 62).

Source: National Academy of Sciences. 1991. *Policy Implications of Greenhouse Warming.* Washington: National Academy Press; Office of Technology Assessment. 1991. *Changing by Degrees: Steps to Reduce Greenhouse Gases.* Washington: Office of Technology Assessment (February).

efficiency: 37.2 percent of present oil consumption could be eliminated with an increase of automobile efficiency to 71 mpg, and at zero cost.[10] A total of approximately 64 percent of US oil use could be eliminated at a marginal cost of less than $10 per barrel, according to the authors. Once again, the Lovins and Lovins estimates appear to lie on the optimistic end of the range.[11]

Table 5.3 reports the NAS and OTA estimates, consolidated into categories considered by the NAS authors to be the leading candidates for obtaining greenhouse gas reductions at modest cost. In this presentation, the cutbacks are

10. This evaluation is apparently based on the authors' finding that "two prototypes, a 71-mpg Volvo and a 92-mpg Peugeot, are said to cost about the *same* to build as ordinarily inefficient cars of comparable size" (Lovins and Lovins 1991, 7, emphasis in the original).

11. Note that both the oil and the electricity cost estimates appear to be formulated in gross terms before deducting the cost of the energy saved. The estimates thus imply net savings so long as the cost per energy unit (kilowatt-hour, barrel) is lower than the market price.

expressed in millions of metric tons of carbon and should be interpreted against the 1990 absolute emissions base of 1.3 GtC for carbon dioxide and 0.9 GtC for other trace gases.[12] The OTA estimates in table 5.3 are converted so that they are on a comparable 1990 scale.[13]

The NAS estimates refer to the "maximum feasible" cutback in each category. They are arrayed in order of cost per metric ton of carbon-equivalent that is reduced from greenhouse gas emissions. The first two entries (buildings and vehicle efficiency) show net benefits (B), indicating that the NAS authors believe that carbon reductions can be achieved in these areas at net savings rather than costs to consumers and businesses. The next three entries involve unit costs that are either net benefits or "low" costs (B-L), no higher than $36 per ton of carbon-equivalent.[14] They are followed by low-cost categories (L) and, finally, low- to medium-cost areas (L-M) with the unit cost of reduction no greater than $367 per ton of carbon-equivalent (M). Importantly, the NAS estimates include three categories that deal with greenhouse gases other than carbon dioxide: landfill gas (methane), CFCS, and agriculture (nitrous oxide from fertilizer and methane from rice paddies and ruminant animals).

The NAS estimates indicate that up to 327 million tons of carbon annually, or 25 percent of carbon emissions and 15 percent of all greenhouse gas emissions, can be eliminated at a net benefit (the first two categories). Up to 491 million tons of carbon-equivalent (38 percent of carbon emissions and 22 percent of total greenhouse gases) can be eliminated at either "net benefits" or at a low cost of under $36 per ton of carbon (the first five categories). The three non-carbon categories (primarily CFCS) provide the next tranche of cost-effective savings, bringing total greenhouse gas reductions at less than $36 per ton of carbon to the equivalent of 980 GtC annually (45 percent of total greenhouse gas emissions). If the final two categories are added with unit costs up to $367 per ton of carbon (M), the total cutback can be extended to as much as 1,306 million tons of carbon-equivalent, or 59 percent of total greenhouse gases. In this case, 817 million tons of carbon from carbon-source emissions (63 percent of the carbon-origin total) would be eliminated.

In table 5.3 the OTA estimates for the groupings corresponding to those in the NAS report broadly confirm those of the NAS. Thus, the OTA "moderate" measures

---

12. The original NAS data are in tons of carbon dioxide. They are converted here by dividing by 3.67. Correspondingly, all estimates of cost per ton are multiplied by 3.67.

13. The original OTA estimates are a hybrid figure that expresses absolute 2015 carbon changes as percentages of the 1987 absolute emissions base. For comparability with the NAS 1990 base, the OTA percentage estimates are reduced by the multiple 0.7 to take account of the ratio of the 1987 to 2105 baseline emissions; these reduced percentages are then applied to the 1990 absolute base.

14. The original NAS cost ranges are as follows: $B \leq 0$; $L = 1 to $9 per ton of carbon-dioxide-equivalent; $M = 10 to $100 per ton of carbon dioxide.

produce annual carbon savings (against a 1990-scale base) of 291 million tons of carbon at zero or negative cost, about the same as the total for the first two "benefit" categories of the NAS. When "tough" measures are considered, the overall OTA carbon savings stand at 717 million tons annually, again about the same as the 817 million tons estimated for the full range of carbon-relevant measures considered by the NAS.

The NAS authors suggest that actual implementation might be expected to lie somewhere between 25 percent and 100 percent of their "maximum feasible" estimates. Overall, they summarize their findings as follows:

> The United States could reduce its greenhouse gas emissions by between 10 and 40 percent of the 1990 levels at low cost, or perhaps some net savings, if proper policies were implemented. (NAS 1991a, 106)

In view of the percentage range for implementation suggested in the NAS report, its central estimates may be interpreted as indicating between 25 percent and 100 percent adoption of the technical improvements that were examined. Under this assumption it is possible to derive a central expected cost curve for emissions reductions. For comparability with the OTA estimates (and those of top-down models), it is useful to limit the analysis to carbon dioxide categories.

Figure 5.2, derived from the NAS and OTA estimates, presents cost curves for carbon reduction. The horizontal axis shows the percentage by which carbon is reduced, and the vertical axis shows the cost as a percentage of GDP. For the OTA, the two "observations" developed above are displayed. For the NAS, the estimates are calculated as follows. The intercept on the horizontal axis is set at the cumulative reductions for the first five categories in table 5.2. Thus, it is assumed that in the marginal category (power plant heat rate) the range from benefit (negative cost) to low cost (B-L) works out on average to zero cost. Using the average between low and full implementation, total carbon reductions through this group amount to 307 million tons, or 23.6 percent of 1990 emissions. The first NAS cost curve observation is thus that a 23.6 percent reduction in carbon emissions may be obtained at zero cost.

The second NAS observation incorporates the final two groups of table 5.3 (skipping the noncarbon trace gases). As the floor unit cost per ton of carbon (tC) for these two categories (L) is $36 and the ceiling (M) is $367, it is assumed that average cost is the midpoint, or $202 per tC. With the central quantity estimate, carbon reductions in these two categories amount to 203.8 million tons (15.7 percent of the total). Multiplied by the estimated average cost, the total annual cost amounts to $41.2 billion, or 0.75 percent of 1990 GNP. The second "observation" on the NAS cost curve is thus a cumulative 39.3 percent reduction in carbon emissions at a cumulative cost of 0.75 percent of GNP. Because this approach makes no allowance for savings in the initial "benefit"

Figure 5.2 Engineering-based estimates of carbon reduction costs

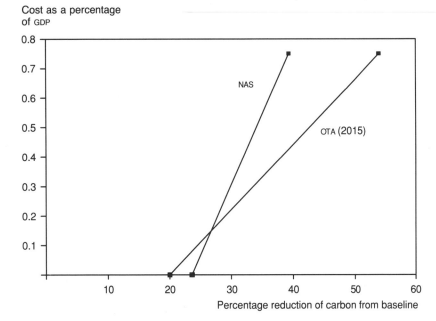

Cost as a percentage
of GDP

NAS

OTA (2015)

Percentage reduction of carbon from baseline

NAS = National Academy of Sciences; OTA = Office of Technology Assessment

Sources: National Academy of Sciences. 1991. *Policy Implications of Greenhouse Warming.*
Washington: National Academy Press; Office of Technology Assessment. 1991. *Changing by Degrees: Steps to Reduce Greenhouse Gases.* Washington: Office of Technology Assessment (February).

categories (treating them instead as zero-cost or "benefit"), it may overstate cumulative cost.

The resulting cost curves in figure 5.2 show considerable similarity between the NAS and OTA estimates. Both curves show that approximately the first 20 percent to 25 percent of carbon emissions cutbacks can be achieved at zero cost (and perhaps a significant net benefit, as the initial portions of the curves lie either along the zero cost line or below it). The two estimates place a cost of 0.75 percent of GNP annually for the reduction of carbon emissions by a range of approximately 40 percent to 55 percent. However, the NAS central estimates imply more rapidly rising costs than do those of the OTA. On the other hand, bottom-up estimates from sources such as the Lovins and Lovins study would tend to show even lower incremental costs than do the OTA estimates.

Like the OTA results discussed above, the cost line for the NAS results lies below the range typically estimated from the top-down economic models.[15] The analysis below considers both classes of estimates to obtain a synthesis view of abatement costs.

In reaching the overall conclusion that some 20 percent to 25 percent of carbon emissions in the United States might be eliminated at zero cost by a move to "best practices," it is important that there not be a misguided inference that dealing with the greenhouse problem will be cheap over the longer term. As of early 1992, debate within the United States seemed to be divided between the view that an international target of limiting emissions by the year 2000 to their 1990 levels would be costless (largely on the basis of the engineering approach reviewed here) and the alternative view that costs could be high. This formulation of the debate missed the point. Serious action to curb global warming would involve emissions restraints over a period of two to three centuries, not just through the year 2000. Whether the first step is low-cost (or even no-cost) is significant but of limited help in gauging the eventual costs.

The central point is that a *one-time* gain from elimination of inefficiencies would shift the entire curve of baseline emissions downward but still leave future emissions far above present levels. Consider the period through the year 2100. As indicated in chapter 2, a central baseline estimate calls for approximately 20 GtC of global carbon emissions by that year. As developed in chapter 7, an aggressive program to limit global warming would mean restricting emissions to approximately 4 GtC annually. Suppose the engineering approach is correct that, say, 20 percent of emissions can be eliminated for free. Such gains would still leave emissions at 16 GtC in the year 2100, far above the 4-GtC ceiling needed to substantially curb the greenhouse effect. The remaining cutbacks would have to be achieved through more costly industrial reductions in energy availability beyond those achievable through costless efficiency gains. In short, the "best practices" school provides a basis for expecting that addressing the global warming problem may be less costly than otherwise might be thought, but it by no means warrants the conclusion that action will be costless over the longer term.

---

15. The NAS report presents a graph that suggests that the upper and lower bounds of the engineering-based cost estimates bracket the range of the economic model estimates (NAS 1991a, figure 6.4, 62). Yet the "central" NAS estimate derived here yields a cost curve below the midrange of the economic models. All of the explicit discussion of cost ranges and cutback potential in the NAS report points toward relatively low costs, so that the high-cost, low-cutback curve included in the report's illustration is implicitly less relevant. The report's statement that "technology costing and energy modeling are in rough agreement" (NAS 1991a, 49) would thus appear misleading.

Implementation: Obstacles and Instruments

Whatever the slope of the cost curve, there is no particular puzzle about why changes that would incur net costs have not been adopted. If the first 20 percent to 25 percent of carbon emissions reductions would indeed generate net benefits, however, as suggested in the engineering studies, the question arises as to why these improvements are not automatically adopted. The NAS report notes that "technological costing studies are often criticized as presenting overly optimistic estimates" because of this gap between implementation and hypothetical savings. The report explains the paradox on these grounds: "Realizing such savings . . . would require a set of conditions not now in existence [and] overcoming private or public barriers of various kinds" (NAS 1991a, 49).

Lovins and Lovins (1991, 68) maintain that "distinctive, well-known market failures" explain the nonadoption of energy improvements with net benefits. They cite poor access of consumers to information; a wide divergence between the (high) rate of discount applied by the consumer for electricity demand and the (much lower) rate adopted by utilities in developing supply; a divergence of interests between builders and occupants; and perverse incentive regimes that lead utilities to seek increased electricity sales even though the reduction of volume would provide greater efficiency and potential profit if companies could keep or share in the savings. On the discount rate, Lovins and Lovins (1991, 34) argue that the consumer typically expects a payback on energy investment within two years, whereas utility companies apply discount rates of 5 percent to 6 percent, stretching the payback period to 12 to 14 years.

Similarly, the OTA study suggests that "many individuals prefer low first-cost options over low life-cycle cost options"; yet the cutting-edge technologies tend to have higher first-cost (capital cost) and lower life-cycle cost. The OTA (1991, 13) also cites distortions from fragmented decision making, including the divergence between builder-developer and occupant.

The *discount rate* issue is formally one of capital market failure. If consumers had access to finance for energy investments at rates close to those used by the utility companies, the wedge between the two rates of return would be narrowed, and distortions favoring increased electricity supply rather than lesser use would be reduced.

Information cost is another obstacle. As an example, in 1987 US consumers spent approximately $10 billion on electricity for air conditioning (US Department of Energy, Energy Information Administration, *Annual Energy Review*, 1989). If it is assumed that about one-third of homes had air conditioning, the average cost was some $375 per year per household covered. Over a 10-year horizon (i.e., the lifetime of new equipment being considered), the discounted present value of these electricity expenses would amount to about $3,000 (discounting at rates in a range of 2 percent to 5 percent per year).

In principle, the reconversion decision is complicated; potentially it should involve making forecasts for electricity prices over the lifetime of the new system; and it requires information on efficiencies of alternative systems (including greater home insulation and double-glazed windows). Suppose that the head of household had a typical income of $35,000 (about $18 per hour, or some 50 percent above the manufacturing average to allow for a tendency toward greater coverage of air conditioning for upper-income homes). If the decision required two days, the decision cost would amount to $280. On this basis, just to cover the information cost for the decision, the household head would have to have a confident expectation that the annual bill for air conditioning could be cut by some 10 percent. In effect, there would be a 10 percent subsidy on the price of electricity used in existing air conditioners as opposed to new systems because of the information cost.

This problem has the nature of a public good. If a pool of similar households could contract an independent entity to make the sophisticated calculations required to identify an optimal cooling system, the total amount that could be spent on the decision would equal the sum of the fees across households (near zero with a large pool); yet each could use the information without reducing the benefit of its consumption by any other household in the pool. Some form of collective action by a centralizing entitity (e.g., the nation, in the case of the public good of an army) is normally the solution to a public good problem. In principle, the electric utility could serve this centralizing role, although there would be the problem of householder suspicion that the diagnosis was not being offered by a disinterested party.

Demand-side management is an important instrument for addressing such obstacles as divergent discount rates and high information costs relative to multiple small decisions. In these programs, electric utilities design changes for customers that reward the saving of energy. The instruments include financing at favorable rates for investments in improved energy efficiency, rebates for reductions in electricity use, the free distribution of high-efficiency light bulbs, and "feebates" that impose a fee for hookup to the power grid for customers with low efficiency and a rebate to those with high efficiency (OTA 1991, 18; Lovins and Lovins 1991, 37–38). An important parallel measure is to restructure utility rate regimes so that the utility has an incentive to encourage energy efficiency.[16]

It is unclear just how far the elimination of market failure would go to secure adoption of energy efficiency measures that have net benefits. On the basis of the above review, however, it does not seem unreasonable to suggest that some 15 percent to 20 percent of carbon emissions could be eliminated at zero cost

---

16. Thus, beginning in 1990 the Pacific Gas and Electric Company was to be allowed to keep as extra profit 15 percent of certain energy savings by consumers (Lovins and Lovins 1991, 39).

with the assistance of a more concerted public program aimed at realizing energy savings.

Regulation is an alternative and more traditional approach to environmental problems. In principle it, too, is premised on the correction of market failure, namely, the failure of private prices to incorporate the external diseconomies of environmental pollution. The regulatory approach runs the risk of all "command and control" solutions: by setting inflexible targets, it may impose extremely high costs in some instances. There may be some broadly agreed range of minimum standards, however, that can provide for some closing of the gap between actual and best practices. Labeling requirements are mild regulations that can help overcome the problem of information cost by revealing life-cycle efficiency. More generally, however, regulation by itself is less likely than demand-side management to secure whatever negative-cost improvements may exist. Consumers and firms already have the option of doing voluntarily whatever the regulation would mandate, and they would thus likely perceive that the mandated changes would impose costs.[17]

Officially supported research and development is another important instrument for implementation of improved energy and greenhouse gas efficiency. US federal funding for renewable energy sources has fallen from $1.3 billion in 1980 to only $135 million in 1990 (in 1990 dollars; OTA 1991, 16). A reversal of this trend would be consistent with the move toward large research funding in other areas of the greenhouse problem.

Forestry Measures

In public perception of the greenhouse problem, a popular view is that planting trees can make a major contribution by withdrawing carbon from the air. At a simplistic level, trees tend to be seen as "scrubbers" that cleanse the atmosphere. The important point to recognize about afforestation, however, is that it is essentially a temporary and limited solution.

Conceptual Framework

Afforestation is a temporary remedy because a forest stores additional carbon only when it is expanding; once it reaches a steady state, the carbon released

---

17. In principle, however, a well-designed regulation could be imposed that would replicate exactly the optimal solution the consumer would arrive at if he or she participated in a pool that contracted for a centralized decision-suggesting entity, overcoming the information-cost problem discussed above but otherwise not pressing the consumer to move into a range of options that have positive life-cycle costs.

by dying trees offsets that sequestered by new and growing trees. In economic terms, the issue is one of stock versus flow: afforestation contributes to the reduction of carbon emissions only so long as there is a positive flow in the form of expanding forest mass. Once the flow ceases and the stock of trees reaches a steady state, there is no further contribution. From this standpoint, it does not matter for further carbon reduction whether the forest is N million hectares or $2N$; steady-state forest size does not influence net carbon withdrawal.

Afforestation is a limited solution because there are limits to the area that can be put into forest in the extreme, the earth's entire land surface. More relevantly, the need for agricultural (and urban) land limits the area that can be placed in forest. Another limiting factor is the consideration that global warming is expected to cause forest loss over a century or more; as the forests seek to migrate poleward, the rate of migration of the new-growth perimeter will be considerably slower than that of the die-off border (EPA 1989a). It may thus be difficult to avoid deforestation, let alone counter carbon emissions by achieving net afforestation.

Despite these caveats, the forestry options warrant close consideration for three reasons. First, reducing existing deforestation (primarily in developing countries) is likely to be one of the lowest-cost alternatives for reducing carbon emissions. Second, even if afforestation is temporary, it might provide an important window of policy response over some 30 to 40 years and thereby buy time for technological change in noncarbon energy sources to take place. Third, and perhaps most important, if afforestation is carried out in a coherent strategy linked to eventual use of the resulting biomass for renewable energy that would replace fossil fuel energy, then the forestry option can provide a much more lasting contribution to resolving the greenhouse problem. If energy is obtained through growing trees and then using their biomass for fuel, the carbon emissions from burning the biomass are canceled out by the carbon that was absorbed from the atmosphere during the growing stage. There is a closed cycle of zero net emissions. In contrast, burning coal, oil, or natural gas releases carbon from a sequestered underground source with no offsetting removal from the atmosphere.

Figure 5.3 illustrates these features of afforestation. In the upper panel, one hectare of new forest grows to maturity over a period of M years. During this period, it sequesters a tons of carbon annually. The cumulative carbon stored is shown in the line CS. In the lower panel of the figure, the corresponding costs and benefits per hectare are illustrated. The annual cost of afforestation is shown as the opportunity cost of the land that is diverted, or R dollars per hectare per year. The annual benefit of the program is shown in the broken line beginning at ap_c on the vertical axis but falling to zero at time M. This benefit curve indicates that, at a going price of p_c for each ton of carbon sequestered, the annual benefit is a tons times price p_c during the initial phase of forest growth and expansion, or up until maturity year M. However, thereafter there is no further benefit (no

Figure 5.3 Economics of afforestation for carbon sequestration

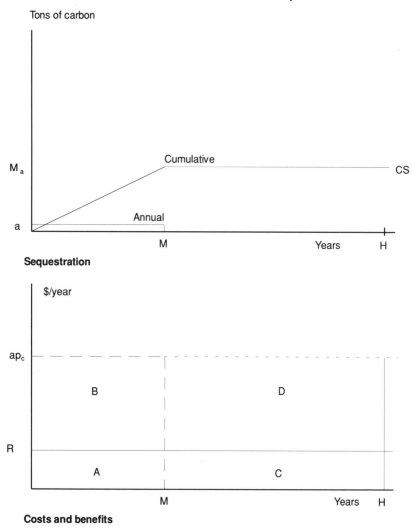

Tons of carbon

M_a

Cumulative

CS

Annual

a

M

Years

H

Sequestration

$/year

ap_c

B

D

R

A

C

M

Years

H

Costs and benefits

additional net sequestration after steady-state forest stock on the hectare of land), but the annual opportunity cost of the land that is diverted continues indefinitely, or until H, the most distant year considered in the horizon under analysis.

In the simple afforestation case, the costs and benefits will depend on the rate of carbon sequestration, the price of carbon per ton, the land opportunity cost per hectare, and the length of the planning horizon (H) relative to the period of forest maturity (M). In the lower panel of the figure, total cost over the horizon will be areas $A + C$ (annual cost times H years). Total benefit over the period will be areas $A + B$, equal to the annual benefit during the growing phase (ap_c) times the number of growing years (M). There will thus be net benefits from the program only if area B exceeds area C. The longer the planning horizon (H), the less likely it is that there will be net benefits, because area C keeps growing over time, whereas area B does not. Discounting costs in the future makes the calculus more favorable to afforestation (because the gains from storing carbon come early, whereas the indefinite immobilization of land extends into a distant, discounted future). However, the issues remain essentially the same.

Now consider instead a program of afforestation combined with earmarked use of the forest for renewable energy from the biomass. The costs and benefits are the same as before up until maturity year M. However, suppose that thereafter a fraction $1/M$ of the forested hectare is harvested and replanted. Suppose that the harvested biomass is used to produce energy. Suppose further that the alternative sources of energy that the biomass displaces have exactly the same carbon content as the amount contained in the biomass feedstock (and, equivalently, the new carbon being stored in the planting on the harvested area). Under these assumptions, the program takes on a benefit profile that turns the broken-line benefit curve from a steep decline at M into a horizontal line extending to the indefinite future, and thus through H. Benefits will now equal areas $(A + B) + (C + D)$, and the program will have net benefits so long as $ap_c > R$.

A few parameters suffice to provide the broad outlines of afforestation costs and benefits. Let a be the number of tons of carbon per hectare sequestered during the growing phase, M the number of years to maturity, and H the number of years to the end of the planning horizon. Let R be the annual opportunity cost of the land, ρ the annual discount rate, and p_c the going price per ton of carbon for other abatement programs, such as energy conservation. Then the net benefit per hectare, z, for simple afforestation will be:

$$(5.1) \quad z = \sum_{t=1}^{M} ap_c/(1 + \rho)^t - \sum_{t=1}^{H} R/(1 + \rho)^t.$$

If there is no time discounting (i.e., $\rho = 0$), this net benefit simplifies to $z = Map_c - HR$.

If the program is one that incorporates biomass energy production, let β be the number of tons of carbon displaced annually by the avoidance of alternative fossil fuel production once the hectare is at full forest growth and enters the harvesting period. In this case, the net benefit per hectare becomes:

$$(5.1') \quad z' = \sum_{t=1}^{M} ap_c/(1 + \rho)^t - \sum_{t=1}^{H} R/(1 + \rho)^t + \sum_{t=1}^{H} \beta p_c/(1 + \rho)^t$$

where the final term shows the value of the carbon emissions averted by biomass energy use once the area has reached the mature, harvesting phase.

Deforestation

Although few estimates exist, there is near consensus among analysts that relatively low-cost reductions in carbon emissions may be obtained through the reduction of deforestation (e.g., Nordhaus 1990b, 20). Recent estimates for Brazil, Indonesia, and Côte d'Ivoire are available from Darmstadter and Plantinga (1991, 54–57). The authors adopt estimates by Haughton et al. for the amount of carbon emissions annually from deforestation in the three countries (336 million metric tons [mmt], 192 mmt, and 100 mmt annually in 1980, respectively). They then estimate the value of agricultural and logging production that would be sacrificed in a program that halted deforestation. On this basis, Darmstadter and Plantinga estimate that the cost per ton of carbon of avoiding carbon emissions from deforestation amounts to $2.30 in Brazil, $15 in Indonesia, and $8 in Côte d'Ivoire. The higher costs in Indonesia and Côte d'Ivoire derive from the greater value of logging activities over alternative uses for the land in these countries than in Brazil, where cattle grazing has a relatively high value.

Reis and Margulis (1991) have provided an in-depth analysis for Brazil. They place recent carbon emissions from Amazon deforestation at 389 mmt of carbon annually. I have calculated that, even if the entire amount of agricultural production in the Amazon were eliminated to avoid deforestation, the corresponding cost would be only $4 per ton of carbon annually (Cline 1991b). If a more reasonable but still large estimate of a 25 percent sacrifice of agricultural output is used, the cost falls to $1 per ton of carbon.

Overall, the Darmstadter-Plantinga and Cline (1991b) estimates imply that some 680 million tons of carbon emissions could be avoided annually at an average cost of only $6.35 per ton of carbon in just these three developing countries.[18] This abatement would amount to 42 percent of the 1.6 GtC ($\pm$ 1 GtC) annual emissions from deforestation estimated by the Intergovernmental Panel on Climate Change (1990b, 14).

A marginal cost of some $6 per ton of carbon is smaller by an order of magnitude or more than typical carbon taxes estimated by the economic-energy models for major reductions in carbon dioxide emissions (chapter 4). It is not implausible that an aggressive program of forest conservation could cut defo-

---

18. This estimate uses the Reis-Margulis estimate for Amazon deforestation emissions, applies an average between the Cline (1991b) and Darmstadter-Plantinga estimates of cost per ton for Brazil, and otherwise uses the estimates from the latter source.

restation emissions globally by, say, 1 GtC annually, or by about 15 percent of total anthropogenic emissions. Moreover, Reis and Margulis (1991) use a projection model to calculate that Amazon deforestation emissions could triple by the year 2030, so the proportionate share of deforestation in the emissions baseline could hold relatively constant or at least not fall by much over the next several decades. On this basis, a cut of as much as 5 percent to 10 percent of total global emissions from baseline at low cost through deforestation abatement might be achievable. This assessment means that, in the cost curve of figure 5.1, there is a second reason beyond the "net benefit" opportunities in the engineering approach for dislocating the origin toward the right (or, more precisely, allowing for a nonzero but low-cost initial segment of the cost curve to the right of point z_0 in the figure): the reason is that significant low-cost reductions should be available from limiting deforestation.

Afforestation

The literature suggests a much wider range of costs for carbon removal through afforestation, with costs potentially much higher than for reduced deforestation. A closer examination of existing estimates suggests, however, that the costs of carbon removal through afforestation are also far lower than the tax range of $100 to $250 per ton of carbon typically proposed by top-down energy-economic models.

For the United States, the best available estimates for afforestation are by Moulton and Richards (1990). The two authors carefully build up a marginal cost curve that ranges from $5 to $10 per ton of carbon for the first 60 million tons of carbon sequestered annually (on the first 25 million acres) to some $35 per ton as total annual sequestration rises from 700 million to 800 million tons (and land area from 300 million to 340 million acres). They consider soil type and current land use. To minimize economic costs, their ordering tends to place into forestation only land of lower quality (land capability classification groups V through VII, rapidly eroding lands, and land with excessively wet soils). They identify 224 million acres of cropland and 120 million acres of land in pasture or sparse forest as available for afforestation (Moulton and Richards 1990, tables 1A and 2).

Moulton and Richards estimate annual costs per acre as comprised of rental cost (in the range of $60 per acre) and planting costs annualized at a 10 percent discount rate. They assume a 40-year planting cycle, and their estimates do not take account of land opportunity cost thereafter. Table 5.4 reports their resulting schedule of marginal costs and sequestration rates (converted to metric tons and hectares). As indicated, these rates are in the range of $12 to $25 per ton for the first 400 million tons of carbon stored annually and rise to $40 per ton at

Table 5.4 Afforestation costs in the United States

Annual carbon sequestration (millions of tons)	Cost per metric ton (dollars)	Sequestration rate (tons of carbon per hectare per year)
0–100	12.2	5.4
100–200	18.2	4.5
200–300	22.9	5.8
300–400	24.6	5.6
400–500	26.0	7.1
500–600	31.2	5.6
600–700	38.6	6.7
700–800	40.7	6.2

Source: Calculated from Robert J. Moulton and Kenneth R. Richards. 1990. *Costs of Sequestering Carbon Through Tree Planting and Forest Management in the United States.* Washington: US Department of Agriculture, Forest Service, table 1A.

800 million tons annually. The sequestration rates are about six tons of carbon per hectare per year (and rise slightly in higher-cost areas because of higher-quality land).

The central finding of the two authors is that the United States could sequester up to 429 million short tons of carbon annually (389 million metric tons), or 30 percent of annual US carbon emissions, at an average cost of $17.91 per short ton ($19.75 per metric ton; Moulton and Richards 1990, table 11). This amount of annual carbon storage would require 197.6 million acres (80 million hectares) of land. Sequestration could be pushed even further but at rising marginal cost. In sum, the study implies that in the United States a relatively large amount of carbon could be sequestered through afforestation at a cost of less than $20 per ton.

Sedjo and Solomon (1989, 113 15) have estimated even lower costs. They calculate that newly planted forests can remove 6.2 tons of carbon per hectare annually in both temperate and tropical regions. They place the maturation ("rotation") period at 30 to 50 years. Using the shorter period, the maximum carrying capacity would thus amount to 186 tons of carbon per hectare of mature forest.[19] The authors estimate that in the United States it costs $400 per hectare to plant new forested area and another $400 to $1,000 per hectare to purchase the land. Using the higher price for land purchases, the total cost (once-and-for-all, because the annual rental cost is collapsed into the price for purchasing land) thus amounts to $1,400 per hectare, or $7.50 per ton of carbon ($1,400/186) sequestered by the fully mature afforested area.[20]

---

19. A longer maturation period with unchanged annual carbon sequestration would imply higher eventual carrying capacity and lower carbon reduction costs.

20. Using the Sedjo and Solomon estimates, Darmstadter and Plantinga (1991) place the figure for the United States at $4 per ton of carbon, as they apply the lower alternative

Sedjo and Solomon suggest that land purchase could be practically free in the tropics, although the costs of establishing forests are comparable to those in the United States. If one conservatively applies a land price for the tropics equal to the lower land price alternative *for the United States,* the corresponding cost per ton of carbon sequestered would amount to $4.30 ($800/186) in the tropics. Specific studies for afforestation projects in Guatemala and Costa Rica designed to offset carbon emissions from a new power plant in Connecticut (United States) identify much lower costs in the tropics: only $0.82 to $1.37 per ton of carbon sequestered (Andrasko et al. 1991, 12). On the basis of these various studies, then, carbon sequestration through afforestation may be conservatively estimated to cost no more than $5 per ton of carbon in the tropics and $20 per ton in temperate, developed regions.[21]

The principal exception to this cost range is the estimate by Nordhaus (1990b, 21) that carbon removal through reforestation costs $100 per ton of carbon. Nordhaus calculates that 210 million hectares could be planted in temperate zones and 300 million hectares in tropical areas, for a total of 510 million hectares. He places the annual carbon removal attainable on this area at 0.2 billion tons. By implication (200 million/510 million), Nordhaus' sequestration rate is only 0.4 tons of carbon per hectare per year. This rate is an order of magnitude smaller than the carbon storing rates applied by Moulton and Richards and by Sedjo and Solomon and is presumably one source of the much higher Nordhaus cost estimate.

Nordhaus (1990b, 21) in turn has "relied upon the EPA estimates of the cost of reforestation." However, early EPA estimates of afforestation costs appear to have been misleading.[22] More recent analyses by experts in the agency rely on the Moulton-Richards cost estimates (Andrasko et al. 1991, 13).

---

for the purchase price of land. Darmstadter and Plantinga also note, however, that the cost per ton could more than triple if account is taken of the eventual harvesting costs at maturity. But in this calculation they rely on the Sedjo-Solomon harvesting cost, which is specified to include *permanent storage* of the carbon, or "tree-pickling." That option is a different concept from the simple option of afforestation, however, as it involves much greater carbon removal (altering the calculation for cost per ton). Essentially, tree-pickling permits the annual sequestration attainable during maturation to continue after the terminal date of forest maturity, because there is no carbon release from dying trees to offset the carbon uptake of new trees.

21. A recent survey by the Organization for Economic Cooperation and Development has found similarly low estimates in the literature. Hoeller et al. (1991, 69) cite estimates by Blok et al. that the cost of reforestation would amount to only $0.70 per ton of carbon. The same survey cites Dixon et al. as calculating that carbon removal costs through afforestation would amount to $4 to $8 per ton.

22. Thus, the EPA (1989c, table 7-21) implies that to store 50 million tons of carbon would require 4.5 million to 13 million hectares and a planting cost (excluding land cost) of $1.9 billion to $5.6 billion or a range of $38 to $112 per ton of carbon. But the same table reports the *annual* sequestration rate at 3.5 to 10 tons of carbon per hectare per

In sum, the appropriate range for the cost of carbon removal through afforestation would appear to be approximately $20 per ton in temperate (developed-country) areas and $5 per ton in tropical areas.[23]

In a personal communication (6 April 1992), William D. Nordhaus has suggested that an estimate of $20 per ton for carbon sequestration in temperate areas is too low. He argues that:

> Currently, timber on the stump sells for $20 to $200 per cubic meter, depending on the location. At 0.25 tons C [carbon] per cubic meter, this is $80 to $800 per ton C. Why should reforestation be able to produce wood so much more cheaply than current managed forestry operations?

We may address this question as follows. Suppose that an afforestation project grows 1,000 cubic feet of merchantable wood. On average, this wood will yield some 450 cubic feet of lumber and some 550 cubic feet of chips and other scrap wood for pulp, with the second category priced at some 13 percent of the price of the former (Robert J. Moulton, personal communication, 8 May 1992).[24] In 1989, lower-priced timber (the type relevant for a carbon-sequestering afforestation project) sold for $118 per thousand board-feet (this is the price for southern yellow pine sawtimber; *U.S. Industrial Outlook*, 1990, 6-3). One cubic foot contains 12 board feet. On this basis, the value of the 1,000 cubic feet of merchantable wood would amount to $637 for lumber ($= [450 \times 12 /1,000] \times \$118$) and $101 for chips and scrap ($= [550 \times 12 / 1,000] \times 0.13 \times \$118$). The merchantable value of the wood would thus amount to $738, or an average of 74 cents per cubic foot.

For its part, the carbon sequestered in the trees and other components of the forestry ecosystem associated with this 1,000 cubic feet of merchantable wood

---

year. Applying the midpoint, and assuming even a short rotation life of five years, it should require only 1.5 million hectares to store 50 million tons of carbon at maturity (50 million tons/[5 years $\times$ 6.75 tons per hectare per year] = 1.48 million hectares). The unit cost would be correspondingly lower. The problem is essentially confusion of annual with life-cycle sequestration.

23. This conclusion means that the NAS report's classification of afforestation in the low-to-medium cost class, or from $37 to $370 per ton of carbon (table 5.3 above), is far too high. Note that the $20 figure adopted here for developed (temperate) areas takes into consideration the fact that, although the Moulton-Richards estimate ignores land opportunity costs after the 40th year, the Sedjo-Solomon estimate is much lower. Therefore, $20 per ton seems plausible even on a basis that consolidates all future costs into the horizon of the first 40 years.

24. This estimate is based on the normal relationship that, of the 12 board-feet (of 12" $\times$ 12" $\times$ 1" each) contained in one cubic foot of merchantable wood, 5.4 board-feet are in sawn boards and the other 6.6 board-feet are in trimmed chips and scrap.

would amount to 23.7 metric tons.[25] Thus, carbon sequestration would have to be worth $31 per metric ton to be as valuable as the opportunity cost of selling the wood (= $738/23.7). After taking account of the fact that wood types selected for carbon content and minimum growing cost, rather than for lumber value, would be likely to have parameters more favorable than the medians, these estimates are consistent with the estimate of $20 per ton of carbon sequestered. Afforestation thus passes the stumpage opportunity cost test.[26]

What is the plausible scope for the afforestation option? In the United States, there are 400 million hectares in farmland and 300 million in forested area, plus another 70 million hectares in unused land (US Department of Agriculture 1990; EPA 1989a, 73; 1989b, VII-234). Against this reservoir of land, it might be reasonable to envision the afforestation of some 80 million hectares, the area identified by Moulton and Richards as sufficient to offset 30 percent of US annual carbon emissions. Thus, the United States could set aside into new forested area about one-sixth of its land not currently in forests and expand the forested area by about one-fourth.

Against this benchmark, it might be plausible to reforest another 30 million hectares in other temperate, developed regions. For the tropics, an area of, say, 150 million hectares would seem feasible. The total area of 260 million hectares globally would sequester 1.6 billion tons of carbon annually (at the rate of approximately six tons per hectare per year used by both Moulton-Richards and Sedjo-Solomon), or 55 GtC over a conservative 35-year maturation phase (e.g., from 1995 to 2030).

Total global carbon emissions are expected to rise from about 6 GtC to some 10 GtC annually by 2025 (chapter 2), so that cumulative emissions over the 35-year period should amount to approximately 300 GtC. Thus, the afforestation option could reduce net global carbon emissions by an average of 18 percent (55/300) over the next 35 years. Although this contribution would be a "tem-

---

25. From Moulton and Richards (1990, table 4), the median mass of carbon per unit of merchantable wood is 14 pounds per cubic foot. Therefore 1,000 cubic feet of merchantable wood contains 14,000 pounds, or 6.4 metric tons, of carbon. From the same source, the median multiple of total forest ecosystem carbon to carbon contained in merchantable wood is 3.7. Thus, 1,000 cubic feet of merchantable wood corresponds to 23.7 metric tons of carbon sequestered through afforestation (= 6.4 × 3.7).

26. The difference between this estimate and the Nordhaus figure in part reflects the following. The Moulton-Richards estimate for total carbon per cubic feet of merchantable wood is 0.84 ton per cubic meter (one cubic meter contains 35.3 cubic feet, and the estimate developed here is 0.0237 metric ton of carbon per cubic foot of merchantable wood), or 3.3 times the Nordhaus figure. In contrast, the price of merchantable wood is approximately the same here ($26 per cubic meter, = 74 cents per cubic foot, in turn equal to $740 per 1,000 cubic feet) as Nordhaus's lower range. On this basis, it would appear that the principal difference is that the figures suggested by Nordhaus do not take account of the multiplier from merchantable wood carbon to total forest carbon, (i.e., incorporating roots, leaves, etc.).

porary" remedy because it could not be extended much further thereafter (for the reasons set forth above, mainly the distinction between stock versus flow), it would be a significant contribution. Moreover, the weighted-average cost for this abatement would amount to only about $11 per ton of carbon, using the estimate of $20 per ton for temperate areas and $5 per ton for tropical areas.

As noted above, afforestation may be an even more attractive option than suggested by these estimates. If biomass is used for renewable energy production that replaces fossil fuel burning, there is a net reduction in carbon even after the maturity terminal date.

Nordhaus has suggested, however, that afforestation would reduce the albedo (reflectivity) of the earth's surface, thereby causing increased warming per unit of atmospheric carbon dioxide concentration that would offset the increment in concentration achieved by the extra carbon sequestration (personal communication, 6 April 1992). My own consultations with agricultural and meteorological experts indicate, in contrast, that the albedo change would be too limited to provide a major offset. The principal reason is that, in the areas that would be suitable for afforestation, there would already be some vegetative cover (such as grassland), and that the reduction in albedo in the shift from such cover to forest is relatively small (the reduction in albedo from a shift from barren land to grasses or forest cover would be considerably larger).

More specifically, in a personal communication (20 May 1992), Piers Sellers of the NASA Goddard Space Flight Center has calculated that afforestation of 260 million hectares as proposed here would cause albedo reduction that would offset at most one-fourth, and more likely only one-eighth, of the global cooling effect from carbon sequestration. Sellers notes that albedo declines by about 3 percent for an area that changes from grassland to forest. Citing work by Nobre et al., he indicates that in a "worst case" there is a global increase of about 30 wm^{-2} in net radiation when grassland is changed to forest (fixed clouds). As the area to be placed in forest amounts to 0.5 percent of the total area of the world, the maximum radiative forcing from reduced albedo would amount to 0.15 wm^{-2} ($= 30 \times 0.005$). In contrast, Sellers estimates that the reduction in net radiation from the 55 GtC carbon sequestered in afforestation would amount to 0.6 to 1.2 wm^{-2}. My own calculation would place the radiative reduction impact of afforestation in the middle of this range.[27]

On this basis, the offsetting influence of increased albedo would seem unlikely to exceed one-sixth of the favorable effect of carbon sequestration through

---

27. Against an atmospheric stock of carbon averaging some 800 GtC in the relevant period, the 55 GtC sequestered would reduce direct radiative forcing from 1.81 wm^{-2} to 1.36^{-2} (from 6.3 ln[800/600] to 6.3 ln[745/600], by the Wigley formula, chapter 1). Applying the average IPCC total feedback multiplier of 1.9 (chapter 1), the corresponding total reduction in radiative forcing amounts to 0.86 wm^{-2}.

afforestation. For its part, the IPCC (1990b) does not provide an estimate of the change in albedo for a shift toward forest. The albedo-sequestration trade-off discussed here is an important issue to add to the agenda for scientific research in the first policy phase proposed in chapter 8 of this study.

A Synthesis of Abatement Costs

The cost estimates of the top-down models, the engineering approaches, and those developed here for forestry options may be integrated to obtain an overview of the costs of carbon abatement. Most of the estimates from economic models are for global carbon emissions, and the forestry effects just discussed are also global. Estimates from economic models for the United States do not give significantly different results from those for global effects (chapter 4). Although some of the economic models show high costs for carbon reduction in developing countries, particularly China (see Manne and Richels 1990c), other top-down models do not show exceptionally high costs for these areas (see Burniaux et al. 1991a), and one relatively high-cost estimate for a developing country (Egypt) may be overstated for methodological reasons (Blitzer et al. 1991, as reviewed in chapter 4). Similarly, although the bottom-up estimates discussed above are for the United States, there is a considerable literature suggesting that the opportunities for low-cost carbon emissions are equally or more available in developing countries (Goldemberg et al. 1987). For these reasons, the analysis that follows is meant to be representative of global costs, even though costs for individual areas will vary.

In chapter 4, the following summary regression was estimated on the basis of cost calculations for several energy-economic (top-down) models:

$$(5.2) \quad \%Y = -1.16 + 0.091 \ \%C - 0.0246 \ t; \ R^2 = 0.75$$
$$ (0.68) \quad (0.024) \quad (0.012)$$

where $\%Y$ is economic cost as a percentage of GDP, $\%C$ is the percentage of carbon emissions cut from baseline, and t is the number of years after 1990 (standard errors in parentheses). This estimate yields a zero cost at 22.2 percent reduction of carbon emissions in 2025 and is thus closely consistent with the OTA and NAS bottom-up estimates of the extent of zero-cost carbon reduction possibilities.

It is useful to reformulate the estimate in terms that force the influence of time to operate solely on the slope of the cost curve, as in figure 5.1, rather than on the vertical intercept. Otherwise, the zero-cost intercept on the horizontal, carbon-reduction axis moves to the right over time, eventually suggesting an implausibly high percentage of reductions at zero cost. It is also useful to force the cost curve through the origin of a redefined percentage-cut axis that dislocates the previous origin to the right by the amount of the zero-cost reductions possible. If we define the adjusted cut as $C' = C - 22$ (that is, the intercept on the zero-cost horizontal axis was at 22 percent carbon reduction), the summary top-down equation may be reestimated as:

$$(5.3) \quad \%Y = 0.0842 \ \%C' - 0.00039 \ (\%C')(t'); \ R^2 = 0.60$$
$$\qquad\qquad (0.011) \qquad\quad (0.00019)$$

where $t' = t - 2024$ (i.e., the time horizon begins in 2025, the year for which the 22 percent zero-cost cutback is estimated). This form may be rewritten as:

$$(5.3') \quad \%Y = \%C' \ (0.0842 - 0.00039 \ t')$$

with the resulting effect of producing a single linear cost curve passing through the (dislocated) origin and having a slope that swivels downward as the year for the estimate becomes more distant (and more technological options become available).

This reformulated cost curve for the leading top-down models is applied to calculate the cost estimates in table 5.5 for alternative reductions of carbon emissions (as a percentage from baseline) and alternative future dates.[28] As indicated, the first 20 percent of carbon reduction comes at zero cost regardless of the time horizon. Reductions of 50 percent from baseline require a sacrifice of 2.3 percent of GDP in 2025 but only 1.5 percent by 2100. By the latter year, carbon emissions may be cut by 80 percent from baseline at a cost of 3.2 percent of GDP.

The second panel of the table integrates the information of the bottom-up estimates discussed above. There is no change required for the zero-cost intercept on the horizontal axis, because both the NAS and the OTA studies imply the same range of 22 percent for this intercept, as already suggested by the linear equation for the top-down models (figure 5.2). However, the bottom-up estimates do provide a basis for estimating a gentler slope of the cost curve (as in the second panel of figure 5.1).

Specifically, whereas the slope of the cost curve for a date of 2025 is 0.0842 in equation 5.3' for the top-down models, it is only 0.0478 for the NAS study and 0.023 for the OTA study.[29] Thus, whereas an extra 10-percentage-point reduction in carbon emissions (for 2025) costs 0.84 percent of GNP in the energy-economic models, it costs only 0.48 percent of GNP in the estimates derived here from the NAS report, and just 0.23 percent of GNP in those of the OTA report. The average slope for the two bottom-up studies is 0.0354.

---

28. That is, with C as the desired cutback, Y is estimated as $(C - 22) \times [0.0842 - 0.00039 \times (\text{year} - 2024)]$.

29. That is, $(0.75 - 0)/(39.3 - 23.6)$ and $(0.75 - 0)/(54 - 21.9)$, respectively; see the discussion above.

Table 5.5 Alternative estimates of global costs of carbon reductions, 2025–2100 (percentages of GNP)

Percentage cut from baseline	2025	2050	2075	2100
Top-down models				
20	0.0	0.0	0.0	0.0
30	0.7	0.6	0.5	0.4
40	1.5	1.3	1.2	1.0
50	2.3	2.1	1.8	1.5
60	3.2	2.8	2.4	2.1
70	4.0	3.6	3.1	2.6
80	4.9	4.3	3.7	3.2
90	5.7	5.0	4.4	3.7
Adjusted for engineering estimates				
20	0.0	0.0	0.0	0.0
30	0.5	0.5	0.4	0.3
40	1.2	1.0	0.9	0.7
50	1.9	1.6	1.3	1.1
60	2.6	2.2	1.8	1.5
70	3.2	2.8	2.3	1.8
80	3.9	3.3	2.8	2.2
90	4.6	3.9	3.3	2.6
Adjusted for engineering and forestry estimates				
20	0.0	0.0	0.0	0.0
30	0.05	0.2	0.2	0.2
40	0.05	0.7	0.7	0.6
50	0.5	1.3	1.1	1.0
60	1.2	1.9	1.6	1.3
70	1.9	2.5	2.1	1.7
80	2.6	3.1	2.6	2.1
90	3.2	3.6	3.1	2.5

Source: See text.

The procedure adopted here is to apply a weight of two-thirds to the top-down studies and one-third to the NAS–OTA bottom-up studies to reestimate the cost curve slope. In part the higher weight is placed on the economic models because they are more in keeping with standard economic theory, but in part the objective is to err on the cautious rather than the optimistic side. The resulting "hybrid" cost equation becomes:

(5.4) $\%Y = \%C' \, (0.0678 - 0.00039 \, t')$

The second panel of table 5.5 reports the cost estimates obtained with the hybrid top-down, bottom-up equation. Thus, a carbon reduction of 60 percent from baseline in the year 2050 requires a GNP loss of 2.2 percent in the hybrid model, as opposed to 2.8 percent of GNP in the equation from the top-down models alone.

Finally, the table incorporates the effect of the forestry options discussed above. For this purpose, it is first necessary to place the forestry cost and carbon reduction estimates into terms that are compatible with the estimates of the percentage of GNP and the percentage of global emissions in the table 5.5 synthesis. The elements for this analysis appear in table 5.6. That table first presents baseline

Table 5.6   Forestry options: carbon reduction and global costs, 1990–2100

Year	1990	2025	2026	2050	2075	2100
Carbon emissions, baseline (GtC)	7	11.7	11.8	15	19	24
World GNP (trillions of dollars at 1990 prices)						
Developed countries	15	28	29	44	57	73
Less developed countries	4	13	13	30	48	79
Total	19	41	42	74	105	152
Carbon reductions from:						
Curtailed deforestation	0.7	0.7	0.7	0.7	0.7	0.7
Afforestation	1.6	1.6	0.0	0.0	0.0	0.0
Total	2.3	2.3	0.7	0.7	0.7	0.7
Percentage of baseline	32.9	19.7	5.9	4.7	3.7	2.9
Cost of forestry measures (billions of dollars at 1990 prices)						
Curtailed deforestation	4.5	4.5	4.5	4.5	4.5	4.5
Afforestation	17.2	17.2	0.0	0.0	0.0	0.0
Total	21.7	21.7	4.5	4.5	4.5	4.5
Percentage of world GNP	0.11	0.05	0.01	0.01	0.00	0.00

GtC = gigatons of carbon.

Source: See text.

global carbon emissions through 2100, the average from the main economic models surveyed in chapter 2 above. The original baseline has been increased by 1 GtC over the whole period (and thus stands at 7 GtC in 1990 rather than the more usual 5.7 GtC used in the models) because the analysis seeks to incorporate emissions from deforestation.[30]

Next the table presents an estimate of global GNP over the next century, in trillions of 1990 dollars. The estimate uses the economic growth assumptions of Edmonds and Barns (1990) through 2050 and Manne and Richels (1990c) thereafter.[31]

The carbon reductions from forestry options are then shown. On the basis of the analysis above, some 0.7 GtC annually might be eliminated at an average cost of $7 per ton from reduced deforestation (elimination in just Brazil, Indonesia, and Côte d'Ivoire, or proportionately smaller but more widely applied reductions). The annual cost amounts to $4.5 billion, or 0.023 percent of world GNP. The analysis of afforestation presented above suggests that a total of about 260 million hectares globally could be placed into new forested area, with-

---

30. If, instead, deforestation emissions keep growing in the baseline, as suggested by Reis and Margulis (1991), the contribution from reduced deforestation would be potentially larger.

31. Specifically, real GNP grows at 1.85 percent in developed countries and 3.3 percent in developing countries through 2050. Thereafter, the respective rates are 1 percent and 2 percent. Note that somewhat different growth assumptions, with greater detail for specific time periods, are applied in the benefit-cost analysis of chapter 7.

drawing 1.6 GtC annually over 35 years at an average cost of $11 per ton, or $17.2 billion annually (initially 0.09 percent of world GNP). Together, the two forestry measures would reduce carbon emissions by 2.3 GtC annually at an initial cost of 0.11 percent of world GNP.

After 35 years, afforestation would provide no further carbon reductions, because the forest would reach a steady state. In the formulation here, afforestation costs would also terminate (in contrast to their continuation in figure 5.3). The reason is that the annualized costs in the initial 35 years are sufficiently high to incorporate all subsequent opportunity cost for the land (as noted above).

The broad characteristics of the forestry options discussed above are vividly apparent in table 5.6: the options provide important but only temporary gains. The gains are proportionately largest at the outset, when global carbon emissions may be cut by 33 percent at a low cost of only 0.11 percent of world GNP. However, by 2025 the contribution of the forestry measures is already relatively less significant, because the baseline has grown and the proportionate cutback possible through deforestation and afforestation has fallen to 20 percent. The option truly collapses to minor proportions, however, after the 35-year maturation phase has passed. By 2026 and after, the only remaining forestry contribution—avoided deforestation—falls to 6 percent or less of baseline global carbon emissions. In short, the estimates confirm the view that forestry can provide an important transitional contribution to resolving the greenhouse problem, but only a much more modest portion of any overall solution over the longer term. The chief qualification of this interpretation is that a large-scale use of carbon sequestered in afforestation for the production of sustainable biomass energy could make the option a much more important measure for dealing with the greenhouse problem over the longer term.

Returning to table 5.5, it is possible to translate the forestry estimates into further adjustments in the synthesis cost curve. For the year 2025, at the tail end of the afforestation growing period, 20 percent of global carbon emissions are still being offset by the forestry options. Equation 5.4 is thus applied to a redefined carbon reduction, equal to $C'' = C' - 20 = C - 42$, with the resulting costs added to those for the forestry options. The outcome is that a full 42 percent carbon reduction from baseline in 2025 can be obtained for only 0.05 percent of GNP: that is, zero cost for the first 22 percent and 0.05 percent of GNP for the next 20 percent (from forestry measures). The whole menu of carbon reduction targets similarly shows a considerably lower cost level in 2025 in the third panel of table 5.4, which incorporates forestry, than in the second panel. For example, a 50 percent cut from baseline in 2025 requires a cost of only 0.5 percent of GNP with forestry integrated into the estimates, versus 1.9 percent of GNP from the hybrid top-down, bottom-up estimates without forestry.[32]

---

32. Technically, the bottom-up estimates do include a minor contribution from forestry

By the time forest maturation has arrived, the impact is very different. By 2050 and thereafter, the menu of costs incorporating forestry measures is practically the same as the menu without them (i.e., the third panel in table 5.4 is almost the same as the second for 2050 and beyond).

Conclusion

The central finding of this review is that the engineering-based cost estimates do provide a basis for moderate downward adjustment in the energy-economic-model estimates of costs of carbon reduction. Importantly, both approaches are consistent with the view that the first 20 percent or so of carbon reduction can be obtained at zero cost through greater adoption of efficient energy practices. Moreover, incorporation of the engineering-based estimates suggests a gentler slope for the cost curve relating the percentage of GNP cost impact to the percentage of carbon reduction from baseline.

Consideration of forestry measures suggests that the past view of deforestation is correct: there are important carbon emissions reductions available at low cost. It also suggests that, despite the past view of a widely disparate level of afforestation costs, more recent and reliable estimates place the cost of carbon sequestration through this vehicle at a modest level as well, although higher than that for emissions reductions through reduced deforestation. However, the analysis strongly confirms the less favorable point that afforestation is only a temporary solution, because of limits to afforestation area and the absence of a further contribution after maturity unless the option is transformed into one of sustainable biomass energy.

Overall, a synthesis of the three sets of estimates (top-down, bottom-up, and forestry) concludes that carbon reductions of some 50 percent to 60 percent from baseline may be purchased at some 2 percent of world GNP or less at the middle of the 21st century (and considerably more cheaply at the beginning of the century because of startup gains from afforestation). Reductions of up to 80 percent from baseline by late in the 21st century would cost on the order of 2 percent of GNP. The increase in cost for the higher percentage cutback is considerably less than might otherwise be expected because of the swiveling of the cost curve toward a gentler slope at more distant dates, when a wider array of technological opportunities is available.

---

measures (see tables 5.2 and 5.3). However, in part because the bottom-up estimates are given less weight than the top-down in the hybrid, there is little bias from double-counting here.

6

Time Discounting
for Global Warming Analysis

6

Time Discounting
for Global Warming Analysis

Benefit-cost analysis of policy response to the greenhouse effect requires inter-temporal comparisons over extremely long horizons. As discussed in chapter 2, in the absence of special action warming can be expected to continue for at least some 250 to 300 years. After that there is a potential for a partial reversal of warming, because of a greater withdrawal of carbon dioxide into the ocean through increased mixing into its vast deeper layers. Some conventional ranges of discount rates for project analysis, on the order of 5 percent to 10 percent real per year, make values at such distant future dates virtually disappear.[1] Thus, discounting at 10 percent, the present discounted value of one dollar 200 years in the future is one-half of one millionth of óne cent. At a 5 percent discount rate, the present discounted value is still only six one-thousandths of a cent. In contrast, discounting at 1 percent, a dollar to be received 200 years in the future is worth 14 cents today (table 6.1). As the benefits of avoided greenhouse damage tend to be realized much later than the costs imposed on the economy from restriction of greenhouse gas emissions, a discount rate that is inappropriately high will tend to bias policy toward inaction.

The potential conflict between long-term environmental policy and standard discounting may be summarized in a logical syllogism:

- Very-long-term environmental effects are important.

- With discount rates in the range of 5 percent to 10 percent, often used in public investment project analysis, very-long-term effects are not important.

---

1. At least some "conventional" discounting in public policy is at considerably lower rates. See the discussion below of US Congressional Budget Office (CBO) and General Accounting Office (GAO) practices.

Table 6.1 Impact of time discounting over 200 years

Discount rate (percentages per year)	Amount of $1 compounded to year 200[a]	Present value of $1 received 200 years in future
0.0	1.00	1.00
0.1	1.22	0.82
0.2	1.49	0.67
0.3	1.82	0.55
0.4	2.22	0.45
0.5	2.71	0.37
0.6	3.31	0.30
0.7	4.04	0.25
0.8	4.92	0.20
0.9	6.00	0.17
1.0	7.32	0.14
1.1	8.92	0.11
1.2	10.9	0.09
1.3	13.2	0.076
1.4	16.1	0.062
1.5	19.6	0.051
2.0	52.5	0.019
3.0	369	0.0027
4.0	2,551	0.00039
5.0	17,293	0.000058
6.0	115,122	0.0000087
7.0	752,929	0.00000133
8.0	4,839,110	0.000000207
9.0	30,600,000	0.0000000327
10.0	189,900,000	0.00000000527

a. Future value of $1 invested today at rate indicated with compounding.

■ Therefore, discount rates in the range of 5 percent to 10 percent are inappropriate for analysis of very-long-term environmental effects, despite their frequent use in other public policy contexts.

This chapter develops an analysis based on standard discounting theory to identify discount rates more appropriate for examination of the greenhouse effect. The method chosen follows the theoretical trend in recent years to convert all capital and consumption effects to "consumption-equivalents" and then to discount at the "social rate of time preference." The analysis gives special attention to proper identification of the social rate of time preference for very-long-term environmental purposes.

Investment Versus Consumption Sourcing

There is a long tradition in the social benefit-cost literature of taking into account the sourcing of the funds for an investment project. It is widely recognized that the appropriate discount rate for consumption (or the "social rate of time preference") tends to be lower than the rate of return on investment. The major reason is that the existence of a tax on capital income introduces a wedge between the two, but, more generally, imperfections in the capital market contribute to the divergence. Many analysts have argued that the discount rate should thus be a weighted average of the two. As Lind (1982, 32–33) puts it:

> The idea underlying this work is that the social rate of discount should reflect both the consumption rate of return insofar as consumption is displaced and the marginal rate of return on private investment insofar as private investment is displaced. Therefore, it has been argued that the social rate of discount should be a weighted average of the two rates, the weights being established in proportion to the percentage of the public investment drawn from consumption and from private investment (Krutilla and Eckstein 1958, Harberger 1968, Haveman 1969, Sandmo and Drèze 1971).

An important feature of discounting for greenhouse action is that in this area policy involves the raising of resources out of the general economy rather than the use of resources withdrawn primarily from either private investment or from alternative public-sector investments within a constrained capital budget. The usual project under consideration by a government entity or international development agency (for example, construction of a dam) is undertaken out of a given investment budget, and must compete against other investment projects. For such "marginal" project decisions, the opportunity cost is the rate of return on alternative public-sector investments.

In contrast, for greenhouse action the bulk of resources comes not from investment (private or public) but from consumption. If a carbon tax is used to discourage emissions, for example, the tax revenue comes out of the general economy. Similarly, if a quota limit is set on emissions, and less efficient means of production must be substituted for fossil fuels, the resulting reduction in production comes from the economy at large. In either case, the sourcing of the resource cost of the policy will reflect the general shares of consumption and investment in the economy. As a result, some 80 percent of the resources withdrawn for the greenhouse action is likely to come from consumption and only some 20 percent from investment.[2]

A major reason to expect the discount rate for greenhouse analysis to be relatively low, therefore, is that within a framework of weighting discount rates by origin of resource, policy actions will tend to draw resources primarily out of consumption, where the appropriate rate is the social rate of time preference, rather than out of private investment, where the appropriate rate is the (higher) rate of return on private capital. For their part, public-sector investments are in turn appropriately discounted by some intermediate rate reflecting resource sourcing in general revenue measures.[3] With revenue constraints, the marginal

---

2. This is a reasonable global average. For the United States, the historical investment rate is closer to 15 percent to 17 percent of GDP.

3. But not necessarily just the weighted average. See the consumption-equivalent approach discussed below.

return on alternative public-sector investments is likely to be higher than this cutoff, because the queue of potential public-sector investments will contain projects with rates of return that warrant implementation but do not fit within budget ceilings (or, for international agencies, borrowing limits).

As developed below, recent social discount analysis builds on the concept of investment versus consumption sourcing by converting all of the investment consequences of a project into their consumption-equivalent through the use of a "shadow price of capital," and then applying a single discount rate, the consumption-based social rate of time preference.

Issue- and Policy-Specific Discount Rates

As an outgrowth of the approach of differentiating between consumption and private investment as the two alternative sources for public investment, various authors have stressed that the appropriate rate of discount will depend on the nature of the project. Stiglitz (1982) goes so far as to suggest that because of varying possible situations with respect to government debt and taxation (e.g., the government's ability or lack thereof to impose nondistortionary lump-sum taxes), in principle there should be a different discount rate for each project. Although perhaps extreme for operational purposes with respect to typical smaller public investments, this principle strongly implies that for a policy area with effects as massive as greenhouse measures—where potentially hundreds of billions of dollars are involved annually over scores or hundreds of years—there should be a careful development of the discounting procedure rather than the simple application of an "off-the-shelf" discount rate from existing operational handbooks.

Intergenerational Comparison

There is a major additional reason why time discounting in greenhouse analysis requires special examination: the issue involves intergenerational comparisons. Among others, Mishan (1975) has identified the essential arbitrariness that enters when the affected generation is not present to participate in the decision. He argues that in this case perhaps even a zero discount rate is appropriate:

> There is little difficulty about the concept of a single individual's time preference. . . . If, at any moment of time, a 10 percent rate of time preference is universal we are justified in valuing 100 next year at about 91 today, and 100 the year after at about 83 today. But are we justified in valuing 100 in 50 years' time as equivalent as $100(1.10)^{-50}$? Not if the 100 in 50 years' time will accrue to different people. If in 50 years' time the 100 accrues to a person B of a new generation, the enjoyment

he derives therefrom might be every bit as great as that derived from it now by a person A of the existing generation. Person A would therefore have no business in evaluating the future worth of 100 by discounting it for 50 years at 10 percent when he himself is not, in any case, going to receive it. . . . Whenever inter-generation comparisons are involved . . . it is as well to recognize that there is no satisfactory way of determining social worth at different points of time. In such cases, a zero rate of time preference, though arbitrary, is probably more acceptable than the use today of existing individuals' rate of time preference or of a rate of interest that would arise in a market solely for consumption loans. (Mishan 1975, 208–09)

Taken literally, Mishan's admonition would rule out benefit-cost analysis of the greenhouse effect. However, public policy decisions must be taken, and the practical thrust of his argument implies the use of a low (indeed, close to zero) discount rate for intergenerational comparisons of consumption.

Weiss (1989, 25) has argued from a legal perspective that "each generation is entitled to inherit a planet and cultural resource base at least as good as that of previous generations." She cites precedents in international law in support of her call for a "Declaration of the Planetary Rights and Obligations to Future Generations" (Weiss 1989, 349).[4]

In the context of the greenhouse problem, d'Arge et al. (1982) suggest that initially warming might be beneficial but that it could impose severe damage on subsequent generations. They emphasize that in the few existing attempts to apply benefit-cost analysis to long-term environmental problems (in areas such as ozone depletion, possible global cooling from supersonic transport emis-sions—an earlier concern now discarded—and the greenhouse problem), "the process of economic discounting of the future has led to small present values for even almost catastrophic future economic losses" (d'Arge et al. 1982, 251). They then examine alternative conceptual frameworks for intergenerational discounting. They note that standard analysis assumes the "utilitarian (Ben-thamite)" framework whereby the objective is to maximize utility in the present generation (U_1) and expected utility for the future generation ($E[U_2]$). An al-ternative, "egalitarian (Rawlsian)" approach would seek instead to maximize the minimum possible outcome for a generation sent randomly into the world; accordingly, the objective would be to maximize the minimum of U_1 and $E(U_2)$. There are other frameworks as well, for example, the elitist and the Paretian-

---

4. Precedents on concern for future generations include the United Nations Charter, drafted after World War II, which opens, "We the peoples of the United Nations, deter-mined to save succeeding generations from the scourge of war . . ."; the 1972 Stockholm Declaration on the Human Environment, which states, "To defend and improve the environment for present and future generations has become an imperative goal for man-kind . . ."; and legal instruments in areas such as fishery rights, marine pollution, and the conservation of living resources (Weiss 1989, 28–29).

libertarian; within the latter the objective is to maximize U_1 subject to the constraint that $E(U_2)$ is no lower than its initially expected position.

D'Arge et al. show that the proper discount rate depends on whether compensation to the future generation can be made through investment, and on the philosophical framework. Thus, in the Rawlsian case with no investment compensation possible and a higher utility today than expected in the future, the discount rate should equal -1 (there is an infinite penalty for transferring consumption from the poorer future to the richer present).

The Environmental Complication

Sen (1982) adds a qualitative complication to discounting intergenerationally for environmental issues when he argues, somewhat similarly to Weiss, that a special right of the future generation may be violated when its environment is degraded by the current generation. In the same spirit as his earlier work with respect to the issue of individuals' rights as opposed to patterned welfare measures of personal income distribution, Sen argues:

> Suppose the investment project in question will eliminate some pollution that the present generation will otherwise impose on the future. Even if the future generation may be richer and may enjoy a higher welfare level, *and* even if its marginal utility from the consumption gain is accepted to be less than the marginal welfare loss of the present generation, this may still not be accepted to be decisive for rejecting the investment when the alternative implies long-term effects of environmental pollution. The avoidance of oppression of the future generations has to be given a value of its own. [Thus,] the question of pollution . . . in the context of the liberty of future generations . . . [implies] a rejection of "welfarism," which judges social states exclusively by their personal welfare characteristics. (Sen 1982, 347, 349)

More generally, long-term environmental issues and concern for the welfare of future generations tend to merge because of the inherent relevance of permanent environmental damage for distant generations. Like that of Mishan but for a different reason, Sen's warning would preclude benefit-cost analysis, at least in the absence of a means of placing a value on the future generation's sacrifice of its "liberty."[5]

---

5. At the high level of abstraction of Sen's caveat, however, one may justifiably raise a prior question. With the availability of birth control technology, the existence of a future generation at all is solely the consequence of the goodwill of the present generation. This formulation suggests that the issue is not one of adversarial rights of one generation against the other, but rather inclusion of proper valuation of descendants' living conditions in the utility of the present generation, under the assumption that the one cares about

A more operational approach is to return to the framework of welfarism (valuation of consumption and utility) but to pay special attention to the division of consumption between environmental and other goods. Conceptually, the two issues of intergenerational comparison and environmental conditions may be maintained separate by distinguishing between the overall level of well-being of future generations, on the one hand, and the composition of their well-being as between environmental (E) goods and all other goods and services (GS), on the other. The first panel of figure 6.1 shows a "production possibility curve" between these two classes of goods. With today's resources, society may produce alternative combinations of GS and E goods along the $Q_0 Q_0$ frontier. Its preferred combination, at point a, is given where production possibilities touch the highest "indifference curve" between the two classes of goods, at utility level U_0. In the future, society will have greater productive power to generate goods and services, but can do little to increase environmental goods potential. The future production possibility frontier is $Q_1 Q_1$. Future society will choose a combination of GS and E goods at point b, where the production frontier is tangent to the (higher) indifference curve U_1.

Now consider the two separable components of consideration for the future: a general concern and concern about the environment. The first may be illustrated by considering an action that shifts today's production possibility frontier outward everywhere but as a result shifts inward the future's production possibility curve, as shown in the middle panel of figure 6.1. That is, the new production frontier for today is higher at $Q_0' Q_0'$ but only as a consequence of damaging future production potential by shifting $Q_1 Q_1$ inward to $Q_1' Q_1'$.

In contrast, a decision today that reduces the future's environmental options but *compensates* by providing larger production potential in other goods and services involves no discrimination against the future per se. Thus, in panel C decisions are made today that swivel the future production possibility frontier toward more goods and services and fewer environmental goods. In this case, the altered $Q_1' Q_1'$ curve crosses the originally anticipated $Q_1 Q_1$ curve rather than lying wholly within it. So long as the altered production possibility curve is tangent to the same indifference curve, U_1 (or one that is even higher), the future generation has not been made worse off. Thus, the future combination of GS and E selected will now move from b to c, generating the same well-being as originally anticipated but with fewer environmental goods (E) and more other goods and services (GS).

---

the other. (If it did not, it presumably would not go to the expense and bother of procreation, at least excepting low-income countries, where children may be seen as old-age insurance.) The exception to this formulation would be if it were believed that "society" had interests in the future generation that somehow transcended those of individual forbearers.

Figure 6.1 The trade-off between environmental and other goods and services

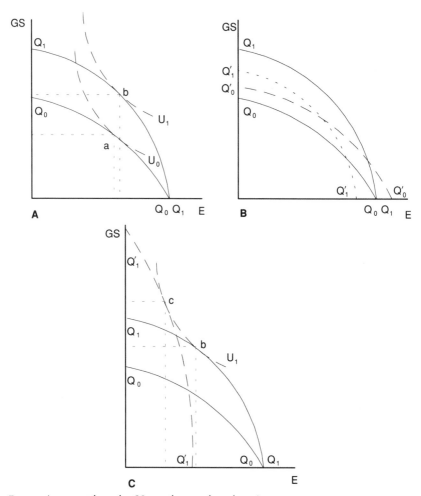

E = environmental goods; GS = other goods and services

The proper way for benefit-cost analysis to ensure that generalized discrimination against the future (as in the middle panel) does not occur is, first, to be certain that an appropriate time discount rate for consumption, or social rate of time preference, is applied (a low rate, if Mishan is followed), and second, to take special account of investment as opposed to consumption effects. The second component of the analysis will give credit to the enhancement of future production capacity that arises from investment-increasing rather than from investment-reducing actions.

Separably, the proper way to ensure that the analysis takes account of the environment-specific issue—the changing composition between environmental goods and other goods and services (as in the third panel of figure 6.1)—is *not* to adjust the time discount rate, but instead to be certain that the future valuation of environmental goods reflects the change in their relative scarcity. Thus, the price ratio between GS and E goods is given by the slope of the tangent of the indifference curve (U) to the production possibility curve (QQ). In the third panel of figure 6.1, the decision to boost future GS production at the expense of E generates a much higher relative price of E goods versus GS goods, as the slope of indifference curve U_1 is much steeper at equilibrium c than at the previously expected future equilibrium b. Essentially the analysis of prospective future damage from global warming (as in Chapter 3) seeks to do just this, by identifying (at least in principle) broad magnitudes for the value of such effects as species loss and valuation of human disamenity from heat waves, thereby implicitly measuring the leftward shift in the future production possibility curve along the E-goods axis from $Q_1 Q_1$ to $Q_1' Q_1'$.[6]

This analysis highlights a potentially serious limitation of benefit-cost analysis of environmental issues. Such analysis must assume that it is possible to identify the price line, or trade-off, between environmental goods and all other goods under conditions when the future environment has been degraded. In some contexts this price line could become extremely or infinitely steep. It is conceivable that there is simply no amount of additional videocassette recorders and automobiles (GS goods) that would compensate the future generation for loss of lands to sea-level rise, loss of species, desertification of certain continental areas, and other damage that might arise from global warming.[7] The practical thrust of this consideration for policy analysis is that valuations placed on prospective environmental damage may need to be extremely large, at least under the more severe scenarios.

Preferred Method

In view of all of the above considerations, the best approach to time discounting for greenhouse analysis would appear to be as follows. First, the central method may apply the technique that has increasingly gained favor in recent years:

---

6. Or, more precisely, the value of the leftward quantity shift when measured at an appropriate price, such as the average between the ex ante and the ex post price.

7. This inability to place a finite valuation on the loss of environmental goods would correspond to Sen's rejection of "welfarism" because no proper price of the loss of "liberty" of the future generation could be identified.

All resources should be valued in terms of consumption units. All consumption gains and losses should be discounted at r^* [the social rate of time preference]. (Gramlich 1990, 102)

Second, this method should be applied with special attention to the use of a social rate of time preference appropriate for very-long-term, intergenerational analysis.

The consumption-equivalent technique is an outgrowth of the practice of weighting the social rate of time preference and the investment discount rate by the respective shares of consumption and investment in the sourcing of resources for the project. Lind (1982a, 41) summarizes the method as follows:

[T]he appropriate procedure is to compute the shadow price of capital and to multiply the costs of public investment that represent a displacement of private capital by this shadow price to obtain the true opportunity cost in terms of consumption. . . . [T]he adjusted stream of benefits and costs should then be discounted at the social rate of discount. To make this procedure operational, we need to be able to compute the shadow price on private capital, to estimate the share of each dollar of project costs that comes from displaced private investment and consumption, and to estimate the impact that future benefits from the project will have on private investment.

The method derives primarily from Arrow (1966), Feldstein (1970), Arrow and Kurz (1970), and Bradford (1975). Arrow had recommended that the dilemma between discounting public investment at the social rate of time preference and the higher marginal rate of return on private investment be resolved by explicitly formulating the project confronting the government as an optimization problem and obtaining the correct discount rate from the solution to this problem.[8]

Although the approach of converting to consumption-equivalents and discounting at the social discount rate has been applied primarily in the context of general public investment, Kolb and Scheraga (1990) have examined it in the context of environmental regulations. They use a shadow price of capital of 2.94, a return of 10 percent on private capital, and a social time preference rate of 3 percent. They then consider the effects of the approach in a comparison with standard discounting, using as a benchmark the 10 percent rate indicated

---

8. Arrow concentrated on the question of the optimal public capital stock and reached the conclusion that if the private marginal propensity to save is fixed, the optimal government policy is to invest to the point at which the marginal rate of return on public capital equals the marginal social rate of time preference, regardless of the rate of return on private capital. In contrast, Bradford focused on "whether a project producing certain output flows should be accepted or rejected" (Bradford 1975, 887).

by the Office of Management and Budget (OMB) in 1981.[9] For a capital outlay on antipollution equipment expected to last 20 years, they consider five alternative benefit structures. At one (early) extreme, benefits flow uniformly over the first 20 years. At the other (delayed), there are no benefits during the first 20 years, but thereafter benefits flow uniformly for a 50-year period. The authors find that, in the early extreme, the two-stage method (i.e., conversion to consumption-equivalents and then discounting at the social rate) yields results identical to standard discounting. However, in the extreme-delay case just described, the two-stage approach gives a benefit-cost ratio 5.5 times as high as that of conventional discounting, and the conventional discount rate would have to be reduced from 10 percent to 4.6 percent to yield the same outcome.

In general the two-stage procedure gives higher benefit-cost ratios than does the conventional approach, and the divergence widens "as the period over which the benefits occur lengthens or as the lag between costs and benefits increases" (Kolb and Scheraga 1990, 387). The authors conclude that, "for some regulations, the use of OMB's recommended 10 percent discount rate creates a significant bias against government intervention" (Kolb and Scheraga 1990, 387).[10]

What is true for some antipollution regulations can be especially true for greenhouse policy, where the lag between costs and benefits can be much longer. The central benefit-cost approach of this study adopts the Arrow-Bradford-Feldstein-Kurz strategy of converting to consumption-equivalents and discounting at the social rate of time preference. The discussion that follows examines the proper means for estimating the shadow price of capital; the division of policy effects into investment and consumption components; and the identification of an appropriate social rate of time preference for greenhouse analysis.

Shadow Pricing Capital Effects

Annex 6A develops the following measure for the shadow price of capital:

$$(6.1) \quad v_c = \sum_{t=1}^{N} A_{r,N}/(1 + i)^t$$

---

9. The OMB procedure is discussed below. Note also that Kolb and Scheraga use Lind's method to calculate the shadow price of capital. As developed in annex 6A, however, under alternative assumptions that method can generate extreme values for the shadow price.

10. Note, however, that if Kolb and Scheraga had used a weighted average of the rate of return on private investment and the social time preference rate to discount rather than the OMB's 10 percent (implicitly, just the private return on capital), the two-stage procedure would not necessarily have shown the same systematic pattern of divergence from results with direct discounting.

where r is the real rate of return on private capital; $A_{r,N}$ is the annual payment of a (real) annuity with a life span of N years and present discounted value of unity discounting at r; and i is the social rate of time preference.[11] As discussed in the annex, this formulation is similar to that of Lind (1982a) in that it takes account of the life span of the typical physical capital investment (Lind uses $N = 15$ years), whereas the earlier formulation by Bradford considers returns over only a single year.[12] If the capital life is assumed to stretch to infinity, this shadow price simplifies to $v_c = r/i$. Thus, if the private rate of return on marginal investments is 8 percent real and the social rate of time preference is 2 percent real, infinite-lived capital would carry a shadow price of 4. That is, each unit of capital would be worth 4 units of consumption.

More typical values would assume capital life of, say, $N = 15$ years. The shadow price may be rewritten as:

(6.1') $$v_c = A_{r,N} \, \Psi_{i,N} N,$$

where

$$\Psi_{i,N} = \left\{ \sum_{t=1}^{N} [1/(1 + i)^t] \right\} \bigg/ N.$$

The term $\Psi_{i,N}$ is merely the ratio of the discounted present value of $1 received annually over N years to N, discounting at rate i. Consider the case $r = 0.08$, $i = 0.02$, and $N = 15$. The payment on a 15-year annuity with present value of $1 discounting at 8 percent ($A_{0.08,15}$) amounts to 11.68 cents per year (note 11 below). The present discounted value of $1 received annually over 15 years and discounting at 2 percent is $12.85, so that $\psi_{0.02,15} = 12.85/15 = 0.857$. Then, in this case, the shadow price of capital is 1.50 (that is, $0.1168 \times 0.857 \times 15$). This shadow price is higher than the typical range identified by Bradford, although lower than the central range of 3 to 5 indicated in the principal examples suggested by Lind (annex 6A).[13]

The question then arises as to what the consumption and investment components of the effects of greenhouse policy are. The approach that will be taken

---

11. The annual annuity payment is calculated as: $A_{r,N} = r/[1 - (1 + r)^{-N}]$.

12. Note, however, that the approach here omits the influence of assumed saving and reinvestment on the public investment project itself—s in Bradford's analysis—as well as the corresponding concept z in Lind's approach, which incorporates the savings represented by depreciation. As noted in annex 6A, the incorporation of reinvestment effects in the shadow price of capital itself would appear to be double-counting, as the method already takes account of the investment versus consumption sourcing of the resources. As analyzed in the annex, this double-counting seems to be the source of the unstable, explosive nature of Lind's shadow price of capital.

13. Again, however, as Lind's method can generate shadow prices of less than zero or up to positive infinity, it is unreliable.

in this study (chapter 7) is as follows. For the economic costs of greenhouse abatement (i.e., those discussed in chapters 4 and 5), it will be assumed that 20 percent come at the expense of investment and 80 percent at the expense of consumption. These figures are based on displacement at "general-economy" rates, as discussed above. For the benefits of abatement (discussed in chapter 3), it is possible to make a further division. Several of the classes of benefits are in the category of "consumption" (human amenity, species loss, sea-level rise, loss of life, migration costs, leisure activities, pollution effects). Others are general production effects (agriculture, forestry). Still others are appropriately divided between consumption and general production (electricity requirements, water supply). On the basis of the rough estimates presented in chapter 3, the division between consumption-specific and general-production benefits of greenhouse warming abatement would appear to be about half and half.

On this basis, and again assuming an investment-saving share of 20 percent out of general production, the shadow price of capital would apply to 20 percent of half of the total benefits. Overall, the conversion of greenhouse policy effects to consumption-equivalents may thus be estimated as:

$$(6.2) \quad C^*_t = 0.8C_t + 0.2C_t(1 + v_c) = C_t(1 + 0.2v_c)$$

and

$$(6.3) \quad B^*_t = \phi_{bc}B_t + (1 - \phi_{bc})B_t(1 + 0.2v_c)$$

where the star indicates the consumption-equivalent after shadow pricing capital, C_t is the cost of the policy (i.e., production sacrificed) in year t, and B_t is the benefit of greenhouse abatement in year t. That is, 20 percent of the costs will be expanded by the capital shadow price. The fraction of the benefits that is consumption-specific (ϕ_{bc}) will have no expansion, but the remaining fraction will have the same expansion factor as that for the costs, on the grounds that this portion of the benefits reflects general output and that the saving-investment fraction of this output is the same as on the cost side (20 percent).

Estimating the Social Rate of Time Preference

The social rate of time preference (SRTP) tells the rate at which society evaluates future consumption versus consumption today. If the SRTP is i per year, then society requires $1 + i$ units of consumption one year into the future to be compensated for the sacrifice of one unit of consumption in the present. Identification of a meaningful SRTP for analysis over a 250-year horizon warrants careful consideration of past theory and empirical applications.

Growth Theory

One basis for identifying the very-long-term SRTP is to invoke important concepts developed in the theory of optimal economic growth. The "Golden Rule," developed by Phelps (1966) and others, states that, in the long-term "steady state," where maximum per capita consumption is achieved and held constant, each generation should do unto the next as it would have the former generation do unto it—by providing capital investment sufficient to hold the capital-labor ratio constant and thereby assure continuation of the standard of living. In this (neoclassical) tradition, production per worker (q) is a function of capital per worker (k). Population (and thus labor supply) grows at rate n. To keep the capital-labor ratio k constant, the amount nk of each worker's output must be devoted to capital accumulation. That is, suppose labor growth is 2 percent annually. Then new capital equal to 2 percent of last year's capital stock must be added; or equivalently, of each worker's output an amount equal to 2 percent of the worker's capital must be set aside for investment.

With these assumptions, the Golden Rule model demonstrates that maximum sustainable per capita consumption is achieved where the marginal product of capital is equal to n, the rate of population growth.[14] If less capital is accumulated, it will be possible to raise long-term per capita consumption by investing more today. If more capital is accumulated than advised by the Golden Rule, the economy will begin to have to divert so much of its output just to keeping this excessive capital endowment constant per capita that it will have less left over to consume. Because the economy is in a steady state, with output per worker and capital per worker constant, total production and the total capital stock also grow at the rate of labor-force growth, n.

In this situation, the SRTP equals the marginal product of capital, which equals the labor-force growth rate n. With steady-state per capita consumption, future consumption should not be further discounted on the grounds that the next generation will be richer, and time discounting arises solely from the side of capital opportunity cost rather than that of diminishing marginal utility (or for that matter, "myopic" pure time preference, discussed below).

Gramlich (1990, 105–09) has cited the Golden Rule as one means of identifying the proper SRTP. He suggests that the expected medium-term growth rate of the economy (on the order of $2\frac{1}{2}$ percent for the United States) might be interpreted as the Golden Rule rate n and thus the SRTP. However, this approach masks the difference between the present rate of population growth (about 1 percent) and the growth rate of the economy that arises because it is not at a

---

14. The proof is as follows. With C for consumption and L for labor, we have: $C/L = f(k) - nk$; $d(C/L)/dk = f'(k) - n = 0$ (where prime indicates a derivative); and thus $f'(k) = n$. See Jones (1975, 211).

steady state and per capita (or per worker) income is rising. The same divergence arises to a lesser extent for the very long term. Thus, for the period 2050 to 2100, World Bank estimates suggest that global population should rise only from 9.5 billion to 10.4 billion (Zacharia and Vu 1988), or at an annual rate of about 0.25 percent. However, because per capita income is likely to keep rising as developing areas catch up to industrial-country standards of living, total GDP would be rising at a rate of perhaps 1 percent higher. On this basis, the SRTP for a horizon of one or two centuries would be on the order of 1 percent to 1½ percent if based on output growth and ½ percent or less if based on population growth. Golden Rule theory thus suggests that the SRTP is somewhere in the range of 1 percent annually for purposes of greenhouse analysis over the very long term.

Log-Linear Utility Function

An alternative theoretical basis for the SRTP may be derived from utility theory or, more specifically, Benthamite welfarism (to use the terms of d'Arge et al. 1982 and Sen 1982). In this approach, the discount rate arises from the lesser inherent value of additional consumption at future points in time. This decline in turn stems from two sources: impatience ("myopia") and the expectation of higher standards of living and therefore lower marginal utility of incremental consumption in the future. Thus, we might write:

$$(6.4) \quad \mathrm{SRTP}_u = \pi_m + \pi_u$$

where subscript u denotes the utility approach, π_m denotes the discount rate arising solely from myopia or impatience, and π_u represents the discount element attributable to expected declining marginal utility.

Ramsey (1928, 543), a Cambridge philosopher and mathematician, rejected π_m on the following grounds: "[W]e do not discount later enjoyments in comparison with earlier ones, a practice which is ethically indefensible and arises merely from the weakness of the imagination." Whatever one thinks about Ramsey's rejection of "pure impatience" with respect to discounting over horizons such as 10 to 20 years, his admonition surely takes on additional force when the horizon stretches over two centuries or more. Impatience or "myopia" may be a legitimate basis for a single individual's preferring consumption earlier rather than later in his lifetime, but from society's standpoint it is hardly a justifiable basis for making intergenerational comparisons.

If with Ramsey we reject π_m, that leaves π_u to evaluate. This discount rate should reflect the expected diminishing marginal utility of consumption associated with the expected rise in per capita income over time. The analysis that follows first uses one standard "utility function," the logarithmic function (per capita utility equals the logarithm of per capita income) to arrive at the following conclusions:

- The utility-based SRTP should equal the rate of growth of per capita income.

- The rate of trade-off between the value of additional consumption for two representative individuals at two different points in time should equal the inverse of the ratio of their consumption levels.

The analysis then turns to generalization to a broader class of utility functions.

Suppose we postulate an exogenously determined future path of per capita consumption, rather than seek to identify what that path should be after taking into account investment opportunities. That is, consider a "positive" very-long-term growth forecast, as opposed to a "normative" rule for identifying rates of saving and investment. Suppose in this outlook, per capita consumption grows at the annual rate g.

Let λ_t be defined as the ratio of the number of additional units of consumption in future year t to the number of additional units of consumption in the base year 0 required to generate identical increases in utility in the two years. Define u' (which equals $u'[c]$, where c is consumption) as marginal utility. Then:

$$(6.5) \quad \lambda_t = u'_0/u'_t.$$

If marginal utility is constant, $u_0 = u'_t$ and $\lambda_t = 1$. However, under the standard utility assumptions—$u = u(c); u' > 0, u'' < 0$—there is diminishing marginal utility. Thus, with $c_t > c_0, u'_t < u'_0$ and $\lambda_t > 1$.

In the logarithmic utility function,

$$(6.6) \quad u = \ln c$$

where u is (per capita) utility and c is (per capita) consumption. Marginal utility is:

$$(6.7) \quad \delta u/\delta c \equiv u'(c) = 1/c.$$

From equations 6.5 and 6.7,

$$(6.8) \quad \lambda_t = [1/c_0]/[1/c_t] = c_t/c_0.$$

Equation 6.8 provides one of the two results postulated above: the rate of trade-off in the value of additional consumption between two individuals across time is the inverse of the ratio of their respective consumption levels.

The SRTP, or i, may be identified by applying the following proposition: the rate of discount should be such that it equates λ_t extra units of consumption in time t to 1 extra unit of consumption in base year 0. Thus:

$$(6.9) \quad \lambda_t/(1 + i)^t = 1.$$

Correspondingly,

(6.10) $\lambda_t = (1 + i)^t$.

From equations 6.8 and 6.10, we have

(6.11) $c_t/c_0 = (1 + i)^t$.

Considering that the exogenous per capita consumption growth rate is g, after t years the level of per capita consumption will be

(6.12) $c_t = c_0 (1 + g)^t$.

From equations 6.11 and 6.12 it follows that $i = g$, confirming the first of the two conclusions stated at the outset. That is, given a postulated long-term path of per capita consumption, the SRTP for comparing consumption over time should be simply the growth rate of per capita consumption, under the logarithmic utility function.

This conclusion helps provide a narrowing of the range of plausible discount rates for long-term analysis. As indicated in chapter 7, real per capita income in the United States has grown at about 1.7 percent annually over the past century. During the past four decades, per capita income in both the industrial and developing countries has grown at an average of about 2 percent (World Bank, *World Development Report 1991*, 17). Dismal results in Africa and Latin America in the 1980s suggest caution about the simple assumption that positive per capita income growth is guaranteed in the future. Over the very long term, diminishing returns to the accumulation of human and physical capital per worker would tend to cause growth rates to moderate. Overall, if we use the logarithmic utility function to conclude that $\pi_u = g$, then an SRTP on the order of 1 percent annually would seem appropriate for the very long term.

The rate could be even lower if the focus of attention is *global* per capita income growth. Because population growth is likely to be much higher in developing countries than in industrial countries, the share of the poor countries in total income will rise even if both areas have identical per capita income growth rates. This reallocation of the center of gravity means that world average per capita income will grow more slowly than per capita income in each area even if the area per capita growth rates are identical. With plausible "stylized magnitudes," a 1 percent per capita growth rate in both rich and poor countries over 100 years would translate into an average global per capita growth rate of about 0.5 percent.[15] With less favorable assumptions (e.g., lower but still positive

---

15. The share of industrial countries in today's world population is about 20 percent, that of developing countries about 80 percent (World Bank, *World Development Report 1991*, 205). The average real per capita income in industrial countries is about five times

per capita income growth rates in each area), it would even be possible for average worldwide per capita income to fall over the next century because of the rising population share of the poorer area.

Considering global rather than area-specific per capita income growth does imply a willingness to take the welfare of citizens of other countries into account in the utility of residents of a (richer) country, whereas the low levels of international concessional assistance suggest that at present the weight of this welfare is relatively small. However, the weight of those more distant from oneself in one's utility function may rise as the horizon stretches past the present generation. That is, the relative importance of conditions in India (or "global society") to conditions in Washington or Wichita may rise in the utility function of an American as the time horizon moves from the present to two centuries or more from today, if for no other reason than the fact that the present-day American knows his living, named kin but does not know his subsequent descendants.

Other Utility Functions

The logarithmic utility function has the feature that the rise in consumption just exactly offsets the declining absolute marginal utility of consumption, so that *the absolute response of utility to a proportionate change in consumption is constant.* That is, if a 1 percent decrease in the consumption of a person consuming $1,000 today permits a 1 percent increase in the consumption of a person consuming $5,000 one hundred years from now, society will be just as well off. The marginal utility of consumption declines at just the right rate to make the absolute gain of $50 in the future just offset the absolute loss of $10 today. More generally, a 1 percent sacrifice of income today will be compensated by a 1 percent increase in income in the (richer) future, because of the larger absolute base to which the future percentage change will apply. Formally, this property of the logarithmic utility function is called the "unitary elasticity of marginal utility with respect to consumption."[16]

---

that in developing countries after taking into account purchasing power parity (Kravis et al. 1982). If population grows at an annual rate of 0.1 percent in industrial countries and 1.5 percent in developing countries, after 100 years the population shares will be about 5 percent and 95 percent, respectively. Per capita income growth of 1 percent in each area would permit per capita income to rise by about 150 percent over the period in each area. Applying the terminal population weights to the respective terminal per capita incomes, the global average at the end of 100 years is only 67 percent, not 150 percent, higher than in the base year, for average annual growth of 0.5 percent.

16. For any monotonic function of a variable, in this case $u(c)$, the elasticity equals the marginal value, $u'(c)$, divided by the average relationship of the function to the variable, $u(c)/c$, where the prime indicates a first derivative. The elasticity of marginal utility with respect to consumption is thus $\theta = u''(c)/[u'(c)/c]$, where the double prime indicates a

It is an open question whether this "proportionality rule" is appropriate. The principle of progressive taxation would say that it is not. That is, where the tax system provides that a richer person should pay a higher *percentage* of her income in tax than a poorer person, not just a higher *absolute* tax, the implication is that the dropoff in marginal utility as consumption rises is faster than can be compensated for by the absolute increase in consumption. If θ is the elasticity of marginal utility with respect to consumption, then progressive taxation implies that $|\theta| > 1$, whereas the logarithmic utility function has $\theta = -1$ and $|\theta| = 1$. In practice, however, after taking into account payroll taxes, deductions, and so forth, the US income tax system has tended to have a broadly proportional rather than progressive structure. This was the case even before the reduction of marginal tax rates in the highest brackets in the 1986 US tax reform (Pechman and Okner 1974, 5–7). There is, of course, the additional question of whether comparison across individuals of different incomes at a given time is the appropriate basis for judging the comparison of representative individuals at different times.

Blanchard and Fischer (1989) review alternative classes of utility functions. They note that the logarithmic form is a specific case of the more general constant relative risk aversion (CRRA) function, which has the form:[17]

(6.13) $u(c) = [c^{1-\gamma}]/[1 - \gamma]$ for $\gamma \neq 1$;

(6.13') $u(c) = \ln c$ for $\gamma = 1$.

The term γ is the coefficient of risk aversion and is equal to the negative of the elasticity of marginal utility, that is, $-u''(c)c/u(c)$. The authors also note that the elasticity of substitution between consumption at two points in time, $\sigma(c_t)$, is the inverse of the negative of the elasticity of the marginal utility of consumption. They report:

> Substantial empirical work has been devoted to estimating σ under the assumption that it is indeed constant, by looking at how willing consumers are to shift consumption across time in response to changes in interest rates. Estimates of σ vary substantially but usually lie around or below unity. (Blanchard and Fischer 1989, 44)

The implication is that empirical work on risk aversion tends to identify a coefficient of risk aversion that implies a near-unitary elasticity of marginal utility of consumption. The further implication is that the logarithmic utility function

---

second derivative. For $u = \ln (c)$, because $u'(c) = 1/c$, we have $u''(c) = -1/c^2$. In turn, $u(c)/c = (1/c)/c = 1/c^2$. The quotient gives $\theta = -1$.

17. Other utility forms include the constant absolute risk aversion (CARA) and quadratic functions. These are more tractable mathematically but less consistent with economic theory.

used above to derive a utility-based SRTP is not inconsistent with the empirical evidence available. This inference requires the assumption that utility relationships across time and generations for varying levels of consumption behave similarly to those for varying levels of consumption of an individual facing alternative risk-return opportunities.[18]

The CRRA utility function may be used to generalize the relationship between the SRTP and the growth rate of per capita income. In an exogenously determined time path, the SRTP merely equals the growth rate of per capita consumption in the case of the logarithmic utility function, as shown in equations 6.5 to 6.12. From equation 6.13 and the fact that the constant elasticity of marginal utility, θ, is the negative of the coefficient of risk aversion, γ, we may write the CRRA utility function as:

$$(6.14) \quad u(c) = c^{1+\theta}/[1 + \theta].$$

Marginal utility is thus:

$$(6.15) \quad u'(c) = c^{\theta}.$$

The ratio of the number of units of additional consumption required at time t to compensate for the loss of a single unit of consumption at time 0 becomes:

$$(6.16) \quad \lambda_t = c_0^{\theta} / c_t^{\theta} = [c_t/c_0]^{-\theta}.$$

As before, we seek an SRTP i such that, compounded over t years, it generates this trade-off, or $\lambda_t = (1 + i)^t$ (as in equations 6.9 and 6.10 above). Considering that with the exogenous per capita consumption growth rate of g we have $c_t/c_0 = (1 + g)^t$, then from equations 6.10 and 6.16 we have:

$$(6.17) \quad (1 + i)^t = [(1 + g)^t]^{-\theta}.$$

Taking the tth root of both sides, we have:

$$(6.18) \quad 1 + i = (1 + g)^{-\theta}.$$

With plausible ranges of g, we have as a close approximation:

$$(6.19) \quad i \approx -\theta g.$$

In the special case of the logarithmic utility function, $\theta = -1$, and the generalized form yields the same result as found above: $i = g$.

---

18. Giovannini and Weil (1989,i) have proposed a methodology that distinguishes between the elasticity of marginal utility with respect to risk and that with respect to intertemporal preference. They find the empirical evidence is consistent with "a unit coefficient of relative risk aversion and an elasticity of intertemporal substitution different from 1." However, they do not report the corresponding value of the intertemporal elasticity of marginal utility.

Fellner (1967) has suggested that, on the basis of statistical estimates of consumption functions for the United States, the elasticity of marginal utility (θ) is on the order of -1.5.[19] In the example at the beginning of this section, with c_1 equal to 5,000 and c_0 equal to 1,000, using $\theta = -1.5$ we would have $u'(c_0)/u'(c_1) = (5,000/1,000)^{1.5} = 11.2$, so that to compensate for a sacrifice of 10 units of consumption at time 0 would require a gain of 112 units of consumption in period 1. In contrast, the required compensation would amount to only 50 units of consumption using the unitary elasticity of marginal utility, (that is, $50 \times u'[c_1] = 10 \times u'[c_0]$, because $u'[c_1]/u'[c_0] = c_0/c_1 = 1/5$). Similarly, in this and all other cases with $|\theta| > 1$, it will require a greater-than-1-percent increase in consumption in the (richer) future to compensate for a 1 percent reduction in consumption in the (poorer) present.

If the range of $\theta = -1.5$ is valid, then the generalized CRRA utility function would indicate an SRTP equal to one and one-half times the growth rate of per capita consumption. With a plausible value of g being somewhere near 1 percent over the very long term (as suggested above), the SRTP would then be set at $i = 1.5$ percent.

Relationship to Discounted Utility Maximization

The approach of this study (chapter 7) is to compare absolute magnitudes of benefits and costs across time by converting to consumption equivalents (shadow pricing capital effects) and then discounting at the SRTP. An alternative approach frequently applied in optimization analyses (e.g. Blitzer et al. 1991, Nordhaus 1992b) is to maximize the "discounted sum of utility" over time. Typically such studies apply a logarithmic utility function, but in principle the utility function may be of the more general CRRA form indicated in equation 6.12 (or still other forms). Usually, such studies then additionally discount utility across time by applying a further discount rate for time preference.

It is important to recognize that analyses that incorporate *both* an explicit utility function *and* time discounting are essentially discounting twice: once implicitly through the utility function, for declining marginal utility, and a second time explicitly through the "discount rate." In such formulations the explicit discount rate is what may be called the "pure" rate of time preference (as, e.g., Nordhaus 1992b uses the term). This concept is the same as the component of the discount rate for "myopia," term π_m in equation 6.4. To see that there is an additional, "first" layer of discounting through the utility function, it need

---

19. Fellner bases this calculation on the proposition that the elasticity of marginal utility equals the ratio of the income elasticity of demand to the income-adjusted price elasticity of demand. These he derives from statistical estimates of demand functions for food in the United States (Fellner 1967, 59–63).

only be recognized that, like discounting, the application of a logarithmic (or other CRRA) utility function has the effect of shrinking the value of consumption at future dates (when marginal utility is lower because of higher per capita income).

In effect, the contribution of consumption c in a future year t to present value of discounted utility is often formulated in utility maximization models as:

$$(6.20) \quad PV(u(c_t)) = \{[c^{1-\gamma}]/[1 - \gamma]\}/(1 + \pi_m)^t$$

In contrast, the corresponding contribution of extra future consumption to present value in the approach of this study is:

$$(6.21) \quad PV(c_t) = c_t/(1 + \pi_u)^t$$

As developed above, if per capita income and consumption are strictly rising at rate g, these two formulations give identical results so long as $\pi_m = 0$ and $\pi_u = -\theta g$, where θ is the elasticity of marginal utility with respect to consumption.

An important implication of this correspondence between the two different approaches is that typical optimization analyses may well apply an excessive total discount rate, at least if one accepts the argument here that discounting for "pure" time preference (myopia) should be excluded. A corresponding implication is that optimization studies of greenhouse policy may often be biased toward delaying action (costs) toward late in the horizon, because by discounting not only for declining marginal utility but also for myopia they place an undue preference on current rather than future consumption.

Reality Check: An Intuitive Approach

Suppose the question of time discounting is formulated in the following way. How much should one dollar taken away from your granddaughter's grandson—call him Joseph—be worth to you today? Two hundred years is on the order of six generations. Suppose one is willing to take away one dollar from Joseph in order to consume 50 cents more today. Then one's implicit discount rate is only 0.4 percent per year (table 6.1). Or suppose one would be willing to take away one dollar from Joseph just to obtain five cents for additional consumption today. Then the discount rate is still only 1.5 percent.

As discussed above, the principal reason for discounting future consumption is that in the future people may have higher incomes than today, and a lower marginal utility of consumption. Given the extent to which people today are richer than people in America at the time of the Revolutionary War, how large would an appropriate 200-year discount factor be on the basis of past experience? The difference in the standards of living (assuming one is speaking of averages, not the poorest) might justify a shrinkage factor of, say, five to one (that is, society would have been better off if one could take away one dollar today in order to have made one's grandfather's grandfather 20 cents better off), implying a time discount rate of 0.8 percent annually. However, standards of living have simply not advanced enough in the past 200 years to justify taking away one dollar from today's consumption to make one's grandfather's grandfather only, say, two cents better off (a discount rate of 2 percent annually; table 6.1). It would be implausible in the extreme to argue that intertemporal America would have been better off to take away one dollar of consumption from a person today just to make her great-great-grandfather better of by six one-thousandths of a cent. Yet that is the bargain implied by a discount rate as high as 5 percent (table 6.1).

The SRTP for discounting consumption is essentially the "demand" side of intertemporal maximization, as opposed to the "supply" side, which takes into account capital productivity. The capital-supply side is taken into account through capital shadow pricing, as discussed above. For the consumption-demand side, these illustrations tend to suggest that for the extremely long-term comparisons required in analysis of global warming the SRTP should be in the range of 1 percent per year or perhaps less. Intuitive reflection thus tends to confirm the analysis above. Moreover, if one is pessimistic about future per capita income growth, there is an intuitive case for not discounting consumption at all.

Observed Market Rates

Actual applications of social benefit-cost analysis have tended to cite historically observed interest rates and rates of return as the basis for identifying appropriate magnitudes to use for time discounting.

The Social Rate of Time Preference

For the consumption-based SRTP, analysts have tended to refer to the real rate of return on treasury obligations as an indicator of the safe yield consumers expect in postponing consumption. Lind (1982a, 82) reports that from 1926 to 1978 the real after-tax rate of return on US Treasury bills (for the 20 percent tax bracket) was on average negative. Lind decides:

> We will . . . use 1 percent as a first approximation of the real rate of time preference associated with a safe asset such as US Treasury bills and 2 percent as the real rate of time preference on safe long-term assets such as long-term US government bonds, with which the primary risk is a change in interest rates. (Lind 1982a, 87)

Because risk is more appropriately incorporated in the projected benefits and costs under alternative scenarios rather than through an increase in the discount rate (Gramlich 1990, 99), and because the risk of a cyclical fluctuation in the real interest rate is of little relevance for very-long-term analysis, Lind's 1 percent rate (which itself rounds up from below zero) would seem the more appropriate of the two.

Kolb and Scheraga (1990, 386) note:

> After-tax rates of return on savings instruments that are widely available to the public or returns on stock portfolios have been used to estimate the consumption rate of interest, which is taken to be a proxy for the social rate of time preference.

They calculate that, from 1946 to 1980, real after-tax rates of return on three-month US Treasury bills were −1.1 percent annually on average, but that in the 1980s this return was in a positive range from 2 percent to 4 percent. The authors state that "returns to stocks averaged about 5 percent over the past 60 years" (Kolb and Scheraga 1990, 386). On this basis, they place the consumption rate of interest in the range of 1 percent to 5 percent and select 3 percent for their central value.

The real return on treasury bills would appear to be the more meaningful basis for an empirical estimation of the SRTP. Return on stocks includes a large component of risk, and the desired concept is a risk-free rate of return. Abel et al. (1989, 2) report estimates by Ibbotson (1987) showing that the average real rate of return on US Treasury bills from 1926 through 1986 was only 0.3 percent. For the period 1960–90, the average real return on treasury bills for the seven major industrial countries amounted to 0.3 percent.[20]

Overall, on the basis of the various empirical estimates of real rates of return on treasury bills, the best benchmark estimate for the consumption rate of discount and thus the SRTP (i) is 1 percent per year. Even this rate would appear to be an overstatement rather than an underestimate. An empirical range of 1 percent for the SRTP is consistent with the theoretically based value of 1½ percent developed above, on the basis of expected long-term growth in per capita income and the elasticity of marginal utility of consumption.

Whereas the standard empirical practice is to consider either the treasury bill or the treasury bond rate as a proxy for the SRTP, it may be asked whether other, higher rates applicable to consumer borrowing should be taken into account as well. Thus, home mortgage rates and, especially, rates on credit cards and other consumer credit will tend to be higher. Are these not revealed rates at which consumers show they are prepared to discount the future?

---

20. This estimate is obtained by deflating by consumer prices and weighting by 1990 GDP shares. Calculated from International Monetary Fund, *International Financial Statistics*, 1990. For France and Japan, the rate on bank deposits is used rather than that on treasury bills.

There are two components to the difference between the consumer rate on credit cards and the treasury bill rate. First, in one case the consumer is a borrower, and in the other a lender. Second, the borrower is a risky client in the case of consumer credit (which is unsecured), whereas it is absolutely safe in the case of the treasury bill.

There are several arguments for using the risk-free consumer lending (treasury bill) rate rather than the risk-inclusive consumer borrowing rate for the SRTP in greenhouse analysis. First, if the consumer discount rate is to be disaggregated by household type to distinguish between net borrowers and net lenders, failure to conduct a similar household disaggregation by income class may bias the analysis by failing to take account of the poor in the future and thereby over-stating the decline of marginal utility. Instead, the analysis implicitly treats a representative household. Because overall households, weighted by income, are net creditors (otherwise there could be no net government debt), so is the "representative" household, and the appropriate time preference rate for this household is the safe return on assets (the treasury bill rate).

Second, some components of consumer credit involve high rates that the consumer pays because of misinformation or high transactions costs (relative to small transactions volumes). The high rates consumers pay on credit cards incorporate some component for the transactions costs the consumer can avoid by not bothering to consolidate the relatively small outstanding obligations into a larger, longer-term loan. Such lending is surely irrelevant to a long-term, societywide decision such as greenhouse policy. For such decisions, the "plan-ner" may be seen as an agent of net-borrower households who arrives at an accounting discount rate by considering what the households would pay for larger, longer-term borrowing.

Third, during its life cycle a household may move from an initial position of net borrower (e.g., for education and setting up a home) to an eventual position of net lender. For long-term analysis, what is of interest is the average position of the household over time. That position is one of net lender rather than borrower. Thus, single-household averaging longitudinally over time arrives at the same implication as multiple-household averaging cross-sectionally at a point in time: the representative household is a creditor rather than a debtor.[21]

Fourth, because risk in social benefit-cost analysis is appropriately taken ac-count of in the underlying projection scenarios, it is again the risk-free rate we seek for discounting purposes. On this basis, the risk component in the high observed interest rates for credit cards, automobile loans, and even home mort-gages should be eliminated. Removal of risk should largely eliminate the wedge between the return on treasury bills and that on high-interest consumer loans.

---

21. Any household that bequeaths more assets than it inherited is a net creditor longi-tudinally.

Table 6.2 Weighted consumer discount rate: premium above Treasury bill

Decile	Borrower premium (percentages per year) A	Net lender share (percentages)[a] B	Income share (percentages)[b] C	Weighted-average discount rate premium (percentages)[c] D
1,2	5.3	10	4.6	4.8
3,4	3.0	14	10.6	2.6
5,6	2.5	29	16.5	1.8
7,8	1.8	32	23.7	1.2
9	0.9	36	16.6	0.6
10	0.0	90	28.0	0.0
Total			100.0	1.2[d]

a. Percentage share of households in this income category that are net lenders.

b. Percentage of total income accruing to households in this income category.

c. $D = A \times (100 - B)/100$.

d. Weighted by column C.

Source: Calculated from R. H. Haveman. 1969. "The Opportunity Cost of Displaced Private Spending and the Social Discount Rate." *Water Resources Research* 5, no. 5 (October); Joseph A. Pechman and Benjamin A. Okner. 1974. *Who Bears the Tax Burden?* Washington: Brookings Institution; and US Department of Commerce, *Statistical Abstract of the United States,* 1991, 455.

In short, the standard practice in the discount literature of concentrating on the real treasury bill (or bond) rate, or the safe consumer lending rate, would seem conceptually preferable to an alternative approach that incorporates, in addition, the rates on risky consumer borrowing.

Nonetheless, it is of interest to consider how much difference inclusion of consumer borrowing rates might make to the estimated SRTP. One of the few studies that follows this approach is by Haveman (1969), who estimates a weighted average of consumer borrowing and lending rates. His calculation yields a US consumer interest rate of 7.3 percent nominal for 1966. As US inflation was 3.0 percent that year, the corresponding real rate is 4.3 percent annually, far higher than the SRTP of 1 percent to 1½ percent suggested above.

Table 6.2 presents an alternative estimate of the same concept, but with appropriate adjustments. The table specifies the various consumer rates in terms of the spread above the US Treasury bill rate, which stood at 4.9 percent in 1966 (*Economic Report of the President,* February 1991, 368). The premiums for borrowing rates by income class are calculated from Haveman (1969).[22] How-

---

22. Except for the arbitrary 20 percent to 25 percent nominal rate assumed by Haveman for those lower-income households that do not lend but cannot borrow for lack of cre-

ever, on the household lending side it is assumed that the US Treasury bill rate is the appropriate marginal risk-free rate. Haveman instead uses an average return on nonlabor income (about 6½ percent nominal), which is neither marginal nor risk free.

The Haveman income classes are converted into income distributional deciles using data also for 1966 reported by Pechman and Okner (1974, 46). The corresponding shares of households in total national income are for 1989 (*Statistical Abstract of the United States* 1991). Haveman's estimates are applied for the division of each income class between net debtors and net creditors.

As indicated in table 6.2, the weighted-average premium of household borrowing and lending rates above the Treasury bill rate amounts to 1.3 percent. Considering that the long-term average for US Treasury bill rates is 0.3 percent real (as noted above), adding this premium would place the SRTP at 1.6 percent, even when estimated under an approach incorporating consumer borrowing as well as household risk-free lending rates.[23] This approach thus does not significantly alter the empirical result for the SRTP in the central estimates above (set at 1½ percent).

Rate of Return on Private Capital

The second real interest rate required for social benefit-cost analysis is the return on private capital (r), for calculation of the shadow price of capital (discussed above). Feldstein and Summers (1977, 216) have calculated that the real rate of return on nonfinancial corporate capital in the United States was an average of 11.5 percent from 1948 to 1969 and 7.9 percent for 1970–76, or 10.5 percent for the three-decade period. Kolb and Scheraga (1990, 385) cite Ibbotson and Sinquefield (1982) to the effect that real rates of return on equities before corporate tax averaged between 10 percent and 12.9 percent over the last 60 years, and they cite various other sources placing the average rate of return on investment in the nonfinancial sector in a range of 8 percent to 13 percent.

It is important to distinguish between the marginal and the average rate of return on private capital. When resources are withdrawn from private investment, it is the lowest-return projects that will be discontinued first. Therefore, the appropriate measure for the opportunity cost on private capital is somewhat

ditworthiness (about 40 percent of the first two deciles). This treatment would seem excessive, and, instead, these households are added here to the borrowing households in the same income groups.

23. This rate is lower than Haveman's because the long-term average real Treasury bill rate is lower than the 1966 rate (accounting for 1.9 − 0.3 = 1.6 percent difference) and because of the methodological changes applied here (which account for the other 1.1-percentage-point divergence).

lower than the measured average rate of return. Kolb and Scheraga place the marginal rate in a range of 5 percent to 10 percent, or about two-thirds the level of the average rates they review.[24]

The real rate of interest on lending to the corporate sector provides an alternative measure of the marginal rate of return on private capital. That is, the rate of return on the marginal project must cover the interest cost of financing incurred to undertake the project. Note that the difference between before- and after-tax returns does not enter the calculation. Because interest is a deductible expense, the firm will borrow up to the point at which the interest rate equals the before-tax rate of return on the project. For the seven major industrial countries, the average real lending (or prime) rate in the period 1960–90 amounted to 4.6 percent per year, weighting by 1990 GDP shares and deflating by the wholesale price index (calculated from *International Financial Statistics,* 1990).

Overall, a central estimate for the marginal real rate of return in the private sector would appear to be in the range of 8 percent per year. In view of the real lending rates for large industrial countries, this estimate would tend to be on the high side rather than an understatement.

A Declining Social Rate of Time Preference?

A nascent but suggestive literature indicates that consumers may apply a much lower discount rate for the distant future than for more proximate events. Unfortunately, most of this literature concerns relatively short time horizons. The studies tend to be based on experiments in which students or others are asked to state their preferences among alternative sums of money (or other benefits) at alternative time periods, usually covering no more than a few months. Such studies typically find extremely high discount rates for short periods such as a few days but successively lower rates for periods further into the future (Winston and Woodbury 1991, Thaler 1981, Loewenstein 1987).

Of much greater relevance for the extremely long time horizon involved in global warming, Cropper et al. (1991) have conducted an intriguing survey on the public's implicit discount rate for comparison of lives saved at different points in time. This issue is of relevance for benefit-cost analysis by regulatory agencies. The authors conducted telephone surveys of approximately 1,600 households in the Washington, DC, metropolitan area. They asked (for example) whether the respondent would prefer antipollution measures that would save 100 lives

---

24. Note that the marginal versus average distinction is appropriate, whereas the after-tax versus before-tax distinction is inappropriate. What matters to society is the loss of return before tax when a private-sector investment is withdrawn. The fact that the after-tax return to the firm's shareholders is lower is not relevant for the calculation of r for use in estimating the shadow price of capital.

now or 200 lives 50 years from now. Converting their findings to a form $d = a + bt$, where d is the discount rate and t is the year, they found that the implicit discount rate fell from 7 percent at $t = 0$ to 3.5 percent at $t = 50$ and zero at $t = 100$.[25]

The Cropper et al. results are provocative but difficult to interpret. Their study provides perhaps the only existing empirical information on the behavior of discount rates over the extremely long time horizons relevant to global warming.[26] Its findings suggest the desirability of further survey work to examine the time discount rates people would apply to the general effects of the greenhouse problem, rather than to human lives. In the absence of such work, the results would at least seem to provide partial support of the proposition considered at the outset (and Mishan's formulation in particular): the discount rate for very-long-term, intergenerational matters is likely to be lower than that for more conventional choices.

Policy Differences Among Government Entities

During the 1970s and 1980s, the American public, in a new type of "checks and balances" unanticipated by the founding fathers, systematically elected Republicans to control the executive branch of the federal government and Democrats to control Congress. Republicans have traditionally favored a limited role for government, whereas the Democrats have favored a more activist role. Considering that a higher discount rate means fewer government projects approved, the philosophical difference may help explain the divergent discounting approaches of the two branches. In the past two decades the executive branch has tended to insist on high real rates of return for government projects under guidelines of the Office of Management and Budget (OMB), whereas the two relevant congressional entities—the Congressional Budget Office (CBO) and the General Accounting Office (GAO)—have followed policies tending toward lower discount rates.

Over this period the OMB has called for a real discount rate of 10 percent on government investments (OMB Circular no. A-94 rev., 27 March 1972). OMB

---

25. These results exclude the 40 percent of respondents who placed an infinite discount rate on lives saved later rather than at the present time. These respondents appeared to be assuming that technological change would resolve death hazards in the future.

26. Note, however, that at least one of the authors (Cropper) is reluctant to interpret the results as a general indication that the discount rate falls over time under very long time horizons. She considers the near-term discount rate on lives overstated, as she would instead expect a near-zero, but more constant, discount rate on lives, apparently because they differ qualitatively from goods and services (statement at a National Bureau of Economic Research workshop, Cambridge, MA, 15 August 1991).

economists in the early 1970s sought to head off a tendency toward lower rates based on the emerging literature on social discounting. Their analytical case was based on the argument that it would be inefficient for the economy to have two rates of return, a higher one in the private sector and a lower one in government. Their approach identified the 10 percent norm as the outcome of prevailing real rates of return in the private sector, on the one hand, and the size of the income tax "wedge," on the other. A chief architect of this approach considers it still valid, but notes that with divergent changes in the private rate of return (lower) and the tax wedge (smaller), the particular rate relevant today might no longer be 10 percent.[27]

In contrast, "GAO and CBO base their analyses of public investment decisions on the Treasury borrowing rate" (Winter and Grosshans 1991, 29). Historically, this approach reflects the perceived opportunity cost to the public sector of funds borrowed for investment purposes. However, Winter and Grosshans demonstrate that, under reasonable assumptions, this rate is close to a weighted-average interest rate reflecting the private sector before-tax rate of return, on the one hand, and private households' after-tax interest rate on safe assets, on the other.[28] Thus, it is arguably close to consistency with the literature calling for a weighted-average approach. The authors also review the consumption-equivalent social discounting approach, but note its "empirical challenges to implementation" because of its sensitivity to parameters for the shadow price of capital (Winter and Grosshans 1991, 29).

The most recent GAO guidelines thus reaffirm the agency's use of the Treasury borrowing rate for the maturity closest to the project life, although they encourage sensitivity analysis using shadow-pricing or weighted-average approaches (Winter and Grosshans 1991, 21). For the period 1956–91, the average real interest rate on long-term US Treasury bonds was 2.6 percent.[29] The GAO

---

27. William Niskanen, Cato Institute, personal communication, 21 October 1991.

28. In their terms, $w = ic + r(1 - c)$, where w is the weighted discount rate, i is the interest rate faced by consumers, and r is the return to private capital. They assume that the Treasury borrowing rate, b, equals the rate of return to private capital after tax, or: $b = r(1 - t_c)$, where t_c is the corporate tax rate. They further assume that the net return to consumers equals the Treasury rate less taxes at the personal income tax rate, or $i = b(1 - t_p)$. Substituting, $w = bf$, where $f = c(1 - t_p) + (1 - c)/(1 - t_c)$. Simulating reasonable values for the parameters, they conclude that f is relatively close to unity, so that the Treasury borrowing rate is a reasonable approximation of the weighted average of the rates of return to private capital and consumers.

29. Calculated from *Economic Report of the President*, February 1991, 351, 368. The 10-year bond rate is used, as this series extends back to the 1950s and for the past decade the average spread between 10-year and 30-year Treasury bonds has been *de minimis* (*Federal Reserve Bulletin*, various issues, table 1-35, and Federal Reserve data sheets). The deflator is consumer price inflation with weights of 0.35, 0.28, 0.22, and 0.15 for the current and three previous years, respectively, for regressive expectations.

approach thus implies a real discount rate on the order of 2½ percent. The similar CBO approach applies a central real discount rate of 2 percent (Hartman 1990, as cited in Winter and Grosshans 1991, 14).

The Investment Fund Alternative

As clarified at the outset of this chapter, the approach here is to convert all effects to consumption-equivalents by shadow pricing capital effects, and then to discount at the social rate of time preference. Some would argue, in contrast, that greenhouse policy should use the investment or capital rate of return to discount, because governments could invest resources at this rate and build up their economies so as to make future generations even better off than under the alternative of a greenhouse abatement program that merely achieves the lower rates of return discussed here. Let us analyze this alternative by considering the establishment of a Fund for Greenhouse Victims (FGV).

There are several problems with the investment fund alternative. First, it is highly vulnerable to the issue of the proper trade-off in valuation between environmental and other goods and services (as discussed above and illustrated in figure 6.1). It is quite possible that, even with high rates of return on investment in the production of videocassette recorders and toasters, no additional amount of such goods can compensate the distant future generations for a parched grain belt (in part because they will already have so many VCRS and toasters). As noted, this difficulty is reflected in the risk of undervaluing benefits of greenhouse abatement for lack of sufficient attention to loss of consumer surplus of environmental categories.

Second, in terms of political economy the "investment alternative" school of discounting requires an implausible commitment to a conscious setting aside of additional investment funds today to compensate the future generation for global warming. In effect, governments would have to tell their publics that an extra income (or other) tax was to be levied, and all proceeds would be invested in the FGV. Unless such action would be in fact undertaken, the *possibility* that such extra investment might more efficiently compensate the future generation than a conscious greenhouse abatement program is simply irrelevant. The question then becomes whether the public is more likely to accept a carbon tax (or other disincentive to greenhouse gas emissions) or a tax for investment in the FGV. Acceptability of the latter is by no means likely to be greater than that of the former, especially in view of the rebate of carbon taxes through reduction in other taxes.

Third, the FGV approach contains no remedy for an unexpected catastrophe from global warming, whereas the more straightforward approach of limiting greenhouse gas emissions does.

Fourth, it is by no means clear that a government investment fund could find capital investment projects that would yield the relatively high real rates of return typically supposed for private capital. IBM may be able to earn a real return of 8 percent annually, but how would the managers of the FGV do so? If the fund invested through financial intermediaries, it would earn no more on a risk-compensated basis than the long-term government bond rate, a return much closer to the SRTP than to the rate of return on private capital investment. If the FGV entered directly into investment in production, the issue of state enterprise activity in the economy would arise, with its risks of inefficiency and vulnerability to political capture (e.g., subsidies to state-sponsored aircraft).

Fifth, and more profoundly, there may be a physical limit on the feasibility of intergenerational transfer. Investment today is usually in machines and factories to produce consumer goods for a tomorrow that is 3 to 15 years hence, not 200. In principle the FGV should invest in factories that construct only "producer goods" (machines) that produce a subsequent generation of producer goods and so forth in an unbroken chain with no consumer-goods output until the distant target date for compensation of the future greenhouse victims. It is unclear what these machines might be, and even more uncertain what the ultimate consumer goods might be.[30] In short, it may be easier to make a meaningful transfer to the future generation through preservation of the environment than through a program to build up production capacity for future consumer goods to be offered as an alternative compensation for environmental deterioration, even if it might seem more efficient to adopt the latter strategy under today's conditions of capital productivity and consumer tastes.

Overview

Central Method

On the basis of the theoretical and empirical considerations set forth in this study, the following method would seem the most appropriate for benefit-cost analysis of global warming. First, all effects should be divided into their investment and consumption components. This division may be based on "general economy" shares for production effects, but consumption-specific effects should be identified as such where possible. Second, these respective consumption and investment effects over time should be converted to consumption-equivalents through the application of a shadow price of capital. Third, the resulting consumption-equivalent magnitudes should be discounted at the estimated SRTP.

---

30. Canned foods come to mind, in view of agricultural prospects under very-long-term warming.

For the SRTP, a central value of 1½ percent real per year would appear appropriate. This rate emerges from consideration of a broad class of utility functions, from which it may be shown that the SRTP equals the expected growth rate of per capita income multiplied by the absolute value of the elasticity of marginal utility of consumption (with any further allowance for pure myopia ruled out). A central expectation of 1 percent for the former and 1.5 for the latter over the long term yields the estimate of 1½ percent for the SRTP. This estimate is consistent with the Golden Rule of growth theory, although that basis might recommend a somewhat lower long-term rate in view of the expected plateauing of population in the middle of the 21st century. The 1½ percent rate for the SRTP is also on the high side if, as argued above, the real treasury bill rate is the best empirical measure of the risk-free consumer rate of time preference, as that rate may be estimated at well under 1 percent.

For the rate of return on private capital, which is needed to calculate the shadow price on capital, a central estimate of 8 percent real per year would appear appropriate. This rate is consistent with the various empirical observations discussed above. With these rates (SRTP = i = 0.015, and r = 0.08), a 15-year average capital life will generate a shadow price of capital of 1.56 (from equation 6.1).

It should be emphasized that this central methodology stands squarely in the mainstream of recent benefit-cost analysis. There is no special adjustment of the discount rate to take account of either the issue of intergenerational comparison (Mishan) or the loss of "liberty" associated with a degraded environment (Sen), even though on both grounds some reduction in the rate might be appropriate for greenhouse analysis.

Sensitivity Analysis

Many economists will consider the SRTP of 1½ percent to be low. An entire generation of benefit-cost analysis emerged in the economics literature from analysts frustrated with what they perceived to be the use of excessively low discount rates to justify public dam projects. This literature made the important contribution of pointing out the need to take into account the opportunity cost of effects on private capital. However, once careful account of the sourcing of investment and the opportunity cost of private capital are incorporated into the analysis, it would err in the opposite direction to call for still higher interest rates, as will likely be the case in an approach such as OMB's (which implicitly attributes complete weight to private capital return and none to resources drawn from consumption).

The empirical estimates by Kolb and Scheraga provide one basis for an alternative set of calculations for purposes of investigating the sensitivity of results.

They use 3 percent as the SRTP, a value of 2.9 for the shadow price of capital, and 10 percent as the real return on private capital. Because the capital return is at the high end of their empirical range (5 percent to 10 percent), these parameters may be considered unfavorable to greenhouse abatement action.

Alternative sensitivity tests may be applied with standard discounting at 2 percent and 3 percent, to reflect the CBO and GAO standards, respectively. For further comparison, standard discounting with a real rate of 5 percent, as well as OMB's 10 percent, may be considered. Under the last alternative the best greenhouse policy will almost certainly be to do nothing.

Broader Implications for Public Policy

The approach identified here could well lead to public policy that in effect carries out investment in the greenhouse area at lower rates of return than in other areas. That possibility arises because of the fundamental second-best nature of public decision when the gap has not been closed between the SRTP and the rate of return on private capital. Several implications follow.

First, with the SRTP at 1½ percent and the shadow price of capital (r_c) at 2 or less (units of consumption equivalent to one unit of capital), the overall equivalent discount rate is in the vicinity of 2 percent. That does not mean that any project with a rate of return of 2 percent or more should be undertaken. Consider the World Bank. Its projects typically have a rate of return in the range of 10 percent. It has a queue of such projects because of a constraint on capital borrowing. Essentially, a whole portfolio of potential projects might have a benefit-cost ratio above unity under the parameters proposed here, but because of the institution's lending constraint the cutoff for projects implemented would be at a benefit-cost ratio considerably in excess of unity.

Second, this illustration should clarify that a favorable benefit-cost ratio identified for greenhouse action by no means purports to argue that such action is the highest-return public endeavor available. Suppose that the greenhouse policy has a benefit-cost ratio of 1.5 on the method set forth here, but programs for preschool instruction of inner-city children have a benefit-cost ratio of 2.0 on the same method. There is no claim that greenhouse measures should be taken in preference to social investment in inner-city schooling.

Third, what *is* argued here is that *if the political process makes it feasible to implement greenhouse measures* whereas political support is absent for undertaking other public initiatives with even higher measured benefit-cost ratios, *the proper role of economic analysis is to confirm whether the greenhouse undertaking has a positive benefit-cost evaluation* rather than to oppose the greenhouse measure on the grounds that some other area might have an even more favorable benefit-cost relationship.

Fourth, this principle surely applies to public policy more generally. Those projects that must compete within a limited budget constraint should do so under an ordering by benefit-cost performance, and after the budget constraint is exhausted there should be no further projects in the queue implemented even though several remain with favorable benefit-cost ratios. However, if there is a policy area that is capable of generating wide political support and thereby breaking the budget constraint *for that area,* and if projects in that area show a favorable benefit-cost profile, they should be undertaken even though other projects with higher benefit-cost prospects in the budget-constrained areas remain unimplemented.[31] This is in the nature of the second best.

Fifth, economists will do well to interpret the political reaction to alternative public initiatives as perhaps conveying information otherwise left out of the calculations. In environmental areas in particular, if the public is willing to undertake action that has a favorable benefit-cost ratio but one that is lower than some alternative public initiatives the public is unwilling to undertake, then there are two alternative interpretations. Either the public is naive and sentimental and cannot make consistent calculations when it comes to the environment as opposed to other goods and services, or the public may be appropriately attaching some valuation in the environmental case that the economic analysis has failed to measure (e.g., Sen's "liberty" for future generations). It should not be assumed automatically that the former is the case.

---

31. This conclusion applies to intraenvironmental issues as well as to the trade-off between environmental and other areas. In some countries, the rate of return to investment in nongreenhouse environmental improvement may be higher than that in greenhouse abatement. If that is the case, that fact should not stand in the way of undertaking greenhouse measures if there is public support and willingness to break the budget constraint for such measures but not for the higher-return actions on the alternative environmental issues.

Annex 6A

Shadow Pricing Capital in Benefit-Cost Analysis: A Note on Bradford Versus Lind

Seminal work by Arrow (1966) and Feldstein (1970) suggested that the proper approach to public investment analysis is to use a shadow price on capital to convert all effects of a project to consumption-equivalents, and then to discount at the social rate of time preference. In this way the dilemma of whether to discount at the rate of return on private capital (r) or the (usually lower) rate of social time preference (i) can be resolved. Building on this concept, Bradford (1975) argued that the net benefit of a one-period public-sector investment is:

$$(6A.1) \quad B = -(1 - a + av_B) + [(1 + \rho)/(1 + i)][1 - \alpha + \alpha v_B]$$

where ρ is the rate of return on the public project, i is the social rate of time preference, a is the amount by which private capital formation is decreased by a dollar of public investment, α is the amount by which private capital is increased as a consequence of an increase of \$1 in public-sector output, and v_B is the shadow price of capital.[1]

Correspondingly, a public-sector project should be undertaken only when:

$$(6A.2) \quad \frac{1 + \rho}{1 + i} \geq \frac{1 + a(v_B - 1)}{1 + \alpha(v_B - 1)}$$

In turn, Bradford estimates the shadow price of capital as:

$$(6A.3) \quad v_B = \frac{(1 - s)\gamma}{1 - s\gamma}$$

where s = the marginal propensity to save out of disposable income and $\gamma = (1 + r)/(1 + i)$.[2] When a and α are equal, a rate of return on government

---

1. The notation here omits Bradford's time subscripts, as the rates of return and reinvestment are assumed constant. The subscript B is added to identify the Bradford shadow price of capital.

2. This expression may be derived, somewhat differently from Bradford, as follows. With the private return on capital at r, in each period output equals $(1 + r)$ times investment in the previous period. Investment equals s times output, and consumption equals $(1 - s)$ times output. Thus, with 1 invested at time 0, in period 1 output is $(1 + r)$, and the amount $s(1 + r)$ is reinvested. In period 2, output is $[s(1 + r)](1 + r) = s(1 + r)^2$, investment equals $s^2(1 + r)^2$, and consumption equals $(1 - s)s(1 + r)^2$. More generally, consumption in period n (including $n = 1$) will equal $(1 - s)s^{n-1}(1 + r)^n$. The present value of consumption is thus $(1 - s)\Sigma_n s^{n-1}\gamma^n$, where Σ_n denotes summation over n

investment (ρ) equal to the social time preference rate (i) will be sufficient to warrant the investment, because the right-hand side of 6A.2 goes to unity. In the extreme, where all the resources come out of private investment ($a = 1$) and there is no positive effect of the project's output on private investment ($\alpha = 0$), the public investment rate of return ρ must equal or exceed the private rate, r.[3] Most cases will be in between, and Bradford (1975, 887) concludes that "The policy of discounting according to a pure time preference rate turns out to be surprisingly robust to plausible variations in the parameters."

However, an important reason for this conclusion is that the shadow price on capital is close to unity. With ranges of $r = 0.05$ to 0.15; $i = 0.02$ to 0.08; and $s = 0.10$ to 0.30, the extremes of Bradford's v are 0.97 and 1.19 (Bradford 1975, 894). If the capital conversion factor is close to unity, it may not be so surprising that discounting consumption-equivalents by the social time preference rate yields results close to those discounting by the same rate with no special treatment of capital effects.

Lind (1982a) has criticized Bradford's results on the grounds that the shadow price of capital is likely to be considerably higher. Lind argues that, in calculating the effect of displaced private capital, Bradford erroneously assumes that after a one-period investment project the amount reinvested would be only sr, the marginal saving rate times the rate of return. Instead, Lind argues, the amount reinvested would normally include full principal. On this basis, the fraction of total return (including original capital) that is reinvested is:

$$(6A.4) \quad z = \frac{1 + rs}{1 + r}$$

rather than the much lower s.

Lind then proposes the following rather cumbersome alternative for the shadow price of capital:

(from 1 to infinity) and $\gamma = (1 + r)/(1 + i)$. This may be rewritten as $[(1 - s)/s]\Sigma_n(s\gamma)^n$. With $s\gamma < 1$, this is a power series with $\Sigma_n(s\gamma)^n = (s\gamma)/(1 - s\gamma)$. The present value of the consumption stream is thus:

$$\frac{(1 - s)s\gamma}{s(1 - s\gamma)} = \frac{(1 - s)\gamma}{1 - s\gamma}, \text{ the result in equation 6A.3.}$$

3. That is, in this case $(1 + \rho)/(1 + i) \geq v_B$, from equation 6A.2). Bradford (1975, 893) states that "generally" $v_B > \gamma = (1 + r)/(1 + i)$, so that with $a = 1$ and $\alpha = 0$, ρ will "generally" have to exceed r. However, note the instability caused by the difference in the denominator of the right-hand side of equation 6A.3. To be sure, as $s \to 0$, $v_B \to \gamma$. Moreover, at typical values, such as $s = 0.2$, $r = 0.1$, and $i = 0.03$, v_B is still close to γ (in this example, $v_B = 1.02\gamma$). But we may see that as $s \to (1 + i)/(1 + r)$, $v_B \to \infty$. The explosive tendency of Lind's shadow price of capital, discussed below, is thus already latent (but more unusual) in Bradford's shadow price. Moreover, at high s, the return on public investment will have to be very high for acceptability even in Bradford's approach.

$$(6A.5) \quad v_L = \frac{Ax(1 - z)}{1 - Axz}$$

where A is the annual payment in an annuity of N years with a present value of \$1 discounted at r, and x is "the expression that, when multiplied by a single payment of an N-period annuity, gives the present value of the annuity discounted at the rate i (Lind 1982a, 53). For its part, z, the reinvestment fraction on total return, is calculated as:

$$(6A.6) \quad z = \frac{D + (A - D)s}{A}$$

where D is depreciation. That is, the fraction D/A of the annual annuity payment automatically goes to depreciation reinvestment, and of the remainder, the fraction s is saved and reinvested.

Lind's approach essentially stretches Bradford's out to a horizon associated with the lifetime of typical capital equipment (N) and takes account of restoration of original capital to reinvestment. Lind reports values in the range of 3 to 5 for v_L, the shadow price of capital, using $N = 15$, $s = 0.2$, $i = 0.02$ to 0.075, and $r = 0.05$ to 0.15 (Lind 1982a, 86). On closer examination, however, Lind's method can give explosive results, with the shadow price of capital ranging from below zero to infinity. The method is thus less reliable for policy analysis than it might appear at first glance.

To understand this outcome, it is first useful to consider that Lind's x is merely the inverse of A_i, where A signifies an annuity payment as before but the discount rate is i rather than r. Present value is still \$1, but in the normal case where $i < r$, $A_i < A_r$ (where A_r equals Lind's A). We may then rewrite Lind's shadow price of capital, equation 6A.5, as:

$$(6A.7) \quad v_L' = \frac{(1 - z)\lambda}{1 - z\lambda}$$

where λ is defined as $\lambda = A_r/A_i$. In this form, Lind's approach looks very much like Bradford's (equation 6A.3), except that z has been substituted for s, and λ for γ.

Despite the similarity, Lind's version is explosive (singular in the vicinity of $z\lambda = 1$), whereas Bradford's is relatively stable. The central reason is that, although the denominator in equation 6A.3 is positive and "generally" well behaved, typically somewhere in the range of 0.65 to 0.90, the denominator in equation 6A.7 is far more variable, can approach zero (causing v_L to approach infinity), and can be negative (causing a negative shadow price of capital). Yet an infinite shadow price of capital is highly improbable (although it has an economic meaning, as noted below), and a negative shadow price contradicts theory (capital can never be a "bad" rather than a good, even if $r < i$).[4]

The instability of Lind's method is already implied in his reported estimates for some of the cases calculated by Bradford (thus, for $s = 0.2$, $i = 0.02$, and $r = 0.10$, Bradford obtains $v_B = 1.10$ but Lind obtains $v_L = \infty$). Lind's final table of well-behaved shadow prices (ranging from about 3 to 5) is possible only because of the constraining assumption that $0.4 \leq i/r \leq 0.5$ (Lind 1982a, 86). He bases this relationship on the argument that the social rate of time preference equals the private rate of return after tax. However, it is not difficult to envision circumstances in which the spread between the two rates is considerably higher (as in the Bradford example just cited). For example, countries with poorly developed domestic capital markets and credit rationing on funds from abroad could have a large wedge between the two rates.

As an alternative, I would propose the following approach. Return to the basic concept of the shadow price of capital. Consider the choice between a loaf of bread this period and a machine that produces q loaves of bread annually for N years $(0 < q < 1)$ and then breaks down entirely. If the bread machine has an internal rate of return of r, then:

$$(6A.8) \quad q = A_{r,N}$$

where, as before, A refers to an annual annuity payment, and the time horizon N is added for clarity. In bread-loaf units as the numeraire, the value of this machine will be the stream of q over N years discounted at the social rate of time preference. But the value of a current loaf of bread is unity. Therefore the shadow price of the machine in consumption units is the present value just mentioned divided by unity, or:

$$(6A.9) \quad v_c = \sum_{t=1}^{N} A_{r,N}/(1 + i)^t.$$

Suppose that $r = 0.10$, $i = 0.02$, and $N = 15$; then $v_c = 1.68$, a more plausible number than Lind's -28.3 (note 4 above).

This alternative shadow price takes the life horizon of the typical investment into account, as urged by Lind. It has the intuitive appeal that, as this time horizon approaches infinity, the shadow price of capital approaches r/i. That is, to hold the rate of return down to r as the annuity horizon stretches to infinity, the component of the annual payment representing depreciation vanishes, leav-

---

4. As an example of a negative capital shadow price under Lind's formula, consider the case of $N = 15$, $s = 0.2$, $i = 0.02$, and $r = 0.10$. The depreciation rate $D = 1/15 = 0.0667$. Lind's formula for annuity value is $A_{r,N} = r/[1 - (1 + r)^{-N}]$. With $A = 0.131$, from equation 6A.6 z equals 0.608. $A_i = 0.0778$, so that $\lambda = 1.683$. The resulting value of v_L is -28.3.

ing only r paid annually, and the present discounted value of an infinite stream of r discounting at i is r/i.

At the other extreme, as the horizon approaches a single year, the shadow price approximates $(1 + r)/(1 + i)$. In this case, the expression is equivalent to Bradford's shadow price on capital, v_B, if the marginal propensity to save, s, is zero (equation 6A.3). This difference provides a clue to what may have gone wrong in both the Bradford and the Lind analyses: they appear to have double-counted the influence of saving and reinvestment. That is, Bradford takes the impact of reinvestment into account once when he considers the private and government-output-induced reinvestment rates (a and α, respectively, in equation 6A.1), and he does so a second time when he builds a reinvested share into the shadow price of capital (s in equation 6A.3). Lind does the same thing, but with a longer horizon (N years) the effect of double-counting reinvestment becomes much more explosive.

Operationally, under plausible ranges for r, i, and N, equation 6A.9 generates estimates of the shadow price of capital that make sense from a policy evaluation standpoint. The values of v_c are typically in the range of $1\frac{1}{2}$ to 2, higher than the Bradford range but lower than Lind's measures with the same s, i, and r. The shadow price suggested here becomes explosive (tends toward infinity) only as i approaches zero and N approaches an infinite horizon. This is the exception that proves the rule, as under these conditions it will always be desirable to undertake an investment project with any positive return whatsoever, so that investment is infinitely to be preferred to consumption.

7

Benefit-Cost Synthesis

7

Benefit-Cost Synthesis

General Approach

This chapter draws upon the findings of the previous analysis of the benefits of global warming abatement (chapter 3) and the corresponding costs (chapters 4 and 5) to arrive at an overall benefit-cost evaluation. In this process, the preceding discussion of the discount rate (chapter 6) informs the choice of this crucial parameter.

The fundamental policy examined is one of a worldwide program of aggressive action to limit global warming. Its centerpiece is the cutback of carbon emissions to 4 billion tons annually, and a subsequent permanent freeze at this level. As developed below, afforestation and reduced deforestation play a central role in this cutback for the initial decade or two, but thereafter increasingly deep reductions in fossil fuel emissions become necessary as well. Those reductions initially draw upon the backlog of low-cost improvements perceived by the technology community, but increasingly require the more costly curtailments analyzed by the cadre of carbon-energy-economic modelers.

The overall pattern that emerges is one in which there is a phase of initially low-cost carbon reductions, followed by a period when these costs rise to a peak in the vicinity of $3\frac{1}{2}$ percent of world GDP, a level that then tapers off to some $2\frac{1}{2}$ percent of GDP as the passage of time permits a wider range of technological alternatives. On the benefits side, the pattern is one of initially minimal gains (because of the long delays in warming), followed by a relatively steady, geometric rise. Depending on the scenario chosen, after some decades the benefits of damage avoidance exceed the cost of action. Thereafter this wedge of net gain continues to expand. A horizon through the year 2275 is chosen for the analysis because of the prospect of partial warming reversal thereafter through deep-ocean mixing of carbon dioxide from the atmosphere (chapters 1 and 2). The overall benefit-cost ratio of aggressive policy action is obtained by discounting the stream of benefits and the stream of costs and taking the ratio of the former to the latter. A ratio of unity or above indicates the desirability of action, from a social economic benefit-cost standpoint.

Table 7.1 provides a summary view of the benefit-cost analysis, and figure 7.1 illustrates its results. Figure 7.1 depicts the costs of aggressive action (a 4-GtC annual emissions ceiling) as a percentage of world GDP. It also shows two alternative "benefits" curves: the base and high cases (a principal "low" case is also evaluated but not shown in the figure). In both cases, the costs of action exceed the benefits in the initial decades. The possibility of a favorable evaluation of action is considerably greater in the high-benefits case. For all cases, the comparison of benefits and costs depends crucially on the discount rate.

Because there are alternative assumptions in each of several dimensions of the analysis, the number of possible outcomes is large (over 200). The analysis identifies the preferred or central evaluation. However, the results reported for the array of alternative estimates provide a menu of outcomes for the reader's inspection, so that he or she may choose alternative entries according to taste on such key issues as the discount rate, the likelihood of greater or lesser warming, and the chances of more or less severe economic damage associated with a given amount of warming.

The Benefit-Cost Model

The model for calculating benefits and costs derives from the analysis of the preceding chapters. The following discussion first sets forth the structure of the calculations and then turns to a description of the values applied for the estimated results. The reader not concerned with the algebra of the model may wish to proceed directly to the subsequent section on assumptions for values used in the calculations.

The analysis first calculates real per capita income (y) and population (P) for developed (D) and less developed (L) countries for the year in question (t), based on assumed growth rates (g for per capita income, n for population) from the base year (year 0).[1]

(7.1) $y_t^D = y_0^D(1 + g_D)^t$

(7.1') $y_t^L = y_0^L(1 + g_L)^t$

(7.2) $P_t^D = P_0^D(1 + n_D)^t$

(7.2') $P_t^L = P_0^L(1 + n_L)^t$

Gross world product (Y) is then the sum of developed- and developing-area per capita incomes times their respective populations:

---

1. As discussed below, these growth rates taper off over future time periods.

Table 7.1   Central features of the benefit-cost analysis

Aggressive abatement	A global ceiling of 4 gigatons of annual carbon emissions permanently. Achieved initially by reduced deforestation, increased afforestation, and a move to best practices in energy use. Subsequently achieved through cutbacks in carbon dioxide emissions throughout the economy.
Very-long term warming	In the absence of action, global warming reaches a central estimate of 10°C by 2275; the upper bound is 18°C by 2275.
Damage function	Damage d_0 is 1 percent of GDP at carbon-dioxide-equivalent doubling for 2.5°C warming, central case, or 2 percent, high-damage case. Damage rises exponentially with warming (at exponent 1.3, central, or 2.0, high).
Benefits	Equal 80 percent of damage, the fraction that is assumed avoidable through action
Costs	Forestry measures are low cost; general economy-wide emission cutbacks are free for the first 22 percent, from a move to best practices. For larger cutbacks, costs rise according to a formula based on carbon-energy-economic models
Discounting	All investment effects are converted to consumption equivalents using a capital shadow price. All consumption-equivalent magnitudes are then discounted at a social rate of time preference (SRTP), with a base case value of 1.5 percent annually.
Economic scale	Damage, benefit, and cost estimates are estimated as percentages of GDP and then applied to future world GDP. Prospective GDP is based on world population that reaches 10.5 billion by the middle of the 21st century, and per capita income growth averaging 1 percent annually over the next 2½ centuries
Sensitivity	Tests are included for alternative values of the SRTP climate sensitivity parameter, damage function exponent, and damage at 2.5°C warming.

Figure 7.1 Costs and benefits of aggressive abatement of greenhouse warming, 1990–2270

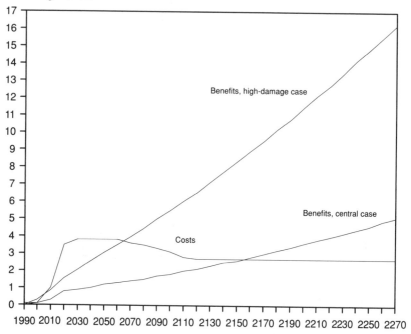

Percentages of GDP

(7.3) $Y_t = y_t^D P_t^D + y_t^L P_t^L$

An exogenous projection of global carbon emissions (E) is then compared for each year to the target ceiling emission (K) set in the abatement program. The difference is the amount by which emissions must be reduced (R):

(7.4) $R_t = E_t - K$

The amount of global warming at a future year t, expressed in degrees Celsius, is W_t. The path of warming is linear (chapter 2). It passes through the amount S, the climate sensitivity parameter for carbon-dioxide-equivalent doubling, in the year 2050 (for 2025 concentration doubling plus an ocean thermal lag of 25 years); and through the amount W^* for very-long-term warming, set in the year 2275. For years before 2050 ($t = 60$), warming is set by linear interpolation between zero at the outset (with $t = 1$ at 1991) and S. Accordingly:

(7.5a) $W_t = S + [(W^* - S)/225](t - 60)$, $t \geq 60$;

(7.5b) $W_t = S(t/60)$, $t < 60$

The amount of economic damage from warming is assumed to be geometrically related to the amount of warming. Benchmark economic damage is estimated for carbon-dioxide-equivalent doubling, set at d_0 percent of world GDP. As the benchmark is calibrated for a climate sensitivity of 2.5°C, the resulting damage function is:

$$(7.6) \quad d_t = d_o \left[\frac{W_t}{2.5} \right]^\gamma$$

where γ is the exponent in the geometrical relationship of damage to warming. The function expresses damage (d_t) as a percentage of world GDP. The linkage to GDP is discussed further below.

The benefit of the abatement policy by year t equals that portion of the damages that can be avoided as a result of the policy. The avoidance proportion is set at μ, so that:

$$(7.7) \quad b_t = \mu d_t$$

The costs of abatement arise from the need to set aside land for afforestation (FA), to curtail frontier agricultural land use and thereby carbon release from deforestation (FD), and to reduce fossil fuel emissions and therefore output (Q) in the rest of the economy. The amount of carbon that can be reduced through afforestation is set at a constant (R_0^{FA}) over a 30-year growing period, and then falls to zero as the new forest reaches its steady state. Thus, afforestation reduces emissions by:

$$(7.8) \quad R_t^{FA} = R_0^{FA}, 1 \le t \le 30; = 0, t > 30$$

The reduction of deforestation to a lower rate and the commitment to hold it indefinitely at that rate provides a constant annual flow of emissions reductions:

$$(7.9) \quad R_t^{FD} = R_0^{FD}$$

The reductions in emissions from afforestation and reduced deforestation only partially meet the need to cut back emissions from the baseline. The remaining reduction that must be obtained from the rest of the economy is thus:

$$(7.10) \quad R_t^Q = R_t - R_t^{FA} - R_t^{FD}$$

The cost of afforestation is calculated in a manner that incorporates all current and future costs within the initial growing period on a constant annualized basis, at C_0^{FA}. Expressed relative to world GDP (and in percentage points), this cost is thus:

$$(7.11) \quad c_t^{FA} = 100 \left[\frac{C_0^{FA}}{Y_t} \right], 1 \le t \le 30; = 0, t > 30$$

For its part, the cost of forgone deforestation (C_0^{FD}) continues indefinitely. Expressed as a percentage of world GDP, it is:

$$(7.12) \quad c_t^{FD} = 100 \left[\frac{C_0^{FD}}{Y_t} \right]$$

The cost of carbon reduction through fossil fuel cutbacks depends on the extent of the proportionate reduction (chapter 4) as well as initial gains from improved technical efficiency (chapter 5). The percentage reduction in carbon from economywide fossil fuel cutbacks is:

$$(7.13) \quad z_t^Q = 100 \left[\frac{R_t^Q}{(E_t - E_0^F)} \right]$$

where E_0^F is the base-year emission contribution from deforestation so that the right-hand side denominator is the baseline value of all other (e.g., economywide fossil fuel) emissions.

As developed in chapter 5, the cost function for carbon reductions in the general economy depends on the percentage cutback, but with adjustments that provide for an initial "free" reduction (z_0) and take account of a downward swiveling over time of the curve relating cost to percentage cutback because of improving technological opportunities. Thus (and with parameter β less than zero), we have:

$$(7.14a) \quad c_t^Q = [z_t^Q - z_0] [\alpha + \beta (t - 35)], t \geq 35;$$

$$(7.14b) \quad c_t^Q = \alpha [z_t^Q - z_0], t < 35$$
$$s.t. \ c_t^Q \geq 0; \ c_t^Q \geq 2 \ for \ z_t^Q \geq 50$$

Note that in the second formulation (equation 7.14b) there is no time-dependent downward shift in the cost curve before the year 2025 ($t = 35$), as the various model estimates on which the cost curve is based are for that year or later. Note further that the final set of restrictions places a floor of 2 percent of GDP on the cost of carbon reductions in excess of 50 percent. Without this floor, the time-dependent cost curve would fall to much lower levels over more distant periods, but the underlying model estimates do not include such distant years, and there is no assurance that costs would continue to decline.

The calculations then introduce the gains from alleviation of the excess burden of the existing tax system (discussed below). The required carbon tax rate (τ, in dollars per ton) is estimated as:

$$(7.15) \quad \tau_t = [z_t^Q - z_0] h_0, 0 \leq \tau \leq H^*$$

where for each additional percentage-point cutback in carbon a specified incremental dollar amount of tax per ton, h_0, must be imposed, up to a ceiling long-range tax of H^* based on the backstop noncarbon energy source (as discussed below).

Because the emission of only K tons of carbon annually is permitted to continue, tax revenue (T) will equal the tax rate times this base:[2]

$$(7.16) \quad T_t = \tau_t K$$

Where the existing structure of taxation is inefficient and each dollar of additional tax revenue causes a partially offsetting loss equal to the fraction ρ of a dollar (i.e., ρ is the marginal efficiency cost of taxation), the new source of revenue from carbon taxes will permit a benefit from reduction of the excess tax burden amounting to:

$$(7.17) \quad B_t^{\tau} = T_t \rho$$

The carbon tax will of course have its own excess burden, but that cost is already incorporated on the cost side of the analysis (equations 7.11 to 7.14).

The overall cost of the abatement program equals world GDP multiplied by the sum of the three cost sources (converted from percentages of GDP to fractions): economywide (Q), afforestation (FA), and reduced deforestation (FD). This cost is expanded by the proportion ω to take into account likely costs associated with curtailing *all* greenhouse gases in a way commensurate with reducing carbon dioxide emissions. The cost is further increased by considering the portion of the cost—essentially production sacrificed—that would have gone into investment (π_k^c), and applying a shadow price of capital (p_k^*) to this component to convert it to consumption-equivalents (chapter 6). Thus, the absolute magnitude of global abatement cost in year t is:

$$(7.18) \quad C_t = .01 Y_t [c_t^Q + c_t^{FA} + c_t^{FD}] [1 + \omega] [(1 - \pi_k^c) + p_k^* \pi_k^c]$$

For its part, the shadow price of capital is estimated as set forth in chapter 6, annex 6A:

$$(7.19) \quad p_k^* = A_{r,N} \psi_{i,N} N$$

where $A_{r,N}$ is the annual payment of an annuity with lifetime N years and interest rate r; $\psi_{i,N}$ is the present discounted value of a stream of unity annually over N years discounted at interest rate i, divided by N; and the two discount rates are the rate of return on private capital (r) and the social rate of time preference (i), respectively.

On the benefits side, the gains from avoidance of warming equal the percentage of GDP benefit (converted to a fraction) multiplied by world GDP. This

---

2. Note that because some emissions from deforestation will continue, the implication is that the tax will be imposed on this source as well.

magnitude is further expanded to take into consideration the fact that some of these gains accrue to production going into investment. A fraction ϕ_{bc} is consumption-specific (e.g., human amenity from avoided heat waves). For the remainder, the fraction π_k^b represents production that goes into investment, and this component is expanded by the shadow price of capital (symmetrically with the treatment on the cost side). Finally, the absolute benefit from reduction of the excess tax burden is included. The overall benefits are thus:

$$(7.20) \quad B_t = .01\, Y_t b_t \{\phi_{bc} + (1 - \phi_{bc})\, [(1 - \pi_k^b) + p_k^* \pi_k^b]\} + B_t^\tau$$

The present discounted value of benefits from the base year 1991 through the terminal year 2275, discounting at the social rate of time preference, is thus:

$$(7.21) \quad V_b = \sum_{t=1}^{285} \frac{B_t}{(1 + i)^t}$$

Similarly, the present discounted value of costs of abatement over the same horizon amounts to:

$$(7.22) \quad V_c = \sum_{t=1}^{285} \frac{C_t}{(1 + i)^t}$$

The ratio of the present discounted value of benefits to that of costs is thus:

$$(7.23) \quad q = \frac{V_b}{V_c}$$

If q exceeds unity, the program for abatement of global warming is socially efficient in economic terms; if q is below unity, the program of aggressive abatement is socially inefficient because the benefits do not warrant the costs.

Variable Baselines and Parameter Values

Population and Income Growth

Table 7.2 reports the values applied for the parameters of the benefit-cost model and for the baseline projections of key variables. The world is divided into developed countries (including the former Soviet Union and Eastern Europe) and developing countries. Their populations in 1990 were an estimated 1,235 million and 4,075 million, respectively. The projected population growth rates in table 7.2 are derived from the assumptions used by the Intergovernmental Panel on Climate Change (IPCC) through the year 2100 (IPCC 1990d, 20).[3] World

---

3. The IPCC estimates in turn were based on Zacharia and Vu (1988).

population reaches a plateau by the mid-21st century at about 10½ billion, and after the year 2100 population growth is zero in both areas.

Per capita income in 1990 constant dollars is set at $14,100 for the developed region. This level is considerably lower than the World Bank's estimate of $19,000 for member countries of the Organization for Economic Cooperation and Development (OECD; World Bank, *World Development Report 1991*, 205). The figure here is calibrated to reflect the much lower per capita income of the former Soviet Union and Eastern Europe.[4]

The estimated per capita income of $3,400 for developing countries is based on a purchasing power parity concept. Kravis et al. (1982, 15) have estimated that at cross-sectional purchasing power exchange rates, which take account of lower-priced nontradeables (especially labor-intensive services) in developing countries, real per capita income in these countries is about one-sixth (1/5.6) the level in industrial countries (excluding the former Soviet Union and Eastern Europe). The resulting world GDP for 1990 is $31.3 trillion, of which $17.4 trillion is in the developed countries and $13.9 trillion in the developing countries.[5]

For the period 1990–2100, growth of per capita income by region is set equal to the lower alternative applied in the IPCC emissions scenario (IPCC 1990d, chapter 2). Beyond the year 2100, per capita income growth is assumed to fall gradually below 1 percent, to rates of ½ percent or lower in the 23rd century. Per capita income growth remains somewhat higher over a longer period in the developing countries than in the developed countries. Over the entire period, average per capita income growth is close to 1 percent in both regions. Although the rate may appear modest, the power of compound interest is such that it implies per capita incomes of $185,000 by the year 2275 for developed countries and $63,000 for developing countries. By that year, global GDP stands at a remarkable $837 trillion (at 1990 prices), or about 26 times today's global output.

The possibility of such high per capita income in the long term raises the question of why the present generation should make any sacrifice at all to avoid a greenhouse-imposed loss to future generations, so long as that loss does not exceed the difference between per capita income today and in the long term. The formal answer to this question is that the analysis already takes account of higher future income by discounting the future on the basis of expected rising per capita consumption (chapter 6). As developed below, the loss of long-term

---

4. World Bank, *World Development Report 1991*, places OECD population at 722.6 million and GDP at $13.8 trillion in 1989. Collins and Rodrik (1991, 6–8) estimate the combined population of the former Soviet Union and Eastern Europe at 422.8 million and 1988 GDP for the area at $2.4 trillion. The combined "developed country" estimates amount to a population of 1.15 billion and per capita income of $14,150 for 1988–89.

5. Without the correction for purchasing power parity in developing countries, world GDP is approximately $20 trillion.

per capita income from global warming could be on the order of 6 to 20 percent or more, even with no unexpected catastrophe. With global per capita annual income in 2275 at about $80,000, versus about $6,000 today (purchasing power parity), a 15 percent loss of 2275 income would be a reduction by some $12,000. If, say, only 2 percent of today's income need be paid to avoid this loss (as discussed below), then the trade-off is $12,000 near the end of the 23rd century in exchange for $120 today. This trade-off of 100 to 1 can be attractive, unless the discount rate is high.

Some might argue that there should be more emphasis on the greater relative value of an extra dollar to today's person with $6,000 than to his descendant with $80,000. The extreme version of this view would hold that no person should ever be asked to give up a single dollar to a descendant who will be at a higher per capita income than himself, regardless of how large the resulting increase in the descendant's income could be. In formal terms, that approach would represent a value of infinity for the elasticity of marginal utility of income (discussed in chapter 6). Any small increase in income would cause marginal utility to plunge to zero, so that even a highly leveraged bargain such as the one just discussed would be dismissed out of hand. In contrast, the analysis here makes some allowance for greater- than-unitary elasticity of marginal utility (the elasticity is set at 1.5) but leaves sufficient marginal utility even at high future incomes that the leveraged bargain just outlined may make sense.

It seems likely that, in the broader public discussion of the greenhouse effect, there is a much different wager at stake. Many of those who stress the dangers of the problem appear to have a much grimmer future in mind. In their future scenario, on a scale of two to three centuries the typical inhabitant of the earth may not be much richer than today even without global warming, and the scope of possible greenhouse damage is catastrophic rather than limited to, say, 10 percent to 20 percent of income. Indeed, in this type of approach, the possible damage is so great that the world's future inhabitants are worse off than those today. The grounds for discounting future income disappear or the discount rate even turns negative (with falling per capita consumption, marginal utility is rising rather than falling and an extra dollar is worth more in the future than today). The equity case for a transfer of income to the more impoverished becomes an argument for shifting income from the richer, present generation to the poorer, future one.

Without going to the extreme of fearing a secular decline in future per capita income, the choice between the forecast of a prosperous or a stagnant future is not as obvious as it might seem simply on the basis of past growth. Suppose that the average rate of growth of per capita income is ½ percent instead of 1 percent, and the growth of population is ½ percent higher than expected. Neither proposition is implausible, yet the consequences over two to three centuries are dramatic. By the late 23rd century, world GDP—and thus (to a first approximation) carbon emissions—would reach just as high as in the base case. However, world per capita income would reach only about $24,000 rather than the $80,000 under the baseline scenario.

The thrust of the growing attention to "sustainable development" (e.g., Bruntland et al. 1987) is precisely that lower per capita growth than in the past may be difficult to avoid. Multiplication of global real GDP by some 25-fold as in the baseline here would raise serious doubts of feasibility in the minds of many in the sustainable development school, which stresses limits of the global resource and environmental base. Moreover, this approach argues that past observed growth has been substantially overstated by the failure to take account of resource depletion and environmental deterioration (cf. Repetto 1989). On this basis, a projection of past growth trends in per capita income that is accurately measured might show future rates considerably below the baseline used here. If so, any equity objections to taking even small amounts from the present to avoid even large losses in a richer future would be further ameliorated.

Although the base case expectaton is that per capita income will keep rising, there is no guarantee that future generations will be richer than the present one. To take into account the possibility of stagnation of living standards over the long term, the analysis below includes one variant for a "Malthusian scenario" in which population growth is high and per capita income remains unchanged (zero growth in living standards). This scenario has somewhat lower emissions (especially at first) but also a lower social rate of time preference, set at zero because of zero growth in per capita income.

Nonetheless, the baseline projections of approximately 1 percent annual growth in per capita income do not seem high, at least on the basis of US experience over the past century and using data unadjusted for resource depletion and environmental deterioration. From 1870 to 1930, an index of US production showed annual growth of 3.7 percent (Schumpeter 1942, 64), or per capita growth of 1.7 percent. From 1929 to 1990, real US GDP grew by an annual average of 3 percent (calculated from *Economic Report of the President*, February 1991, 288), or by 1.8 percent annually per capita.[6] This sustained growth confirmed the optimistic half-century forecast of the famous economist Joseph Schumpeter (1942), but it proved insufficient to achieve his corresponding prediction that "this would do away with anything that according to present standards could be called poverty, even in the lowest strata of the population" (Schumpeter l942, 66). The complication of uneven income distribution adds further to grounds for caution about the assumption of a (uniformly) richer future.

---

6. US population rose from 39.8 million in 1870 to 122.8 million in 1930 and approximately 251 million in 1990 (*Statistical Abstract of the United States*, 7; International Monetary Fund, *International Financial Statistics*, 1991).

One further word is warranted on the implications of the baseline incomes. They do suggest that international implementation of an abatement policy should include special measures to minimize the current losses imposed on the developing countries, whether through compensatory transfers, the sale of developing-country emission permits, or otherwise. The sharp contrast between present and future expected per capita income in the developing area implies a steeper trade-off for marginal utility over time than in the industrial countries.[7] This divergence adds to the case for differential burden sharing based solely on present income differences between the two regions.

Carbon Emissions and Abatement

As shown in table 7.2, global emissions rise from 6.7 billion tons of carbon (GtC) in 1990 to approximately 14 GtC in 2050, 22 GtC in 2100, 39 GtC in 2200, and 57 GtC by the end year, 2275. This path is the average of the projections in chapter 2 based (through 2100 and then extended) on three leading energy-economic models (Reilly et al. 1987, Nordhaus and Yohe 1983, Manne and Richels 1990c), plus 1 GtC annually from deforestation. For the first century, the projection is approximately the same as that indicated by the IPCC for its "2030 High-Emissions Scenario," which "depicts a world in which few or no steps are taken to reduce emissions in response to concerns about greenhouse warming" (IPCC 1990d, 10).[8]

It may be asked whether this emissions baseline is consistent with the economic growth baseline just discussed, in view of the fact that the growth assumptions here adopt the lower of two IPCC variants (rather than an average). The ratio of emissions to global GDP provides a gauge of this consistency, as a rising or even constant emissions-production ratio would suggest overstatement of future carbon emissions. Instead, the baseline of table 7.2 shows a steady decline in this ratio, from 0.21 billion tons of carbon per trillion (1990) dollars of world GDP in 1990 to 0.13 in 2050, 0.10 in 2100, 0.07 in 2200, and 0.07 in 2275. For the period as a whole, carbon emissions grow at 0.7 percent annually, whereas world GDP grows at 1.2 percent annually. This divergence provides room for both autonomous energy efficiency growth and response to rising real

---

7. Thus, the ratio of per capita income in 2275 to per capita income in 1990 is 12.8 for developed countries, but 17.3 for less developed countries. When we apply the generalized utility function of chapter 6 with an elasticity of marginal utility of -1.5, the trade-off ratio between a dollar in the year 2275 and a dollar today is about 60 percent higher for the developed countries (at 2.18 cents on the dollar) than for the less developed countries (at 1.39 cents on the dollar; calculated from equation 6.15).

8. That scenario places 2050 carbon emissions at 15.2 GtC and 2100 emissions at 22.4 GtC.

prices of fossil fuel resources. In short, the carbon baseline appears compatible with the economic growth assumptions. Moreover, as shown in chapter 2, it is consistent with the availability of fossil fuel reserves.

The abatement policy examined cuts global emissions to a ceiling of 4 GtC annually (K, table 7.2). This level is approximately the same as that identified by the IPCC for an aggressive abatement stance of "accelerated policies."[9]

Greenhouse Warming, Damage, and Abatement Benefits

The climate sensitivity parameter (S) for warming at carbon-dioxide-equivalent doubling is set at the three benchmarks identified by the IPCC: 1.5°C for the lower bound, 2.5°C for the "best guess," and 4.5°C for the upper bound (IPCC 1990b, chapter 5). The corresponding estimates for warming in the very long term (see chapter 2 above) are 6°C, 10°C, and 18°C, respectively. As noted, the calculations set the years 2050 for $2 \times CO_2$-equivalent warming and 2275 for very-long-term warming ($t = 285$, table 7.2). Warming in intermediate years is determined by linear interpolation.

The damage estimates are based on those for the United States developed in chapter 3. The use of US patterns as a proxy for global effects should not be seriously misleading and provides a basis for a first estimate that should ideally be followed up with regional estimates. As discussed in chapter 3, damages could be higher in developing countries because of a greater share of agriculture in GDP (but with some offset because warming should be less in the lower latitudes where developing countries tend to be located). Damages could be proportionately lower at the high latitudes because of possible favorable effects on agriculture, less relevance of air conditioning, and lesser water supply reduction in view of increased precipitation.

The central estimate for economic damage from global warming is set at 1 percent of world GDP at benchmark $2 \times CO_2$ warming, as developed in detail in chapter 3 above. Because of the likelihood that this estimate understates the value of some key effects (e.g., species loss) and simply omits others (human disamenity, side benefits of reduced pollution), the alternative estimate of 2 percent of GDP is examined as well. Nordhaus (1991a) also uses 1 percent of

---

9. In its "accelerated policies" scenario, the IPCC sets carbon emissions at 5.6 GtC in the year 2000, 5.1 GtC in 2025, 2.9 GtC in 2050, 3.0 GtC in 2075, and 2.7 GtC in 2100. For global warming there should be little difference between the plateau of 4 GtC used here and the 3 GtC applied in the later portion of the IPCC scenario. Only half the difference would accumulate in the atmosphere, so that over 200 years the additional atmospheric stock would amount to 100 GtC. By comparison, present atmospheric stock is approximately 750 GtC. On the other hand, reducing the ceiling to 3 GtC after 2050 would not raise costs much, as the percentage cutback from baseline would not differ radically (86 percent cutback by 2100, versus 82 percent using $K = 4$).

Table 7.2 Variables and parameter values

Variable or Parameter	Concept	Value
t	Time (years)	1991 = 1
y_0^D	Initial per capita income, developed countries	$14,100
y_0^L	Initial per capita income, less developed countries[a]	$3,400
P_0^D	Initial population, developed countries	1,235 million
P_0^L	Initial population, less developed countries	4,065 million
g_D	Per capita income growth, developed countries (percentages per year)	1.9, 1.2, 1.2, 1.2, 1.0, 0.8, 0.5, 0.2[b]
g_L	Per capita income growth, less developed countries (percentages per year)	1.6, 1.3, 1.5, 1.5, 1.0, 1.0, 0.5, 0.5[b]
n_D	Population growth, developed countries (percentages per year)	0.4, 0.4, 0, 0, 0, 0, 0, 0[b]
n_L	Population growth, less developed countries (percentages per year)	1.6, 1.4, 0.8, 0.3, 0.2, 0, 0, 0[b]
E_t	Global carbon emissions (GtC)	6.7, 7.1, 10.9, 13.8, 17.3, 21.6, 25.5, 29.7, 34.3, 39.2, 44.7, 50.6, 57.2[c]
K	Aggressive abatement carbon ceiling (GtC)	4
S	Climate sensitivity parameter	Base: 2.5°C; low: 1.5°C; high: 4.5°C
w^*	Very-long-term warming	Base: 10°C; low: 6°C; high: 18°C
d_0	Greenhouse damage at 2.5°C warming (percentages of GDP)	Base: 1.0; high: 2.0
γ	Damage function exponent	Base: 1.3; high: 2.0
μ	Damage avoidance potential	0.8
R_0^{FA}	Emissions reduction from afforestation	1.6 GtC per year, 1991–2020
R_0^{FD}	Emissions reduction from lower deforestation	0.7 GtC per year, 1991–2275
E_0^F	Base year deforestation emissions	1.0 GtC
C_0^{FA}	Annualized cost of afforestation	$17.2 billion, 1991–2020; zero thereafter

Symbol	Description	Value
R_0^{FD}	Annual cost of reduced deforestation	$4.5 billion
α	Abatement cost parameter	0.0678 (chapter 5)
β	Abatement cost parameter	−0.00039 (chapter 5)
z^0	Percentage carbon reduction at zero cost	22 (chapter 5)
h_0	Carbon tax parameter	$5 per ton per percentage-point cut
H^*	Carbon tax, long-term backstop	$250 per ton
ρ	Marginal efficiency cost of tax burden	0.33
ω	Proportionate cost expansion for other greenhouse gases	0.2
P_K^*	Shadow price of capital	1.6; depends on social rate of time preference, rate of return on capital
π_K^c	Investment share of cost	0.2
π_K^b	Investment share, nonspecific benefits	0.2
ϕ_{bc}	Consumption-specific share of benefits	0.5
i	Social rate of time preference (percentage per year)	Base: 1.5; Other: 1, 2, 3, 5, 10
N	Capital life	15 years

GtC = gigatons of carbon.

a. At purchasing power parity.

b. In 1990–2000, 2001–2025, 2026–2050, 2051–2075, 2076–2100, 2101–2150, 2151–2200, 2201–2250, 2251–2275, respectively.

c. In 1990, 2000, 2025, 2050, 2075, 2100, 2125, 2150, 2175, 2200, 2225, 2250, 2275, respectively.

GDP as the "medium" estimate of greenhouse damage for carbon dioxide doubling, and 2 percent of GDP as the "high" estimate.[10]

When the high-damage case of 2 percent of GDP at the central climate sensitivity parameter ($S = \Lambda = 2.5°C$) is translated into damage for upper-bound warming ($S = 4.5°C$), economic damage reaches 4.3 percent of GDP for $2 \times CO_2$ ($= 2$ percent $\times [4.5/2.5]^{1.3}$). The central and high-damage estimates for very-long-term warming with $S = 2.5°C$ (that is, 10°C warming) are 6 percent and 12 percent of GDP, respectively. With upper-bound very-long-term warming (18°C), damage reaches 13 percent to 26 percent of GDP (that is, 6 percent to 12 percent multiplied by $[4.5/2.5]^{1.3}$) under the central damage exponent case ($\gamma = 1.3$).

The exponent in the geometric function relating damage to warming is set at 1.3 in the base case and 2.0 in the high-damage case. The parameter 1.3 is derived from the weighted average for various effects, discussed in chapter 3. The higher, quadratic damage function is easily plausible, however. It is widely recognized that there are strong reasons to expect damage to be nonlinear in warming, and the degree of nonlinearity suggested in chapter 3 may be an understatement. Thus, in one model variant Nordhaus (1990a) applies a quadratic damage function (i.e., $\gamma = 2$).

Application of the damage function to world GDP raises the question of whether the impact of a given amount of warming in the distant future would be proportionate, relative to GDP, to the impact imposed on today's world economy. As discussed in chapter 3, there is no strong reason for expecting the overall effect to rise less or more than proportionately with GDP. Some components would tend to rise by less than GDP (for a given warming)—for example, agricultural damage in view of the likely decline of the share of agriculture in GDP over time. Others could rise more than proportionately, including the valuation of human lives lost and of species loss.

Abatement benefits are determined by the amount of prospective damage that can be avoided through policy action. The damage avoidance fraction μ is set at 0.8. Thus, even with aggressive policy action, it is assumed that 20 percent of the prospective baseline damage is unavoidable. This fraction is based on the evaluation that, in the very long term, about the best that can be expected from aggressive abatement policy is to hold the ceiling global warming to the amount associated with carbon dioxide doubling, or 2.5°C in the central case. The amount of damage avoided, expressed as a percentage of GDP, thus becomes the difference between baseline damage in the very long term and that for a doubling of carbon-dioxide-equivalent. As discussed in chapter 3, the base-case analysis places very-long-term warming damage at 6 percent of GDP, so that this difference amounts

---

10. The differences between the Nordhaus damage estimates and those of this study are discussed below.

to $6 - 1 = 5$ percent of GDP. Forceful action can thus avoid five-sixths of the potential damage. The use of 80 percent here provides a conservative estimate of the fraction of damage avoided, especially for the case of the quadratic damage function. In that more extreme case (but still applying only the central IPCC value for climate sensitivity, S), very-long-term damage reaches 16 percent of GDP (1 percent $\times$ $[10°C/2.5°C]^2$). In that case, the damage avoided would be $16 - 1 = 15$ percent, so the avoidance fraction would be as high as 94 percent.

Cost Parameters

The estimate for emissions reduction from afforestation, 1.6 GtC annually for 30 years, is developed in chapter 5. A worldwide program for planting 260 million hectares in new forest would be required for this purpose. The estimated cost, including land purchase, would amount to $17.2 billion (1990 dollars) annually during the first 30 years and zero thereafter.[11] Similarly, the estimate of 0.7 GtC for annual emissions reduction from curtailment of deforestation is developed in chapter 5, on the basis of potential effects in just three major developing countries (Brazil, Indonesia, and Côte d'Ivoire). This program would cost only $4.5 billion annually, but the cost would recur over the entire time horizon. Base-year deforestation emissions (and, in the baseline, constant deforestation emissions thereafter) are set at 1 GtC.[12]

Table 7.2 next reports the parameters in the cost function for reduction of emissions in industry and elsewhere in the economy (excluding forestry). As developed in chapter 5, the estimates assume that a reduction of up to 22 percent of emissions can be achieved at zero cost, on the basis of the body of engineering estimates. As noted, the term that shifts cost downward over time (reflecting improved technological opportunities) is restricted from lowering cost below 2 percent of GDP, where large cuts (over 50 percent) are involved even in the distant future.

---

11. An alternative formulation could use the cost of land rental rather than purchase, with lower costs initially but recurrent and rising costs over the whole, long-term horizon.

12. The IPCC (1990d, chapter 2) no-abatement baseline ("high scenario") uses 0.7 GtC in 1985, 1 GtC in 2000, 1.4 GtC in 2025–50, 0.7 GtC in 2075, and 0.4 GtC by 2100, thereby allowing for the impact of forest exhaustion. The IPCC's use of a lower figure for its emissions projections than the central value of 1.6 GtC identified in its scientific volume (IPCC 1990b, chapter 1) reflects a wide range of uncertainty regarding the current extent of deforestation.

Tax Parameters

The carbon tax parameters are based on the models surveyed in chapter 4. From those models, it may be estimated that, for the period from approximately 2025 to 2050, for each percentage point reduction in the economy's carbon emissions a carbon tax of $5 per ton (1990 dollars) is required. To provide a conservative estimate of tax revenue, it is assumed that the relevant "percentage cut" is the total less that which can be achieved at zero cost (or 22 percent, z_0). The maximum tax is $250 per ton, which reflects the cost differential for backstop noncarbon energy sources and thus is sufficient for high cutbacks over an indefinite range.

To estimate tax revenue, the tax rate is applied to the volume of emissions still permitted, or 4 GtC. On this basis, the maximum tax revenue is $1 trillion annually.[13] The marginal efficiency cost of existing taxes, ρ, is set at 0.33. Thus, for each dollar of existing revenue that can be replaced by carbon tax revenue, there is a savings of 33 cents for the economy because of reduction in the excess tax burden—the loss to inefficiencies from tax-induced distortions in resource allocation. This parameter is based on the estimate by Jorgensen and Yun (1990) that, in the United States (after the Tax Reform Act of 1986), the marginal efficiency cost of the tax system was 0.383.[14] With $\rho = 0.33$ and maximum carbon-tax revenue at $1 trillion, the maximum benefit from tax burden reduction reaches $330 billion in 2060, or about 0.25 percent of world GDP.

Other Greenhouse Gases

The factor for expansion of cost estimates to incorporate reduction of noncarbon greenhouse gases (ω) is set at 0.2. This range is consistent with the following considerations. First, under "business as usual," carbon dioxide is expected to account for about two-thirds of the increase in radiative forcing from all greenhouse gases over the next century (IPCC 1990b, table 2.7). Second, Nordhaus (1990b) has emphasized that the reduction of chlorofluorocarbons is the lowest-cost means of reducing global warming. Third, carbon dioxide has spectrum-based saturation effects that makes its radiative forcing logarithmic in concentration, whereas with lower saturation the radiative forcing of other trace gases is closer to linear (chapter 1). The implication of this last point is a high payoff

---

13. Note, however, that revenue does not reach this maximum until approximately 2060, when it amounts to only 0.8 percent of world GDP.

14. The marginal efficiency cost falls to 0.335 if tax rates are cut by 20 percent, and to 0.307 if they are cut by 30 percent. The estimates here suggest that carbon revenue would be only a modest percentage of GDP, so that the lower marginal efficiency costs at still steeper general tax reductions are not relevant.

to prevention of expansion of other trace gases relative to that for carbon dioxide. Fourth, as discussed in chapter 8, many of the measures that cut carbon emissions should also reduce emissions of other greenhouse gases.

These four considerations together imply that the ratio of abatement cost expansion for other trace gases to that for carbon dioxide is substantially less than implied by the relative shares in the buildup of radiative forcing (about 50 percent, i.e., $\frac{1}{3} \div \frac{2}{3}$). On this basis, expansion by 20 percent would appear reasonable, or perhaps even excessive, to translate carbon abatement costs into costs for a corresponding reduction in total trace gases.

Shadow Pricing of Capital

Table 7.2 next reports the shadow price of capital for the central value of the social rate of time preference (i), estimated on the basis of equation 7.19 above (and using a capital lifetime of 15 years). At $i = 1\frac{1}{2}$ percent, this shadow price is approximately 1.6, so that one unit of displaced investment is worth 1.6 units of displaced consumption. The share of investment (π_k) is set at 20 percent on both the side of abatement cost (c) and the side of non-consumption-specific benefits (b). It is assumed, however, that half of the benefits of greenhouse damage avoidance are consumption-specific.

Adaptation

The National Academy of Sciences (NAS 1991a, 1991b) has stressed the importance of adaptation as an approach to the greenhouse problem. Adaptation reduces greenhouse damage but it also imposes a new cost in the "baseline." The benefit-cost calculus after incorporation of adaptation thus involves a reduction in the benefit from abatement (less damage to be avoided). However, it also involves a reduction in the net costs of the abatement policy, because the costs of the *alternative* strategy of adaptation may now be deducted in assessing the abatement option.

This formulation of mutually exclusive alternatives of abatement and adaptation is useful conceptually, but in practice public policy on global warming is likely to involve a mixture of both. What is really at issue, then, is a comparison between two broad strategies: one with heavy emphasis on abatement and lesser reliance on adaptation, and the other the reverse. The implicit assumption of this study is that, in view of the possible extent of very-long-term warming, the amelioration possible through adaptation will be limited, and the primary strategy if a meaningful response is to be mobilized, will have to be abatement.

The discussion of agriculture in chapter 3 suggests that adaptation can help but is unlikely to fundamentally alter the qualitative dimensions of potentially large greenhouse damage, especially in the very long term.[15] More generally, the range of changes in the benefit-cost calculation resulting from consideration of adaptation seems likely to be modest compared with the already wide range of uncertainty regarding the underlying warming effects and damage functions.

In the absence of explicit measures for the impact of adaptation, the approach taken here is simply to register that the benefit-cost ratio of a particular abatement scenario may be a modest overstatement for lack of direct inclusion of adjustments for the adaptation alternative.

Benefit-Cost Results

Table 7.3 reports the results of the benefit-cost calculations for 36 principal cases using combinations of alternative assumptions for key parameters. It should be noted that, whereas the discount rate selected affects both the cost and the benefit side, variation of the other three parameters—climate sensitivity (S), the damage function exponent (γ), and benchmark damage (d_0)—affects only the benefit side.[16]

The broad picture that emerges is that, under the combinations of lower rates of social time preference and greater greenhouse damage, it will be socially efficient to undertake aggressive abatement action, whereas with higher discount rates and lesser damage, action will not be warranted. From the standpoint of the analysis in chapter 6, the most meaningful results are those that apply a social rate of time preference of 1½ percent (with a corresponding shadow price of capital of 1.56). Of the 11 cases reported for this discount rate, six show a benefit-cost ratio (q) in excess of unity for aggressive abatement action. With the IPCC's best-guess climate sensitivity parameter ($S = 2.5°C$), three of the four cases have $q > 1$, and with the upper-bound warming ($S = 4.5°C$), all three cases show $q > 1$. In contrast, if the lower-bound climate sensitivity parameter is applied ($S = 1.5°C$), the benefit-cost ratio is strictly less than unity, although it approaches unity in the case with the highest economic damage assumptions ($d_0 = 2$ percent of GDP at 1.5°C warming and damage function exponent $\gamma = 2.0$).

If a single case were to be chosen as the central estimate, it would be case 1. Here the climate sensitivity parameter is at the IPCC central value, and the economic damage parameters are set at the central magnitudes developed in chapter 3. The ratio of the present discounted value of benefits to the present discounted value of costs for this case is 0.74. If it were certain that these were the stakes of global warming, the implication would be that abatement is too costly relative to the prospective damage and no action should be undertaken.

---

15. See, in particular, the interpretation in chapter 3 of the MINK results.

16. The climate sensitivity parameter S is that referred to as Λ in chapters 1 and 2.

As discussed below, however, the outlook is far from certain. A more appropriate approach to decision making is to take into account a weighted average of the alternative scenarios. The degree of policymaker risk aversion will also enter into this calculation. For the moment, however, it is useful to consider the further implication of the finding of $q = 0.74$ for the base case. This result indicates that, of every dollar spent on greenhouse abatement, there would be an outright loss of about 26 cents. More specifically, as the abatement costs are on the order of 2½ percent of GDP over time, the implication is that about 0.6 percent of GDP would be a pure loss. One way to think about this outcome is that this is the price of purchasing greenhouse insurance—an insurance policy that yields benefits covering only three-quarters of its costs but provides protection against the contingency of higher, unexpected losses.

The remaining cases in table 7.3 are reported for purposes of sensitivity analysis with higher social rates of time preference. As expected, there are fewer instances of benefit-cost ratios in excess of unity when this rate is set at 3 percent or 5 percent instead of the preferred 1½ percent. However, even with these discount rates, the benefits of action outweigh the costs in several cases where the warming and damage functions are high. This is the outcome for 3 of the 11 cases estimated with a discount rate of 3 percent (cases 16, 22, 23) and for one of the cases with the discount rate at 5 percent (case 34). The principal implication of this finding is that, even with higher discount rates than proposed in this study, abatement action may be warranted if emphasis is given to the possible outcomes with higher damage.

The potential scope of the damage is very large in several of the scenarios considered in table 7.3. Whereas in the base case (case 1) greenhouse damage in the very long term amounts to 6 percent of GDP, if the damage function exponent is raised from 1.3 to 2.0 this estimate increases to 16 percent of GDP ($1 \text{ percent} \times [10°C/2.5°C]^2$). For climate sensitivity $S = 2.5°C$, the maximum very-long-term damage reaches 32 percent of GDP (e.g., case 4); with $S = 4.5°C$, this maximum reaches 52 percent of GDP (e.g., case 11). The highest possible damage combination ($S = 4.5°C$, $\gamma = 2$, $d_0 = 2$) is ruled out, because it gives very-long-term damage in excess of 100 percent of GDP.[17]

Policy Choice Under Uncertainty with Risk Aversion

Cases 1, 5, and 9 in table 7.3 represent the central calculations of this study for the three alternative warming scenarios of the IPCC: best-guess, lower-bound,

---

17. For the seven other combinations involving $S = 2.5°C$ or $4.5°C$, $\gamma = 1.3$ or 2.0, and $d_0 = 1$ or 2, greenhouse damage at very-long-term warming amounts to 6 percent of GDP in one, 12 percent to 16 percent of GDP in three, 26 percent to 32 percent in two, and 52 percent in one.

Table 7.3 Results of benefit-cost analyses of abatement of greenhouse warming, principal cases[a]

Case	Key parameters				Benefit-cost ratio (q)
	i	s	γ	d_0	
1	1.5	2.5	1.3	1	0.74
2	1.5	2.5	1.3	2	1.42
3	1.5	2.5	2.0	1	1.33
4	1.5	2.5	2.0	2	2.60
5	1.5	1.5	1.3	1	0.41
6	1.5	1.5	1.3	2	0.76
7	1.5	1.5	2.0	1	0.51
8	1.5	1.5	2.0	2	0.97
9	1.5	4.5	1.3	1	1.52
10	1.5	4.5	1.3	2	2.99
11	1.5	4.5	2.0	1	4.18
12	1.5	4.5	2.0	2	n.a.
13	3	2.5	1.3	1	0.44
14	3	2.5	1.3	2	0.80
15	3	2.5	2.0	1	0.58
16	3	2.5	2.0	2	1.09
17	3	1.5	1.3	1	0.26
18	3	1.5	1.3	2	0.45
19	3	1.5	2.0	1	0.26
20	3	1.5	2.0	2	0.44

21	3	4.5	1.3	1	0.86
22	3	4.5	1.3	2	1.63
23	3	4.5	2.0	1	1.71
24	3	4.5	2.0	2	n.a.
25	5	2.5	1.3	1	0.33
26	5	2.5	1.3	2	0.57
27	5	2.5	2.0	1	0.33
28	5	2.5	2.0	2	0.56
29	5	1.5	1.3	1	0.22
30	5	1.5	1.3	2	0.34
31	5	1.5	2.0	1	0.18
32	5	1.5	2.0	2	0.26
33	5	4.5	1.3	1	0.61
34	5	4.5	1.3	2	1.12
35	5	4.5	2.0	1	0.85
36	5	4.5	2.0	2	n.a.

i = social rate of time preference, in percentages per year; S = climate sensitivity factor (degrees Celsius warming for a doubling of carbon-dioxide-equivalent); γ = damage function exponent; d_0 = damage from 2.5°C warming (in percentages of GDP); n.a. = not applicable.

a. All cases *include* the benefits from tax burden reduction and apply a shadow price of capital ranging from 1.56 (i = 1.5 percent) to 1.21 (i = 5 percent).

and upper-bound, respectively. Cases 10 and 11 represent upper-bound warming in combination with high-damage functions ($d_0 = 2$ and $\gamma = 2$, respectively). Suppose that the probability of the best-guess case is 50 percent, and the probability of either the upper- or the lower-bound is 25 percent. Suppose further that policymakers are risk averse, so that they attach more weight to avoiding unpleasant surprises than to enjoying pleasant ones. An informal way to arrive at the policy decision is to weight the (present discounted values of) benefits of the alternative scenarios by a combination of their underlying probabilities and a factor that takes account of risk aversion. Note that the costs of the alternative cases are all identical, because their abatement cutbacks of carbon emissions are the same.

Suppose that, because of risk aversion, the weight for the upper-bound warming case should be three times the weight for the lower-bound case. Suppose further that the weight for the central case is unity times its probability of occurrence. On this basis, the respective weights might be, for example, 0.5 for the central case, 0.125 for the lower-bound case, and 0.375 for the upper-bound case.

For the upper-bound damage case, an average of scenarios 9 and 10 may be used. In case 9, damage is 1 percent of GDP at benchmark CO_2 doubling and rises to 13 percent in the very long term; in case 10, damage is 2 percent of GDP at benchmark warming and reaches 26 percent of GDP in the very long term. These two cases suggest that the most meaningful estimate for high damage with very long term warming is a loss of 20 percent of GDP annually (the average of the two cases). With the weights just discussed applied to the present discounted value of benefits of cases 1 (central), 5 (lower-bound), and an average of cases 9 and 10 (upper-bound), respectively, and then divided by the present discounted value of costs, the resulting weighted benefit-cost ratio is 1.26. Thus, *using the central assumptions of this study, if there is weighting of outcomes to take account of risk aversion, the benefit-cost analysis finds that aggressive abatement action is warranted.*[18]

This result may be seen further by returning to figure 7.1. The figure shows the abatement-cost curve (as a percentage of GDP) and two alternative benefit curves: that for the central case and the average of high-damage cases 9 and 10 (the low case is omitted from the diagram). Once the magnitude of growing world GDP is taken into account, on the one hand, and values are discounted at the social rate of time preference, on the other, the effect is that the area under the cost curve in the figure is less than a weighted average of the areas

---

18. Note also that this approach is conservative in at least one regard. If the highest-damage case (11) is used to represent the high-risk outcome rather than the less severe high-damage alternatives (cases 9 and 10), the risk-weighting procedure gives a benefit-cost ratio of 1.98.

under the two alternative benefit curves, so that the weighted benefits exceed costs (present discounted value).[19]

Sensitivity Analysis

Table 7.4 reports the benefit-cost ratios of the abatement program under alternative assumptions. The table indicates the sensitivity of the outcome to the discount rate, the shadow price of capital, and inclusion or exclusion of tax burden effects. The first 40 cases (37 through 76) apply traditional discounting with no special conversion of capital effects into consumption- equivalents (i.e., $p_k^* = 1$).[20] Perhaps the biggest surprise of the tests is that, even with a discount rate of 10 percent, one variant of the high-damage outcome shows a benefit-cost ratio for abatement in excess of unity (case 74, with $q = 1.07$). The benefit-cost ratio is also above unity for the corresponding high-damage case using a discount rate of 5 percent (case 70, with $q = 1.15$). These results suggest that, even with the higher discount rates frequently used in medium-term public investment projects, a program of aggressive abatement is warranted under the high-damage assumptions.[21] At the other end of the spectrum, if a discount rate

---

19. Note that visual inspection of the central case shows the area under the benefits curve to be closer in size to the area under the cost curve than the benefit-cost ratio for this case, $q = 0.74$. (The ratio of the strictly nonoverlapping components of these two areas and thus the difference between benefits and costs as a percentage of GDP—may be seen by visual inspection to be smaller, but it is the ratio of total benefits to total costs that matters.) The contrast between the measured q and the visual comparison indicates that the net effect of the conflicting influences of time discounting and GDP growth is dominated by the former. That is, because the diagram reports results as percentages of GDP, a corresponding diagram of absolute amounts would show much larger areas toward the right of the figure (from growing absolute GDP); but once discounted by the time discount rate, these larger absolute areas would be more than proportionately shrunk in comparison with the areas of net cost in the earlier decades. In part the reason for this outcome is that GDP is growing more slowly in the latter part of the time horizon than in the earlier part.

20. In terms of the discussion of chapter 6, the range of 2 percent to 3 percent may be considered to represent the approaches of the Congressional Budget Office and the General Accounting Office, whereas the extreme of 10 percent may be seen as representing the approach of the Office of Management and Budget.

21. A nuance in this regard is that, with high discount rates, earlier damages matter more than eventual damage magnitudes. For example, case 74 has a higher benefit-cost ratio than case 75 even though very-long-term damage is higher in the latter (52 percent of GDP rather than 26 percent). The reason is that the damage occurs earlier ($d_0 = 2$ percent in case 74 and 1 percent in case 75). The higher discount rates also emphasize an anomaly of the earlier years. The higher the damage exponent (γ), the lower the damage prior to 2050. In these years, the ratio $W_t/2.5$ in equation 7.6 is less than unity, so a higher exponent γ causes lower damage. Thus, the benefit-cost ratio is lower in case 75 than in case 73. However, this difference is essentially spurious and would reverse if linear in-

Table 7.4 Sensitivity analysis of benefits and costs of abatement of greenhouse warming[a]

Case	Key parameters i	S	γ	d_0	Benefit-cost ratio (q)
37	1	2.5	1.3	1	0.96
38	1	2.5	1.3	2	1.86
39	1	2.5	2.0	1	1.87
40	1	2.5	2.0	2	3.70
41	2	2.5	1.3	1	0.64
42	2	2.5	1.3	2	1.20
43	2	2.5	2.0	1	1.03
44	2	2.5	2.0	2	2.00
45	3	2.5	1.3	1	0.46
46	3	2.5	1.3	2	0.84
47	3	2.5	2.0	1	0.61
48	3	2.5	2.0	2	1.13
49	5	2.5	1.3	1	0.34
50	5	2.5	1.3	2	0.59
51	5	2.5	2.0	1	0.34
52	5	2.5	2.0	2	0.58
53	10	2.5	1.3	1	0.33
54	10	2.5	1.3	2	0.56
55	10	2.5	2.0	1	0.24
56	10	2.5	2.0	2	0.37
57	1	4.5	1.3	1	2.00
58	1	4.5	1.3	2	3.94
59	1	4.5	2.0	1	5.96
60	1	4.5	2.0	2	n.a.
61	2	4.5	1.3	1	1.29
62	2	4.5	1.3	2	2.50
63	2	4.5	2.0	1	3.19
64	2	4.5	2.0	2	6.32
65	3	4.5	1.3	1	0.89
66	3	4.5	1.3	2	1.70
67	3	4.5	2.0	1	1.78
68	3	4.5	2.0	2	n.a.
69	5	4.5	1.3	1	0.62
70	5	4.5	1.3	2	1.15
71	5	4.5	2.0	1	0.87
72	5	4.5	2.0	2	n.a.
73	10	4.5	1.3	1	0.59
74	10	4.5	1.3	2	1.07
75	10	4.5	2.0	1	0.54
76	10	4.5	2.0	2	n.a.
77	1.5	2.5	1.3	1	0.66
78	1.5	2.5	1.3	2	1.28
79	1.5	2.5	2.0	1	1.19
80	1.5	2.5	2.0	2	2.34
81	1.5	4.5	1.3	1	1.37
82	1.5	4.5	1.3	2	2.69
83	1.5	4.5	2.0	1	3.76
84	1.5	4.5	2.0	2	n.a.
85	1.5	2.5	1.3	1	0.68
86	1.5	2.5	1.3	2	1.37
87	1.5	2.5	2.0	1	1.27
88	1.5	2.5	2.0	2	2.54
89	1.5	4.5	1.3	1	1.47
90	1.5	4.5	1.3	2	2.93
91	1.5	4.5	2.0	1	4.12
92	1.5	4.5	2.0	2	8.24

i = social rate of time preference, in percentages per year; S = climate sensitivity factor (degrees Celsius warming for a doubling of carbon-dioxide-equivalent); γ = damage function exponent; d_0 = damage from 2.5°C warming (in percentages of GDP); n.a. = not applicable.

a. All cases except cases 85 to 92 *include* the benefits from tax burden reduction. The shadow price of capital is 1 for cases 37 to 76, 3 for cases 77 to 84, and 1.56 for cases 85 to 92.

of only 1 percent is applied (e.g., on grounds that intergenerational comparison calls for a low discount rate), the benefit-cost ratio exceeds unity in five out of six of the cases considered, and reaches nearly 6:1 in the highest-damage variant.

Cases 77 to 84 in table 7.4 examine the influence of the shadow price of capital. These cases are identical to their counterparts in the initial section of table 7.3 (using the central social rate of time preference, $i = 1.5$ percent), except that they arbitrarily assign a higher shadow price of capital ($p_k^* = 3.0$ rather than 1.56). The higher shadow price does not markedly alter the benefit-cost ratios. Thus, for the central case (case 1, table 7.3) the shift to the higher shadow price reduces the benefit-cost ratio only from 0.74 to 0.66 (case 77). In the high-damage range, the change is also modest (from 4.18, case 11, to 3.76, case 83).

Cases 85 to 92 report the influence of omitting the reduction in excess tax burden from the benefits side of the analysis, for example on grounds that governments might independently shift to optimal tax structures with no help from carbon tax revenue. Otherwise the assumptions are as in the central cases (with the social rate of time preference at 1.5 percent and the shadow price of capital according to equation 7.19 above). It is evident that the influence of the tax revenue effect is minor. Thus, in the central case its omission lowers the benefit-cost ratio only from 0.74 to 0.68 (case 1 versus case 85), and in the highest-damage case from 4.18 to 4.12 (case 11 versus case 91).

Overall, the tests in table 7.4 show that the benefit-cost ratio is highly sensitive to the social rate of time preference, but that the desirability of abatement holds up more robustly than expected under high discount rates if high-damage variants are considered. The tests also show that the shadow price of capital and the inclusion of excess tax burden effects have only minor influences on the results. In short, the sensitivity tests broadly confirm the findings of the central analysis.

Catastrophe Analysis

The main analysis of this study presumes steadily rising greenhouse damage from modest levels by the first half of the 21st century, with varying degrees of severity over the very long term. These scenarios might be described as "moderate progressive decay," and they are superimposed on a baseline of rising per capita income so that the end result is to leave future incomes higher than today but lower than attainable in the absence of global warming damage. Evaluation with relatively low (but theoretically justifiable) discount rates tends to find

---

terpolation were used for damage in the early years. The phenomenon becomes apparent only when high discount rates are used, because they tend to make all but the early years of little importance.

favorable benefit-cost ratios for abatement action; calculation with higher rates (5 percent to 10 percent) tends to find that the costs of action outweigh the benefits except in the high-damage cases.

It is useful to consider an alternative approach that applies a relatively conventional discount rate of, say, 5 percent and then asks the following question: how high would the probability of catastrophe have to be to make the expected (i.e., weighted) benefit-cost ratio greater than unity? As discussed in chapter 1, possible catastrophic effects could include the release of vast reservoirs of carbon-equivalent trapped in methane clathrates, the disintegration of the West Antarctic ice shelf under very-long-term warming, and fundamental shifts in ocean currents.

Let us postulate a catastrophe that is large and relatively sudden. Suppose that it is sufficient to reduce per capita incomes worldwide by 20 percent from present levels and freeze them at that plateau thereafter. Suppose that the catastrophe arrives in the year 2050.

Now return to the risk-weighted analysis considered above, but with reformulations to discount at a higher rate but also incorporate the chance of a catastrophe. First, we apply a discount rate of 5 percent. Second, we calculate the risk-weighted benefit-cost ratio as above. Third, we set a probability p for the catastrophe occurring and $(1 - p)$ for the (risk-weighted) principal scenarios. We may then examine how high the probability of the catastrophe would have to be to raise the overall benefit-cost ratio for aggressive abatement action to above unity.

Cases 29, 25, and 34 in table 7.3 represent the low, central, and high-damage cases with 5 percent discounting. Using the same technique as discussed above, the risk-weighted benefit-cost ratio for these three cases is 0.61. The catastrophe scenario would have to have a probability of 7.8 percent to raise this ratio to unity.[22] The implication of this exercise is that, if a discount rate of 5 percent is applied, it requires only a relatively modest probability of the catastrophe scenario to boost the (risk-weighted) benefit-cost ratio calculated from the principal scenarios to the threshold of unity required for social profitability of an aggressive abatement program.

This conclusion is sharply reinforced if it is kept in mind that there should be an interdependency between the discount rate and the probability of catastrophe. If future incomes are lower than today's because of catastrophe, the social rate of time preference should be lower and in fact, under the analysis of

---

22. The present value of the cost of abatement over 285 years, discounting at 5 percent, is $18.3 trillion. The risk-weighted present value of benefits of the three noncatastrophe scenarios is $11.3 trillion. The present value of benefits of abatement in the case of the catastrophe scenario is $101 trillion. Thus, $(0.078 \times 101) + (0.922 \times 11.3) = 18.3$.

chapter 6, negative.[23] A second version of the catastrophe analysis may thus appropriately apply a weighted average in which the 5 percent discount rate holds for the three noncatastrophe scenarios, but the catastrophe evaluation applies a discount rate of zero. If this approach is adopted, then the probability of catastrophe needs to be only one-hundredth of one percent to raise the weighted-average benefit-cost ratio to unity.[24]

My own expectation is that, even in the very long term, global warming is unlikely to be so catastrophic that it would reduce world income sharply below today's levels. Thus, my preference is for a methodological approach that applies the central value of the social rate of time preference developed here (1.5 percent), in which case the risk-weighted analysis finds aggressive abatement action socially attractive even without considering the possibility of catastrophe. Others may prefer to impose a higher discount rate such as the 5 percent just examined.[25] The principal point is that, even under that approach, abatement remains attractive if just a small probability is attached to catastrophic consequences.

A Malthusian Scenario

Approximately two hundred years ago the English economist Thomas Malthus predicted that population growth would surpass that of production (the first being geometric and the second arithmetic, he argued). The result would be chronic poverty among the lower classes unless population growth was checked by "moral restraint" or war. In the event, technological change has permitted production to outstrip population. However, as the discussion of sustainable development in chapter 8 suggests, concern remains that the global economy could stagnate over the long term and fail to increase standards of living above those of today for much of the world's population. If that occurred, the con-

---

23. With $i = g\theta$, where i is the social rate of time preference, g is the rate of per capita consumption growth, and θ is the elasticity of marginal utility of consumption (absolute value), an initial value of $i = 5$ percent where g is only 1 percent (the baseline consumption growth of the analysis) implies that the agency or analyst believes the elasticity of marginal utility is a high value, 5. In the catastrophe case, $g = -0.3$ percent for 1991–2050 and zero thereafter. Consistency would then require discounting at -1.5 percent, at least over the first 60 years.

24. With $i = 0$, the present discounted value of benefits under catastrophe is $72.5 quadrillion. Following note 22, we have: $(72,532 \times 0.000097) + (11.3 \times 0.999903) = 18.3$.

25. Indeed, my own expectation is that whereas the probability of the catastrophe specified above is likely to be less than the threshold 7.8 percent indicated in the calculation, this probability could easily exceed the level of 0.01 percent required if the catastrophe analysis is conducted in the theoretically consistent way.

sequence would be a slow-motion economic catastrophe comparable in impact to the more abrupt natural catastrophe postulated and examined above. It is useful to consider the implications of a Malthusian scenario for the benefit-cost analysis of greenhouse policy.

The central features of a Malthusian world are rapid population growth, minimal technological change, and constant rather than rising per capita income. Population projections are thus the place to begin in formulating such an outcome. As noted above, in the basic projections here, world population stabilizes by the year 2100 at 10.5 billion. One recent study suggests, however, that under unfavorable assumptions world population could reach 28 billion by 2150 (Harrison 1992). An alternative, somewhat less extreme formulation, is to reconsider the population growth rates of the projections here and simply assume that in developing countries these rates do not fall to zero.

In table 7.1, population growth in developing countries is shown to decline from 1.6 percent annually at present to 1.4 percent, 0.8 percent, 0.3 percent, and 0.2 percent in the successive 25-year periods of the next century, and to zero thereafter. If instead it is assumed that the rate remains constant at 0.8 percent annually from the middle of the 21st century on, world population reaches 15.6 billion by 2100, 22.6 billion by 2150, 33 billion by 2200, and 48 billion by 2250. The 2150 level is actually smaller than the 28 billion suggested in the study just cited.

Because there is no growth in production per capita, the economy expands in size strictly in proportion to population. With no technical change, the ratio of carbon emissions to population (and thus to output) remains constant. Today the global average of carbon emissions amounts to approximately 1 ton per person per year. On this basis, the scenario calls for carbon emissions to rise to 15.6 GtC by 2100, considerably below the baseline amount of 20.6 GtC. However, eventually emissions nearly catch up with those in the baseline. Thus, by 2250 the Malthusian case shows emissions at 48.8 GtC, versus 50.9 GtC in the main projections. The absence of technical change and the much higher population growth eventually compensate for the absence of growth in output per capita in generating baseline carbon emissions.

With zero growth in per capita income, the social rate of time preference becomes zero. There is no longer any reason to give a higher weight to consumption today than to consumption in the future, because people in the future will no longer be richer than today. However, the shadow price of capital rises, because the discount rate at which capital earnings over the life of equipment is discounted falls to zero. With the social rate of time preference at zero and the rate of return on capital at 8 percent, the shadow price of capital rises to 1.75 (equation 6.1, chapter 6).

When the benefit-cost model is run applying these projections and parameters, it turns out that the discounted present value of benefits of an aggressive action program exceeds the discounted present value of the costs even for the central case (where Λ = 2.5°C, d_0 = 1 percent of GDP, and γ = 1.3)—that is, the analogue of case 1 in table 7.3 but with the social rate of time preference i = zero. The central Malthusian case shows the benefit-cost ratio at q = 1.09:1. If the higher benchmark damage alternative is used (d_0 = 2 percent), the benefit-cost ratio rises to 2.07. If in addition warming is set at the upper bound (Λ = 4.5°C), the benefit-cost ratio rises to 4.28:1.

The simulations for the Malthusian scenario thus reinforce the main findings above that aggressive action to limit global warming seems warranted. The effect of somewhat lesser and later warming, as the consequence of a slower rise in carbon emissions from slower per capita income growth, is more than offset by the fact that the proper rate to use for the social rate of time preference is zero under these circumstances. Although this scenario is not the principal case of this study, it has considerable importance because it represents what is perhaps a major theme of public concern: that future generations will be no better off than the present, and therefore that burdening them with greenhouse damage would be inequitable.

Comparison With the Nordhaus Results

Annex 7A to this chapter examines the optimization models developed by William D. Nordhaus for analysis of greenhouse policy. The central findings of Nordhaus's earlier, best-known greenhouse model were the following (1991a, 936):

> For the low damage function—which includes only identified costs and uses a middle discount rate [1 percent pure rate of time preference]—we estimate the marginal damage of greenhouse gases to be about $1.83 per ton of C [carbon] in CO_2 equivalent, which suggests very little CO_2 abatement. For the medium damage function, which assumes damage from greenhouse warming of 1% of GNP, the cost is reckoned at $7.33 per ton carbon; in this case, the efficient reduction is 11% of total GHG [greenhouse gas] emissions. In this case, CFCs are substantially reduced, and CO_2 emissions are reduced by about 2%. In the high damage case, with damages taken to be 2% of total output and with no discounting, GHG emissions are reduced by about one-third.

The main thrust of the Nordhaus analysis is that little action needs to be taken on greenhouse abatement unless one is pessimistic about damages. In contrast, the analysis of this study suggests that an aggressive course of abatement is warranted, at least with risk aversion. A major difference between the two studies is that Nordhaus focuses on the impact of a doubling of carbon-dioxide-equivalent rather than very-long-term warming.

A central problem with the Nordhaus analysis is that it assumes a future in which resources are in a "steady state"; there is no population growth and no rise in per capita income except from technical change. By implication, greenhouse gas emissions are also in a steady state. Yet as the projections of chapter 2 indicate, emissions could rise some tenfold over the very long term. By the year 2100, a 2 percent cut in carbon dioxide emissions (the central Nordhaus result above) would still leave them at more than three times their present level.

As discussed in annex 7A, Nordhaus has subsequently stated that the steady-state formulation was inadequate, and has constructed a dynamic model (the DICE model) that allows for rising population, per capita income, and baseline emissions. The revised analysis considers a 400-year horizon and allows for nonlinear damage from warming, both key improvements compatible with the approach of the present study. Nonetheless, the initial results of the DICE model continue to find relatively modest optimal abatement, with cutbacks from baseline on the order of 10 percent initially and 15 percent by 2100, and carbon taxes of only $5 to $20 per ton. As discussed in annex 7A, however, it seems likely that, with arguably appropriate parameter modifications and explicit attention to upper-bound warming and risk aversion, the DICE model would yield optimal abatement much closer to the aggressive policy examined here.[26]

In short, the new Nordhaus results may be less indelibly contrary to stiff abatement measures than were the earlier results. In at least one regard, even the previous estimates were similar to those here. As discussed in chapter 3, Nordhaus arrived at direct estimates of damage from global warming equal to ¼ percent of GDP for benchmark carbon-dioxide-equivalent doubling, and he suggested 1 percent of GDP as a central damage estimate and 2 percent for high damage. The estimates developed in the present study also amount to 1 percent to 2 percent of GDP for benchmark doubling.

However, there is an important distinction. In the analysis of this study, warming at the upper-bound climate sensitivity parameter ($\Lambda = 4.5°C$) is considered as well as warming at the central parameter ($\Lambda = 2.5°C$). With the upper-bound variant, the high-damage estimate at benchmark doubling in the present study amounts to 4.3 percent of GDP ($= 2$ percent $\times [4.5/2.5]^{1.3}$). In this sense, then, the high-damage case in this study indicates about twice as much damage as the high case in the Nordhaus analysis, even without considering very-long-term warming.

When in addition the impact of very-long-term warming is taken into account, the differences between the initial Nordhaus results and those here become evident. At 10°C, the central estimate of damage is 6 percent of GDP, and the higher-damage cases amount to some 20 percent of GDP (the average for cases

---

26. One such modification would be removal of the 3 percentage points Nordhaus incorporates into the discount rate for pure (myopic) time preference.

9 and 10, table 7.3) or even higher (case 11). With a linear damage function, the early, steady-state Nordhaus results did not reach damages anywhere near this high.

Nordhaus's analysis does include a sophisticated treatment of other trace gases, and he usefully examines the rank ordering of cost-effectiveness in reducing greenhouse gas emissions through cutting CFCs, planting trees, and reducing fossil fuel emissions. As discussed in chapter 5, the analysis of the present study finds forestry measures relatively more attractive than does Nordhaus. His findings on the high cost-effectiveness of reducing CFCs would have made eminent sense had it not been for the subsequent scientific findings suggesting that their warming effect has been relatively neutral because of their ozone-stripping impact (chapter 1), such that focusing attention on CFCs does not go far toward reducing global warming.

In sum, for several reasons, but especially because of the inclusion of more dramatic effects associated with nonlinear damage and very-long-term warming, the policy conclusion in this study differs from that found in the Nordhaus steady-state analysis. The results here indicate that a program holding global carbon emissions to 4 GtC per year—which would amount to a 71 percent reduction from baseline by 2050, an 82 percent reduction by 2100, and a 90 percent reduction by 2200—is warranted under risk aversion. The broad finding of aggressive action contrasts with Nordhaus's conclusion that only very limited action is optimal. It remains unclear whether appropriate reformulation of Nordhaus's more recent dynamic model (the DICE model) would reach a conclusion closer to that of the present study.

Insurance and the Value of Information

The approach of this chapter (and the more recent Nordhaus analysis) is to treat the damages from global warming as a continuous (geometric) function and to consider whether these damages are likely to warrant aggressive abatement measures.[27] Manne and Richels (1990b) offer an alternative approach that attempts to circumvent a lack of estimates on the damages (benefits) side by simplifying the policy choice to one between inaction after scientific progress shows the greenhouse effect is not dangerous, and intense action if new research discovers that greenhouse damage would be catastrophic.

Annex 7B outlines the conceptual framework and principal results of the Manne-Richels insurance analysis. Essentially, it says that policymakers will be

---

27. Nordhaus seeks to identify the optimal level of intervention; the analysis here specifies a particular, aggressive action scenario and seeks to determine whether it has a favorable benefit-cost ratio.

better off to take only moderate action during an initial period of three decades, and thereafter—when more scientific information is available—to take massive steps if necessary, or otherwise to phase out abatement efforts altogether. The authors suggest that this strategy could save the United States a total of $90 billion (present discounted value), compared with an approach that attempts to pursue abatement from the start.

As noted in annex 7B, because the probability of near-catastrophic consequences may be higher than suggested by Manne and Richels and for other reasons—the same model might more appropriately place the value of "waiting and learning" at, say, one-third of the $90 billion total indicated by the authors. But even the full $90 billion is a small gain if considered against the possible damages.

The wait-and-learn strategy assumes that in the second, catch-up phase, strong measures can fully deflect the path of trace gas buildup back to one that converges at the permissible ceiling. However, it would seem more realistic to conclude that a "go slow" initial phase would inevitably leave the total eventual buildup and warming higher than under a policy of more aggressive action undertaken from the start. One reason is the irreversibility of the atmospheric accumulation. Another is the political implausibility of a sudden intensification of international effort as opposed to a steady but gradual tightening of measures.

The 30-year waiting period suggested by Manne and Richels would by itself be enough for a global "commitment" to the doubling of carbon-dioxide-equivalent (chapter 1). The implication is that the total warming commitment expected over a 300-year horizon under the program of aggressive action described in this chapter would already be fully exhausted after the first 30 years (or at least nearly so, depending on just how minimal the Manne-Richels measures are during this first period). As complete avoidance of further buildup after the first three decades would seem highly unlikely, the net result would seem capable of boosting global warming by perhaps at least 1°C, compared with the alternative of earlier forceful action.

If ultimate warming rises from 2.5°C to 3.5°C, the damage function of this chapter would indicate additional damage of about ½ percent of GDP.[28] Half of 1 percent of US GDP is approximately $30 billion even at today's economic scale. The implication is that the entire present discounted value of the gains from "waiting" in the Manne-Richels analysis ($90 billion according to the authors, $30 billion if scaled down as suggested here) could be offset by just one to three years' worth of damages from the likely net increase in warming.

There is nonetheless an important element of truth in the Manne-Richels insurance analysis. It correctly implies that, during at least some initial period,

---

28. With d_0 at 1 percent for $S = 2.5°C$ and $\gamma = 1.3$ (table 7.2), damage reaches 1.5 percent of GDP instead of 1 percent $(1.0[3.5/2.5]^{1.3} = 1.5)$.

the phase-in of measures might appropriately be gradual and that considerable effort should be dedicated to research. An initial phase-in period of 10 years would seem considerably safer than 30 years, however.

These issues are explored further in the discussion of international policy in chapter 8 below. However, in terms of the analysis provided in the present chapter, it may be noted that the initial stage of the response relies primarily on low-cost initiatives (reduced deforestation, afforestation, and a move toward state-of-the-art technology). This initial modest level of costs helps resolve the tension between the need to begin a relatively aggressive program of action sooner rather than later, on the one hand, and the high return to further scientific verification, on the other.

Overview

In sum, benefit-cost analysis suggests that the benefits of an aggressive program of abatement warrant the costs of reducing greenhouse gas emissions if policy-makers are risk averse, or if one is pessimistic and concentrates attention on high-damage cases (especially even a slim chance of an economic catastrophe).

Some will argue that the issue cannot be decided in this way, and in particular that it is the unquantifiable ecological effects that should dominate the analysis rather than the measurable impacts considered here. However, that argument reinforces the result here rather than reversing it, because the analysis concludes that aggressive abatement action is justifiable on economic grounds alone and thus would be all the more warranted if further ecological considerations were added.

These findings contradict the principal conclusion of the only other benefit-cost analysis of global warming to date. Nordhaus (1991a, 936) finds instead that the optimal amount of cutback in greenhouse gases amounts to only 11 percent; that most of this reduction should be in CFCs; that carbon emissions should be reduced by only 2 percent; and that the optimal carbon tax is only $7.33 per ton. The principal reasons for the divergence between the two results are that the estimates here consider much greater warming for the very long term and associated nonlinear damage, whereas the Nordhaus analysis focuses on carbon-dioxide-equivalent doubling; and that the central discount rate applied here is lower.

Annex 7A

The Nordhaus Optimal Emissions Models

Nordhaus (1991a, 1990b) has published results of an optimization model that has received widespread attention among economists and policymakers. This model, which for purposes of clarity we may refer to as NORD1, found that only modest reductions in carbon emissions from baseline were economically optimal. In subsequent unpublished work, Nordhaus (1992a; 1992b) has acknowledged that NORD1:

> had a number of shortcomings, but one of the most significant from an analytical point of view was the inadequate treatment of the dynamics of the economy and the climate. The earlier work examined a "resource steady state". . . . The previous approach is unsatisfactory primarily because of the extraordinarily long time lags involved . . . [such that] dynamics are of the essence. . . . (Nordhaus 1992a, 2–3)

Because of the great policy influence of NORD1, especially in the United States, it seems useful to review more specifically its results and problems. This annex first examines NORD1 and then considers the results of the more recent Nordhaus model, DICE (for Dynamic Integrated Climate-Economy model).

The NORD1 Model

Table 7A.1 reports the equations of the earlier Nordhaus model. T is cumulative greenhouse warming; subscript t indicates the year; M is the atmospheric stock of anthropogenic greenhouse gases (carbon-equivalent); and the overdot indicates a change in the variable in question. The first equation states that the change in temperature is a function of the difference between equilibrium warming for the given stock of M (as indicated by function g) and warming to date. The second equation indicates that the change in M is determined by the fraction β of annual emissions E retained in the atmosphere, less a decay rate δ for absorption into the deep ocean. The third equation linearizes the first.

Equation 7A.4 states that per capita consumption c depends on a steady-state level y^* for constant resources, as augmented by technological change at the rate h (e in the equation denotes the base of the natural logarithm). In addition, consumption varies positively with the steady-state level of emissions, E^*, and negatively with the amount of warming in the steady state, T^*. In equation 7A.5, the objective function to be maximized, V, is the discounted sum of utility of consumption, discounting at the pure time preference rate ρ.

The model then posits a one-time burst of emissions, ΔE, at the initial year. The resulting change in temperature in any given future year is shown in equa-

Table 7A.1 Nordhaus model equations

(1) $\dot{T}_t = \alpha\{g(M_t) - T_t\}$

(2) $\dot{M}_t = \beta E_t - \delta M_t$

(3) $\dot{T}_t = \alpha\{\mu M_t - T_t\}$

(4) $c_t = y^* e^{ht}\{g(E^*) - \phi(T^*)\}$

(5) $V = \int_0^\infty u(c_t)e^{-\rho t}\,dt$

(6) $\Delta T_t = \dfrac{\Delta E\mu\beta\alpha[e^{-\delta t} - e^{-\alpha t}]}{(\alpha - \delta)}$

(7) $\Delta c_t = y^* g'(E^*)\,\Delta E,\ t = 0$

$\qquad = -y^* e^{ht}\phi'(T^*)\,\Delta T_t,\ t > 0$

$\quad \rightarrow y^* g'(E^*)\,\Delta E = \int_0^\infty y^* e^{ht}\phi'(T^*)\,\Delta T_t e^{-rt}\,dt$

(8) $g'(E^*) = \mu\beta\phi'(T^*)\,\dfrac{\alpha\left[\dfrac{1}{r+\delta-h} - \dfrac{1}{r+\alpha-h}\right]}{(\alpha - \delta)}$

(9) $g'(E^*) = \mu\beta\phi'(T^*)\,\Gamma$

Source: William D. Nordhaus. 1991. "To Slow or Not to Slow: The Economics of the Greenhouse Effect." *The Economic Journal* 101, no. 6: 920–37. Reprinted with permission.

tion 7A.6. The first line of equation 7A.7 reports the gain in consumption in the initial year from the extra emissions. The second line reports the loss in consumption in any future year as a result of the corresponding additional warming. The final line of equation 7A.7 sets the initial consumption gain equal to the present discounted value of future consumption losses to identify the optimal size of the one-shot burst of extra emissions. This optimal level occurs where the marginal consumption gain equals the present discounted value of the future marginal consumption losses, as shown in the left- and right-hand sides of equation 7A.8, respectively. Equation 7A.9 is a restatement that consolidates discount and decay terms into a single multiplier Γ.

As Nordhaus has now recognized, the fundamental problem with NORD1 is that it attempts to use a steady-state or comparative static framework to investigate a problem that is inherently dynamic. In the simplest of terms, the baseline for emissions identified in chapter 2 of this study finds a rise from about 6 GtC annually today to approximately 50 GtC by late in the 23rd century—hardly a static, steady-state world.

In policy terms, the static-versus-dynamic problem may be seen as follows. NORD1 concludes under central parameters that greenhouse gases should be cut back by 11 percent, primarily from CFC reduction, and carbon dioxide emissions should be reduced by only 2 percent (through a carbon tax of only $7.33 per ton). The implication is that these cuts are from baseline. But in a real, dynamic world, the baseline is rising rather than steady-state. By the year 2100, for example, a 2 percent cut in carbon emissions would still leave them at about 19½ GtC annually, or more than three times today's level rather than 2 percent below it.

There are other problems with NORD1. It is evident in equation 7A.7 that the model has an asymmetry between its treatment of the gains from extra emissions and the costs from extra warming. The gains are treated as occurring instantaneously and are therefore not discounted. The damages, on the other hand, are spread over time and discounted. In reality, the forgoing of emissions would also occur over time, so that losses from a restraint program (or gains from extra emissions) should be phased over time and discounted. The asymmetry biases the results toward higher optimal emissions.

A crucial problem with NORD1 is that it sets a linear damage function, Φ. This function is based on 1 percent of world GDP loss from 3°C warming (benchmark carbon-dioxide-equivalent doubling), or $200 billion. Each degree Celsius of warming imposes damage of $(200/3) billion. This formulation misses the more-than-linear damage to be expected with warming, and thus the much greater damage for warming beyond 3°C.

A closely related problem is that NORD1 is specified for benchmark carbon-dioxide-equivalent doubling. It thereby misses the damages associated with much higher very-long-term warming, as emphasized in this study.

The DICE Model

Nordhaus's new, dynamic model is a major improvement over NORD1. The DICE model allows for growing population and per capita income over time. It maximizes the discounted sum of utility of per capita consumption multiplied by population, with a logarithmic utility function. Production in the economy is a Cobb-Douglas function of capital and labor (population), multiplied by a term for technological change. In addition, production at any given year is shrunk by a summary factor that takes account of the cost of emissions cutbacks as well as damage to the economy from global warming. This factor is:

$$\Omega_t = \frac{1 - .0686 \ (\mu_t)^{2.887}}{[1 + .00144 \ (T_t)^2]}$$

Here the term μ_t is the proportionate cutback in greenhouse gas emissions from baseline in the year in question, and T is the amount of global warming. Thus, both the abatement cost and the warming damage functions are nonlinear (the former nearly cubic, and the latter quadratic).

Importantly, the DICE model extends the time horizon to 400 years, a crucial change compatible with the much longer term horizon suggested in the present study. Nonetheless, in the results reported in the model version of Nordhaus (1992a, 19), the optimal policy is again found to be a relatively mild reduction in emissions from baseline (as in the static NORD1 model). Optimal emissions are only 10 percent below baseline in the near future, "rising to 15 percent late in the next century." These cutbacks are accomplished by a carbon tax of $5 per ton initially, rising to $20 per ton by 2100.[1]

It seems quite possible that reasonable alternative parameters and modest respecification of the DICE model could yield results much closer to those found here, for several reasons.

First, the results just cited do not take account of a probabilistic distribution of lower- and upper-bound warming (in contrast to the risk-averse treatment in the present study). DICE applies 3°C for benchmark carbon-dioxide-equivalent doubling and a damage of 1.33 percent of GDP for that level. This damage does not consider even the 2 percent high case applied in NORD1. Nor does it consider upper-bound warming (climate sensitivity Λ = 4.5°C). If the DICE damage function is applied to upper-bound warming, all damages are 2.25 times as high (= $[4.5/3.0]^2$). If Nordhaus's earlier high-damage case of 2 percent of GDP is considered in conjunction with upper-bound warming, all damages are 3.4 times as high (= $[2.0/1.33] \times 2.25$).

---

1. However, the study does not report cutbacks and carbon taxes for subsequent years, or more than two-thirds of the horizon.

Second, the specification of transient (i.e., actual time-dependent) warming as the consequence of specified atmospheric concentration of carbon-dioxide-equivalent may yield an understatement of warming. Thus, in the DICE baseline, global warming is only 3°C by the year 2100, whereas the IPCC (1990b, figure 6.11) places realized baseline warming by that year at 4.2°C (despite a lower climate sensitivity, $\Lambda = 2.5°C$). The DICE model's 50-year thermal lag may be overstated.[2]

Third, whereas the abatement cost function seems reasonable for cutbacks of 50 percent from baseline (about 1 percent of GDP), for the very high cutbacks that are eventually required for stiff emissions limits the function may overstate costs. Thus, at a 90 percent cutback, abatement costs amount to almost 7 percent of GDP. This level is far above the 2½ percent plateau identified in the present study. One reason is that the overall cost curve is linear in percentage cutback in the present study, and the degree of nonlinearity in the DICE formulation may be overstated. Another reason is that the DICE cost curve makes no allowance for declining cost over time with widening technological alternatives, in contrast to the treatment here.[3]

Fourth, the DICE model applies not only a logarithmic utility function, which is an implicit means of discounting future income by the growth rate of per capita income (as demonstrated in chapter 6 of this study), but in addition it applies a 3 percent discount rate for "pure" time preference (i.e., myopia, which means discounting even at unchanged per capita income). The net result is much higher discounting than in the methodology applied here. Curiously, whereas the earlier steady-state analysis contained sensitivity analysis with the pure rate of time preference equal to zero (Nordhaus 1991a, 927), the DICE results reported in Nordhaus (1992a) do not.

In sum, the reformulated Nordhaus analysis might be considerably more consistent with the results found here if the DICE model were further extended for risk aversion with attention to upper-bound warming; declining abatement costs with wider technological choice over time; shorter thermal lag; and elimination of the myopia component of discounting. Even as formulated, the model

---

2. Note further that DICE continues the ambiguity of NORD1 with respect to whether the atmospheric stock M is total greenhouse gas or merely the anthropogenic component. Its value is set at 677 GtC for 1965 (Nordhaus 1992b, 21), whereas anthropogenic carbon-equivalent in the atmosphere today is only about 150 GtC for carbon dioxide and, say, 200 GtC for total greenhouse gases. The atmospheric buildup equation (Nordhaus 1992b, 21) yields the curiosity that, if emissions cease immediately, total atmospheric stock falls to its preindustrial level within about 25 years. If emissions remain at zero, within a century the atmospheric stock of carbon dioxide is down to nearly half its natural level. As this instance suggests, the model's parameters would seem appropriately subject to revision.

3. Note further that the DICE model makes no allowance for "free" emissions reductions from a move to best practices, or for low-cost forestry measures.

contains some disturbing implications. As developed in chapter 2 of this study, baseline warming may be expected to be approximately linear in time under business as usual. Even with just 3°C warming by 2100, the DICE model thus implies warming of about 9°C by 2300, similar to the very-long-term warming of 10°C identified in the present study. The model's damage function would generate annual losses of 12 percent of GDP for this much warming (and an implied 27 percent of GDP for $\Lambda = 4.5$°C).

Overall, the DICE model would seem to hold promise for policy guidance, although parameter values in its initial application would seem to lead to an understatement of optimal abatement.

Annex 7B

The Manne-Richels Model of Greenhouse Insurance

Manne and Richels (1990b) have attempted an indirect measurement of the merits of policy action to avoid the greenhouse effect. Their approach incorporates in-depth estimates on the cost side of carbon restraints, based on their Global 2100 carbon-energy-economic model. However, on the benefits side, instead of a continuum of warming damages avoided, they apply a dichotomy between two outcomes: a catastrophe that must be avoided at all cost, on the one hand, or a mild annoyance that may safely be permitted to run its course, on the other.

Their initial example considers the merits of a "learn, then act" strategy. They examine a two-period horizon where fraction x of cutback is taken in the first and $1 - x$ in the second (if necessary). The initial probability of catastrophe is denoted p. By the end of the first period, science knows for sure whether the catastrophic threat is real. If it is, the rest of the action is undertaken; otherwise, no further action is required. With a cost function that rises with the square of action, expected cost is $C = 0.5x^2 + 0.5p(1 - x)^2$ and optimal $x = p/(1 + p)$.[1] Thus, if the chances of catastrophe are 50-50, the optimal hedge is to commit 33 percent (0.5/1.5) of the required reduction in the near term and 67 percent later, if necessary. With optimal $x = 0.33$, expected cost is $C = 0.167$. If the catastrophe were known for certain, it would be optimal simply to do half of the adjustment in the first period and half in the second ($x = 0.5$), in which case $C = 0.125$. The value of perfect information is thus 25 percent of total cost. The simple initial model thus provides two lessons. First, if there is any uncertainty at all, it pays to do less early and (contingently) more later. Second, there is value to information.

The authors then adopt a threefold world: greenhouse warming is harmless (case A); it is sufficiently serious to warrant a 20 percent cutback in carbon emissions from the 1990 level (case B); or it is so serious that the cutback should be 50 percent from that level (case C).

Manne and Richels allow 30 years to find out which state of the world is true. In 2020, policymakers either make up the shortfall of needed carbon dioxide cutbacks (case B or C is true) or eliminate restraints (case A is true). In case A, US emissions rise to nearly 3 billion tons of carbon annually by 2050; in case C, they are cut from their current 1.25 billion tons to 0.62 billion. In a

---

1. Cost is minimized at $dC/dx = 0$, or $x - p(1 - x) = 0$. Rearranging, $x + px = p$, $x(1 + p) = p$, and $x = p/(1 + p)$.

hedged "act first" approach, emissions rise only slightly through 2020, then diverge depending on whether case A, B, or C is true.

The authors calculate the value of improved information by considering how much cost could be saved through earlier knowledge of the true state (A, B, or C). If the probability of A is 60 percent, that of B 27 percent, and that of C 13 percent, in the extreme the savings from complete certainty by the first year in the forecast (2000) amount to $90 billion based on the Global 2100 model (discounting at 5 percent). This savings arises from being able to avoid the abrupt shifts from a hedged emissions path to the ideal one at the end of 30 years of research. Under either case B or case C, the long-term tax on carbon is $250 per ton, but there is a temporary bulge of taxes up to $500 per ton if case C is true and the strategy does not achieve cost-smoothing through improved information.

Manne and Richels then explore the value of information under alternative assumptions. One key influence is the probability of case A (that global warming is no problem). The value of perfect information peaks at $90 billion if this probability is 60 percent, but is only $20 billion if it is 5 percent and $30 billion if it is 95 percent. That is, if it is highly likely that something will have to be done about the greenhouse effect, there is less value in delaying for purposes of further confirmation; and if it is highly likely that the greenhouse effect is no problem, the initial hedged strategy without further information will not be far different from business as usual (so that a complete shift to business as usual would provide only limited gains). Hence the authors' third lesson: information is worth less if the probability is high that the greenhouse effect is either very severe or very mild, essentially because the proper action in each case is obvious and needs little further investment in information.

The value of information also depends on the likelihood that the new information is accurate (lesson four). If there are two chances in five of the research being incorrect, the value of information drops from a maximum of $90 billion to only $10 billion. Technology optimism also matters (lesson five). If future availability of low-cost nonrenewable energy (e.g., biomass) is twice the base-case assumption (10 quads annually rather than 5) and the autonomous energy efficiency increase twice as high (1 percent annually rather than 0.5 percent), the maximum value of perfect information falls from $90 billion to $45 billion. That is, if one expects it to be easy to dispense with fossil fuels, the cost of reducing carbon emissions will be low, so that savings from avoiding abrupt future cutbacks through improved knowledge will also be low. Conversely, if these two technology changes are pessimistically set at zero, perfect information value rises to nearly $150 billion (for p in the range of 60 percent).

The key policy conclusion of Manne and Richels (1990b, 25) is that "there can be a big payoff to reducing climate-related uncertainties—something of the order of $100 billion for the U.S. alone." However, this conclusion appears somewhat exaggerated even in terms of the model itself. Probabilities of only about 20 percent for case A and 40 percent each for cases B and C would seem to be a distribution more in keeping with the findings of the Intergovernmental Panel on Climate Change (1990a). This assessment sharply reduces the value of waiting for more information. Technology optimists would further cut these gains, as just discussed (note that the Global 2100 model does not include the initial range of zero-cost improvements suggested by the engineering estimates; see chapter 5 above). Furthermore, the model does not provide a persuasive bridge from the maximum value of perfect information available immediately to a plausible value related to how much we will know and by when.

More fundamentally, the structure of the exercise, although conceptually illuminating, seems inadequate to the task. A threefold classification is insufficient for evaluating the size of warming damage. The idea of waiting 30 years while additional research is carried out also seems questionable, especially if policymakers erroneously interpret the authors as saying there need be no action in the interim (instead, even their second-best strategy is the fixed hedge based on *a priori* probabilities, with considerably less emissions than under business as usual). In the absence of action, carbon-dioxide-equivalent doubling is likely to occur by 2025 (chapter 1).

Overall, the Manne-Richels insurance analysis is an important qualitative reminder that there is a value to obtaining further scientific information before embarking on draconian measures. However, its specific quantitative estimates may be misleading. In particular, the economic damages from delaying action too long could be much larger than the Manne-Richels waiting period of 30 years would imply, as suggested in the illustrative calculation in the main text of this chapter.

8

Toward an International Policy Strategy

8

Toward an International Policy Strategy

International efforts toward action on the greenhouse problem had moved much further by early 1992 than most scientists, economists, and policymakers would have predicted five years earlier. There was a significant chance of a meaningful framework agreement on global warming by the time of the June 1992 United Nations Conference on Environment and Development (UNCED), or "Earth Summit," in Rio de Janeiro. Whatever the outcome of that landmark event, however, there were likely to be strong, persistent characteristics of the problem that would somehow have to be dealt with in the following years. This concluding chapter outlines these policy features, reviews the positions of the major players, and proposes a strategy for action. This "contingent" policy strategy envisions a milder, more voluntary regime in an initial decade as further scientific confirmation is obtained; the regime would move to a much more forceful stage after such confirmation.

The analysis of chapter 7 suggests that it is desirable on economic grounds to pursue a global policy of aggressive abatement of greenhouse gas emissions from levels they would otherwise reach. Many issues must be addressed if such a policy is to become a reality. The principal questions include how international cooperation can be attained when each country individually has an incentive to let the others bear the abatement burden; how equity can be incorporated to take account of different income levels and growth needs among countries; what the interrelationship between policy action and the evolution of scientific certainty should be; what instruments (e.g., taxes, quotas, tradeable permits) should be applied; what role can be played by related areas of policy such as that on population growth; what approaches can stimulate technological advances on alternative energy sources; how energy uses can be moved closer to the existing "best practice" frontier; what role should be played by forestry measures; how far adaptation can go as an alternative to abatement; and what the potential scope is for a resolution of the problem through "geoengineering." It is also necessary to address the broader conceptual framework by placing the problem of global warming in its historical context of North-South negotiations and considering the recurrent theme of "limits to growth" and the more recent emphasis on "sustainable development." This chapter first explores these issues and reviews the state of play in policy on global warming for the major countries. It then presents a proposed timetable and strategy for policy action under uncertainty.

Overarching Issues

Before turning to the individual aspects of a policy strategy, it is appropriate to seek additional perspective on the significance of the preceding analysis and its implications for action.

First, it is reasonable to ask whether any policy can be based on a 300-year horizon. Looking backward, we may ask what could American colonists in the year 1690 have divined about today's world? Would they have been willing to pay a price to avoid environmental damage for the present generation?

It is important to distinguish between the near inevitability of certain long-term physical phenomena, on the one hand, and the unpredictability of much human activity, on the other. Thus, one can confidently predict the positions of the planets thousands of years into the future, but not elections, political systems, or technology. Global warming has attributes of both human unpredictability and natural predictability. The central consideration is simply that the largest damage from global warming arises over the very long term, and the issue cannot be properly analyzed if these effects are ignored. For policy purposes, it is appropriate to highlight the argument developed below about technical change. There is no reason to assume that technological change will reduce the prospective damages from global warming by more than it will reduce the costs of avoiding the greenhouse effect; cautious policymakers should not count on pleasant surprises; and inaction can fail to send the right price signal.

The intergenerational issue is at least equally thorny. If people will be richer in the future than today, why pay anything at all to avoid damage to them? One reason is that a relatively small price today might purchase avoidance of enormous damage in the distant future. If so, it could be attractive to a public mindful of its descendants even if the future population would remain better off than the present despite the prospective future losses. Another is that there is no guarantee that people *will* be better off in the future than today. The sorry history of economic retrogression in Africa and much of Latin America in the last decade, and even the failure of real wages to rise in the United States in the last twenty years, are reminders that progress is not inevitable.

With respect to both predictability and concern about future generations, it may well be that differing cultural histories yield divergent views. Europeans daily pass cathedrals built almost a millenium ago, not just 300 years. The experience of the United States is far shorter. The difference could help explain the divergence of positions between the United States amd most European countries on the greenhouse issue to date.

Second, it should be emphasized that the analyis of this study is conservative on the side of benefits in at least one dimension. The central calculations do not take credit for various spillover benefits that could arise from action on global warming. The case of reduced pollution has been discussed, and a rough estimate ventured but not included in the central benefits measurement. Other beneficial side effects have been wholly omitted, such as the opportunity provided by a carbon user fee to address important problems. For the United States, these include infrastructure decay and the burden placed on future generations by the persistent and large US fiscal deficit. The analysis seeks to be austere to avoid undue attribution of gains to action on the greenhouse problem, but these spillovers are present, as the US administration's "no regrets" policy (adopting measures desirable in their own right that also have antigreenhouse effects) recognizes.

Achieving Cooperation

The Free-Rider Problem

Many economists have emphasized the difficulty of international negotiations on global warming caused by the "free-rider problem," in which the individual country has an incentive to take advantage of the benefits of carbon abatement by other nations without bearing the cost of restricting its own emissions.

The classic illustration of the problem of noncooperation is the game of "prisoners' dilemma," in which there is a perverse incentive to an individual actor caused by uncertainty about whether other actors will cooperate. Suppose that two guilty suspects are under interrogation in separate cells. There is a heavy penalty for lying. If the two could communicate, they would both deny the crime and face intermediate sentences (three years, southeast quadrant in figure 8.1) because the evidence against them is merely circumstantial. If both confess, the crime is unequivocal and both receive heavier sentences (five years, northwest). In isolation, each prisoner has an incentive (perverse, from the suspects' viewpoint) to confess. Thus, prisoner A reasons that he is better off to confess whatever B does. If B confesses, A gets a sentence of either five years (northwest) for confessing or ten years for lying and being discovered (southwest). If B does not confess, A gets a light sentence of one year as a reward for cooperating if he confesses (northeast) or the intermediate sentence of three years if he does

Figure 8.1 Prisoners' dilemma: payoff matrix[a]

B

	Confess	Not Confess
Confess	−5, −5	−1, −10
Not Confess	−10, −1	−3, −3

A

a. The first number in each cell reports the payoff for prisoner A (e.g., −1 = a one-year jail sentence), the second for prisoner B.

not confess (southeast). The same incentive to confess whatever A does applies to B's decisions. The point of the game is that noncooperation leads to a suboptimal result from the players' perspective: each prisoner concludes that his safest bet is to confess (northwest).

The same principle of suboptimal action in the absence of cooperation may be seen for global warming abatement in the first panel of figure 8.2. For an individual country, the long-term cost of reducing carbon emissions from baseline (as a percentage of GDP) is shown by curve CC. If no other country takes action, the benefits for the country (the value of greenhouse damage avoided) are shown by curve $B_0 B_0$. If other countries take comparable action, there is a much greater reduction in greenhouse damage, and the benefit curve shifts upward to $B_1 B_1$. In the cooperative case, the equilibrium is at x, with a cutback of z_1 percent. If the country expects its actions to be solely unilateral, the benefit

Figure 8.2   Benefits and costs of abatement of greenhouse warming with and without free riding

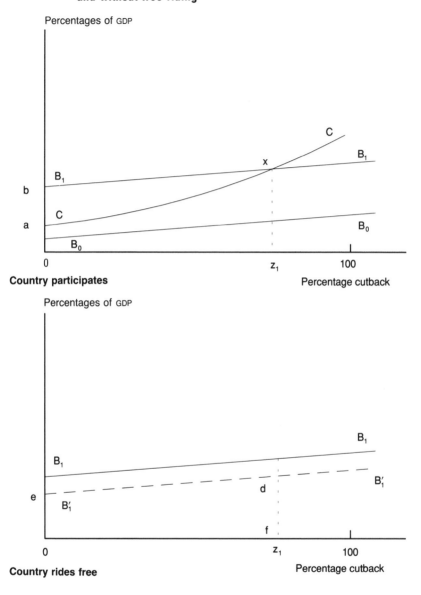

Percentages of GDP

B_1

b

C

a

B_0

C

x

B_1

B_0

0

z_1

100

Country participates

Percentage cutback

Percentages of GDP

B_1

B_1

B_1'

e

B_1'

d

f

0

z_1

100

Country rides free

Percentage cutback

curve lies wholly underneath the cost curve, and it is optimal to take no action at all.[1]

The second panel of figure 8.2 shows the incentive to free-ride. If the country does not undertake abatement, the benefit curve facing the country falls only slightly as long as all other countries pursue abatement: from B_1B_1 to $B_1'B_1'$. The country in question now has zero costs. If it can get away with inaction while other countries continue to cut back emissions by proportion z_1, the country's net benefits will rise from the area abx (under participation, first panel) to the much larger area $0edf$ under free-riding (second panel).

Schelling (1983, 477–81) has emphasized the severity of the free-rider (or prisoners' dilemma) problem of noncooperation in dealing with global warming:

> [A]ny single nation that imposes on its consumers the cost of further fuel restrictions shares the benefits globally and bears the costs internally. . . . Some global rationing scheme . . . would be required if there were to be severe action. . . . In the current state of affairs the likelihood is negligible that the three great possessors of the world's known coal reserves—the Soviet Union, the People's Republic of China, and the United States of America—will consort on an equitable and durable program for restricting the use of fossil fuels through the coming century and successfully negotiate it with the world's producers of petroleum and with the fuel-importing countries, developed and developing.

Despite this theoretical expectation, actual recent experience has shown considerable willingness of individual industrial countries to move ahead toward carbon emissions abatement despite the absence of generalized international participation. As outlined below, the European Community, Japan, Canada, Australia, New Zealand, Finland, Norway, Sweden, and Switzerland have all made commitments of varying degrees to restrain carbon emissions (Schmidt 1991). This list of countries accounts for 22 percent of present emissions of carbon dioxide, excluding that from deforestation (table 8.1).

One reason for the seeming willingness of some countries to move ahead despite the free-rider problem is that there is scope for international cooperation, especially over time. The prisoners' dilemma illustrates the costs of noncooperation, but it is an extreme "game" because cooperation is not only uncertain, it is ruled out. The free-rider incentive illustrated in the second panel of figure 8.2 can in principle be overcome by negotiation in which each party insists on "reciprocity": the individual country is essentially put on notice that it cannot

---

1. Abatement of global warming thus has the properties of a public good like, for example, the national anthem. Country i can enjoy the benefits of global abatement without reducing the amount of such benefits available to country j. For a public good, the optimum equilibrium occurs where the vertical summation of the individual actors' benefit (or "demand") curves intersects with their representative individual cost ("supply") curve.

expect to enjoy the large net gains of free-riding, because if it does not participate, neither will the other countries.

This process of negotiation for reciprocity is familiar from international trade negotiations, where the most-favored-nation principle (which extends tariff cuts to all parties) has long dominated despite its risk of free-riding. The feasibility of overcoming the free-rider problem through negotiation depends in part on the number of principal actors. Just as industrial concentration favors cooperative (collusive) action among producers, concentration of economies by size (and emissions) should facilitate credible negotiations. As Barrett (1989) argues, the smaller the number of actors, the greater the chances for a stable international economic agreement, because "the larger is the effect of exit by any signatory on the abatement level of the remaining cooperators."[2] Thus, he argues, the greater the risk to the exiting country that it will not be able to gain the benefits of abatement from the remaining adherents because of a collapse of the agreement.

Fortunately for global warming action, the distribution of carbon emissions is relatively concentrated among countries. As indicated in table 8.1, the 10 largest emitters of carbon dioxide account for 70 percent of the world total, and the 25 largest account for 87 percent. The special problems raised by the major role of developing countries and the former Soviet Union among these principal actors are discussed below.

Two additional factors seem to account for the readiness of some industrial countries to act without universal agreement. First, the political salience of the environmental movement tends to be high in Europe, in part because of the past adverse experience with local pollution and acid rain. In this context, there may be a higher sensitivity to "doing the right thing" than in some other countries, and a greater influence of the notion of a fiduciary responsibility to future generations (Weiss 1989, Brown 1991) regardless of the more narrow benefit-cost calculations. Second, at least in the case of the European Community, there appears to be a sense that Europe's sway is on the rise (most manifestly in the movement toward monetary and political union as well as geographical expansion) and that the Community's influence can eventually be brought to bear to bring the United States and the former Soviet Union along in a broader abatement program. This factor essentially represents a complication of the free-rider game into one with repeat sessions with learning. That is, the European Community seems to be betting that in future negotiations it can alter

---

2. Barrett (1989) has combined a standard game-theoretic model of abatement with recent theory on cartel stability to analyze the prospects for international economic agreements. He emphasizes that the smaller the number of parties, the greater the chance of a stable agreement. Ironically, because his analysis simplifies to treat all countries as being of identical size, he reaches the opposite conclusion: an agreement on global warming abatement will be extremely difficult to reach.

Table 8.1 The top 50 carbon-emitting countries

	Carbon dioxide emissions (millions of tons of carbon-equivalent)			Economic indicators		Emissions performance				
	Fossil fuels	Land use change	Total emissions	1989 population (thousands)	1989 GNP per capita	Share of world emissions (percentages) A	Share of world population (percentages) B	Share of world GNP (percentages) C	A/B	A/C
United States	1,222	5	1,227	248,800	20,690	17.52	4.78	25.74	3.67	0.68
Soviet Union	1,034	0	1,034	282,830	7,545[a.d]	14.77	5.43	10.67	2.72	1.38
European Community	786	0	786	342,489	13,294	11.22	6.58	22.76	1.71	0.49
China	596	0	596	1,113,900	1,153[d]	8.52	21.40	6.42	0.40	1.33
Brazil	54	390	444	147,300	4,409[d]	6.34	2.83	3.25	2.24	1.95
India	155	118	273	832,500	980	3.89	15.99	4.08	0.24	0.95
Japan	248	0	248	123,100	15,710	3.54	2.36	9.67	1.50	0.37
Indonesia	35	185	220	178,200	1,468[d]	3.14	3.42	1.31	0.92	2.40
Myanmar (Burma)	1	126	128	40,000	984[b.d]	1.82	0.77	0.20	2.37	9.26
Poland	129	0	129	37,900	4,980	1.84	0.73	0.94	2.53	1.95
Colombia	14	101	115	32,300	2,655[d]	1.64	0.62	0.43	2.64	3.83
Canada	110	0	110	26,200	19,230	1.57	0.50	2.52	3.13	0.62
Mexico	82	27	109	84,600	3,763[d]	1.55	1.63	1.59	0.95	0.97
Thailand	16	79	95	55,400	4,190	1.35	1.06	1.16	1.27	1.16
Cote d'Ivoire	1	84	85	11,700	1,700	1.22	0.22	0.10	5.43	12.28
South Africa	78	0	78	35,000	4,327[d]	1.11	0.67	0.76	1.66	1.47
Laos	0	71	72	4,100	735[d]	1.02	0.08	0.02	12.97	67.79
Philippines	10	57	67	60,000	2,280	0.96	1.15	0.68	0.83	1.40
Nigeria	16	49	64	113,800	1,290	0.92	2.19	0.73	0.42	1.25
Czechoslovakia	66	0	66	15,600	5,425[d]	0.94	0.30	0.42	3.13	2.21
Australia	65	0	65	16,800	14,290	0.92	0.32	1.20	2.86	0.77
Romania	58	0	58	23,200	6,083[a.d]	0.83	0.45	0.71	1.87	1.18
Vietnam	5	49	54	64,800	n.a.	0.77	1.24	0.00	0.62	n.a.
Korea (South)	48	0	48	42,400	6,720	0.68	0.81	1.42	0.84	0.48
Peru	6	38	44	21,200	2,362	0.63	0.41	0.25	1.55	2.53
Malaysia	11	32	43	17,400	3,951[d]	0.62	0.33	0.34	1.85	1.80
Venezuela	26	15	41	19,200	4,303[d]	0.59	0.37	0.41	1.59	1.42
Korea (North)	40	0	40	20,600	n.a.	0.57	0.40	0.00	1.44	n.a.
Iran	40	0	40	53,300	4,430	0.57	1.02	1.18	0.55	0.48
Ecuador	4	33	37	10,300	2,378[d]	0.53	0.20	0.12	2.67	4.31

Country				GDP per capita					
Turkey	37	0	37	55,000	4,610	0.53	1.06	1.27	0.50	0.42
Yugoslavia	34	0	34	23,700	2,920	0.49	0.46	0.35	1.08	1.42
Bulgaria	34	29	34	9,000	5,320	0.48	0.17	0.24	2.78	2.01
Zaire	1	29	30	34,500	943[d]	0.43	0.66	0.16	0.66	2.67
Cameroon	2	0	30	11,600	2,070	0.43	0.22	0.12	1.94	3.59
Argentina	30	23	30	31,900	3,951[d]	0.43	0.61	0.63	0.70	0.68
Sudan	1	0	24	24,500	1,428[d]	0.34	0.47	0.17	0.72	1.93
Hungary	21	0	21	10,621	6,200	0.30	0.20	0.33	1.46	0.91
Egypt	21	0	21	51,000	3,160	0.29	0.98	0.81	0.30	0.36
Madagascar	0	19	20	11,300	700	0.28	0.22	0.04	1.29	7.07
Algeria	19	0	19	24,400	4,038[d]	0.28	0.47	0.49	0.59	0.56
Saudi Arabia	18	0	18	14,400	7,907[d]	0.25	0.28	0.57	0.90	0.44
Nicaragua	1	14	15	3,504	2,018[c,d]	0.21	0.07	0.04	3.16	6.01
Sweden	15	0	15	8,500	15,670	0.22	0.16	0.67	1.35	0.33
Pakistan	15	1	15	109,900	1,700	0.22	2.11	0.93	0.10	0.23
Finland	0	0	15	15,230	15,230	0.21	0.10	0.38	2.18	0.55
Malawi	14	13	14	8,200	660	0.19	0.16	0.03	1.23	7.18
United Arab Emirates	1	0	14	1,500	16,859[d]	0.20	0.03	0.13	6.96	1.59
Costa Rica	13	13	13	2,700	3,466[b,d]	0.19	0.05	0.05	3.68	4.07
Iraq		0	13	17,600	5,232[b,d]	0.19	0.34	0.46	0.56	0.41
Subtotal	5,244	1,600	6,844	4,533,744		97.77	87.09		1.12	
Others	456	0	156	672,356		2.23	12.91		0.17	
World	5,700	1,600	7,000	5,206,100		100.00	100.00		1.00	

ICP = (United Nations) International Comparison program; n.a. = not available.

a. GNP estimate is that of PlanEcon; population is from World Bank, *World Development Report*, 1990, 1991.

b. 1988 GDP from International Monetary Fund, *International Financial Statistics*; population from World Bank, *World Development Report* 1990, 1991.

c. 1987 GNP from World Bank, *World Debt Tables*, 1991.

d. ICP estimates of per capita GDP from the equation $\ln(\text{ICP}) = 3.085925 + (0.676735 \times \ln[\text{GDP per capital}])$.

Sources: data on carbon dioxide emissions from World Resources Institute, *World Resources 1990–91*, table 24-1; population and GNP from World Bank, *World Development Report 1990, 1991*, tables 1 and 30, except where noted. World Resources Institute and World Bank data reprinted with permission.

the position of the United States and, eventually, other reluctant nations, by being willing to move ahead without these countries during a first round.

Overall, there are grounds for some optimism that the free-rider problem can be overcome. Its most difficult aspect is likely to be its interaction with the problem of equity, in regard to burden sharing by developing and Eastern European countries and the former Soviet Union.

Winners Versus Losers?

The obstacles to international agreement would be much more severe if an important class of countries clearly stood to gain from global warming. In that case, they might not only refrain from supporting a program of action, but actively oppose it. However, instances of "winners" from the greenhouse effect would be few and highly uncertain. Thus, under benchmark $2 \times CO_2$ warming the agricultural effects would tend to be positive in only a few high-latitude countries (Iceland, Denmark, Finland); effects are expected to be unfavorable even in Canada and neutral in the Soviet Union (table 3.3). High-latitude countries that gain on agriculture would still participate in losses in other areas, such as species extinction. Even some of the winners could turn into losers under the much more extreme climate changes associated with very-long-term warming. The risk of catastrophe and the high degree of uncertainty in the estimates of regional effects further reduce the likelihood that a substantial class of countries would see it in their own interests to facilitate, rather than impede, global warming.

The regional pattern of global warming is expected to be related to latitude. The closer to the poles, the greater the warming is expected to be. Table 8.2 summarizes projected warming for major areas on the basis of calculations by three general circulation models for a doubling of carbon dioxide. Gauged by the amount of warming, the industrial and socialist countries appear to be more affected than the developing countries. The reason is that land masses in the developing areas tend to be closer to the tropics, where the least warming occurs.

However, there are other major influences that would tend to make damages from global warming relatively greater in developing countries than in industrial countries. The much larger share of agriculture in the economy is one factor. Another is the likelihood of lesser adaptability in lower-income economies, where the capacity for response through new investment and technological

---

3. The estimates are derived from figures 2.5 through 2.8, chapter 2.

Table 8.2 Mean temperature increase under carbon-dioxide-equivalent doubling, various countries and regions (degrees Celsius)

	Winter	Summer	Average
United States			
North	6.2	3.7	5.0
South	3.9	1.9	2.9
West	3.3	3.0	3.1
Alaska	3.5	3.0	3.3
Canada			
North	5.1	2.5	3.8
South	4.3	4.0	4.1
Former Soviet Union			
European	4.8	3.7	4.2
Asia-North	6.7	3.5	5.1
Asia-South	5.3	4.8	5.1
Japan	3.5	1.0	2.3
Western Europe	2.4	3.1	2.7
Scandinavia, Greenland	5.0	3.1	4.1
Australia, New Zealand	0.5	0.6	0.5
Central America, Mexico	0.5	0.5	0.5
South America			
Tropical	0.0	0.3	0.2
Temperate	0.9	1.1	1.0
Africa			
Sahara	1.4	1.5	1.5
Sub-Sahara	1.8	0.2	1.0
Middle East	0.9	3.2	2.0
Southeast Asia	1.6	1.9	1.8
Philippines, Indonesia	0.4	0.5	0.5
China	3.8	2.7	3.3

Sources: Figures 2.5 to 2.8, this volume.

change is relatively weak.[4] Third, the incidence of damage from sea-level rise is likely to be relatively high among developing countries. The case of Bangladesh is the best known, but the list of the 50 countries or territories expected to suffer the most severe damage from sea-level rise contains 49 from the developing world and only one (New Zealand) from the developed (chapter 3, table 3.3).

For these reasons, geographical concentration toward the lower latitudes would seem insufficient reason for the developing countries to be substantially less affected by global warming than industrial countries would be. Correspondingly, there is little cause on the side of prospective damages for the developing countries to be disinterested in international action.

In another dimension, there would be a significant class of prospective winners from global warming, or at least from the avoidance of international action to arrest warming. Countries that are heavily dependent on the production and export of fossil fuels would stand to lose from international carbon abatement. The issues affecting these countries are addressed below.

---

4. An ameliorating factor is that the rate of growth of the stock of plant and equipment should be higher than in industrial countries, so that a larger share of the capital stock can be altered annually.

Overall, divergence between winners and losers should pose little difficulty for the development of international abatement action, because few, if any, countries could be assured that they would enjoy actual gains from global warming, and most would be exposed to the risk of damage.

Uncertainty and the Adaptation Alternative

As discussed below, in 1990–91 the official US position was that there was too much scientific uncertainty about the greenhouse effect to warrant costly measures to reduce emissions of carbon dioxide or other trace gases.[5] A closely related position, emphasized by a majority of members of a special review panel on adaptation in the study of global warming by the National Academy of Sciences (NAS 1991b), held that the principal response to global warming, if it occurred, should be the adaptation of agricultural practices and other aspects of economic life.

In mid-1990 the Intergovernmental Panel on Climate Change (IPCC) issued an extensive report that provided authoritative support for the science of the greenhouse effect (IPCC 1990b). Written by some 170 scientists from 25 countries and reviewed by another 200 scientists, the report endorsed a range of 1.5°C to 4.5°C for equilibrium warming from the doubling of carbon-dioxide-equivalent, with a "best guess" of 2.5°C (see chapter 1 of this study). The report rejected several critiques of a vocal minority of scientists who disputed the theory (Kerr 1990).

Uncertainty nonetheless remains, particularly about the extent of warming in the very long term (chapter 2), the severity of economic damage associated with a given amount of warming (chapter 3), and the regional incidence of warming effects. There is a high value to increased information to clarify these issues (chapter 7, annex 7B). The presence of uncertainty can actually favor more aggressive action if policymakers are risk averse, because of the greater possibility of severe damage as opposed to the best-guess case.

The policy strategy suggested in this study deals with the uncertainty issue by dividing action into two phases. As outlined below, the first phase, lasting perhaps a decade, would stress research to narrow the scientific (and economic) uncertainties. Nonetheless, in this phase there would also be institution building and moderate initial abatement measures, to lay the groundwork for more

---

5. Thus, the Council of Economic Advisers concluded: "The highest priority in the near term should be to improve understanding in order to build a foundation for sound policy decisions. Until such a foundation is in place, there is no justification for imposing major costs on the economy in order to slow the growth of greenhouse gas emissions." (*Economic Report of the President*, February 1990, 223).

aggressive action in a second phase, contingent on the findings of research in the first phase.

For its part, the adaptation argument provides little basis for inaction on abatement. The NAS report of mid-1991 stirred considerable controversy among its panel members over the dominant complacent tone—"a virtual paean to human adaptability . . . [which] concludes that both the speed of innovation and the turnover rate of capital investments . . . are faster than the projected rate of climate change" (Roberts 1991b, 1206). Among the more provocative findings of the report was the statement that "People in the United States will have no more difficulty adapting to such future changes than to the most severe conditions in the past, such as the Dust Bowl" (NAS 1991a, 45).

Quite apart from the question of whether the American public would prefer to accept a permanent Dust Bowl or instead take measures to lessen its chances of occurring, the finding raised dissent from one panel member on grounds that it assumed "gradual change, no surprises" and did not "examine the resulting impacts of severe ecosystem disruption on human societies" (NAS 1991a, 45).

There are two fundamental points to recognize about adaptation. First, it is not cost free. If agronomists are occupied designing new varieties of crops to withstand heat stress and drought, they will have less time to develop new varieties that have other favorable features. There will be more running just to stay in place rather than to move ahead. Second, a large contribution from adaptation will be essential even in combination with aggressive abatement action. As outlined in chapters 2 and 3, in the very long term, global warming is likely to reach 10°C in the absence of abatement; but it is also likely to reach 2.5°C even *with* aggressive abatement measures. Considerable adaptation will be required just to deal with the unavoidable component of warming.

In short, there is good reason for skepticism about the view that adaptation alone will suffice. Despite the implications of its adaptation panel, the overall NAS study reached the same conclusion, and in April of 1991 its summary volume urged that "the United States should act promptly to reduce the threat of global warming" through such measures as "raising overall mileage standards for new automobiles . . . federal support for mass transit and reforestation, and developing a new generation of safe and efficient nuclear power plants" (*New York Times*, 11 April 1991, B12; NAS 1991a).

Technological Change

Another reason some would cite in favor of inaction is that technological change will solve the greenhouse problem. Chapters 2 and 3 suggest that, in the "base case," the truly severe damages from global warming can be expected not so much from benchmark carbon dioxide doubling but from much greater warming in the very long term. Some scholars (e.g., Schelling 1983, 453–54) would reply that the very-long-term horizon of 100 to 300 years is so distant that technical change will completely alter all of the calculations and, by implication, eliminate the problem.

Four points should be recognized about technical change.

First, it affects both the cost and the benefit sides of the calculus. If some dramatic technical breakthroughs (e.g., new agricultural varieties, genetic replication of species, miracle insulation materials) reduce the damages of warming and therefore the benefits of abatement, other changes are likely to reduce the costs of abatement. For example, the cost models of chapter 5 make no allowance for nuclear fusion (where an important breakthrough occurred in 1991; Broad 1991) or hydrogen fuel from solar energy (Ogden and Williams 1989) becoming available. There is no presumption that technical change will reduce the benefits of warming avoidance by more than it will reduce the costs of abatement.

Second, technical change is affected by price signals. If there is no such policy signal for the reduction of carbon emissions, the pace of carbon-saving technical change is likely to be slower.

Third, technical change takes time, and time is not on society's side. The IPCC central case is that, under business as usual, the planet will be committed to 5.7°C warming by the year 2100 (IPCC 1991b, 191, figure 6.11). As analyzed in chapter 2, each decade of delay for the arrival of a technological *deus ex machina* costs on the order of .25°C to .5°C in warming that might otherwise be avoided.

Fourth, policymakers should be risk averse. Counting on a technological pleasant surprise to resolve the greenhouse problem is risk-prone rather than risk-averse behavior.

Developing-Country Participation

A crucial question for international cooperation on global warming is whether the developing countries will participate in restraints on the growth of emissions of carbon dioxide and other greenhouse gases. Some argue that, because the industrial countries have been the main emitters in the past, and because developing countries are too poor to undertake the additional burden of carbon restraints, the developing nations must be exempt from any such restrictions.

Although only about 30 percent of nondeforestation carbon dioxide emissions today are from developing countries (excluding Eastern Europe and the former Soviet Union), projections of future emissions show that developing countries are likely to play a massive role in expansion and that any program that exempted their increased emissions would amount to a failure to limit global emissions. Moreover, even today the developing countries account for 40 percent

Table 8.3 Future carbon emissions, excluding deforestation, by region
(GtC except where noted)

Model	Region	1990 GtC	1990 Percentage of total	2100 GtC	2100 Percentage of total	2250 GtC	2250 Percentage of total
Manne-Richels	US	1.25		4.04		n.a.	
	Other OECD	1.31		4.30		n.a.	
	SUEE	1.48		3.23		n.a.	
	Subtotal	4.04	70.9	11.57	43.0	n.a.	
	China	0.63		5.92		n.a.	
	Rest of world	1.03		9.42		n.a.	
	Subtotal	1.66	29.1	15.36	57.1	n.a.	
	Total	5.70	100.0	26.90	100.0	n.a.	
IPCC[a]	US	1.25		2.7		n.a.	
	Other OECD	1.31		2.8		n.a.	
	SUEE	1.48		4.4		n.a.	
	Subtotal	4.04	70.9	9.9	45.6	n.a.	
	China	0.63		3.9		n.a.	
	Rest of world	1.03		7.9		n.a.	
	Subtotal	1.66	29.1	11.8	54.9	n.a.	
	Total	5.70	100.0	21.7	100.0	n.a.	
This study	OECD, SUEE	4.04	70.9	10.6	51.5	24.2	48.8
	Developing countries	1.66	29.1	10.0	48.5	25.4	51.2
	Total	5.7	100.0	20.6	100.0	49.6	100.0

OECD = Organization for Economic Cooperation and Development; SUEE = Soviet Union and Eastern Europe; IPCC = Intergovernmental Panel on Climate Change; GtC = gigatons of carbon; n.a. = not available.

a. Working Group III, chapter 2, table 8, figures 5 and 6; 1990 figures are based on the Manne-Richels estimate from IPCC; 2100 regional detail is based on shares in primary energy consumption.

of emissions if deforestation is included. Table 8.3 reports alternative estimates of carbon dioxide emissions from fossil fuels (i.e., excluding deforestation) by five broad country groupings. The most direct estimates are provided by Manne and Richels (1990c). Their projections indicate that the share of developing countries (China plus their Rest of World category) in global carbon dioxide emissions should rise from 29 percent today to 57 percent by 2100. The two alternative estimates are less direct but also show an increase of the developing-country share to half of global emissions or more.[6]

It is unambiguous that some limitation from baseline will be required in developing countries if global abatement is to occur. By the year 2100, carbon

---

6. The IPCC estimates are for the business-as-usual (or "2030 high") case, with average between low and high economic growth rates. The allocation by region shown in the table is based on shares in primary energy consumption and thus tends to understate the shares of China and the developing countries because of their relatively greater reliance on coal. The figures for this study allocate global emissions totals on a basis of world real GDP shares (at purchasing power parity exchange rates), as adjusted by the base period ratio of emissions share to GDP share.

emissions in these countries alone would be almost twice the entire global level today. What is less obvious is that the cutbacks from baseline have to be high for developing countries *relative* to the cutbacks by industrial countries. Let us suppose that the target is to limit global emissions to 4 billion tons of carbon (GtC). Suppose we identify λ as the ratio of the developing-country percentage cutback to the industrial-country percentage cutback, both expressed relative to baseline. Include the former Soviet Union and Eastern Europe in the industrial-country group. Then, if baseline emissions in 2100 are set at 21 GtC, the overall percentage cutback must be 81 percent. Suppose the industrial countries attempt to cut by 95 percent from baseline. Considering that the developing countries account for at least half of the projected emissions, it would be necessary for these countries to cut emissions from baseline by 67 percent to meet the global target (i.e., $67 \times 0.5 + 95 \times 0.5 = 81$). The ratio of the percentage cutback from baseline required of developing countries to that required of industrial countries, or λ, would thus have to be at least 0.7 (67/95).

As discussed below, there are good reasons to treat the timing and financing of abatement differently for industrial than for developing countries. In particular, it would be appropriate for an initial policy subject to scientific confirmation to concentrate on cutbacks by industrial, rather than developing, countries (aside from reducing deforestation, which does belong in the first phase). However, eventually developing countries will have to participate in restraints, or global abatement will fail.

It is important to recognize that this conclusion does not mean the absolute level of developing-country emissions (excluding emissions from deforestation) would have to fall from present-day levels. In the example given above, a 67 percent cut from baseline by the year 2100 would still leave developing-country carbon emissions at somewhat over 3 GtC, about double present levels.

Moreover, the scope for low-cost carbon reductions in developing countries appears especially large because of two related factors: relatively inefficient energy use today and the widespread presence of energy subsidies. Removal of subsidies would provide an improvement in efficiency (and thus a benefit to the developing economy rather than a burden) while at the same time reducing energy use and carbon emissions.

With respect to low present efficiency, Goldemberg et al. (1987, 74–83) have noted that per capita energy use in developing countries is approximately 0.9 kw, or about 40 percent of the level in Western Europe (2.3 kw per capita), even though per capita income in developing countries is less than one-tenth as high.[7] The authors calculate that if all developing countries attained living standards equal to those of industrial countries in the 1970s and did so using

---

7. Note, however, that the use of purchasing power parity GDP gives a higher ratio of per capita income to industrial-country levels.

the most energy-efficient technologies on the market today (in water heaters, light bulbs, cement plants, paper mills, fertilizer plants, and so forth), the resulting energy requirements would be only 1 kw per capita little higher than today. This dramatic scope for increased efficiency stems in considerable part from the low efficiency—about 0.4 kw per capita—of noncommercial energy presently in use (cattle dung, crop residue, wood). Development toward energy efficiency would involve a sharp reduction in the percentage of energy requirements allocated to residential use and thus permit a reallocation to industry.

The emissions data presented in table 8.1 shed further light on the issue of scope for carbon emissions reductions. They suggest major opportunities for cutbacks in emissions from fossil fuel energy in the former Soviet Union and Eastern Europe. Thus, for the 50 countries with individual detail, the median ratio of energy-based (i.e., nondeforestation) carbon emissions in tons per thousand dollars of purchasing power parity GDP is 0.19 for industrial countries and 0.13 for developing countries, but stands much higher at 0.50 for the former Soviet Union and Eastern Europe. The table also reveals that, although the developing countries' emissions are not particularly high for energy use when properly gauged against purchasing power parity GDP rather than nominal GDP, their emissions are disproportionately high once deforestation is included. Deforestation emissions are negligible in industrial countries and in the former Soviet Union and Eastern Europe, but for the developing countries they boost the median emissions rate fourfold, to 0.56 ton per thousand dollars, or about three times as high as the median ratio for industrial countries. Considering that deforestation emissions are the cheapest to eliminate (chapter 5), these findings suggest that the developing countries can make a major, low-cost contribution to reduction of global emissions through cutbacks in deforestation.

With respect to subsidization, Shah and Larsen (1991, 8) have estimated that nine large developing and Eastern European countries[8] spend $40 billion annually in subsidies to fossil fuels (with China's $15.7 billion the largest). In addition, the former Soviet Union spends subsidies of $89.6 billion annually for fossil fuels. The removal of these subsidies would eliminate an estimated 157 million tons of carbon in annual emissions from the developing group and 233 million tons from the former Soviet Union alone. These cutbacks would represent about 8 percent of global carbon emissions (about 6 percent, if deforestation emissions are included). Subsidization is relatively widespread: a World Bank survey of 60 developing countries (cited in Shah and Larsen 1991, 7) finds that, typically, electricity is priced at 30 percent below long-run marginal cost.

---

8. China, Poland, Mexico, Czechoslovakia, India, Egypt, Argentina, South Africa, and Venezuela.

Finally, table 8.1 suggests that, although per capita emissions are high in industrial countries, they are high because per capita economic activity is high, not because energy is used with gross inefficiency compared with other countries. Thus, whereas the United States' share of global emissions (including emissions from deforestation) is 3.5 times its share of world population, its emissions share is only 0.86 times its share of global production (purchasing power parity GDP), about the same rate as for the European Community. The ratio of the emissions share to real GDP share is even lower for Japan (0.51). These measures suggest that if a global planner arrived from another planet and was assigned the task of reducing emissions at minimum cost to cutbacks in world production, he would focus attention first on some of the countries with much higher ratios of emissions share to GDP share (e.g., China, Brazil, India, Indonesia, Myanmar, Poland, the Philippines, Peru, Turkey; table 8.1, final column). Of course, such a planner would need the flexibility to redistribute world income to compensate developing countries for their costs of reducing carbon emissions, and in practice there are limits to such redistribution. Nonetheless, the thought experiment underscores the importance of including developing countries in international efforts to restrain emissions.

The China Problem

China poses a special challenge for policy on global warming. In part because of its large population, but more directly because of its heavy present and expected future reliance on its massive reserves of coal, the nation already accounts for 11 percent of global carbon emissions (excluding emissions from deforestation), and by the year 2100 its share could reach 22 percent (table 8.3). Manne and Richels (1990c) have estimated that, if China were to attempt to constrain carbon emissions to twice their present levels, the resulting economic costs could reach a range of 8 percent of the nation's GDP by the year 2040, rising to 11 percent by 2100.[9] If, instead, China's emissions were allowed to quadruple, the economy would face minimal losses by 2040, but by 2060 losses would amount to 1 percent of GDP, rising to 8 percent by 2100. Yet at four times present levels, or some 2.6 GtC, China's emissions alone would preempt two-thirds of the global total examined in chapter 7 as a target for aggressive abatement (4 GtC annually).

The coal-specific aspect of the China problem actually applies to the United States, the former Soviet Union, Australia, Germany, and South Africa as well.

---

9. Note, however, that the GREEN model developed at the Organization for Economic Cooperation and Development shows much lower costs for China, as reviewed in chapter 4.

Of the world total of proven recoverable coal reserves (693 billion tons), these five countries account for 27.5 percent, 24.4 percent, 5.2 percent, 5.0 percent, and 3.6 percent, respectively. China has 14.3 percent of proven recoverable world reserves (Edmonds and Reilly 1985, 156), bringing the share of the top six nations to 80 percent. If coal reserves became essentially unusable because of emissions constraints, the losses per person would actually be greater for the United States (760 tons of proved recoverable reserves per capita) than for China (89 tons per capita).

The unique China problem stems from the combination of the country's reliance on coal and its large prospective increase in per capita income and energy use, in view of its low present level of development. Thus, China's energy requirements are expected to multiply about threefold from the year 2000 to 2070 (or from 1.5 billion tons of coal equivalent, or tce, to 4.7 billion tce; Lu 1990)—for a growth rate of about 1.7 percent annually. At present, 70 percent of primary energy comes from coal. In contrast, US energy consumption could approximately double over the same 70-year period.[10]

Lu argues that even this rate of energy expansion for China will require major efforts to improve efficiency, as the elasticity with respect to GDP growth is only 0.6. He notes that China's current energy efficiency is considerably lower than that in industrial countries, as primary commercial energy consumption per dollar of GDP amounts to 2.13 kg of coal equivalent (kgce) in contrast to 1.05 in the United States and 0.51 in Japan. Over the medium term the Chinese government seeks to reduce the energy intensity of industry to developed-country levels, and by 2050 the goal is to reduce it by more than 80 percent (from 3.01 kgce per dollar today to 0.52).

Lu notes that partial deregulation of energy prices and investments for energy conservation has already brought savings of about one-fifth in total energy use during the decade of the 1980s. An investment program of approximately $1.5 billion in energy conservation during the Sixth Five-Year Plan (1981–85) (including a sizable emphasis on cogeneration) contributed to this outcome. However, for future carbon emissions, much will depend on the availability of alternative technology. There is considerable scope for increased hydroelectric power during an initial phase, and perhaps for nuclear power once inherently safe reactors have been more fully developed. The central view from China, however, would appear to be that "International cooperation in the development of inexpensive new energy supply technology will therefore be indispensable for world-wide CO_2 reduction" (Lu 1990, 28).

---

10. The US Department of Energy (1991, A-5) indicates that US energy demand should rise at a rate of between 0.5 percent and 1.5 percent annually through 2030. Applying a 1 percent growth rate, the total would rise by 100 percent over 70 years.

The need for new technology is surely inescapable, not just for China but globally, if carbon emissions are to be severely restrained by the middle of the 21st century. For perhaps a decade, however, the analyses of both Lu (1990) and Shah and Larsen (1991) suggest that there is major scope for restraint through improved efficiency stimulated by a removal of subsidies.

The OPEC Problem

Countries that rely heavily on production and export of oil constitute another special problem for international cooperation on global warming. Whalley and Wigle (1990) have estimated that oil-exporting nations would stand to lose 18.7 percent of their GDP over the period 1990–2030 if national consumption taxes were applied to reduce global carbon emissions by 50 percent from the baseline they would otherwise follow. In contrast, if carbon were restrained by national production taxes, the oil exporters would enjoy a net gain equal to 4.5 percent of GDP over this period.

At a minimum, such calculations highlight the need to pay special attention to the distributional effects of the regime pursued to limit global emissions. However, some caveats would seem warranted. First, several oil-exporting countries (e.g., the United Kingdom, Mexico, and potentially Venezuela) have perhaps more to gain from international cooperation against global warming than they stand to lose, because their economies are (or increasingly will be) dominated by agriculture and industry rather than oil. Second, oil producers typically have natural gas production as well, and gas will be the fuel of choice in an emissions-restraining environment because the carbon emissions of gas are much lower than those of coal (leading to intrafossil fuel substitution; chapter 5). Third, for essentially the same reason, over a long time horizon even oil will tend to be used under carbon restraints; the much vaster reserves of coal, and its higher emissions content, make coal the principal fossil fuel that will be disadvantaged by emissions restraints.[11]

---

11. Thus, Sundquist (1990, 202) indicates that, whereas there are 3.2 trillion tons of carbon-equivalent in identified coal reserves, there are only 97 billion tons in oil and 41 billion tons in natural gas reserves. If global emissions were held to 4 GtC annually and only oil and gas were burned, the identified reserves of the two fuels would still run out in 35 years. Although ultimately recoverable reserves are perhaps two to three times as large, the estimates underscore the fact that there would continue to be a vital market for oil and gas, relative to supply, despite international measures to restrain carbon emissions.

Business Interests

The usual assumption is that business groups will oppose yet more environmental initiatives on grounds that the burden of environmental regulations is already heavy. However, there is a countercurrent within business that sees evolving public attitudes toward the environment as an opportunity to capture a strategic competitive position, including in the area of global warming. This second reaction is most evident in Europe and Japan.

Some European nations (e.g., Germany) have long had national business organizations' "green" seal of approval on environmentally favorable products, and the European Community is moving to establish such "eco-labeling" Community-wide.[12] Data Resources, Inc. (1990) has estimated that the environmental products market in Europe will grow from 1 percent of GDP in 1987, or 34 billion ecus ($39 billion), to 109 billion ecus in 2005 at constant prices (2.4 percent of GDP) under likely policies and to 168 billion ecus (3.7 percent of GDP) under extreme environmental policies. The firm estimates that the market for equipment and services to reduce air pollution (including energy conservation) could grow from a relatively small base of 7.5 billion ecus in 1987 to 49 billion ecus in 2005 under an "extreme" policy scenario.

Just as business advisory services are pointing to prospective markets associated with environmental efforts, some economists have argued that the nations that are the most active in these areas are likely to gain a competitive edge. Porter (1991, 168) has found that "the nations with the most rigorous requirements often lead in exports of affected products." He notes that Germany has perhaps the world's tightest regulations on air pollution and that German companies hold the lead in patenting and exporting technologies designed to limit air pollution. Conversely, the United Kingdom has relatively lax environmental standards, and the ratio of its exports to imports of environmental technology has fallen from 8:1 to 1:1 in the past decade. In the United States, sectors subject to the most stringent environmental requirements have improved external performance, including chemicals, plastics, synthetics, fabrics, and paint.

Japan's response to the prospect of action on global warming has been prototypical of the nation's industrial strategy. The Ministry of International Trade and Industry (MITI) has identified a framework plan for industrial response and initiated a program of research and development. MITI's "New Earth 21" environmental plan for the 21st century (MITI 1991) calls for an initial focus, during the years 1990–2000, on intensified scientific research to resolve uncertainties and on accelerated energy conservation, the phaseout of CFCs, the development of safer nuclear reactors, and reforestation. In the decade 2000–2010, efforts would concentrate on new and renewable energy sources, third-generation CFC

---

12. "EC Agrees Eco-Label for Consumer Goods," *Financial Times*, 13 December 1991, 3.

substitutes, and CO_2-fixation and reutilization technology. In 2010–20, "environmentally friendly" production processes would begin, and biotechnology would be used to reverse desertification through salt- and drought-resistant plants. In the following decade, there would be enhancement of ocean sinks for carbon dioxide. By 2030–40, the plan foresees the availability of nuclear fusion and space solar generation.

Research in progress in Japan's institutions (mostly government) includes work on biotechnology-based CO_2 fixation through the identification and breeding of plankton or bacteria for mass culturing and use as carbon dioxide "sweepers"; catalytic hydrogenation technology for synthesizing CO_2 (separated by membranes) from industrial facilities into useful chemicals such as methanol; and the use of CO_2-consuming bacteria to produce plastics (Miyama 1991). The past pattern of Japanese industrial development would suggest that the Japanese private sector could secure a lead in international production of such technologies on the research base initiated largely by MITI.

In short, business may be more receptive to international action on the greenhouse problem than generally thought, because of an important subgroup of business that considers the issue to be an opportunity for innovation, production, and seizing future markets. So far, the trends suggest more dynamic business-government approaches to developing antigreenhouse technologies in Europe and Japan than elsewhere, including the United States. If so, American firms could ironically stand to lose from a US policy of inaction. If the global warming problem turned out not to be serious, this "loss" would be meaningless, and firms in countries not pursuing abatement measures would gain. However, if the problem is confirmed as serious and international action eventually does turn forceful, the price of waiting could be a loss of competitive position for firms in the countries slowest to act under the assumption that firms build first for the domestic market. Ironically, free-riders would face a longer-term penalty of loss of competitiveness.

Negotiation Principles

The achievement of effective action will depend in part on the approaches adopted for international negotiation and, potentially, administration. A tentative consensus has emerged about some elements of the approach, but not about others.

There has been considerable agreement about the desirability of a framework-protocol structure, as opposed to a comprehensive once-for-all convention. Nations first agree to a general framework accord that sets forth broad goals. They then sign protocols that help implement the framework and provide more specific commitments. A prime example of this structure is the Vienna Convention for the Protection of the Ozone Layer, the framework agreement for the reduction of chlorofluorocarbons (Sebenius 1991). The Montreal Protocol of 1987 committed signatories to reduce CFCS by 50 percent by 1999. The London Adjustments and Amendments of 1990 to the Protocol banned the use of CFCS by the year 2000. Although only 24 countries had signed the Montreal Protocol, 93 nations signed the London Adjustments and Amendments, in part because of the promise of financial and technical assistance to developing countries but also because of the growing evidence of the severity of ozone depletion.

As discussed in Sebenius (1991), the unfavorable experience with negotiation of the Law of the Seas (LOS) Treaty served to discourage the alternative mode of a comprehensive agreement. The LOS convention is a vast codification of rules on the use of the seas. It took from 1970 to 1982 to negotiate. The United States refused to sign (as did Israel, Turkey, and Venezuela); the United Kingdom and West Germany signed but opposed ratification; and by 1991 only 40 of the 60 countries required for entry into force had ratified the treaty.

The framework-protocol structure provides flexibility for action to begin with a nucleus of countries willing to move ahead, rather than requiring universal participation on a consensus basis. Thus, Thatcher (1991) proposes that a climate convention contain a ''Fast Track Plan'' for unilateral action by developed countries at an early date. Moreover, the modular nature of action under successive protocols provides substantive flexibility for adaptation, especially appropriate for climate change because of the evolving scientific evaluation of the problem.

Nitze (1991) proposes a ''conference of the parties'' to a climate convention that would establish an executive council, permanent committees (e.g., on science), and a strong secretariat, for the purpose of monitoring country implementation and upgrading scientific understanding. He urges strong provisions for technology transfer and financial assistance to ensure the participation of such key developing countries as China, Indonesia, and Brazil. He also advocates emissions targets and timetables, primarily as catalysts to action rather than as rigid rules. The issues of explicit targets and assistance to developing countries are at the core of the debate; both are examined below.

Richardson (1991) calls for the entrustment of climate convention responsibilities to an international entity, either a new organization modeled after the General Agreement on Tariffs and Trade (GATT) or the International Monetary Fund, or an expanded version of the existing United Nations Environment Programme. The body would not have enforcement powers, but would have important means of persuasion, including the definition of targets, monitoring, and technical assistance.

Past experience with international organizations suggests that, if a new entity is established, it will be more effective if its executive board has weighted voting, in which country population and economic size are taken into account. Thus, the International Monetary Fund and the World Bank, in which votes are weighted according to economic size, have enjoyed a much greater record of success than many other UN entities, in which the one-nation, one-vote principle applies. Weighted voting will be especially important if an entity is to have discretion over financial resources—for example, for assistance to developing countries in pursuit of emissions reductions. Otherwise, the magnitude of resources forthcoming is likely to be much smaller.

Efficient and Equitable Mechanisms to Limit Emissions

Three central economic issues dominate the question of how to implement an international program for abatement of greenhouse gas emissions: efficiency, equity, and decision under uncertainty. The two-stage phased approach outlined below seeks to deal with the uncertainty issue. The discussion that follows examines efficiency and equity and, for simplicity, takes as given the assumption that uncertainty has been reduced sufficiently that the international community is prepared to take energetic action. Thus, the analysis here is more appropriate for the later stage of global action than for the initial "running in" phase, as discussed below.

Carbon Taxes Versus Quota Ceilings

Pearce (1991) provides a summary of the economic arguments favoring the use of carbon (or greenhouse gas) taxes to reduce emissions rather than nontradeable country quo as on emissions.[13] The most central argument is that environmental taxes accomplish abatement at minimum cost (see Baumol and Oates 1988). A given tax applicable to all polluters will induce abatement by firms with low marginal costs of emissions cutbacks, whereas firms with high marginal abatement costs will find it more attractive to pay the tax. At a more general level, taxation uses the market mechanism to allocate adjustments to the greenhouse problem, whereas explicit quotas on emissions use a "command and control" approach that can be extremely costly. Thus, Tietenberg (1990) finds in a survey of model-based studies of 10 cases of US pollution abatement (regionally and pollutant-specific) that the ratio of command-and-control costs to least-cost measures is a median of 4.[14] He also concludes that the initial experience of trading emission reduction credits, begun by the Environmental Protection Agency

---

13. The alternative of tradeable permits is discussed below.

14. He notes that certain biases (such as model assumptions about ease of retrofitting for optimal technology) tend to understate the least-cost solution, but even so, the wide divergence leaves ample room to demonstrate the high costs of command and control.

(EPA) in the late 1980s under its implementation of the US Clean Air Act, confirms the greater efficiency of a market-oriented approach.

Pearce adds four other advantages of a tax. First, it can raise revenue that can be applied to reduce other taxes and thus the "excess burden" of the existing tax regime (see chapter 7). Second, its revenue potential opens the possibility of channeling resources to developing countries to secure their participation in international abatement. Third, a carbon tax provides an ongoing incentive to technical change, whereas a quantitative regulation does not unless it is continuously revised to set standards just above the best current technical practice. Fourth, the carbon tax is easy to modify in the light of new scientific information, whereas regulations are difficult to change.

There are two principal disadvantages of carbon taxes rather than nontradeable quotas. First, because price elasticities of supply and demand are not well known, especially for the large changes implied by the range of carbon taxes under consideration for major emissions cutbacks, there will be considerable uncertainty about the quantitative amount of abatement accomplished by the proposed tax, whereas a quota (if observed) will provide a precise outcome. Second, the incidence of a carbon tax is usually considered regressive.[15]

As discussed in chapter 4, a related issue for the carbon tax is its macroeconomic impact. Countries that suffer from chronic fiscal imbalance (with consequent high inflation, as, e.g., in Brazil, or high real interest rates, as in the United States in the 1980s) may derive a macroeconomic benefit from the carbon tax that provides a new, politically acceptable way to raise revenue (e.g., as an environmental user fee rather than a "tax"). Otherwise, rebate of the tax is appropriate, to avoid contractionary demand effects and to provide an economic gain from the reduction of efficiency distortions imposed by existing alternative taxes.[16]

---

15. Pearce (1991, 943) indicates that, in the United Kingdom, the lowest income decile (10 percent) of households spends 13.2 percent of income on fuel, whereas the highest decile spends only 3.5 percent. However, Poterba (1991, 81) demonstrates for the United States that a considerable portion of the apparent regressivity of a carbon tax would stem from the overall phenomenon of a higher average propensity to consume all goods in low-income groups than in high. Thus, he estimates that a tax on carbon of $100 per ton would cost the lowest decile 10 percent of income and the highest decile only 1.5 percent; but the impact would amount to 3.7 percent of consumption for the lowest decile and 2.3 percent for the highest. The implication is the need for a more profound understanding of the composition of the lowest income classes; if their members are transitory, consumption is probably a better guide to "permanent income" than is current income, so the less regressive interpretation using consumption data is the more meaningful.

16. These potential effects are large. Poterba (1991, 76) has estimated that a tax of $100 per ton of carbon would raise an average of 2.4 percent of GDP for industrial countries in the Organization for Economic Cooperation and Development (OECD) and 3.42 percent of GDP for the United States.

It is important not to confuse a coordinated program of taxation at the *national* level with a plan for *international taxation* by a supranational body. Schelling (1991) rightly argues that any tax high enough to have a major impact on global carbon emissions would generate so much revenue that nations would be unwilling to entrust the administration of the tax and control of its revenue to an international body.

Perhaps the most serious arguments in favor of quotas rather than taxes have to do with international equity, on the one hand, and certainty of outcome, on the other. An internationally coordinated carbon tax is a market mechanism and as such has the indifference to income distributional consequences inherent in all strictly market transactions. Developing countries would be concerned that the tax approach would mean that the richest countries would be able to bid preemptively for the lion's share of carbon emissions, as consumers and firms in industrial countries would be more able to afford the tax than those in developing countries. The distributional issue is hidden in the case of taxes and transparent in the case of allocated country quotas, but it is present in either approach. It is addressed further below.

With respect to certainty of outcome, imperfect knowledge of the price elasticities of demand and supply for fossil fuels means that a specified tax (e.g., $100 per ton of carbon) could have a greater or lesser abatement impact than expected. Thus, in figure 8.3, the expected carbon cutback from a tax of t per ton is the amount a, with intermediate demand and supply elasticities. However, the cutback may be much smaller than desired if both demand and supply are inelastic (abatement amount b, panel B in figure 8.3). If both are elastic, the cutback will be larger than expected (d, panel D). If either demand or supply is more inelastic than expected, the cutback will be below target. If demand is inelastic and supply elastic, consumers will bear the brunt of adjustment through much higher prices (panel C). Conversely, if demand is elastic and supply inelastic, producers will bear the adjustment burden by absorbing most of the loss of rent to taxes (panel E).

One important possibility is that, because of the low marginal cost of such large fuel suppliers as Saudi Arabia, the bite of carbon taxes would be considerably softened through absorption by producers who accept lower rents rather than by consumers facing higher prices. The more inelastic the fossil fuel supply, the less effective the tax in reducing production and emissions (figure 8.3, F).

Weitzman (1974) has argued that, where there are sharply rising marginal damages from overshooting of the desired ceiling on pollutants or other "bads," and there is uncertainty about the demand and supply elasticities, it will be more efficient to use quantity controls rather than prices.[17] If, in contrast, there

---

17. Weitzman's central result is: $\Delta \approx (\sigma^2 B'')/(2C'^2) + \sigma^2/(2C'')$ where Δ is the "com-

Figure 8.3 Fossil fuel elasticities and the carbon tax

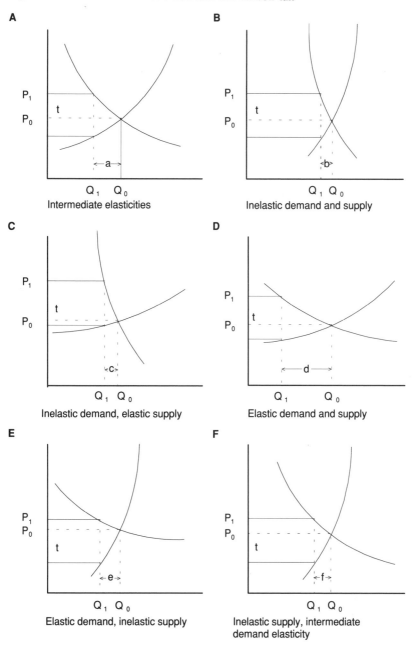

A

P_1
P_0
t

Q_1 Q_0
Intermediate elasticities

B

P_1
P_0
t

Q_1 Q_0
Inelastic demand and supply

C

P_1
P_0
t

Q_1 Q_0
Inelastic demand, elastic supply

D

P_1
P_0
t

Q_1 Q_0
Elastic demand and supply

E

P_1
P_0
t

Q_1 Q_0
Elastic demand, inelastic supply

F

P_1
P_0
t

Q_1 Q_0
Inelastic supply, intermediate
demand elasticity

is great uncertainty about costs of action, marginal costs are steeply rising, and the marginal benefits are relatively constant, there will be an advantage to using prices rather than quantity controls, because the excess costs of setting too ambitious a target will tend to overwhelm the excess benefits.[18]

Epstein and Gupta (1990) have invoked Weitzman's analysis to argue that, for the greenhouse effect, a system of international quotas ceilings is preferable to taxes. There is a crucial aspect of the greenhouse problem that calls the Epstein-Gupta proposition into question, however. Global warming is an extremely long-term process with numerous opportunities for readjustment, rather than a once-and-for-all "game" that requires expert marksmanship on the first shot at the carbon ceiling. If in the first five-year period (for example) the tax imposed to obtain a given carbon emissions outcome proves to be insufficient, the tax can be increased in a subsequent round. Suppose, for example, that over a decade the international regime aims for 4 GtC annual emissions but, instead, emissions amount to 5 GtC. The extra 10 GtC emissions translate to 5 GtC atmospheric buildup, or 0.7 percent—too little to have a significant impact. At the end of the decade the tax regime can be tightened to push the outcome closer to the target.[19]

Another complication of the carbon tax is the divergence among the initial tax positions of different countries. For example, European countries and Japan tend to have much higher taxes on gasoline than does the United States.[20] In an eventual (second phase) regime of internationally coordinated taxation, there would presumably be a need for movement toward harmonization of taxes on fossil fuels. Otherwise, countries with a low initial tax position will enjoy free-riding benefits.

Finally, it is important to stress that taxation of *carbon* (or greenhouse gases more generally) rather than *energy* is necessary for an efficient response to the greenhouse problem. Indeed, a crucial part of the solution to the problem is the substitution of fossil fuel energy by nonfossil fuel energy, and if all energy is taxed there is no incentive for this substitution. As discussed in chapter 4,

---

parative advantage" of prices over quantity targets, σ^2 is the variance of vertical shifts in the cost curve, B is benefit, C is cost, and double prime refers to the second derivative (i.e., the derivative of marginal benefit or of marginal cost). Weitzman argues that "prices can be a disastrous choice far more often than quantities can [considering that] $\Delta \rightarrow -\infty$ if either $B'' \rightarrow -\infty$ or $C'' \rightarrow 0$ (or both)" (Weitzman 1974, 486).

18. In terms of note 17: when σ^2 is high, C'' is high and B'' is low.

19. As Weitzman (1974, 482) himself notes: "In an infinitely flexible control environment where the planners can continually adjust instruments to reflect current understanding of a fluid situation and producers instantaneously respond, the above considerations are irrelevant and the choice of control mode should be made to depend on other factors." Over a time scale of decades, readjustment within five to ten years is close to "instantaneous."

20. In the opposite direction, Germany has important subsidies for coal.

Jorgenson and Wilcoxen (1990b) have conducted simulations for the US economy that show that it is more costly to reduce carbon emissions through a general energy tax than through a tax on carbon emissions.[21]

Tradeable Permits

It is widely considered that a system of tradeable permits can have the same allocative efficiency benefits as a tax (see, e.g., Hoel 1990). If a country has a quota allocation that is small relative to its demand, its firms will bid to purchase quotas from other countries. Other countries will sell a portion of their quotas to the point where the marginal cost of cutting back a ton of carbon emissions at home equals the price of a ton "exported" through the sale of an emissions permit. International abatement will thus be pursued at minimum cost, in a manner similar to the outcome under taxation and in contrast to the result with a rigid, nontradeable quota system. There is a direct mapping between the tax and tradeable permit regimes: in the latter case, the equilibrium price in the market for permits will settle at the same value per ton as the per-ton tax under a tax regime that yields the same outcome in terms of magnitude of abatement.

A specific advantage of both taxes and tradeable permits over rigid country quotas is that both would be more efficient than at least one version of the quota regime that has tended to dominate greenhouse policy discussion so far: proportionate cutbacks of carbon emissions from current levels by all countries. There is little reason to expect the marginal cost of, say, cutbacks of emissions to 80 percent of current levels to be identical across countries. As noted, both taxes and tradeable permits minimize overall abatement cost by allocating the cutbacks to the countries where marginal costs of emissions reductions are the lowest.

However, there are at least two major differences between taxes and tradeable permits, as well as a number of minor ones. By far the most important difference is likely to be the fact that, under a regime of country quotas with tradeable permits, the underlying "equity" value judgment about who gets to use fossil fuels becomes explicit in the initial allocation. The need to decide on quota allocation would raise severe negotiation difficulties. (Quota allocation criteria are discussed below.) In contrast, the taxation approach would be blind with respect to individual countries and parties, and in the first instance would be equivalent to a rise in price because of increased scarcity value (e.g., from technical change or resource depletion).

---

21. Nonetheless, as discussed below, the European Community has tentatively adopted a tax based half on carbon content and half on energy.

Another major difference between taxes and tradeable permits is that, with the latter, it is possible to specify the exact cutback in emissions. The tradeoff between certainty of outcome and exposure to high cost from a specific target thus remains present even when the alternative to taxation is the tradeable permit rather than the nontradeable quota; there is, however, no "unnecessary" component of cost (deadweight loss) if tradeable permits are allowed.

The "minor" differences between taxes and tradeable permits concern administrative costs and the risk of monopolization. A tradeable permit regime will require an administrative infrastructure. Moreover, there is always the possibility that some coalition of firms could buy up a large share of permits in an attempt to extract monopoly profit from their resale. The limited international experience with "auction quotas" in the area of trade restrictions suggests that such concerns tend to be exaggerated (Bergsten et al. 1987). In the environmental area, most countries already have extensive infrastructures in place for monitoring emissions, and it seems unlikely that the marginal administrative costs associated with tradeable permits for carbon emissions would be high.

It is just barely conceivable that, if quotas were allocated internationally on a formula heavily weighted toward country population, a handful of populous but poor countries might be able to monopolize the market for exportable permits. Under most circumstances, however, cartel action by any future Organization of Carbon Permit Exporting Countries (OCPEC) to obtain monopoly rent would be considerably less feasible than the only modestly successful past efforts of OPEC to sustain rents from international trade in oil.

Quota Allocation

As developed below, the best strategy would appear to be to rely on nationally set carbon (or greenhouse gas) taxes during an initial phase-in period; then, in a subsequent phase of regime tightening, to pursue carbon taxes nationally collected but at an internationally agreed rate. However, if such taxes fail to achieve progress toward global emissions targets, it would be appropriate in this second phase to shift to an international system of tradeable permits. In this case, it would be necessary to identify the basis for the initial allocation of emissions quotas.

Allocation on a historical basis—that is, on the basis of existing use—is a conventional means of assigning quotas, an example being the way import quotas are assigned among supplying countries in international trade in textiles. Allocation of quota rights on the basis of existing use would minimize the disruption of current production. In this regard, the historical basis is the most "realistic" or "pragmatic" approach. However, there are two important drawbacks. Historical quota allocation would reward past inefficiency in the use of carbon-based energy. It would also have questionable equity effects, because it would freeze the distribution of emissions rights to the present profile of international income (approximately) and thereby make relatively inadequate provision for developing countries.

A second possible basis for quota allocation is by GDP. Here the reasoning is that, because energy is required for economic production, any severe divergence from the distribution of production could force unnecessary reductions in global output. Using GDP as the basis for quota allocation would avoid the problem of rewarding past profligacy in the use of energy or fossil fuels. It would not, however, avoid the problem of global inequity, as current production is concentrated in the developed countries. Moreover, there are important nuances in evaluating the proper GDP to use. As noted above, the purchasing power parity GDP of developing countries is considerably higher than their GDP at market exchange rates, so the use of GDP as normally measured at market exchange rates would tend to channel a disproportionately small share of emissions rights to the developing countries.

A third possible basis for allocating quotas is simply population.[22] Here, the notion is the ultimate equality-oriented rule: one person, one emissions vote. This basis has the merit of equity. However, it would generate such a severe redistribution of world income from developed countries to poorer countries that it is implausible that the former would be prepared to adopt it. Moreover, the "equal per capita" allocation would build in a perverse incentive to increased population growth, whereas just the opposite is needed to address the greenhouse problem.

If global quota allocation for emissions becomes necessary, then the following formula would seem to have merit:

$$(8.1) \qquad Q_i = Q_g \left[w_h \phi_{o,i}^h + w_Y \phi_i^Y + w_P \phi_{o,i}^P \right]$$

where i signifies the country in question; Q is the emissions quota; subscript g is the global emissions target; w refers to the weight assigned to the criterion (basis) in question (with the sum of $w = 1$); super- and subscripts h, Y, and P refer to historical use, purchasing power parity GDP, and population, respectively; ϕ is the country's share in the relevant global total; and subscript 0 refers to the base year.[23]

This approach weights each of the alternative criteria to obtain an overall quota—a practice that has worked for the International Monetary Fund (where country quotas are determined by such criteria as GDP, external trade, and pop-

---

22. Thus, Epstein and Gupta (1990) cite in their chief example the allocation of quotas based on projected population.

23. Because the sum over all Q_i would be close to, but not equal to, Q_g, it would be necessary, in addition, to normalize all country quotas by the multiple $Q_g / \Sigma Q_i$.

ulation). The allocation would take realism, efficiency, and equity into account, and the use of base-year shares for the historical emissions and population criteria would remove the problem of perverse incentive.

If applied today, the allocation of formula 8.1 would have the following illustrative results. The United States accounts for 25.7 percent of world GDP, 17.5 percent of world emissions (including emissions from deforestation), and 4.8 percent of world population (table 8.1). The simple average of the three shares amounts to 16 percent. If the global emissions target were set at 4 billion tons of carbon, the initial US share would amount to 640 million tons. Current US emissions are 1.2 billion tons (table 8.1); therefore, a cutback by approximately 50 percent would be required. A similar calculation for Japan would show a share of 5.2 percent in global quotas, or 208 million tons of carbon—a cutback of 16 percent from present levels. In contrast, India's share would amount to 8 percent, or 320 million tons of carbon. India would thus have an excess of 47 million tons to sell in carbon permits, or, alternatively, a cushion of 17 percent above current levels for further expansion of emissions.

It would be appropriate for the three weights to shift over time toward the population criterion and thus equity. For example, the initial assignment of weights might be one-third each for present emissions (w_h), GDP (w_Y), and population (w_P). Over a period of, say, 20 years, the historical criterion might be phased out. Over a longer period—say, 40 years—the GDP criterion could be phased out, leaving only the base-year population criterion.

For its part, the population criterion could usefully be refined to reflect a measure of "projected population under maximum population control effort," to make some allowance for the population growth already in the pipeline from the age structure in the base year (say, 2000). This measure could be calculated using, for example, the assumption of birth and mortality rates identical to those in industrial countries but applied to the age structure of the country in the base year.

The approach here would seem to stand the best chance of support by both industrial and developing countries. It would give heavy weight to the "realism" concerns of industrial countries at the beginning of the period but provide large scope for a shift over time toward the equity concerns of developing countries.[24]

---

24. Grubb (1989, 37) has suggested that the adult population should be the criterion for allocation. His intent is to find a measure that reduces the incentive to population growth and achieves a distribution more palatable to industrial countries than simple equal per capita allocation. The latter effect obtains simply because of the younger age structure of developing countries. However, the use of base year population more effectively avoids the problem of perverse incentive to population growth. As for increasing the share for industrial countries, the "adult population" criterion is a rather transparent subterfuge that has no more merit than basing global emissions rights on, say, the number of left-handed dentists—as the industrial-country share will also be larger on this criterion than

Revenue Sharing

The importance of including developing countries in international measures for restraining and reducing emissions, and the political and equity considerations that seriously limit the amount of growth these countries can be expected to sacrifice to help avoid global warming, strongly point to the need to channel some of the revenue from a carbon tax from industrial countries to assist developing countries that are prepared to take measures to reduce deforestation and configure future energy development along lines that minimize carbon emissions. In an initial phase of policy response, in which the principal actors are industrial countries and the primary instrument is the carbon tax, it would be appropriate to devote perhaps 10 percent of revenue to such programs and to research and other efforts toward the transfer of noncarbon energy technology. As discussed below, the Group of Seven industrial countries has already reached tentative agreement with Brazil for a $1.5 billion fund for the preservation of the Amazon forest and thus a reduction of deforestation.

The UNCED Secretariat has estimated that resource flows to developing countries would have to be increased from $55 billion annually at present to $125 billion to meet the goals of Agenda 21, the UNCED program for environmental improvement and sustainable development in the next century (*New York Times,* 3 March 1992; Reuters, 3 March 1992). The increment of $70 billion annually would seem ambitious for at least the next few years. For the component associated with global warming, however, an appropriate interim program might involve resource flows on the order of $5 billion to $10 billion annually.

As noted, it would be appropriate to channel perhaps 10 percent of carbon tax revenue to developing countries willing to participate in programs to limit deforestation and increase fossil fuel efficiency. Over the next few years, the average of moderate carbon taxes in industrial countries might be on the order of $25 per ton of carbon. As these countries emit about 4 GtC annually, the revenue would amount to some $100 billion per year, so that 10 percent would generate a flow of $10 billion annually. Viewed from another perspective, if the developing countries undertook cutbacks in deforestation and increased afforestation for a total effect of some 1 GtC annually, at an average cost on the order of $6 to $10 per ton, the level of additional costs would be in the range of $6 billion to $10 billion annually, and resource flows to cover the bulk of these costs would again be in the range just suggested.

---

on the basis of simple population. Adult population might arguably be a germane criterion only if it were thought that the "excess population" represented by the high share of the young in developing countries was likely to die off over the planning horizon. In short, it is better to address the "realism" consideration directly through GDP and present emission shares than indirectly through a distorted population variant.

If a second stage of intensified international action arrives, more formal revenue sharing, made conditional on developing-country abatement efforts, would be an appropriate part of a strengthened and internationally harmonized system of (nationally collected) greenhouse taxation. If it becomes necessary to move toward quotas with tradeable permits in this second phase, the allocational formula suggested above would automatically provide a redistribution of revenue to developing countries, because their population shares would generally exceed their emissions shares (see, e.g., the penultimate entry for India in table 8.1). Developing countries would thus tend to be in a position to be net exporters of emissions permits and to obtain corresponding "export" earnings.

Enforcement

In an initial phase of global policy response, it would be appropriate for action to remain largely voluntary, motivated by moral suasion and national self-respect for preservation of the environment. However, it is not difficult to envision a situation early in the 21st century in which scientific confirmation and perceived urgency of action are greater than today. Under these circumstances, a considerably wider network of countries would be likely to be willing to participate in measures to restrain emissions of carbon dioxide and other greenhouse gases. However, important emitters could still refuse to cooperate. The first and most desirable response to this situation would be to proffer the positive incentive of international assistance just outlined, at least if the country is a developing country.

At some point, however, negative incentives could become necessary as well. If so, the most plausible instrument would be trade penalties. For example, countervailing duties levied against carbon-intensive products could compensate for the implicit subsidy in the exporting country that fails to take emissions-restraining measures. An overall tariff surcharge could also be applied to all imports from such a country, to address the subsidy-equivalent of cheaper energy on a basis too widespread among products to be captured in individual energy-intensive goods.

Trade penalties would be the most likely instrument for negative incentives, simply because trade is the economic interface among nations.[25] Free trade is optimal in general but not sacrosanct; as sanctions against Iraq have illustrated most recently, other international objectives can override the general presumption in favor of free trade. The precedent of penalties on trade is already estab-

---

25. Other alternatives, such as an "environmental withholding tax" on interest earned by foreign countries on US Treasury bonds, are conceivable but implausible, in part because free-rider countries would be unlikely to be the countries holding net external assets.

lished in the Montreal Protocol on CFCs. However, as indicated by the 1991 GATT panel decision on the conflict between the United States and Mexico over dolphin mortality in tuna fishing (*GATT Focus*, January-February, October 1991), the present rules of the GATT may well be too narrowly drawn to permit trade penalties for environmental violations (and could be found in conflict with the trade sanction provisions of the Montreal Protocol on ozone depletion).[26] For this reason, it would probably be necessary for a new phase of GATT agreements in the environmental area to lay the groundwork for such measures. With or without the GATT's blessing, it is not difficult to foresee the development of trade sanctions from the combination of an environmental political movement and a business community unprepared to accept the undermining of its competitiveness by free-rider countries.[27]

Global Development Context

Global warming introduces a new difficulty for the process of long-term economic development. The broad perspective of international development is thus helpful in interpreting the implications of the greenhouse problem. Two development themes in particular are relevant: the increasingly popular (but ill-defined) notion of "sustainable development" (with overtones of North-South division) and the all-important issue of population growth.

Sustainable Development

As discussed below, the United Nations Conference on Environment and Development (UNCED), to be held in Rio de Janeiro in June of 1992, will be an important forum for the launching of any international program to address global warming. The intellectual framework for this conference has emphasized heavily the concept of "sustainable development." Popularized by the Bruntland Commission (Bruntland et al. 1987), this term means many things to many people but is centered on the idea that economic development should take account of conservation of the environment, cautious use of nonrenewable resources, and the use of renewable resources (e.g., fisheries) at rates that can be maintained over the long term.

---

26. The GATT decision turned on the fact that dolphins in international waters were extraterritorial to US interests. Unfortunately, the global commons are extraterritorial to everyone.

27. This dynamic was already evident in the US–Mexico negotiations for a North American Free Trade Area in 1991, although labor groups played a larger opposition role than did business.

Principal expositions of the sustainable-growth viewpoint include those by Daly (1987) and MacNeill et al. (1991). In essence, like the Club of Rome's "limits to growth" theory of the 1970s (Meadows et al. 1974), this more recent school is a restatement of the classical position of the early 19th-century economist Thomas Malthus. As noted in chapter 7, Malthus held that economies would stagnate at the subsistence level because of the conflict between the geometric growth of population and the linear growth of food production. Today's sustainable development similarly stresses finite limits to production from the limitations of ecology and natural resources. The historical refutation of Malthus resided in technological change far beyond what he expected. Similarly, the urgency of moderating or reformulating economic development to make it "sustainable" depends importantly on the prospects for continued technological change to offset the finite limits imposed by resource reserves.

An extreme formulation of the sustainable development school calls for a revision and/or reduction in consumption patterns in industrial countries on the grounds that present consumption patterns are so lavish they cannot physically be replicated by developing countries, in view of absolute resource limits. Thus, the UNCED secretariat avows: "The lifestyles of the rich are also the source of the primary risks to our common future. They are simply not sustainable. Those who enjoy these lifestyles are all 'security risks'" (UNCED 1991). Similarly, researchers at the Indira Gandhi Institute of Development Research calculate that the developed countries have only 24 percent of the world's population but much higher shares of world consumption (reaching 86 percent for copper and aluminum and 92 percent for automobiles; Parikh et al. 1991). They argue that "the present patterns of consumption of the rich is [sic] unsustainable with the currently available technology" (Parikh et al. 1991, iv). However, they also argue that economic development for poor countries is important to reduce environmental degradation caused by poverty and that population growth needs to be curtailed.

It has by no means been demonstrated, however, that current standards of living in industrial countries could not be generalized across developing countries because of absolute resource and environmental constraints. Careful analysis—for example, using input-output techniques and making plausible assumptions about rates of technological change—would be required to reach such a verdict. Indeed, just the opposite is assumed in the long-term projections of chapter 7, with the implicit supposition that technological change will circumvent any such absolute obstacles.

It would seem that a far more productive analytical framework would be one that incorporates appropriate long-term social pricing of nonrenewable resources and the environment in product pricing as the central response to making development "sustainable." In this approach, there would be no automatic presumption that it would be impossible to replicate the high levels of automobile ownership in the United States for Africa because of the resulting demands on oil and pollution effects. Instead, a "full-cost pricing" approach would indicate that technical change, such as a shift toward biomass fuel (e.g., the Brazilian sugar alcohol fuel) or even hydrogen fuel could be expected eventually in response to appropriate prices.

The scope for ongoing growth with environmentally sound pricing cannot be resolved within these few paragraphs. However, it is important to note that the political-economic context of greenhouse negotiations includes a considerable appeal to "sustainable development" ideas, which in turn sometimes approximate recommendations of "no growth" or "negative consumption growth" for rich countries.

This context revives another aspect of international negotiations: the North-South dialogue, also known as the New International Economic Order (NIEO). The greenhouse effect could be the occasion for the resurgence of "demands from the South." In an earlier episode, the oil price increase of the mid-1970s seemed to provide leverage for developing countries to insist on increased financial "transfers" (essentially, grants) from the North, based on the potential threat of use of the oil weapon as well as a proliferation of cartels to impose price increases on an array of other commodities produced by developing countries. In the end, oil-exporting countries proved not primarily interested in forcing new transfers on behalf of other developing countries, and the scope for commodity cartels was demonstrated to be thin indeed. There is a risk that global warming negotiations could be diverted into a North-South confrontation in the framework of a new source of leverage for the South: the threat of noncooperation on global warming and other environmental concerns.

A confrontational approach would be no more likely to bear fruit than in the commodity power–conscious NIEO negotiations of the 1970s. Scientific uncertainty remains sufficiently high that industrial countries would be unsusceptible to much arm-twisting for net increases in transfers on these grounds. Ironically, the further into the future the analysis goes, the more it is the residents of the developing countries themselves that stand to lose from global warming, simply because their numbers come to dominate world population even more dramatically than they do today. So there is a second limit to the threat potential in the issue: those in the South cannot raise the threat of global pollution without threatening their own descendants.

A far more positive incorporation of the sustainable development framework is, as suggested, the concept of full-cost pricing, implemented in a mutually beneficial way among all nations. In this process, there is ample room for revenue sharing to ensure that a significant portion of the *extra costs* faced by the developing countries is undertaken by the rich countries. However, as just outlined, there would seem to be little potential for use of the global warming issue as a lever for the South to pry more net grants out of the North.

Population Policy

The eventual severity of the greenhouse problem will be greatly affected by the eventual steady-state population of the earth. The calculations of chapter 7 apply the World Bank's 1987 assumptions, also used by the IPCC, which anticipate that world population will rise from its present level of approximately 5 billion to a plateau of 10½ billion by the middle of the next century. However, recent United Nations (1992a) projections indicate that the central expectation is for population to keep rising to a level of 11½ billion by the year 2150, and a high assumption would place population by that year at 28 billion (Harrison 1992).

Higher population means a greater scale of economic activity and thus, under most assumptions, higher levels of emissions of greenhouse gases and other pollutants. The relationship is probably less than linear, however, because more rapid growth comes partly at the expense of growth in production per capita.[28] Slower per capita growth under higher population growth is consistent with basic economic theory, as labor has less capital and land to work with if there is faster population growth and a larger resulting labor force. A more thorough analysis would need to incorporate the influence of the emissions intensity of demand structure (e.g., income elasticity for automobiles).

It is useful to consider a quantitative trade-off between population restraint and carbon restraints.[29] The annual emissions ceiling suggested in chapter 7 is 4 GtC annually. If population stabilizes at a level of 10 billion or more, this emissions level amounts to 0.4 ton of carbon per capita. If one additional person is added to the steady-state population, another 0.4 ton of carbon annually must be removed from the general emissions base to provide for that person's emissions rights. On the basis of the models of chapter 4, the marginal cost to remove one ton of carbon from industrial production is on the order of $100 to $250. Suppose the figure is set at $175 per ton. Then the carbon cost of an extra person amounts to $70 annually.

This cost is recurrent, not only during the lifetime of the extra individual but also in perpetuity, under the assumption that the increase is in the permanent

---

28. Thus, Levine and Renelt (as cited in Fischer 1991, 6) have estimated the following growth equation for 101 countries over the period 1960–89 (in percentages per year):

$$GYP = -0.83 - 0.35\, R_{GDP60} - 0.38\, G_N + 3.17\, SEC + 17.5\, INV$$

where GYP is per capita real growth, R_{GDP60} is real income per capita in 1960, G_N is the population growth rate, SEC is the 1960 rate of secondary school enrollment, and INV is the share of investment in GDP. The population growth variable is significant at approximately the 10 percent level. It indicates that an extra 1 percent population growth translates to additional GDP growth of only 0.62 percent, because per capita income reaches lower levels than otherwise.

29. The author is grateful to Lawrence H. Summers for the initial inspiration for the calculation that follows.

steady-state population. The discounted present value of this cost is thus $70/
0.02 = $3,500 if the discount rate is set at 2 percent (a level approximately
compatible with the 1½ percent social rate of time preference suggested in
chapter 6), and amounts to $700 even if a high discount rate of 10 percent is
used. Thus, *the global warming value of an extra birth avoided is on the order of
$1,000 to $3,000.* The range would still be relatively high, say $500 to $1,500,
if it is assumed that half of the impact is offset by lesser growth per capita and
resulting moderation of the economic scale and emissions effects of higher
population. It would seem that a considerable amount of population restraint
could be purchased for even this price range, in terms of family planning programs, investment in basic health and education, education of women, reform
of social security systems, and so forth.

The central point here is that major efforts to restrain population growth
would appear to be a necessary part of a cost-effective global strategy to limit
greenhouse warming.

The State of Play

At the beginning of 1992, the policy positions of major players on the greenhouse
problem stood as summarized in table 8.4.[30]

European Community

In October of 1990, the European Community agreed to a target of stabilizing
carbon dioxide emissions at their 1990 levels by the year 2000 (Schmidt 1991).
By September of 1991, the EC Commission had moved to put teeth into this
pledge by proposing a tax equivalent to $10 per barrel of oil, to be levied half
on carbon content and half on energy (Btu) and to be phased in gradually over
the decade. Despite skepticism that national governments would accept the
proposal, in December the environmental and energy ministers of member countries approved the proposal in principle (*Los Angeles Times,* 14 December 1991;
Wall Street Journal, 14 December 1991). However, it was expected that there
would be temporary exemptions for energy-intensive sectors, including steel,
chemicals, and pulp and paper. Only Spain expressed reluctance about the tax,
on the grounds that it might impede economic development; France preferred
a carbon rather than energy base, in view of its heavy reliance on nuclear energy.
A final proposal was expected by May of 1992, in advance of the Rio conference
(discussed below).

---

30. For a discussion of the outcome of the final negotiating session of the International
Negotiating Committee in May of 1992, see the postscript to this chapter.

Table 8.4 Country policy positions on greenhouse warming as of mid-1991

Country	Carbon dioxide stabilization		Comment
	At level of:	By:	
European Community	1990	2000	Tax equivalent to $10 per barrel of oil pending, to be levied half on carbon content, half on energy.
Belgium	1990 minus 5%	2000	
Denmark	1988 minus 20%	2005	
France	See comment.	2000	Ceiling of 2.0 metric tons per capita. Currently 1.8 metric tons.
Germany	1987 minus 25%	2005	Cutback of 25% to 30% from 1987 expected for unified Germany.
Italy	1990 minus 20%	2005	
Netherlands	1989–90 minus	2000	
United Kingdom	3% to 5% 1990	2005	Cut contingent on action by other countries. Measures to cut methane are planned.
Finland			EFTA members have agreed in principle to EC target.
Norway	1989	2000	Goal is preliminary. Depends on research and results of international negotiations.
Sweden			EFTA members have agreed in principle to EC target.
Switzerland	1990	2000	Parliamentary approval pending.
United States	None		Cutback of CFCs was expected to leave total greenhouse gas emissions by 2000 at 1990 levels.
Japan	1990	2000	Stabilization of CO_2 emissions per capita.
Canada	1990	2000	
Australia	1988 minus 20%	2005	
New Zealand	1990 minus 20%	2000	
Soviet Union	None		
China	None		
Brazil	None		Measures in process to arrest deforestation.

Source: Karen Schmidt. 1991. *Industrial Countries' Responses to Global Climate Change.* Washington: Environmental and Energy Study Institute (July). Reprinted with permission.

The prospective tax of $10 per barrel of oil is equivalent to approximately $75 per ton of carbon (based on the relationships identified in Congressional Budget Office 1990, as discussed in chapter 4), and amounts to about 25 cents per gallon of gasoline. This level is substantial and is well within the range that the more sensitive models (e.g., Jorgenson-Wilcoxen) show would be required to have a major impact in reducing carbon emissions.[31] Thus, by early 1992 the European Community appeared well on the way to serious action, despite the free-rider problems facing any single actor (as discussed above).

As analyzed in chapter 4, the efficiency of a tax based partly on energy rather than strictly carbon dioxide is subject to serious question. Nonetheless, it would appear that political feasibility was greater for the combined energy-carbon tax, in part because of the influence of such groups as coal producers in Germany. One of the arguments used in support of the broader tax was that other forms of energy have their external diseconomies as well, such as the need to maintain a military capacity to secure supplies of foreign oil or the costs for disposal of nuclear waste (Jo Leinen, Minister of Environment of the state of Saarland, Germany, at the Malente Symposium IX, November 1991).

Within the European Community, Germany has gone the furthest to specify targets for cutbacks in carbon emissions. Thus, the government has set a target of 25 percent reduction of carbon emissions from 1990 levels by the year 2005. In late 1991, an exhaustive study by the Bundestag (parliament) called for a 30 percent reduction in carbon dioxide emissions from 1987 levels by the year 2005, as well as a 30 percent cut in methane emissions, a 50 percent reduction in nitrogen oxides, a 60 percent cut in carbon monoxide, and an 80 percent reduction in nonmethane volatile organic compounds (Deutscher Bundestag 1990, 48).

Japan, Canada, and Other OECD Countries

As indicated in table 8.4, by 1991 most other OECD nations had also stated targets for emissions of carbon dioxide. In late 1990, the Japanese government adopted an action program that provided:

> . . . based on the common efforts of the major industrialized countries to limit CO_2 emissions. . . . The emissions of CO_2 should be stabilized on a per capita basis in the year 2000 and beyond at about the same level as in 1990. . . . Efforts should also be made . . . to stabilize the total amount of CO_2 emission in the year 2000 and beyond at about the same level as in 1990. . . . The emission of methane gas

31. Although other models, especially the Manne-Richels model, place the tax needed to restrain emissions at 1990 levels in the range of $250 per ton by the mid-21st century; see chapter 4.

should not exceed the present level. To the extent possible, nitrous oxide and other greenhouse gases should not be increased (Government of Japan 1990, 4).

The Japanese government has not yet announced taxation measures, but it has taken research and development initiatives (as discussed above).

As indicated in table 8.4, most other OECD nations have also adopted carbon ceilings at about 1990 levels by the year 2000 and after.

The United States

Among industrial countries, the United States is the principal exception to the pattern of emerging commitments to limits on carbon dioxide emissions. As noted earlier in this chapter, US officials have stressed scientific uncertainty as grounds for refraining from any targets or taxes that would restrain greenhouse gases for reasons of global warming. However, they have also emphasized that measures undertaken for other environmental reasons will have the effect of limiting total greenhouse gas emissions.

The Bush administration has cast the issue as one of balancing environmental concerns, on the one hand, and economic costs, on the other. At the White House Conference on Science and Economics Research Related to Global Change, in April 1990, US spokespersons emphasized the scientific uncertainties associated with the greenhouse effect and the burdensome economic costs of curtailing carbon emissions, especially for developing countries. At the first meeting of the UN International Negotiating Committee for a Framework Convention on Climate Change (Chantilly, Virginia, February 1991) US officials for the first time acknowledged the greenhouse as a "potential threat" that justified "taking action now." However, the US position in 1991 offered only to stabilize trace gas emissions through the year 2000 (not thereafter) and to do so almost entirely through phasing out CFCs—a commitment already made under the Montreal Protocol undertaken internationally in response to the danger of depletion of the stratospheric ozone layer (Kerr 1991a).[32]

Cristofaro and Scheraga (1990) have calculated that existing US policy commitments should hold total US greenhouse gas emissions constant at 2.3 billion tons of carbon-equivalent from 1987 until the year 2000. Carbon dioxide itself would rise by 193 million tons (from 1.31 GtC to 1.5 GtC), or about 15 percent. However, there would be a reduction of 111 million tons of carbon-equivalent in CFCs (from 0.37 Gt carbon-equivalent to 0.26 Gt, a cutback of 30 percent), and a combined reduction of 76 million tons carbon-equivalent in other green-

---

32. The US position has been close to what one well-known analyst has advocated as the limited extent of action that is justified on a benefit-cost basis (Nordhaus 1991a; see chapter 7, annex 7A, of this study).

house gases as the result of the Clean Air Act. Thus, the cutbacks would amount to 11 percent for methane, 33 percent for volatile organic compounds, 9 percent for nitrogen oxides, and 14 percent for carbon monoxide; emissions of nitrous oxide should be held constant.

This approach was criticized by other countries as taking undue credit for reduced greenhouse impact from CFCS, which are to be cut back in any event under the Montreal and London protocols. If CFCS were excluded, US carbon-equivalent emissions would rise by 6 percent, as the 15 percent rise in carbon dioxide emissions more than offset the 12 percent cut in other non-CFC greenhouse gas emissions. The reliance of the US strategy on a phaseout of CFCS was also vulnerable to subsequent scientific findings that the net effect of CFCS for global warming may have been neutral (United Nations Environment Programme 1991). As discussed in chapter 1, ozone depletion by CFCS has been greater than expected, and ozone itself is a greenhouse gas (with heat-trapping emissions sensitive to altitude and only poorly known). If CFCS are neutral for global warming, reducing them provides no offset to rising emissions of carbon dioxide.

More fundamentally, the US energy strategy continues to rely heavily on fossil fuels. Total US oil consumption is projected to rise from 16.8 million barrels per day (mbpd) in 1990 to 18.8 mbpd by 2010 (US Department of Energy 1991, 77). Domestic oil production is to rise through the administration's requested opening of the Arctic National Wildlife Refuge (ANWR) to exploration, advanced recovery technology, and leasing of the outer continental shelf for oil exploration. US coal production would rise from approximately 1 billion short tons in 1989 to central estimates of 1.2 billion by 2010 and 2.2 billion by 2030 (US Department of Energy 1991, 98). The strategy usefully stresses increased use of natural gas, which has decreased by 10 percent since 1970, in large part because of regulatory rigidities.

The US administration's National Energy Strategy called for carbon dioxide emissions to rise by about 25 percent by the year 2015 and stabilize thereafter through 2030 (the latest year examined). However, the reduction of CFCS, carbon monoxide, methane, and other greenhouse gases was to hold total greenhouse gas emissions (carbon-equivalent) "at or below the 1990 level through at least 2030" (US Department of Energy 1991, 179). The strategy called for the displacement of oil by alternative fuels (compressed natural gas, electricity, and alcohol from natural gas, biomass, and coal; US Department of Energy 1991, 77).

In late 1991, the US Congress defeated the administration's energy bill, partly because of the environmental risks of drilling in the ANWR but more broadly because the proposed legislation was interpreted as an oil production bill that gave too little emphasis to moderation of energy demand (despite the proliferation of energy conservation measures at the state level; Mathews 1991). At the beginning of 1992, US energy policy thus remained uncertain. Policy formation was not fully insensitive to global warming, as indicated by the administration's efforts to show a freeze in "comprehensive" greenhouse gas emissions and by references to alternative fuels in the energy strategy. However, the fundamental policy remained one of "no regrets," in which no policy should be undertaken for reasons of global warming that would not be implemented for its own purposes.[33] Technically, "no regrets" means zero weight on global warming (i.e., in a project's benefits there should be no valuation whatsoever placed on reduction of greenhouse gas emissions).

In February of 1992, the US position changed modestly. Although US negotiators continued to reject commitment to a specific target (and in particular the EC target of limiting CO_2 emissions to 1990 levels by the year 2000), they outlined a series of measures that were expected to yield results that "compared favorably" with European efforts (Bureau of National Affairs 1992). The measures included higher efficiency standards for appliances and equipment; incentives for electric utilities to conserve energy; increased government purchases of alternative-fuel vehicles; afforestation; and voluntary public-private programs to improve lighting efficiency. Notably, the new position included the announcement of a unilateral provision of $75 million to assist developing countries in the restraint of greenhouse gas emissions (New York Times, 28 February 1992, A6).

Aside from the new initiatives to provide assistance for developing countries, it was unclear just how much change the revised US position represented. It was not explicit about expected levels of future carbon dioxide emissions. Some observers interpreted the position as a compilation of existing programs and commitments in proposed transportation and energy legislation that, combined with lower projected growth rates for GNP, could mean a stabilization of carbon dioxide emissions through the year 2000, rather than the 13 percent increase expected in the 1991 National Energy Strategy (Mathews 1992). In any event there was hope that the reformulation would provide grounds for agreement

---

33. A stylized political fact in Washington was that the opposition of coal producers in particular would be a difficult obstacle to any serious policy for reducing carbon emissions. Producers of high-sulfur coal in the eastern states had been formidable adversaries of the Clean Air Act and were represented by strategically placed legislators. Yet the number of coal mining jobs in the United States was moderate: 163,000 in 1987 (U.S. Industrial Outlook 1990, 2-1). As a tax of $100 per ton of carbon would raise on the order of $100 billion annually in the United States, earmarking just 1 percent of the tax revenue over five years would be sufficient to provide a severance payment of $30,000 to each and every one of these workers. Moreover, the move toward textile liberalization in the Uruguay Round suggested that even a much larger work force (2 million textile and apparel workers) might not suffice to block action when international, rather than solely domestic, issues are at stake.

with EC and other representatives in the negotiations leading up to the "Earth Summit" in Rio de Janeiro.

Rio 1992

The United Nations Conference on Environment and Development scheduled for Rio de Janeiro in June of 1992 provided a potentially important decision point for international policy on global warming. The Rio conference was to be an umbrella event that could generate an earth charter promising protection of tropical forests and endangered species as well as the limitation of greenhouse gases. As the conference grew closer, there was concern that "squabbling between the rich and developing countries" could stalemate the conference (*Financial Times*, 7 November 1991, 7). There was some risk that the focus of the conference would be diverted from cooperation on global environmental issues to confrontation on NIEO issues resuscitated from the past (as discussed above).

The key negotiations on global warming were taking place in a parallel Intergovernmental Negotiating Committee, comprised of representatives of 160 nations and established by the same UN resolution that had established the Rio conference itself. As of early 1992, the central negotiating issues concerned whether there would be commitments to emissions targets and what provisions, if any, would be made for transfers of technology and financial resources to developing countries.

My own view is that the United States and other countries would do well to reach agreement with the European Community and most other industrial countries to *make best efforts* to limit carbon emissions to 1990 levels by the year 2000, but with no binding commitment. That stance would send an important signal to producers and households that it would be advisable to plan on diversifying away from fossil fuels. Yet the policy would be flexible enough to be compatible with the contingent, two-stage approach outlined below. Such a compromise would emphasize the principle of "emulatory initiative," whereby the countries most intent on carbon cutbacks would be encouraged to move at their own, more rapid speed. In this approach, the countries preferring to go more slowly in the initial phase would be exposed to the risk of loss of dynamic competitive advantage, in exchange for lower initial extent and costs of cutbacks.

A Blueprint for Action

The answer to the positive question of what nations will do in practice remains to be seen. The normative question of what they *should* do may be explored with the help of the findings in the previous chapters.

The central analysis of this study suggests that, over the very long term, global warming could impose heavy damages on the world economy and that the benefits of avoiding this outcome outweigh the costs of reducing emissions of carbon dioxide and other greenhouse gases. However, because these costs are so large, and because the potential extent and damage of very-long-term warming have so far received relatively little scientific attention, there is a high return to improved information confirming the prospective severity of the greenhouse problem. The policy strategy developed below thus recommends a contingent response that is divided into two phases. In the first phase, the emphasis is on confirming the scientific diagnosis and the economic evaluation, and on implementing initial measures that set precedents and establish the infrastructure for more decisive action later. This first phase involves a posture of "cautious preventive action." In the second phase, the policy response is *contingent* on what is learned during the first phase.

Phase I: 1992–2000

During the 1990s, the main elements of the international response to global warming should include the following.

Scientific Confirmation

During phase I, there should be intense efforts to obtain further scientific confirmation of the likelihood and extent of future global warming. It is of crucial importance to policy formulation to determine whether warming is more likely be on a path associated with the upper end of the range for climate sensitivity (4.5°C for carbon-equivalent doubling) or the lower end (1.5°C). In the former case, preventive action could be nearly imperative, whereas in the latter case adaptation could well suffice. The range of outcomes is even more extreme at the regional level. The agenda for high-priority scientific research over the next decade is reviewed in chapter 1.

Ideally, the scientific agenda should include increased analysis of the prospects of very-long-term warming as suggested in the present study. Such analysis should incorporate investigation of the impact of such warming on agriculture, sea-level rise, and other key areas of physical impact.

Scientific research should also include further study of the geoengineering options, which would seek to neutralize rather than avoid greenhouse gas buildup by such measures as placing debris into the atmosphere to reflect incoming sunlight, or "fertilizing" the ocean with iron to increase phytoplankton uptake of carbon. Several of the geoengineering measures are considered to involve high risk (National Academy of Sciences 1991a, 58), but they warrant further study because of their possible low-cost resolution of the problem.

Carbon Taxation and Targets

In the first decade, moderate levels of carbon taxes should be introduced progressively by at least the higher-income industrial countries (most OECD members). It would be appropriate to aim for a carbon tax of perhaps $40 per ton (at constant 1991 dollars) by the year 2000.[34] The tax could thus be introduced in annual increments of $5 per ton. If the most optimistic among the carbon-economic models (Jorgenson-Wilcoxen) is right, a $40 rate would be sufficient to reduce carbon emissions by 20 percent from 1990 levels.

As noted, the European Community has already approved a tax equivalent to $10 per barrel of oil, which amounts to about $75 per ton of carbon (chapter 4). However, in the first phase it would not be necessary for all industrial countries to take identical measures. Such an objective would reduce action to the lowest common denominator, thereby forgoing more aggressive action that the European Community and perhaps others would be prepared to take.

On the basis of past positions, the United States would be the most likely OECD country to object to carbon taxes. Ideally, the US position should be changed to accept the approach outlined here. As noted, the minimalist US position to date—holding "greenhouse gases" constant at 1990 levels by the year 2000 (but not thereafter)—stems almost solely from the phaseout of CFCs already committed under the London Protocol.

Quantitative targets, such as the EC ceiling of 1990 levels of carbon dioxide emissions by the year 2000, can have an important political role and provide a significant signal to industry. Adoption of such targets is less important than the implementation of at least a moderate carbon tax, however. More generally, taxes and targets, as well as measures to restrain methane and other noncarbon greenhouse gases, may appropriately be formulated on the principle of "emulatory initiative" during this first phase, whereby leadership provided by some major countries serves as a benchmark for international best-policy practice. Countries where policymakers are more skeptical or subject to more severe

---

34. This tax is relatively high for coal. A ton of coal contains 0.7 ton of carbon and is priced at about $40. The tax of $40 per ton of carbon would thus be about $28 for a ton of coal, or a tax of 70 percent. However, the tax would be modest relative to the price of oil products, and would amount to only about 12 cents per gallon of gasoline—much less than the existing difference between European and US levels of gasoline taxes.

political opposition to action may appropriately take lesser, but still significant, measures in the first phase.[35]

Forestry Measures

As developed in chapters 5 and 7, the lowest-cost means of obtaining major initial reductions in carbon emissions is to reduce deforestation and to place new land in forests. It would thus be important for these measures to be included even in the first phase (1990s). In December of 1991, the Group of Seven industrial countries reached an encouraging agreement with Brazil in this direction (Rubens Ricupero, personal communication, Brazilian embassy in Washington, 1991). Prompted by the G-7's initiative to Brazil at the Houston Summit in 1990, the agreement anticipates a $1.5 billion effort over five years to establish a Rain Forest Trust fund. Administered by the World Bank, the fund will finance "sustainable development" activities compatible with forest preservation in the Amazon. The initiative is important both in its own right and as a precedent for the type of measure likely to be required in at least the first phase: efforts by developing countries to reduce deforestation, financed by industrial countries.[36] If an intensified international regime is called for in a second phase and developing countries are expected to begin to make their own contributions to emissions restraint, reduced deforestation would be a critical component with or without special finance from industrial countries.

Special Measures for the Former Soviet Union, Eastern Europe, and Developing Countries

During the first phase, it would be appropriate for this group of countries to be considered exempt from the obligation to restrict carbon emissions (except for

---

35. As noted for the case of the United States, adjustment assistance for coal miners in particular could be an important political condition for action, and some portion of carbon tax revenue would appropriately be devoted to this end.

36. The repurchase of external debt at a discount has been used on a small scale in some Latin American countries to finance forest reserves. There may be some potential for this vehicle in the case of Brazil. Generally, however, debt for nature faces considerable limitations. Banks are not willing simply to donate their claims, so some entity (public or nongovernmental) must come up with the grant funds to purchase them, even at a discount. Some national authorities are also concerned about the inflationary impact on the domestic money supply, although such effects should be small and manageable where domestic fiscal policy is sound. In any event, bargains in Latin American debt are fast disappearing, as successive nations set their houses in order and the secondary market price of their debt returns to the range of 70 to 80 cents on the dollar and higher.

efforts to reduce emissions from deforestation). However, the presumption would be that this exemption would no longer apply in the second phase if globally intensified efforts are called for by then. Even in the first phase, all international development lending efforts (e.g., by the World Bank and regional multilateral banks) should be subject to review with respect to their impact on greenhouse emissions. Country plans that involve emissions growth of, say, higher than 3 percent to 4 percent annually during the decade would require extraordinary justification. This growth rate should be compatible with economic growth on the order of 5 percent to 7 percent. Moreover, during the first phase these countries should also be expected to eliminate subsidies to fossil fuels and deforestation. As discussed above, the analysis of Shah and Larsen (1991) shows that these subsidies are often large.

Research and Development

In the first phase, there should be considerable effort toward research on technology to reduce greenhouse gas emissions (such as the programs outlined in the discussion of the Japanese government-entrepreneurial response, above). As recommended by the National Academy of Sciences (NAS 1991a), research on geoengineering should be included. Because this alternative approach offers the possibility of a low-cost solution but raises potentially enormous risks, there is a high return to greater certainty about the efficacy and dangers of geoengineering measures. Of course, research on alternatives to fossil fuels should also continue, in particular for inherently safe nuclear reactor design, solar energy, and even nuclear fusion.

Movement Toward Best Practices

During the first policy phase, it would also be appropriate to pursue opportunities for zero- or negative-cost sources of energy (and carbon) saving (as discussed in chapter 5). Improved incentive structures for public utilities to save energy, revised building standards, special financing mechanisms for improvement of household energy efficiency, and increased automotive mileage standards are among the actions that should be considered. In each case, caution should be used to avoid the setting of "command and control" standards that are extremely expensive to implement. Systematic nationwide programs of energy audits and proposed patterns of use could help households achieve efficiency where the decision and information costs are high for each family acting on its own.

Subsidy Removal

During the first phase, there should be an internationally coordinated effort to remove existing subsidies to the use of carbon-based fuels, deforestation (e.g., through tax incentives encouraging land clearing), and other activities that contribute to emissions of greenhouse gases. This reform should apply equally to developing and industrial countries, as such subsidies will generally hinder rather than help economic growth in less developed countries. International lending agencies should review country programs to ensure progressive removal of such subsidies.

Fiscal Incentives

Even in the first phase, there would seem to be merit in the adoption of investment tax credits for research, development, and installation of energy systems that do not use fossil fuels. Such incentives, combined with the moderate but rising carbon tax, could provide the price signal to induce more rapid technical change away from reliance on carbon-based energy.

International Infrastructure

There should also be the development of an international administrative machinery to deal with the greenhouse problem, even in the first policy phase. Rather than a full-fledged new UN entity, something like the GATT secretariat to monitor and implement protocols signed under a framework treaty could be the most appropriate structure.

Public Values Research

It would be useful during the first phase to obtain a clearer idea of the public's attitudes toward the importance of such intangible effects as species loss and climate-related comfort, as well as the appropriate rate for discounting future economic impacts. Survey techniques ("contingent valuation") should be applied for this purpose.

Instrument Linkage

Policy action should ideally seek to maximize impact by linking measures in the various areas. A major consideration in this regard is the use to be made of any revenue collected from a carbon tax. As indicated above, perhaps a tenth of such revenue in industrial countries might appropriately be channeled toward reduced deforestation and investment in nonfossil fuel energy in developing countries. Another significant portion would appropriately be invested in research and development of new, non-carbon-emitting energy technologies. Some revenue could also usefully go to retraining and relocation of coal miners and other affected workers. However, the bulk of revenue would still appropriately be used to reduce existing distortive taxes (or, in countries where necessary, for reduction of fiscal deficits and investment in neglected infrastructure).

Phase II: Beyond 2000

International policy action after the year 2000 should be contingent on the scientific findings obtained during the 1990s. There are essentially three relevant cases:

- the greenhouse effect is confirmed and projected to cause severe eventual damage

- the greenhouse effect is found to be minimal in impact, as more reliable projections are set at or below the current lower-bound estimates

- there is neither substantial confirmation nor rejection of greenhouse science beyond the state of knowledge in 1990–92.

Substantial Confirmation of Likely Serious Damage

This case would amount to confirmation of something like the main analysis of this study and would call for consolidation and intensification of an international regime to limit greenhouse gas emissions. It would be appropriate to phase in a carbon tax of $100 to $200 per ton (at 1990 prices) by, say, the year 2015 (e.g., by adding say $7 per ton annually to the $40 per ton tax present in the year 2000). Intensification of a large-scale afforestation effort along the lines set forth in chapters 5 and 7 would be important to take advantage of the remaining low-cost carbon reduction from forestry measures. The developing countries would begin to have to enter the international program more forcefully. All development programs financed by international entitities would appropriately be contingent on plans to limit greenhouse gas emissions.

If by, say, 2015, progress toward limitation of emissions is disappointing, it would be appropriate to move toward a system of international quotas with tradeable permits as a substitute for taxation. The formula suggested above would be a reasonable basis for initial allocations, with gradual evolution of the formula toward the equity criterion (base-year population) over time. As suggested in chapter 7, the level for acceptable global emissions would probably be on the order of 4 GtC annually, including deforestation. Even before such readjustment, revenue sharing with developing countries would be important to ensure cooperation. By some cutoff date, again perhaps 2015, it would be appropriate to initiate a system of trade penalties on countries not participating in international emissions limitation.

Major Downgrading of Likely Damage

In the second policy case, greenhouse abatement policies could be safely shelved. Whereas there is virtually no likelihood that the underlying theory of greenhouse warming would be rejected, it is indeed possible that the feedback and other parameters will be found to be such that prospective long-term warming would be minimal. Even in this adventitious event, national authorities would be well advised to avoid rolling back the efficiency-improving measures undertaken in the 1990s, such as the elimination of subsidies to fossil fuel energy. This outcome would of course vindicate those countries that had emphasized a go-slow approach based on scientific uncertainty, essentially granting a winning stake to a successful gamble.

No Substantial Change in Scientific Uncertainty

Despite the calendar of important scientific experiments in the 1990s outlined in chapter 1, it is quite possible that there will be little more certainty about the extent of future warming by the year 2000 than today. Some scientists suggest that the time scale for major confirmation is more on the order of 30 years. This case poses the most difficult decision for policymakers. The main thrust of policy in phase II under these conditions would have to be a gradual continuation and intensification of the regime established under phase I, with a new "consolidation decision point" pushed ahead to, say, 2010 in the hope and expectation that by that revised date scientific certainty would be greater. Under this scenario, the period 2000–2010 would essentially become "phase I-A," still a precursor to the phase II of major intensification of the policy regime.

This approach would of course run increasing risk that the most forceful action would be delayed so long that much damage would already be in the pipeline by the time the decision to intensify action was reached. Ocean thermal lag introduces a wedge of perhaps three decades between the commitment and the arrival of a given amount of global warming. Moreover, this third scenario brings out most forcefully an underlying problem of greenhouse science: the only way fully to verify the theoretical projections would be to allow the global experiment to run unimpeded by preventive action. If it is decided that major preventive measures must be adopted, society will never know for sure whether the amount of global warming otherwise predicted would have materialized or not. The issue thus places an unusual burden on public confidence in scientific prediction. The precedent of willingness to act despite uncertainty in the case of ozone depletion by CFCs is encouraging, but as is widely recognized by those who have compared the two cases, global warming involves much larger costs and, arguably, greater scientific uncertainty.

Other Greenhouse Gases

The London Protocol on CFCs holds promise for early elimination of the most powerful greenhouse gases other than carbon dioxide, namely, the chlorofluorocarbons. However, other important gases will need policy action in a successful program to limit global warming. As in the case of carbon dioxide, there is merit in a phased approach providing for some immediate action followed by intensified efforts after an initial period of further scientific confirmation of the prospective severity of the greenhouse effect.

In the business-as-usual projections of the IPCC, noncarbon greenhouse gases account for 28 percent of the increase in global warming potential by the year 2100.[37] With "accelerated policies," the greenhouse impact of methane and CFCs could be reduced to levels below those at present, and the further impact of nitrous oxide and HCFCS (which replace CFCs) could be substantially curtailed.[38]

Fortunately, measures that reduce fossil fuel burning and deforestation to limit carbon dioxide emissions should also go a considerable way toward reducing other greenhouse gas emissions. These two sources account for 80 percent of emissions for carbon monoxide, 25 percent for methane, 56 percent for nitrogen oxides, and 16 percent for nitrous oxide (IPCC 1990d, table 1).[39]

---

37. Total "radiative forcing" above preindustrial levels rises from 2.95 watts per square meter (wm^{-2}) in the year 2000 to 9.9 wm^{-2} in 2100. The contribution of carbon dioxide rises from 1.85 to 6.84 wm^{-2}; methane (including indirect from conversion of methane to stratospheric water vapor), from 0.69 to 1.47; nitrous oxide, from 0.12 to 0.47; the CFCs (CFC-11 and CFC-12), from 0.25 to 0.28 (under moderate application of the Montreal Protocol); and the replacement HCFCs, from 0.04 to 0.59 (IPCC 1990b, table 2.7).

38. To only 0.46 wm^{-2} for methane (including indirect), 0.12 for CFC-11 and CFC-12, 0.56 for HCFCs, and 0.26 wm^{-2} for nitrous oxide, by 2100.

39. The figure for methane refers to biomass burning, coal mining, and gas drilling, venting, and transmission.

About one-third of methane emissions comes from natural sources (wetlands, termites, oceans, fresh waters, methane hydrate destabilization; IPCC 1990d, table 1). Approximately one-third comes from agriculture (enteric fermentation from ruminants; rice paddies), and 7 percent from landfills. Methane emissions can thus be reduced through landfill gas collection systems, flaring, management of livestock wastes, and biogas systems to treat waste water (IPCC 1990d). Moreover, the short atmospheric residence of methane in its initial state (ten years) means that relatively significant reductions in concentration (at least from baseline) should be possible. For its part, nitrous oxide emission can be reduced through the improved formulation and application of fertilizer, in addition to cutbacks possible through reduced fossil fuel burning and deforestation.

The elimination of CFCs in an effort to protect the ozone layer should make an important contribution to the reduction of non-CO_2 greenhouse gases as well. However, this effect should not be overstated. The IPCC (1990b) projections show a total increase of radiative forcing from CFCs, plus their replacement HCFCs, of 0.82 wm^{-2} from 2000 to 2100 under business as usual. This incremental forcing drops to 0.39 wm^{-2} under accelerated policies—an important cutback but still a modest one compared with the total increment in radiative forcing from all greenhouse gases over this period (6.95 wm^{-2}). The contribution would be even more limited if, as recent evidence suggests, the influence of CFCs has been approximately neutral because of the offsetting impact for global warming from ozone-stripping by these gases.

In sum, an international strategy to limit global warming must include efforts to reduce emissions of other greenhouse gases as well as carbon dioxide. A substantial contribution toward this objective can be accomplished by the same measures that cut carbon dioxide emissions: reducing deforestation and the use of fossil fuels. There is thus added reason to focus on these measures in the first policy phase, along with full implementation of the London Protocol on CFCs. Technological change to curtail methane emissions from livestock and rice growing should also be pursued in this period, and some tax on these activities might appropriately be introduced to internalize their external diseconomy of contribution to global warming. However, it would be premature in the first policy phase to seek a tight regime for livestock and rice, especially in developing countries.

Conclusion

The greenhouse effect poses major risks, especially over the very long term of two to three centuries, by which time temperatures could rise by as much as 10° to 18°C (chapters 1 and 2). Benefit-cost analysis suggests that, under risk aversion, policymakers would find it socially favorable to adopt aggressive preventive action by limiting global carbon emissions to perhaps 4 billion tons of carbon (GtC) annually. Despite theoretical expectations of severe free-rider problems, most OECD countries have already expressed the intention of limiting carbon emissions by the year 2000 or after to the levels of 1990. The United States is the principal exception, as US officials have cited scientific uncertainty as grounds for delaying action.

The strategy proposed here calls for a two-phase policy response. In the first phase, lasting about a decade, intense efforts should be made to confirm and clarify the scientific projections. During this phase, the policy principle should be one of "emulative initiative" whereby those countries that prefer to do so (in particular, the European Community) should proceed with relatively aggressive measures, without the requirement that all other nations do likewise. Even in this first phase, however, there should be a gradually rising carbon tax in as many nations as possible, major efforts to reduce deforestation and to plant new forest areas, elimination of CFCs, elimination of subsidies to fossil fuels and forest clearing, revision of standards and other policies that affect the gap between best and actual technical practices in energy use, and intense efforts on research and development of noncarbon energy technologies. Some portion of revenue from carbon taxes should be channeled to developing countries prepared to take measures limiting restrictions.

By the year 2000 a major review of scientific projections should provide the basis for conversion to a second policy phase. If there is substantial confirmation of major prospective damage from global warming, a much more aggressive international response should be mounted. Ideally this second phase would continue to rely on (nationally collected) taxes on carbon, but if by, say, the year 2015 emissions remain too high, it may be necessary to shift to a regime of national quotas allocated on a basis of existing emissions, GDP, and base-year population (shifting toward the latter over time), with trading of emissions permits allowed to maximize efficiency of their use.

The principal risk of the two-stage approach is that delay in a truly aggressive regime until the year 2000 could increase the ultimate extent of global warming. As analyzed above, unavoidable long-term warming is probably on the order of 2.5°C, and very-long-term warming with complete inaction is probably on the order of 10°C (but could be as high as 18°C). As indicated in chapter 2, the cost of delay is failure to restrain avoidable warming by a range of .25°C per decade under the central estimates, and up to .5°C per decade for upper-bound warming. Some portion of this cost of delay would be likely to be paid, because of the moderate nature of the first-phase measures. Nonetheless, this price would probably be worth paying to reduce the risk of massive action later revealed to be an unneeded expense.

For some, even the two-stage approach proposed here will involve excessive action and costs. However, the main thrust of the analysis of this study suggests that the eventual extent and damages of global warming are so severe that there is greater risk in doing nothing. Nor is it plausible to argue that if the large potential warming identified here does become evident, there will be time in the future (perhaps several decades from now) to intervene and prevent this outcome. Global warming is essentially an irreversible process over the scale of two to three centuries; there are long physical lags between committed and realized warming; and there are no doubt long political lags that would make it extremely difficult to adopt wrenching adjustments decades late if there had been no discipline in the direction of more moderate initial measures in preceding decades.

Postscript

As this book went to press in May of 1992, negotiators in the Intergovernmental Negotiating Committee for a Framework Convention on Climate Change (INC), at their final session preceding the Rio Earth Summit, reached an agreement regarding national measures to limit greenhouse gas emissions. The agreement was a compromise in which the United States recognized the need to limit these emissions but did not commit itself to a specific target (such as 1990 levels) by a specific date (such as 2000). At US insistence, the agreement called for countries to submit within six months the specific programs they planned to implement to limit emissions.

The key clauses of the agreement included the following:

> Each of these parties [the industrialized countries, the Eastern European countries, and the successor states of the former Soviet Union] shall adopt national policies . . . limiting its anthropogenic emissions of greenhouse gases and protecting and enhancing its greenhouse gas sinks and reservoirs. These policies and measures will demonstrate that developed countries are taking the lead in modifying longer-term trends in anthropogenic emissions consistent with the objective of this convention, recognising that *the return by the end of the present decade to earlier levels of anthropogenic emissions of carbon dioxide and other greenhouse gases not controlled by the Montreal Protocol would contribute to such modification.* . . . [E]ach of these parties shall communicate, within six months of the entry into force of the convention for it and periodically thereafter . . . detailed information on its policies and measures . . . with the aim of returning individually or jointly to their 1990 levels of these anthropogenic emissions of carbon dioxide and other greenhouse gases not controlled by the Montreal Protocol. (United Nations 1992c, 3, emphasis added)

Many, especially in the environmental community, considered the agreement extremely weak because of its lack of a binding commitment. Nonetheless, the agreement averted the collapse that would have occurred without US participation. Moreover, the US position seemed to be edging toward one of more serious intent. The US position paper released at the INC negotiating session stated that "For some time the scientific community has warned us" of the risk of "global climate change" and that "The United States has taken this warning to heart" (US Department of State 1992, 1). This language seemed to signal a shift from the earlier position emphasizing scientific uncertainty. Indeed, the agreed text provided that "Where there are threats of serious or irreversible damage, lack of full scientific certainty should not be used as a reason for postponing such measures. . . ." (United Nations 1992b, 4).

Moreover, the US position paper contained a list of additional US actions to curb emissions of carbon dioxide and other greenhouse gases. These included a commercial and industrial lighting program that could reduce annual emissions by up to 50 million tons of carbon-equivalent; measures to increase the efficiency of industrial motors and buildings, providing reductions of some 17 million tons annually; changes in appliance standards, saving some 5 million tons annually; and actions in the administration's National Energy Strategy that could save 45 million tons annually (including other efficiency gains, regulatory reform for natural gas, increased use of biomass for fuel, and research and development for renewable energy). Total reductions of US carbon emissions resulting from these initiatives were estimated to amount to 87 million to 121 million tons per year. In addition, 39 million tons of carbon-equivalent were to be removed through control of methane from landfills, and another 13 million from methane reductions in livestock practices. With the addition of other measures, the US program envisioned annual reductions of 125 million to 200 million tons of carbon-equivalent for all greenhouse gases by the year 2000, representing 7 percent to 11 percent of expected emissions by that year (US Department of State 1992, tables 1 to 3).

Importantly, both the US position paper and the INC text emphasized carbon dioxide and other greenhouse gases *aside from* CFCs. By explicitly referring to gases not controlled by the Montreal Protocol, the agreement ruled out the earlier (1990–91) US approach that reduction of CFCs would suffice to address the global warming problem (and could indeed be counted against rising carbon dioxide emissions for this purpose). As noted in chapter 1, this shift was essentially dictated by new scientific findings that the warming effects of CFCs were apparently neutralized by their effect of stripping ozone, itself a greenhouse gas.

The agreed INC text was intentionally ambiguous. Thus, some delegations considered the reference to "1990," in the paragraph immediately following the commitment to reduce emissions to "earlier levels," to mean a target of return to 1990 levels; others (the US representatives in particular) did not.

Overall, the INC agreement represented a significant starting point if the signatory countries subsequently proved serious about taking action. Its provisions were not too far from the "best efforts" approach recommended in this study. However, the agreement was less specific about goals than are the recommendations of this study (a nonbinding target of reduction of emissions to the 1990 level by the year 2000) and made no provision for shifting to a more stringent regime after a period of years pending scientific confirmation. Moreover, the US position made no mention of carbon taxes, an omission perhaps understandable in an election year but a serious shortcoming nonetheless. Instead, the US strategy opted broadly for the "engineering" approach of pursuing low-cost reductions through a move to best practices.

It remained to be seen whether there would be further tightening or other modification of the agreement at the Rio Earth Summit. However, an early consequence of the INC agreement was that the European Commission approved a version of its carbon-energy tax (described above) that was newly conditional on adoption of a similar tax by the United States and Japan (*Financial Times*, 14 May 1992, 1). That modification reflected strong pressure from industrial interests within the Community, who had argued that a unilateral tax would impose a competitive disadvantage (*The Economist*, "Europe's Industries Play Dirty," 9 May 1992, 85–86).

In sum, on the eve of the Earth Summit, international negotiations on climate change had yielded a modest beginning in what seemed likely to be a long process of mobilizing international action to limit global warming. Because the stakes were so high with regard to both the costs of limiting warming and the damages that could occur in the absence of action, it seemed likely that an intensive and probably lengthy debate would be required to sharpen scientific, policymaker, and public opinion to the point of decisive action. This book seeks to inform that debate and outline a responsible strategy for policy action.

References

Abel, Andrew B., N. Gregory Mankiw, Lawrence H. Summers, and Richard J. Zeckhauser. 1989. "Assessing Dynamic Efficiency: Theory and Evidence." *Review of Economic Studies* 56, no. 1 (January): 1–20.

Abelson, P. H. 1990. "Uncertainties About Global Warming [editorial]." *Science* 247, no. 4950 (30 March).

Andrasko, Kenneth, Kate Heaton, and Steve Winnett. 1991. "Estimating the Costs of Forest Sector Management Options: Overview of Site, National, and Global Analyses." Paper prepared for a Technical Workshop to Explore Options for Global Forest Management, Bangkok (24–30 April).

Arrhenius, S. 1896. "On The Influence of Carbonic Acid in the Air Upon the Temperature of the Ground." *Philosophical Magazine* 41, no. 251 (April): 237–77.

Arrow, Kenneth J. 1966. "Discounting and Public Investment Criteria." In A. V. Kneese and S. C. Smith, eds., *Water Research*, 13–32. Baltimore: Johns Hopkins University Press for Resources for the Future.

Arrow, Kenneth J., and Mordechai Kurz. 1970. *Public Investment, the Rate of Return and Optimal Fiscal Policy.* Baltimore: Johns Hopkins University Press.

Ausubel, Jesse H. 1983. "Historical Note." In National Research Council, *Changing Climate*, 488–91. Washington: National Academy Press.

Ausubel, Jesse H. 1990. "Conventional Wisdom About Impacts of Global Change." New York: Rockefeller University (mimeographed, 1 April).

Barrett, Scott. 1989. "On the Nature and Significance of International Agreements." London: London Business School (preliminary, May).

Batie, Sandra S., and Herman H. Shugart. 1989. "The Biological Consequences of Climate Changes: An Ecological and Economic Assessment." In Norman J. Rosenberg, William E. Easterling, Pierre Crosson, and Joel Darmstadter, eds., *Greenhouse Warming: Abatement and Adaptation*, 121–32. Washington: Resources for the Future.

Baumol, William, and Wallace E. Oates. 1988. *The Theory of Environmental Policy*, 2nd ed. Cambridge: Cambridge University Press.

Bazzaz, Fakhri A., and Eric D. Fajer. 1992. "Plant Life in a CO_2–Rich World." *Scientific American* 266, no. 1 (January): 68–74.

Beardsley, Tim. 1992. "Night Heat." *Scientific American* 266, no. 2 (February): 21–22.

Benedick, Richard Elliot, et al. 1991. *Greenhouse Warming: Negotiating a Global Regime.* Washington: World Resources Institute.

Berger, A., J. Imbrie, J. Hays, G. Kukla, and B. Saltzman, eds. 1984. *Milankovitch and Climate.* Dordrecht, Holland: D. Reidel.

Bergsten, C. Fred, Kimberly Ann Elliott, Jeffrey J. Schott, and Wendy E. Takacs. 1987. *Auction Quotas and United States Trade Policy.* POLICY ANALYSES IN INTERNATIONAL ECONOMICS 19. Washington: Institute for International Economics (October).

Blanchard, Olivier Jean, and Stanley Fischer. 1989. *Lectures on Macroeconomics.* Cambridge, MA: MIT Press.

Blitzer, Charles R., Richard S. Eckaus, Supriya Lahiri, and Alexander Meeraus. 1991. "Growth and Welfare Losses from Carbon Emissions: A General Equilibrium Analysis for Egypt." Cambridge: Massachusetts Institute of Technology, Center for Economic Policy Research (mimeographed, December).

Boero, Gianna, Rosemary Clarke, and L. Alan Winters. 1991. "The Macroeconomic Consequences of Controlling Greenhouse Gases: A Survey." *Environmental Economics Research Series*. London: Department of the Environment (November).

Bradford, David F. 1975. "Constraints on Government Investment Opportunities and the Choice of Discount Rate." *American Economic Review* 65, no. 5 (December): 887–99.

Brookshire, David S., Mark A. Thayer, William D. Schulze, and Ralph C. D'Arge. 1982. "Valuing Public Goods: A Comparison of Survey and Hedonic Approaches." *American Economic Review* 72, no. 1 (March): 165–77.

Brown, Peter G. 1991. "Climate Change and the Planetary Trust." College Park: University of Maryland (mimeographed).

Bruntland, Gro Harlem, et al. 1987. *Our Common Future*. Oxford, England: Oxford University Press for World Commission on Environment and Development.

Bureau of National Affairs. 1992. *International Environmental Reporter* 15, no. 5 (March).

Burniaux, J. M., John P. Martin, Giuseppe Nicoletti, and Joaquim Oliveira Martins. 1991a. "The Costs of Policies to Reduce Global Emissions of CO_2: Initial Simulation Results with GREEN." *Working Papers* 103. Paris: OECD Economics and Statistics Department (June).

Burniaux, J. M., John P. Martin, Giuseppe Nicoletti, and Joaquim Oliveira Martins. 1991b. "GREEN—A Multi-Region Dynamic General Equilibrium Model for Quantifying the Costs of Curbing CO_2 Emissions: A Technical Manual." *Working Papers* 104. Paris: OECD Economics and Statistics Department (June).

Carbon Dioxide Information Analysis Center. 1992. *Trends '91*. Oak Ridge, TN: Oak Ridge National Laboratory.

Carlsmith, Roger, et al. 1990. "United States." In William U. Chandler, ed., *Carbon Emissions Controls Strategies: Case Studies in International Cooperation*, 193–220. Washington: World Wildlife Fund.

Center for Environmental Information. 1990. *Conference on "Global Climate Change: The Economic Costs of Mitigation and Adaptation."* (James C. White, ed.), New York: Elsevier.

Cess, R. D., et al. 1989. "Interpretation of Cloud-Climate Feedback as Produced by 14 Atmospheric General Circulation Models." *Science* 245 (August): 514.

Chandler, William U., ed. 1990. *Carbon Emission Controls Strategies: Case Studies in International Cooperation*. Washington: World Wildlife Fund.

Charlson, R. J., J. Langner, and H. Rodhe. 1990. "Sulphate Aerosol and Climate." *Nature* 348 (1 November): 22.

Charlson, R. J., S. E. Schwartz, J. M. Hales, R. D. Cess, J. A. Coakley, Jr., J. E. Hansen, and D. J. Hofmann. 1992. "Climate Forcing by Anthropogenic Aerosols." *Science* 255 (24 January): 423.

Cline, William R. 1989. "Political Economy of the Greenhouse Effect." Washington: Institute for International Economics (mimeographed, August).

Cline, William R. 1990a. "Economic Stakes of Global Warming in the Very-Long Term." Washington: Institute for International Economics (mimeographed, November).

Cline, William R. 1990b. "Global Warming and the Costs of Hurricane Damage." Washington: Institute for International Economics (mimeographed, July).

Cline, William R. 1990c. "Greenhouse Gas Emissions and Global Warming: Parameters and Timetables." Washington: Institute for International Economics (mimeographed, December).

Cline, William R. 1990d. "Greenhouse Restraints: Delaying the Inevitable at High Cost?" Washington: Institute for International Economics (mimeographed, December).

Cline, William R. 1990e. "Grid Analysis in Global Warming Studies: A Methodological Note." Washington: Institute for International Economics (mimeographed, November).

Cline, William R. 1991a. "A Note on Time-Discounting for Consumption." Washington: Institute for International Economics (mimeographed, April).

Cline, William R. 1991b. "Comment on Reis and Margulis." In Rudiger Dornbusch and James M. Poterba, eds., *Global Warming: Economic Policy Responses*, 375–80. Cambridge: MIT Press.

Cline, William R. 1991c. "Carbon Abatement Costs: Engineering Estimates and Forestry Options." Washington: Institute for International Economics (mimeographed, June).

Cline, William R. 1991d. "Economic Models of Carbon Reduction Costs: An Analytical Survey." Washington: Institute for International Economics (mimeographed, June).

Cline, William R. 1991e. "Scientific Basis for the Greenhouse Effect." *The Economic Journal* 100 (September): 904–19.

Cline, William R. 1991f. "Welfare Effects of Agricultural Yield Reductions from Global Warming." Washington: Institute for International Economics (mimeographed, March).

Cline, William R. 1991g. "Estimating the Benefits of Greenhouse Warming Abatement." Washington: Institute for International Economics (mimeographed, May).

Cline, William R. 1992a. "Global Warming: The Long-Term Stakes." Paper presented at the annual meeting of the American Economic Association, New Orleans (3 January).

Cline, William R. 1992b. *Global Warming: The Benefits of Emissions Abatement.* Paris: Organization for Economic Cooperation and Development (May).

Cline, William R. 1992c. *Global Warming: The Economic Stakes.* POLICY ANALYSES IN INTERNATIONAL ECONOMICS 36. Washington: Institute for International Economics.

Collins, Susan M., and Dani Rodrik. 1991. *Eastern Europe and the Soviet Union in the World Economy.* POLICY ANALYSES IN INTERNATIONAL ECONOMICS 32. Washington: Institute for International Economics (May).

Congressional Budget Office. 1990. *Carbon Charges as a Response to Global Warming: The Effects of Taxing Fossil Fuels.* Washington: Congressional Budget Office (August).

Cookson, Clive. 1989. "A Clouded View of the Global Greenhouse." *Financial Times* (22 June).

Council on Environmental Quality. 1991. *Environmental Quality: 21st Annual Report.* Washington: Council on Environmental Quality.

Cristofaro, Alexander, and Joel D. Scheraga. 1990. "Policy Implications of a Comprehensive Greenhouse Gas Budget." Washington: Environmental Protection Agency (mimeographed, September).

Cropper, Maureen L., and Wallace E. Oates. 1990. "Environmental Economics: A Survey." *Discussion Papers* QE90-12. Washington: Resources for the Future (January).

Cropper, Maureen L., Sema K. Aydede, and Paul R. Portney. 1991. "Discounting Human Lives." *Discussion Paper* CRM 91–05. Washington: Resources for the Future (June).

Daly, Herman E. 1987. "The Economic Growth Debate: What Some Economists Have Learned but Many Have Not." *Journal of Environmental Economics and Management* 14, no. 4 (December): 323–36.

d'Arge, Ralph C. 1975. *Economic and Social Measures of Biologic and Climatic Change. Climatic Impact Assessment Program Monographs* 6. Washington: US Department of Transportation, Climatic Impact Assessment Program (September).

d'Arge, Ralph C., William D. Schulze, and David S. Brookshire. 1982. "Carbon Dioxide and Intergenerational Choice." *American Economic Review* 72, no. 2 (May): 251–56.

Darmstadter, Joel. 1991. "Estimating the Cost of Carbon Dioxide Abatement." *Resources* 103 (Spring): 6–9. Washington: Resources for the Future.

Darmstadter, Joel, and Jae Edmonds. 1989. "Human Development and Carbon Dioxide Emissions: The Current Picture and the Long-term Prospects." In Norman J. Rosenberg et al., eds., *Greenhouse Warming: Abatement and Adaptation*, 35–51. Washington: Resources for the Future.

Darmstadter, Joel, and Andrew Plantinga. 1991. "The Economic Cost of CO_2 Mitigation: A Review of Estimates for Selected World Regions." *Discussion Papers* ENR91–06. Washington: Resources for the Future (January).

Data Resources, Inc. 1990. *Green Europe: Economic Implications and Business Opportunities,* vol. 1. Lexington, MA: Data Resources, Inc. (Autumn).

Deutscher Bundestag. 1990. *Protecting the Earth: A Status Report with Recommendations for a New Energy Policy.* Bonn: Deutscher Bundestag Enquête-Commission (October).

Dornbusch, Rudiger, and James M. Poterba, eds. 1991. *Global Warming: Economic Policy Responses.* Cambridge, MA: MIT Press.

Edmonds, Jae, and David W. Barns. 1990. "Factors Affecting the Long-Term Cost of Global Fossil Fuel CO_2 Emissions Reductions." Washington: Pacific Northwest Laboratory (mimeographed, December).

Edmonds, Jae, and John Reilly. 1983a. "A Long-term Global Energy-Economic Model of Carbon Dioxide Release from Fossil Fuel Use." *Energy Economics* (April): 74–88.

Edmonds, Jae, and John Reilly. 1983b. "Global Energy and CO_2 to the Year 2050." *The Energy Journal* 4, no. 3 (July): 21–47.

Edmonds, Jae, and John Reilly. 1985. *Global Energy—Assessing the Future.* New York: Institute for Energy Analysis, Oak Ridge Associated Universities, and Oxford University Press.

Edmonds, Jae, and John Reilly. 1986. *The IDA/ORAU Long-term Global Energy–CO_2 Model: Personal Computer Version A84PC.* Oak Ridge, TN: Oak Ridge National Laboratory.

Emanuel, Kerry A. 1987. "The Dependence of Hurricane Intensity on Climate." *Nature* 326, no. 2 (April): 483–85.

Environmental Protection Agency. 1989a. *The Potential Effects of Global Climate Change on the United States* (Joel B. Smith and Dennis Tirpak, eds.). Washington: Environmental Protection Agency.

Environmental Protection Agency. 1989b. *The Potential Effects of Global Climate Change on the United States,* Appendix C: Agriculture, volumes 1 and 2. Washington: Environmental Protection Agency.

Environmental Protection Agency. 1989c. *Policy Options for Stabilizing Global Carbon: Draft Report to Congress.* Washington: Environmental Protection Agency (February).

Environmental Protection Agency. 1990. *Progress Reports on International Studies of Climate Change Impacts (Draft).* Washington: Environmental Protection Agency (6 November).

Epstein, Joshua M., and Raj Gupta. 1990. *Controlling the Greenhouse Effect: Five Global Regimes Compared.* Washington: Brookings Institution.

Evans, Daniel J., et al. 1991. *Policy Implications of Greenhouse Warming.* Washington: National Academy Press.

Feldstein, M. S. 1970. "Financing in the Evaluation of Public Expenditure." *Discussion Papers* 132. Cambridge, MA: Harvard Institute of Economic Research (August).

Feldstein, M. S. 1972. "The Inadequacy of Weighted Discount Rates." In Richard Layard, ed., *Cost Benefit Analysis,* 311–32. Middlesex, England: Penguin Books.

Feldstein, Martin, and Lawrence Summers. 1977. "Is the Profit Rate Falling?" *Brookings Papers on Economic Activity* 1: 211–27.

Fellner, William. 1967. "Operational Utility: The Theoretical Background and a Measurement." In *Ten Economic Studies in the Tradition of Irving Fisher,* 39–74. New York: John Wiley & Sons.

Fischer, Stanley. 1991. "Growth, Macroeconomics and Development." *NBER Working Papers* 3702. Cambridge, MA: National Bureau of Economic Research (May).

Flavin, Christopher. 1989. "Slowing Global Warming: A Worldwide Strategy." *Worldwatch Papers* 91. Washington: Worldwatch (October).

Giovannini, Alberto, and Philippe Weil. 1989. "Risk Aversion and Intertemporal Substitution in the Capital Asset Pricing Model." *NBER Working Papers* 2824. Cambridge, MA: National Bureau of Economic Research (January).

Glantz, Michael H. 1990. "Assessing the Impacts of Climate: The Issue of Winners and Losers in a Global Climate Change Context." In James G. Titus, ed., *Changing Climate and the Coast.* Washington: Environmental Protection Agency (forthcoming).

Gleick, Peter H. 1987. "Regional Hydrologic Consequences of Increases in Atmospheric CO_2 and Other Trace Gases." *Climatic Change* 10: 137–61.

Glynn, P. W., and W. H. de Weerdt. 1991. "Elimination of the Reef-Building Hydrocorals Following the 1982–83 El Niño Warming Event." *Science* 253 (5 July): 69–71.

Goering, John M. 1990. "The Causes of Undocumented Migration to the United States: A Research Note." *Working Papers* 52. Washington: Commission for the Study of International Migration and Cooperative Economic Development (July).

Goklany, Indur M. 1989. "Climate Change Effects on Fish, Wildlife and Other DOI Programs." In John C. Topping, Jr., ed., *Coping with Climate Change,* 273–81. Washington: The Climate Institute.

Goldemberg, Jose, Thomas B. Johanssen, Amulya K. N. Reddy, and Robert H. Williams. 1987. *Energy for a Sustainable World.* Washington: World Resources Institute (September).

Government of Japan. 1990. "Action Program to Arrest Global Warming." Tokyo: Council of Ministers for Global Environment Conservation (23 October).

Gramlich, Edward M. 1990. *A Guide to Benefit-Cost Analysis,* 2nd ed. Englewood Cliffs, NJ: Prentice Hall.

Grobecker, A. J., S. C. Coroniti, and R. H. Cannon, Jr. 1974. *Report of Findings: The Effects of Stratospheric Pollution by Aircraft.* Washington: US Department of Transportation (December).

Grubb, Michael. 1989. *The Greenhouse Effect: Negotiating Targets.* London: Royal Institute of International Affairs.

Hansen, J., and S. Lebedeff. 1987. "Global Trends of Measured Surface Air Temperatures." *Journal of Geophysical Research* 92, no. 13: 345–72.

Hansen, J., et al. 1989. "Regional Greenhouse Climate Effects." In John C. Topping, Jr., ed., *Coping with Climate Change,* 68–81. Washington: The Climate Institute.

Hansen, James, William Rossow, and Inez Fung. 1990. "The Missing Data on Global Climate Change." *Issues in Science and Technology* 7, no. 1: 62–69.

Harberger, Arnold C. 1968. "On Measuring the Social Opportunity Cost of Public Funds." In *Proceedings of the Committee on Water Resources and Economic Development of the West: The Discount Rate in Public Investment Evaluation.* Denver: Western Agricultural Economic Research Council.

Harberger, Arnold C. 1974. *Taxation and Welfare.* Boston: Little, Brown.

Harrison, Paul. 1992. *The Third Revolution.* London: I. B. Tauris.

Hartman, R. W. 1990. "One Thousand Points of Light Seeking a Number: A Case Study of CBO's Search for a Discount Rate Policy." *Journal of Environmental Economics and Management* 18: S/3–S/7.

Haveman, R. H. 1969. "The Opportunity Cost of Displaced Private Spending and the Social Discount Rate." *Water Resources Research* 5, no. 5 (October).

Hoel, Michael. 1990. "Efficient International Agreements for Reducing Emissions of CO_2." Oslo: University of Oslo (mimeographed, January).

Hoeller, Peter, Andrew Dean, and Jon Nicolaisen. 1990. "A Survey of Studies of the Costs of Reducing Greenhouse Gas Emissions." *OECD Working Papers* 89. Paris: Organization for Economic Cooperation and Development.

Hoeller, Peter, Andrew Dean, and Jon Nicolaisen. 1991. "Macroeconomic Implications of Reducing Greenhouse Gas Emissions: A Survey of Empirical Studies." *OECD Economic Studies* 16 (Spring): 45–78.

Hoffman, J. S., J. B. Wells, and J. G. Titus. 1986. "Future Global Warming and Sea Level Rise." In G. Sigbjarnason, ed., *Iceland Coastal and River Symposium,* 245–66. Reykjavik: National Energy Authority.

Hogan, William W. 1990. "Comments on Manne and Richels." Cambridge, MA: Harvard University (mimeographed, January).

Hogan, William W., and Dale W. Jorgenson. 1991. "Productivity Trends and the Cost of Reducing CO_2 Emissions." *The Energy Journal* 12, no. 1: 67–85.

Houghton, Richard A., and George M. Woodwell. 1989. "Global Climatic Change." *Scientific American* 260, no. 4 (April).

Ibbotson, R. G. 1987. *Stocks, Bonds, Bills, and Inflation: Market Results for 1926–1986.* Chicago: R. G. Ibbotson Associates.

Ibbotson, R. G., and Rex A. Sinquefield. 1982. *Stocks, Bonds, Bills, and Inflation: The Past and the Future.* Charlottesville, VA: Financial Analysts Research Foundation.

Intergovernmental Panel on Climate Change. 1990a. *IPCC First Assessment Report, Volume I: Overview and Summaries.* New York: World Meteorological Organization and United Nations Environmental Programme (August).

Intergovernmental Panel on Climate Change. 1990b. *Scientific Assessment of Climate Change: Report Prepared for IPCC by Working Group I.* New York: World Meteorological Organization and United Nations Environment Programme (June).

Intergovernmental Panel on Climate Change. 1990c. *Potential Impacts of Climate Change: Report Prepared for IPCC by Working Group II.* New York: World Meteorological Organization and United Nations Environment Programme (June).

Intergovernmental Panel on Climate Change. 1990d. *Formulation of Response Strategies: Report Prepared for IPCC by Working Group III.* New York: World Meteorological Organization and United Nations Environment Programme (June).

Intergovernmental Panel on Climate Change. 1990e. "Emissions Scenarios." Report of the Expert Group on Emissions Scenarios (Response Strategies Working Group Steering Committee, Task A) to IPCC. New York: World Meteorological Organization and United Nations Environment Programme (April).

Japan. Ministry of International Trade and Industry. 1991. "Action Program for the 21st Century." *Journal of Japanese Trade and Industry* 2 (March-April): 13.

Jones, Hywel. 1975. *Modern Theories of Economic Growth.* London: Nelson.

Jorgenson, Dale W., and Peter J. Wilcoxen. 1990a. "Global Change, Energy Prices, and US Economic Growth." In American Council for Capital Formation, *Environmental Policy and the Cost of Capital,* 1–45. Washington: American Council for Capital Formation (September).

Jorgenson, Dale W., and Peter J. Wilcoxen. 1990b. "The Cost of Controlling US Carbon Dioxide Emissions." Cambridge, MA: Harvard University (mimeographed, September).

Jorgenson, Dale W., and Kun-Young Yun. 1990. "The Excess Burden of Taxation in the U.S." *Discussion Papers* 1528. Cambridge, MA: Harvard Institute of Economic Research (November).

Kane, Sally, John Reilly, and Rhonda Bucklin. 1989. "Implications of the Greenhouse Effect for World Agricultural Commodity Markets." Washington: US Department of Agriculture (June).

Kerr, Richard A. 1989. "Bringing Down the Sea Level Rise." *Science* 246 (22 December): 1563.

Kerr, Richard A. 1990. "New Greenhouse Report Puts Down Dissenters." *Science* 249 (3 August): 481–82.

Kerr, Richard A. 1991a. "US Bites Greenhouse Bullet and Gags." *Science* 251 (22 February): 868.

Kerr, Richard A. 1991b. "Could the Sun Be Warming the Climate?" *Science* 254 (1 November): 652–53.

Kerr, Richard A. 1992. "1991: Warmth, Chill May Follow." *Science* 255 (17 January): 281.

Kimball, Bruce, and Norman J. Rosenberg, eds. 1990. *The Impact of CO_2, Trace Gases, and Climate Change. Publication* no. 53. Madison, WI: American Society of Agronomy.

Kolb, Jeffrey A., and Joel D. Scheraga. 1990. "Discounting the Benefits and Costs of Environmental Regulations." *Journal of Policy Analysis and Management* 9, no. 3: 381–90.

Kopp, Raymond J. 1991. "The Cost of Controlling US Carbon Dioxide Emissions: Comments." In David O. Wood and Yoichi Kaya, eds., *Proceedings of the Workshop on Economic/Energy/Environmental Modeling for Climate Policy Analysis, October 22–23, 1990,* 378–84. Cambridge, MA: MIT Center for Energy Policy Research (January).

Kravis, Irving B., Alan Heston, and Robert Summers. 1982. *World Product and Income: International Comparisons of Real Gross Product.* Baltimore: Johns Hopkins Press.

Krutilla, J. V., and Otto Eckstein. 1958. *Multiple Purpose River Development.* Baltimore: Johns Hopkins University Press for Resources for the Future.

Lind, Robert C. 1982a. "A Primer on the Major Issues Relating to the Discount Rate for Evaluating National Energy Options." In Robert C. Lind et al., *Discounting for Time and Risk in Energy Policy,* 21–94. Washington: Resources for the Future.

Lind, Robert C. 1982b. "A Reader's Guide to the Papers in this Volume." In Robert C. Lind et al., *Discounting for Time and Risk in Energy Policy,* 95–114. Washington: Resources for the Future.

Lind, Robert C., et al. 1982. *Discounting for Time and Risk in Energy Policy.* Washington: Resources for the Future.

Lindzen, R. S. 1990. "Some Coolness Concerning Global Warming." *Bulletin of the American Meteorological Society* 71: 288–99.

Loewenstein, George. 1987. "Anticipation and the Valuation of Delayed Consumption." *The Economic Journal* 97: 666–84.

Lorius, C., J. Jouzel, D. Raynaud, J. Hansen, and H. Le Traut. 1990. "The Ice-Core Record: Climate Sensitivity and Future Greenhouse Warming." *Nature* 347 (13 September): 139–45.

Lovins, Amory B., and L. Hunter Lovins. 1991. "Least-Cost Climatic Stabilization." Old Snowmass, CO: Rocky Mountain Institute (March).

Lu, Yingzhong. 1990. "The Prospects and Economic Costs of the Reduction of the CO_2 Emission in the PRC." Beijing: Institute for Techno-Economics and Energy System Analysis (mimeographed).

MacDonald, Gordon J. 1990a. "Role of Methane Clathrates in Past and Future Climates." *Climatic Change* 16: 247–81.

MacDonald, Gordon J. 1990b. "Detecting Greenhouse Warming." In G. MacDonald and L. Sertorio, *Climate Change and Ecosystem Modeling.* New York: Plenum Press (forthcoming).

MacNeill, Jim, Pieter Winsemius, and Taizo Yakushiji. 1991. *Beyond Interdependence: The Meshing of the World's Economy and the Earth's Ecology.* New York: Oxford University Press.

Manabe, Syukuro, and Kirk Bryan, Jr. 1985. "CO2–Induced Change in a Coupled Ocean-Atmosphere Model and Its Paleoclimatic Implications." *Journal of Geophysical Research* 90, no. C6 (20 November) 11689–707.

Manne, Alan S., and Richard G. Richels. 1990a. "CO_2 Emission Limits: An Economic Cost Analysis for the USA." *The Energy Journal* 11, no. 2.

Manne, Alan S., and Richard G. Richels. 1990b. "Buying Greenhouse Insurance." Stanford, CA: Stanford University (mimeographed, November).

Manne, Alan S., and Richard G. Richels. 1990c. "Global CO_2 Emission Reductions: The Impacts of Rising Energy Costs." Stanford, CA: Stanford University (mimeographed; subsequently published in *The Energy Journal* 12, no. 1: 88–107, 1991).

Manne, Alan S., and Richard G. Richels. 1990d. "Global 2100: Model Formulation." Stanford, CA: Stanford University (mimeographed, September).

Mathews, Jessica. 1991. "Energy Policy: Where the Real Action Is." *Washington Post* (8 November), A25.

Mathews, Jessica. 1992. "Tiny Steps Toward a Greenhouse Trend." *Washington Post* (8 March), C7.

McKibben, Bill. 1989. *The End of Nature.* New York: Anchor Books.

McLean, Dewey M. 1989. "A Mechanism for Greenhouse-Induced Collapse of Mammalian Faunas." In John C. Topping, Jr., ed., *Coping with Climate Change,* 263–67. Washington: The Climate Institute.

Meadows, Donella H., et al. 1974. *Limits to Growth: A Report for the Club of Rome's Project on the Predicament of Mankind,* 2nd ed. New York: Universe Books.

Mearns, Linda O., Richard W. Katz, and Stephen H. Scheider. 1984. "Extreme High-Temperature Events: Changes in their Probabilities with Changes in Mean Temperature." *Journal of Climate and Applied Meterology* 23 (December): 1601–13.

Mintzer, Irving. 1987. *A Matter of Degrees: The Potential for Controlling the Greenhouse Effect.* Washington: World Resources Institute (April).

Mishan, E. J. 1975. *Cost Benefit Analysis: An Informal Introduction.* London: Allen & Unwin.

Mitchell, J. F. B., C. A. Senior, and W. J. Ingram. 1989. "CO_2 and Climate: A Missing Feedback?" *Nature* 341 (14 September).

Miyama, Hidefusa. 1991. "Efforts to Cut CO_2." *Journal of Japanese Trade and Industry* 2 (March–April): 17–18.

Morgenstern, Richard D. 1991. "Towards a Comprehensive Approach to Global Climate Change Mitigation." *American Economic Review* 81, no. 2 (May): 140–45.

Moulton, Robert J., and Kenneth R. Richards. 1990. *Costs of Sequestering Carbon Through Tree Planting and Forest Management in the United States.* Washington: US Department of Agriculture, Forest Service (December).

National Academy of Sciences. 1991a. *Policy Implications of Greenhouse Warming.* Washington: National Academy Press.

National Academy of Sciences. 1991b. *Policy Implications of Greenhouse Warming: Report of the Adaptation Panel.* Washington: National Academy Press (prepublication manuscript, 23 August).

National Research Council. 1983. *Changing Climate.* Washington: National Academy Press.

Nitze, William A. 1991. "A Proposed Structure for an International Convention on Climate Change." In Richard Elliot Benedick et al., *Greenhouse Warming: Negotiating a Global Regime,* 33–36. Washington: World Resources Institute.

Nordhaus, William D. 1976. "Strategies for the Control of Carbon Dioxide." *Cowles Foundation Discussion Papers.* New Haven: Yale University (mimeographed).

Nordhaus, William D. 1979. *The Efficient Use of Energy Resources.* New Haven: Yale University Press.

Nordhaus, William D. 1990a. "An Intertemporal General-Equilibrium Model of Economic Growth and Climate Change." In David O. Wood and Yoichi Kaya, eds., *Proceedings of the Workshop on Economic/Energy/Environmental Modeling for Climate Policy Analysis, October 22–23, 1990,* 415–33. Cambridge, MA: MIT Center for Energy Policy Research (January).

Nordhaus, William D. 1990b. "To Slow or Not to Slow: The Economics of the Greenhouse Effect." New Haven: Yale University (mimeographed, 5 February).

Nordhaus, William. 1991a. "To Slow or Not to Slow: The Economics of the Greenhouse Effect." *The Economic Journal* 101, no. 6: 920–37.

Nordhaus, William D. 1991b. "A Sketch of the Economics of the Greenhouse Effect." *American Economic Review* 81, no. 2 (May): 146–50.

Nordhaus, William D. 1992a. "Rolling the 'DICE': An Optimal Transition Path for Controlling Greenhouse Gases." New Haven: Yale University (mimeographed, February).

Nordhaus, William D. 1992b. "The 'DICE' Model: Background and Structure of a Dynamic Integrated Climate Economy Model of the Economics of Global Warming." New Haven: Yale University (mimeographed, February).

Nordhaus, William D., and Gary W. Yohe. 1983. "Future Carbon Dioxide Emissions from Fossil Fuels." In National Research Council, *Changing Climate,* 87–153. Washington: National Academy Press.

Office of Technology Assessment. 1991. *Changing by Degrees: Steps to Reduce Greenhouse Gases.* Washington: Office of Technology Assessment (February).

Office of Management and Budget and US Department of Agriculture. 1989. *Climate Impact Response Functions. Report of a Workshop Held at Coolfont, West Virginia, 11–14 September.* Washington: Office of Management and Budget (mimeographed, September).

Ogden, Joan M., and Robert H. Williams. 1989. *Solar Hydrogen: Moving Beyond Fossil Fuels.* Washington: World Resources Institute (October).

Parikh, Jyoti, et al. 1991. *Consumption Patterns: The Driving Force of Environmental Stress.* Bombay: Indira Gandhi Institute of Development Research (October).

Parry, Martin. 1990. *Climate Change and World Agriculture*. London: Earthscan.

Parry, M. L., and T. R. Carter. 1989. "An Assessment of the Effects of Climatic Change on Agriculture." *Climatic Change* 15: 95–116.

Pearce, David. 1991. "The Role of Carbon Taxes in Adjusting to Global Warming." *The Economic Journal* 101 (July): 938–48.

Pechman, Joseph A., and Benjamin A. Okner. 1974. *Who Bears the Tax Burden?* Washington: Brookings Institution.

Phelps, Edmund. 1966. *Golden Rules of Economic Growth*. New York: W. W. Norton.

Porter, Michael E. 1991. "America's Green Strategy." *Scientific American* (April): 168.

Poterba, James M. 1991. "Tax Policy to Combat Global Warming: On Designing a Carbon Tax." In Rudiger Dornbusch and James M. Poterba, eds., *Global Warming: Economic Policy Responses*, 71–97. Cambridge, MA: MIT Press.

Ramanathan, V., R. D. Cess, et al. 1989. "Cloud-Radiative Forcing and Climate: Results from the Earth Radiation Budget Experiment." *Science* 243 (6 January): 57–61.

Ramsey, F. P. 1928. "A Mathematical Theory of Saving." *Economic Journal* 138, no. 152: 543–59.

Raval, A., and V. Ramanathan. 1989. "Observational Determination of the Greenhouse Effect." *Nature* 342 (14 December): 758–61.

Regens, James L., Frederick W. Cubbage, and Donald C. Hodges. 1989. "Climate Change and U.S. Forest Markets." In John C. Topping, Jr., ed., *Coping with Climate Change*, 303–09. Washington: The Climate Institute.

Reid, Walter, Charles Barber, and Kenton Miller. 1992. *Global Biodiversity Strategy: A Policy-Maker's Guide*. Washington: World Resources Institute.

Reilly, J. M., J. A. Edmonds, R. H. Gardner, and A. L. Brenkert. 1987. "Uncertainty Analysis of the IEA/ORAU CO_2 Emissions Model." *The Energy Journal* 8, no. 3: 1–29.

Reis, E. J., and S. Margulis. 1991. "Options for Slowing Amazon Jungle-Clearing." In Rudiger Dornbusch and James M. Poterba, eds., *Global Warming: Economic Policy Responses*, 335–74. Cambridge, MA: MIT Press.

Repetto, Robert. 1989. *Wasting Assets: Natural Resources in National Income Accounts*. Washington: World Resources Institute.

Revelle, Roger R. 1983a. "Methane Hydrates in Continental Slope Sediments and Atmospheric Carbon Dioxide." In National Research Council, *Changing Climate*, 252–61. Washington: National Academy Press.

Revelle, Roger R. 1983b. "Probable Future Change in Sea Level Resulting from Increased Atmospheric Carbon Dioxide." In National Research Council, *Changing Climate*, 433–48. Washington: National Academy Press.

Revelle, R., and H. E. Suess. 1957. "Carbon Dioxide Exchange Between Atmosphere and Ocean and the Question of an Increase of Atmospheric CO_2 During the Past Decades." *Tellus* 9:18.

Richardson, Elliot L. 1991. "Elements of a Framework Treaty on Climate Change." In Richard Elliot Benedick et al., *Greenhouse Warming: Negotiating a Global Regime*, 25–32. Washington: World Resources Institute.

Rind, D., R. Goldberg, J. Hansen, C. Rosenzweig, and R. Ruedy. 1990. "Potential Evapotranspiration and the Likelihood of Future Drought." *Journal of Geophysical Research* 95, no. D7: 9983–10004.

Ritchie, J. T., B. D. Baer, and T. Y. Chou. 1989. "Effect of Global Climate Change on Agriculture: Great Lakes Region." In Environmental Protection Agency, *The Potential Effects of Global Climate Change on the United States*, chapter 1. Washington: Environmental Protection Agency.

Roberts, Leslie. 1991a. "Costs of a Clean Environment." *Science* 251 (8 March): 1182.

Roberts, Leslie. 1991b. "Academy Panel Splits on Greenhouse Adaptation." *Science* 253 (13 September): 1206.

Rosenberg, Norman J. 1988. *Climate Change—A Primer*. Washington: Resources for the Future.

Rosenberg, Norman J. 1992. "Facts and Uncertainties of Climate Change." Washington: Resources for the Future (mimeographed).

Rosenberg, Norman J., and Pierre R. Crosson. 1991. *Processes for Identifying Regional Influences of and Responses to Increasing Atmospheric CO₂ and Climate Change: The* MINK *Project—An Overview* (document no. DOE/RL/01830T-H5). Washington: US Department of Energy (August).

Rosenberg, Norman J., Pierre Crosson, William E. Easterling, Kenneth Frederick, and Roger Sedjo. 1989a. "Policy Options for Adaptation to Climate Change." *Discussion Papers* ENR 89–05 (March). Washington: Resources for the Future.

Rosenberg, Norman J., William E. Easterling, Pierre Crosson, and Joel Darmstadter, eds. 1989b. *Greenhouse Warming: Abatement and Adaptation*. Washington: Resources for the Future.

Rosenberg, Norman J., et al. 1991. *Processes for Identifying Regional Influences of and Responses to Increasing Atmospheric CO₂ and Climate Change—The* MINK *Report I Background and Baselines* (document no. DOE/RL/01830T-H6). Washington: US Department of Energy (August).

Ruddiman, William F., and John E. Kutzbach. 1991. "Plateau Uplift and Climatic Change." *Scientific American* 264, no. 3 (March): 66–75.

Sandmo, A., and J. H. Drèze. 1971. "Discount Rates for Public Investments in Closed and Open Economies." *Economica* 38 (November): 395–412.

Schelling, Thomas C. 1983. "Climatic Change: Implications for Welfare and Policy." In National Research Council, *Changing Climate*, 449–86. Washington: National Academy Press.

Schelling, Thomas C. 1991. "Economic Responses to Global Warming: Prospects for Cooperative Approaches." In Rudiger Dornbusch and James M. Poterba, eds., *Global Warming: Economic Policy Responses*, 197–221. Cambridge, MA: MIT Press.

Schlesinger, Michael E., and John F. B. Mitchell. 1987. "Climate Model Simulations of the Equilibrium Climate Response to Increased Carbon Dioxide." *Review of Geophysics* 25, no. 4: 760–98.

Schmalensee, Richard. 1991. "How Should We Address Economic Costs of Climate Change?" In Center for Environmental Information, *Global Climate Change: the Economic Costs of Mitigation and Adaptation*, 72–76. New York: Elsevier.

Schmidt, Karen. 1991. *Industrial Countries' Responses to Global Climate Change*. Washington: Environmental and Energy Study Institute (July).

Schneider, Stephen H. 1991. "Three Reports of the Intergovernmental Panel on Climate Change." *Environment* 33:25–30.

Schneider, Stephen H. 1992. "Will Sea Levels Rise or Fall?" *Nature* 356 (5 March): 11–13.

Schneider, Stephen H., and R. S. Chen. 1980. "Carbon Dioxide Warming and Coastline Flooding: Physical Factors and Climatic Impact." *American Review of Energy* 5: 107–40.

Schneider, Stephen H., and Norman J. Rosenberg. 1989. "The Greenhouse Effect: Its Causes, Possible Impacts, and Associated Uncertainties." In Norman J. Rosenberg, William E. Easterling, Pierre Crosson, and Joel Darmstadter, eds., *Greenhouse Warming: Abatement and Adaptation*, 7–34. Washington: Resources for the Future.

Schumpeter, Joseph A. 1942/1976. *Capitalism, Socialism and Democracy*. New York: Harper.

Sebenius, James K. 1991. "Negotiating a Regime to Control Global Warming." In Richard Elliot Benedick et al., *Greenhouse Warming: Negotiating a Global Regime*, 69–98. Washington: World Resources Institute.

Sedjo, Roger A. 1992. "Preserving Biodiversity as a Resource." *Resources* 106 (Winter): 26–29. Washington: Resources for the Future.

Sedjo, Roger A., and Allen M. Solomon. 1989. "Climate and Forests." In Norman J. Rosenberg et al., eds., *Greenhouse Warming: Abatement and Adaptation*, 105–19. Washington: Resources for the Future.

Seitz, Frederick, Karl Bendetsen, Robert Jastrow, and William A. Nierenberg. 1989. *Scientific Perspectives on the Greenhouse Problem*. Washington: George C. Marshall Institute.

Sen, Amartya K. 1982. "Approaches to the Choice of Discount Rates for Social Benefit-Cost Analysis." In Robert Lind et al., eds., *Discounting for Time and Risk in Energy Policy*, 325–53. Washington: Resources for the Future.

Shah, Anwar, and Bjorn Larsen. 1991. "Carbon Taxes, the Greenhouse Effect and Developing Countries." Washington: World Bank (mimeographed, November).

Smith, William H. 1991. "Air Pollution and Forest Damage." *Chemical and Engineering News* (11 November).

Solomou, Solomos. 1990. "The Impact of Climatic Variations on Construction Cycles and Economic Activity, 1856–1913." Cambridge, England: Cambridge University (mimeographed, August).

Solow, Andrew R. 1990. "Is There a Global Warming Problem?" Paper presented at a conference on "Economic Response to Global Warming," sponsored by the Instituto Bancario San Paolo di Torino, Rome (September).

Stevens, William K. 1991. "In a Warming World, Who Comes Out Ahead?" *New York Times* (5 February).

Stiglitz, Joseph E. 1982. "The Rate of Discount for Benefit-Cost Analysis and the Theory of the Second Best." In Robert Lind et al., eds., *Discounting for Time and Risk in Energy Policy*, 151–204. Washington: Resources for the Future.

Sundquist, Eric T. 1990. "Long-term Aspects of Future Atmospheric CO_2 and Sea-Level Changes." In Roger R. Revelle et al., *Sea-Level Change*, 193–207. Washington: National Research Council, National Academy Press.

Thaler, Richard. 1981. "Some Empirical Evidence on Dynamic Inconsistency." *Economic Letters* 8: 201–07.

Thatcher, Peter S. 1991. "Alternative Legal and Institutional Approaches to Global Change." In Richard Elliot Benedick et al., *Greenhouse Warming: Negotiating a Global Regime*, 37–59. Washington: World Resources Institute.

Tietenberg, T. H. 1990. "Economic Instruments for Environmental Regulation." *Oxford Review of Economic Policy* 6, no. 1: 17–33.

Titus, James G., ed., 1990. *Changing Climate and the Coast*. Washington: Environmental Protection Agency (forthcoming).

Titus, James G. 1991. "Greenhouse Effect and Coastal Wetland Policy: How Americans Could Abandon an Area the Size of Massachusetts." *Environmental Management Journal* 15, no. 1: 39–58.

Titus, James G., et al. 1992. "Greenhouse Effect and Sea Level Rise: Potential Loss of Land and the Cost of Holding Back the Sea." *Coastal Management* (forthcoming).

Topping, John C., Jr., ed. 1989. *Coping with Climate Change*. Washington: The Climate Institute.

Tyndall, J. 1863. "On Radiation Through the Earth's Atmosphere." *Philosophical Magazine* 4: 200.

United Nations. 1992a. *Long-Range World Population Projections: Two Centuries of Population Growth, 1950–2150* (document no. ST/ESA/SER.A/125). New York: United Nations Department of International Economic and Social Affairs.

United Nations. 1992b. "United Nations Framework Convention on Climate Change" (document no. A/AC.237/L.14). New York: United Nations General Assembly (8 May).

United Nations. 1992c. "United Nations Framework Convention on Climate Change, Addendum 2: Commitments" (document no. A/AC.237/L.14/Add.2). New York: United Nations General Assembly (8 May).

United Nations Conference on Environment and Development. 1991. *In Our Hands: Earth Summit '92*. New York: United Nations.

United Nations Environment Programme. 1991. "Scientific Assesment of Stratospheric Ozone: Executive Summary." New York: United Nations Environment Programme (October).

US Department of Energy. 1991. *National Energy Strategy: Powerful Ideas for America*. Washington: US Department of Energy (February).

US Department of Energy, Energy Information Administration. 1990a. *Energy Consumption and Conservation Potential: Supporting Analysis for the National Energy Strategy.* Washington: US Department of Energy.

US Department of Energy, Energy Information Administration. 1990b. *State Energy Price and Expenditure Report 1988.* Washington: Department of Energy (September).

US Department of State. 1992. "US Views on Global Climate Change." Position paper released to the Intergovernmental Negotiating Committee, New York (4 May).

Waggoner, Paul E., ed. 1990. *Climate Change and US Water Resources.* New York: John Wiley and Sons.

Washington, W. M., and C. L. Parkinson. 1986. *An Introduction to Three-Dimensional Climate Modeling.* Mill Valley, CA: University Science Books.

Waters, Somerset. 1990. *The Travel Industry World Yearbook: The Big Picture.* Madrid: World Tourism Organization.

Weiss, Edith Brown. 1989. *In Fairness to Future Generations: International Law, Common Patrimony, and Intergenerational Equity.* Tokyo and Dobbs Ferry, NY: The United Nations University and Transnational.

Weitzman, Martin L. 1974. "Prices vs. Quantities." *Review of Economic Studies* 41 (October): 477–91.

Weitzman, Martin L. 1991. "On Diversity." *Discussion Papers* 1553. Cambridge, MA: Harvard University Institute of Economic Research (May).

Wendland, Wayne M. 1977. "Tropical Storm Frequencies Related to Sea Surface Temperatures." *Journal of Applied Meteorology* 16, no. 5 (May): 477–81.

Whalley, John, and Randall Wigle. 1990. "The International Incidence of Carbon Taxes." Paper presented at a conference on "Economic Policy Responses to Global Warming" sponsored by the Instituto Bancario San Paolo di Torino, Rome (September).

Wigley, T. M. L. 1987. "Relative Contributions of Different Trace Gases to the Greenhouse Effect." *Climate Monitor* 16: 14–20.

Wigley, T. M. L. 1989. "Possible Climate Change Due to SO2–derived Condensation Nuclei." *Nature* 339 (1 June): 365–69.

Wilhite, Donald A. 1990. "The Enigma of Drought: Management and Policy Issues for the 1990s." *International Journal of Environmental Studies* 36: 41–54.

Wilhite, Donald A., and Michael H. Glantz. 1985. "Understanding the Drought Phenomenon: The Role of Definitions." *Water International* 10: 111–20.

Williams, Robert H. 1989. "Low-Cost Strategies for Coping with CO_2 Emission Limits." Princeton: Princeton University, Center for Energy and Environmental Studies (mimeographed, December).

Winston, Gordon C., and Richard G. Woodbury. 1991. "Myopic Discounting: Empirical Evidence." In *Handbook of Behavioral Economics,* vol. 28, 325–45. Greenwich, CT: JAI Press.

Winter, Sidney G., and Werner Grosshans. 1991. *Discount Rate Policy.* Washington: General Accounting Office (May).

Wood, David O., and Yoichi Kaya. 1991. *Proceedings of the Workshop on Economic/Energy/ Environmental Modeling for Climate Policy Analysis, October 22–23, 1990.* Cambridge, MA: MIT Center for Energy Policy Research (January).

Yohe, Gary W. 1992. "Sorting Out Facts and Uncertainties in Economic Response to the Physical Effects of Global Climate Change." Middletown, CT: Wesleyan University (mimeographed, February).

Zachariah, K. C., and M. T. Vu. 1988. *World Population Projections, 1987–1988 Edition.* Baltimore: Johns Hopkins University Press for the World Bank.

Zwally, H. Jay. 1989. "Growth of the Greenland Ice Sheet: Interpretation." *Science* 246 (22 December): 1589–91.

Index

Adaptation, 295–96
Aerosols, 25–26
Afforestation, 216–27, 370
 and carbon reduction costs, 152
Africa, yield estimates for, 97–99
Agriculture,
 drought calculations, 89–91
 greenhouse effect and, 87–101
 international yield estimates, 97–100
 and very–long–term warming,
  100–01
Albedo, 23
Arrhenius, Svante, 13, 20–21
Arrow, Kenneth, 244, 244n, 270

Barrett, Scott, 239, 329n
Bazzaz, Fakhri A. and Eric D. Fajer,
 90–91, 103
Beckerman, Wilfred, 45
BELM model, 178–82
Benefit–cost analysis, 81–138
 benefit–cost model, 278–84
 investment versus consumption
  sourcing, 236–38
 results, 296–301
 sensitivity analysis, 267–68, 301–05
 shadow price of capital, 245–47,
  270–77, 291–95
 social rate of time preference, 257–63
 of species loss, 104–06
 and utility maximization, 255–56
Benefit–cost synthesis, 277–320
 catastrophe analysis, 303–05
 DICE model, 315–17
 income growth, 284–86
 insurance, 310–11
 Malthusian scenario, 305–07
 model used for, 277–84
 Nordhaus results, 307–09, 312–14
 population growth, 284–88

sensitivity analysis, 301–03
Blitzer, Charles R. See BELM model
Bradford, David, 244, 244n, 246, 246n,
 270–274
Brundtland Report, 15

Callandar, Bruce, 76
Canada, 363–64
Capital, shadow price of, 245–47,
 270–77, 291–95
Carbon abatement costs, 197–232
 attainable efficiency gains, 199–203
 cost parameters, 293
 emissions and, 288–89
 investment versus consumption
  sourcing, 236–38
 model used for, 277–84
 shadow price of capital, 245–47,
  270–77, 291–95
 social rate of time preference, 262–63
 synthesis of factors, 225–32
 tax parameters, 294
 and utility maximization, 255–56
 See also Economic analyses (of carbon
  reduction costs)
Carbon cycle, and greenhouse effect,
 16–17
Carbon dioxide emissions,
 calculations of, 16–17
 time horizon estimations, 46–50
 See also Benefit–cost synthesis
Carbon Dioxide Information Analysis
 Center, 28–29
Carbon reduction costs,
 analysis of, 141–94
 BELM model, 175–82
 carbon taxes, 146–51, 294, 346–51,
  369–70
 CBO–DRI model, 182–83
 of construction sector, 122

Jorgenson and Wilcoxen (JW) model, 162–65

Lahiri, Supriya. *See* BELM model
Larsen, Bjorn, *See* Shah, Anwar and Bjorn Larsen
Leisure activities, and greenhouse effect, 122–23
Lighting, energy efficiency, 199–200
Lind, Robert C., 237, 244, 246, 246n, 257, 270–274
Lindzen, Richard, 22n, 33
Log–linear utility function, 249–52
London Adjustments and Amendments to Montreal Protocol, 18
Lovins, Amory B. and L. Hunter Lovins, 199–201, 203, 208, 212, 214–215, 215n
Lu, Yingzhong, 341–342

Malthusian scenario, 305–07, 358
Manne and Richels (MR) model, 50–51, 152–57, 309–11, 318–20
Marshall Institute, 32
Masking, by urban pollution, 25–26
Matthews, Jessica T., 365, 366
Meeraus, Alexander. *See* BELM model
Methane clathrates, 17, 34–35
Middle East, yield estimates for, 97–99
Migration, and greenhouse effect, 119–20
Milankovitch Effect, 27, 30n
MINK area study, 95–96
Mishan, E. J., 238, 242
Mitchell, John F. B., 15, 76
Morbidity rates, and greenhouse effect, 116–18
Morgernstern, Richard D., 107–109
Moulton, Robert J., 224
Moulton, Robert J. and Kenneth R. Richards, 221–223, 225

National Academy of Sciences (NAS), geoengineering report, 36–37
National Aeronautics and Space Administration (NASA), 28–29
Negotiation principles, 344–46
Niskanen, William, 264n

Nitrous oxide emissions, and greenhouse effect, 18
Nitze, William A., 345
Nordhaus, William D., 43, 86, 88, 223–24, 292
Nordhaus models, 50, 165–70, 307–09, 312–14, 315–17
   DICE model, 315–17
   steady-state model, 312–14

Ocean biomass stimulation, 37
OECD countries, and international policy, 363–64
OECD–GREEN model, 173–77
OPEC, 342

Pearce, David, 346–347, 347n
Personal comfort, and greenhouse effect, 115–16
Phelps, Edmund, 248
Policy considerations,
   adaptation alternative, 334–35
   business interests and, 343–44
   Canada and, 364
   carbon taxes and, 346–51, 369–70
   China and, 340–42
   developing countries, 336–40
   enforcement issues, 356–57
   European Community, 361–63
   free–rider problem, 325–32
   future directions, 368–80
   Japan, 363–64
   negotiation principles, 344–46
   OPEC and, 342
   quota allocation, 352–54
   quota ceilings, 346–51
   revenue sharing, 355–56
   technological change, 335–36
   tradeable permits, 351–52
   United States, 364–67
Pollution,
   CFCs and, 3, 18–19, 46, 59–61
   economic analysis of, 128–30
Population growth,
   benefit–cost synthesis, 284–88
   and international policy, 360–61
Porter, Michael E., 343
Poterba, James M., 347n
Potter, G. L., 24
Prisoner's dilemma, 325–32

See also Benefit–cost analysis; Carbon abatement costs; Discounting

Waggoner, Paul, 100n
Warming commitment, 20–21, 43–44, 51
Water supply, and greenhouse effect, 123–27
Water vapor feedback, global warming and, 22–23
Weiss, Edith Brown, 239, 329
Weitzman, Martin L., 105, 348, 350, 350n
Welfare loss, 138

Whalley and Wigle (WW) model, 170–73
Williams, R. H., 156n, 167
Wigley formula, for radiative forcing, 55
Wilcoxen, Peter. *See* Jorgenson and Wilcoxen model
Window glazing, energy efficiency, 200
World Meteorological Organization (WMO), 14
WW model. *See* Whalley and Wigle model

Zachariah, K. C. and M. T. Vu, 249, 284
Zwally, H. Jay, 30n

Other Publications from the
Institute for International Economics

POLICY ANALYSES IN INTERNATIONAL ECONOMICS Series

Economic Sanctions Reconsidered (in two volumes)
   Economic Sanctions Reconsidered: History and Current Policy
   (also sold separately, see below)
   Economic Sanctions Reconsidered: Supplemental Case Histories
   Gary Clyde Hufbauer, Jeffrey J. Schott, and Kimberly Ann Elliott/
   1985, rev. December 1990

$65.00	ISBN cloth 0-88132-115-X	928 pp.
$45.00	ISBN paper 0-88132-105-2	928 pp.

Economic Sanctions Reconsidered: History and Current Policy
Gary Clyde Hufbauer, Jeffrey J. Schott, and Kimberly Ann Elliott/
   December 1990

$36.00	ISBN cloth 0-88132-136-2	288 pp.
$25.00	ISBN paper 0-88132-140-0	288 pp.

Pacific Basin Developing Countries: Prospects for the Future
Marcus Noland/*January 1991*

$29.95	ISBN cloth 0-88132-141-9	250 pp.
$19.95	ISBN paper 0-88132-081-1	250 pp.

Currency Convertibility in Eastern Europe
John Williamson, editor/*September 1991*

$39.95	ISBN cloth 0-88132-144-3	396 pp.
$28.95	ISBN paper 0-88132-128-1	396 pp.

Foreign Direct Investment in the United States
Edward M. Graham and Paul R. Krugman/*1989, rev. October 1991*

$19.00	ISBN paper 0-88132-139-7	200 pp.

International Adjustment and Financing: The Lessons of 1985–1991
C. Fred Bergsten, editor/*January 1992*

$34.95	ISBN cloth 0-88132-142-7	336 pp.
$24.95	ISBN paper 0-88132-112-5	336 pp.

North American Free Trade: Issues and Recommendations
Gary Clyde Hufbauer and Jeffrey J. Schott/*April 1992*

$42.50	ISBN cloth 0-88132-145-1	392 pp.
$25.00	ISBN paper 0-88132-120-6	392 pp.

American Trade Politics
I. M. Destler/*1986, rev. June 1992*

$35.00	ISBN cloth 0-88132-164-8	400 pp.
$20.00	ISBN paper 0-88132-188-5	400 pp.

Narrowing the U.S. Current Account Deficit: A Sectoral Assessment
Allen J. Lenz/*June 1992*

$40.00	ISBN cloth 0-88132-148-6	640 pp.
$25.00	ISBN paper 0-88132-103-6	640 pp.

The Economics of Global Warming
William R. Cline/*June 1992*

$40.00	ISBN cloth 0-88132-150-8	416 pp.
$20.00	ISBN paper 0-88132-132-X	416 pp.

SPECIAL REPORTS

FORTHCOMING